Lecture Notes in Computer Science 14785

Founding Editors

Gerhard Goos
Juris Hartmanis

The series Lecture Notes in Computer Science (LNCS), including its subseries Lecture Notes in Artificial Intelligence (LNAI) and Lecture Notes in Bioinformatics (LNBI), has established itself as a medium for the publication of new developments in computer science and information technology research, teaching, and education.

LNCS enjoys close cooperation with the computer science R & D community, the series counts many renowned academics among its volume editors and paper authors, and collaborates with prestigious societies. Its mission is to serve this international community by providing an invaluable service, mainly focused on the publication of conference and workshop proceedings and postproceedings. LNCS commenced publication in 1973.

Yu-Ping Cheng · Margus Pedaste ·
Emanuele Bardone · Yueh-Min Huang
Editors

Innovative Technologies and Learning

7th International Conference, ICITL 2024
Tartu, Estonia, August 14–16, 2024
Proceedings, Part I

Springer

Editors
Yu-Ping Cheng
National Chi Nan University
Nantou County, Taiwan

Emanuele Bardone
University of Tartu
Tartu, Estonia

Margus Pedaste
Institute of Education
University of Tartu
Tartu, Estonia

Yueh-Min Huang
National Cheng Kung University
Tainan City, Taiwan

ISSN 0302-9743 ISSN 1611-3349 (electronic)
Lecture Notes in Computer Science
ISBN 978-3-031-65880-8 ISBN 978-3-031-65881-5 (eBook)
https://doi.org/10.1007/978-3-031-65881-5

This Springer imprint is published by the registered company Springer Nature Switzerland AG
The registered company address is: Gewerbestrasse 11, 6330 Cham, Switzerland

Preface

The International Conference of Innovative Technologies and Learning (ICITL 2024), provided a platform for those who are working on educational technology to get together and exchange experiences. Benefiting from using a variety of emerging innovative technologies, the e-learning environment has become highly diversified along the way. Diversified innovative technologies have fueled the creation of advanced learning environments by adopting appropriate pedagogies. Moreover, those technologies not only facilitate learning but also actively help students reach maximized learning performances. However, due to the rapid evolution of new technologies, how to make use of those technologies by complying with effective pedagogies to create adaptive or smart learning environments has been always in demand. Therefore, this conference intended to provide a platform for those researchers in education, computer science, and educational technology to share experiences of effectively applying cutting-edge technologies to learning and to further spark brightening prospects. It is hoped that the findings presented at the conference will enlighten relevant researchers or education practitioners to create more effective learning environments. ICITL is always ready to share their work with the public.

This year's conference was held at the University of Tartu, Tartu, Estonia. This year, we received 131 submissions from 24 countries worldwide. Each submitted article was assigned to three reviewers. 60 papers were selected after a rigorous single-blind review process. The acceptance rate was 45%. These contributions covered the latest findings in the areas, including: 1) Artificial Intelligence in Education; 2) Computational Thinking in Education; 3) Design and Framework of Learning Systems; 4) Pedagogies to Innovative Technologies and Learning; 5) STEM/STEAM Education; 6) VR/AR/MR/XR in Education; 7) Application and Design of Generative Artificial Intelligence in Education. Moreover, ICITL 2024 features 2 keynote presentations and 2 invited plenary presentations by renowned experts and scholars. Sunny S. J. Lin and Wayne Holmes gave us their insights into the keynote topics "Academic Facial Emotion Recognition with AI: Momentary Profiles in Knowledge Construction and Feedback Effect in Learning" and "Artificial Intelligence and Education. A Critical Studies Perspective". The plenary topic, "Revolutionizing Education for Global Competence: The Synergy of 360-Degree Video, VR, and AI in Cross-Cultural Learning" was presented in detail by Rustam Shadiev, and "AI imaginaries in education" was presented in detail by Caroline Pelletier.

We would like to thank the Organizing Committee for their efforts and time spent to ensure the success of the conference. We would also like to express our gratitude to the Program Committee members for their timely and helpful reviews. Last but not least, we would like to thank all the authors for their contribution in maintaining a high-quality conference – we count on your continued support in playing a significant role in the Innovative Technologies and Learning community in the future.

August 2024

Yueh-Min Huang
Margus Pedaste
Ting-Ting Wu
Yu-Ping Cheng
Emanuele Bardone

Organization

Honorary Chair

Yueh-Min Huang	National Cheng Kung University, Taiwan

Conference Co-chairs

Margus Pedaste	University of Tartu, Estonia
Ting-Ting Wu	National Yunlin University of Science and Technology, Taiwan

Technical Program Co-chairs

Yu-Ping Cheng	National Chi Nan University, Taiwan
Emanuele Bardone	University of Tartu, Estonia

Program Committee

Andreja Istenic Starcic	University of Ljubljana, Slovenia
Céline Jost	Université Paris 8, France
Chantana Viriyavejakul	King Mongkut's Institute of Technology Ladkrabang, Thailand
Charuni Samat	Khon Kaen University, Thailand
Chin-Feng Lai	National Cheng Kung University, Taiwan
Claudia Motta	Federal University of Rio de Janeiro, Brazil
Elmarie Kritzinger	University of South Africa, South Africa
Frode Eika Sandnes	Oslo Metropolitan University, Norway
George Ghinea	Brunel University London, UK
Grace Qi	Massey University, New Zealand
Gwo-Dong Chen	National Central University, Taiwan
Hana Mohelska	University of Hradec Králové, Czech Republic
Hanlie Smuts	University of Pretoria, South Africa
Janne Väätäjä	University of Lapland, Finland
Jui-long Hung	Boise State University, USA
Jun-Ming Su	National University of Tainan, Taiwan

Lisbet Ronningsbakk	UiT The Arctic University of Norway, Norway
Maiga Chang	Athabasca University, Canada
Mu-Yen Chen	National Cheng Kung University, Taiwan
Pao-Nan Chou	National Pingtung University of Science and Technology, Taiwan
Qing Tan	Athabasca University, Canada
Ru-Chu Shih	National Pingtung University of Science and Technology, Taiwan
Rustam Shadiev	Zhejiang University, China
Satu-Maarit Frangou	University of Lapland, Finland
Siri Sollied Madsen	UiT The Arctic University of Norway, Norway
Synnøve Thomassen Andersen	UiT The Arctic University of Norway, Norway
Tacha Serif	Yeditepe University, Turkey
Tien-Chi Huang	National Taichung University of Science and Technology
Ting-Sheng Weng	National Chiayi University, Taiwan
Tor-Morten Groenli	Kristiania University College, Norway
Yi-Shun Wang	National Changhua University of Education, Taiwan
Yu-Ju Lan	National Taiwan Normal University, Taiwan
Yuping Wang	Griffith University, Australia

Organizers

Sponsored By

台灣工程教育與管理學會
Association of Taiwan Engineering Education and Management

Contents – Part I

Artificial Intelligence in Education

Computational Thinking in Education

Design and Framework of Learning Systems

Pedagogies to Innovative Technologies and Learning

Contents – Part II

STEM/STEAM Education

VR/AR/MR/XR in Education

Artificial Intelligence in Education

Investigating the Impact of Integrating Prompting Strategies in ChatGPT on Students Learning Achievement and Cognitive Load

Yu-Sheng Huang[1], Wei-Ting Wu[2], Po-Han Wu[2](✉), and Yang-Jui Teng[2]

[1] National University of Tainan, Cheng Shiu University, Kaihsiung City, Taiwan
[2] Department of Information and Learning Technology, National University of Tainan, Tainan City, Taiwan
d11055001@stumail.nutn.edu.tw, phwu@mail.nutn.edu.tw, m11155023@gm2.nutn.edu.tw

Abstract. This study primarily investigates integrating prompting strategies into ChatGPT in instructional applications in elementary school natural science curricula. It examines the effects of different learning strategies (prompting strategies integrated into the ChatGPT natural science instructional group and worksheet tasks integrated into the ChatGPT natural science instructional group) on elementary students' learning achievement and cognitive load in natural science. This study adopted a quasi-experimental research design involving fifty fifth-grade students from two classes in a primary school in Taichung City. The classes are divided into two groups: one integrates prompting strategies into ChatGPT natural science instructional, and the other integrates worksheet tasks into ChatGPT natural science instructional. Both groups use ChatGPT as a learning aid within three sessions of instructional experiments. Pre- and post-tests of natural science learning achievement are conducted before and after the experiments. Additionally, the study explores the impact of integrating prompting strategies into ChatGPT instruction on elementary students' cognitive load in natural science.

The results of this study reveal that: (1) integrating prompting strategies into ChatGPT instruction facilitates the enhancement of elementary students' natural science learning achievement, and (2) the use of a guided questioning system in prompting strategies integrated into ChatGPT natural science instruction demonstrates the potential to reduce students' cognitive load.

Keywords: ChatGPT · Prompting Strategies · Cognitive Load

1 Introduction

This study investigates the impact of integrating prompting strategies into AI technology aids - ChatGPT conversational robot, on elementary school upper-grade natural science curriculum. It aims to examine the effects on students' natural science learning effectiveness and cognitive load. This study applied a quasi-experimental research design, comprising two groups: the experimental group integrates prompting strategies

Y.-P. Cheng et al. (Eds.): ICITL 2024, LNCS 14785, pp. 3–11, 2024.
https://doi.org/10.1007/978-3-031-65881-5_1

into ChatGPT instructional activities. In Contrast, the control group involves worksheet tasks integrated into ChatGPT natural science instructional activities. The study seeks to address the following research questions: (1) Investigating whether integrating the hypothetical questioning strategy into ChatGPT instruction makes a difference in the learning outcomes of elementary school students in natural science. (2) Investigating whether integrating the hypothetical questioning strategy into ChatGPT instruction can reduce cognitive load in elementary school students' natural science learning.

2 Literature

2.1 Problem-Posing Education

In many research papers, it can be observed that the ability of problem-posing has a positive impact on learning in fields such as mathematics [1], science education, and pre-service education. In mathematics education, problem-posing refers to the activity of creating new mathematical problems or questions. Problem-posing involves generating mathematical tasks that require critical thinking, creativity, and a deep understanding of mathematical concepts. It is a complementary skill to problem-solving, enhancing students' thinking abilities and exploring different perspectives in mathematics [2]. Pointed out that the ability to pose problems not only has a positive impact on learning mathematical concepts, but also the activity of problem-posing can have a positive effect on learners' problem-solving skills and metacognition in chemistry and physics [3].

2.2 Generative AI-ChatGPT

Artificial Intelligence Generated Content (AIGC) uses mature natural language generation (NLG) technology and AI models, enabling computer systems to produce various types of content. Current technology can generate drawings, music, videos, code, stories, poems, emails, and marketing copy. The artificial intelligence chatbot ChatGPT developed by OpenAI was launched in November 2022. Many educational institutions have begun integrating it into their teaching in recent years. For example, Sal Khan, the founder of the world's largest nonprofit online education platform Khan Academy, announced the adoption of GPT4 to create the teaching assistant Khanmigo [4].

In a 2023 AI in education survey, HolonIQ, a prominent global education technology research firm, highlighted that the integration of artificial intelligence into learning design and learner experiences holds potential for efficiency gains and the introduction of novel learning methods across diverse educational settings [5].Increasingly prevalent across all educational stages, including higher education, is the importance of artificial intelligence applications in education [6].Whether for personalized learning, computerized assessment, intelligent educational systems, or teacher support, artificial intelligence provides convenient ways to deliver learning outcomes. Chatbots, operated through artificial intelligence, mimic human interaction. What are the advantages of employing ChatGPT in educational contexts? A study examining the potential benefits of ChatGPT utilization in education revealed three potential advantages through interviews with preschool educators: (1) aiding in curriculum preparation and planning, (2) providing references for teaching and knowledge content, and (3) fostering students' creativity through learning activities designed by ChatGPT [7].

3 Research Methods

3.1 Research Design

This study adopts a quasi-experimental research method, dividing participants into two groups based on different learning strategies in instructional activities. The experimental group integrates prompting strategies into ChatGPT-based natural science instruction, while the control group incorporates worksheet tasks into ChatGPT-based natural science instruction. Before the experimental instruction, all two groups undergo underwent an initial assessment of their natural science achievement (O1) as a pretest. During the instructional experiment, teaching activities integrating different learning strategies with ChatGPT are conducted, with the experimental group receiving prompting strategy integration (X1) and the control group receiving worksheet task integration (X2). Following the conclusion of the instructional experiment, a postassessment of natural science learning achievement (O2) is immediately administered. The experimental design of this study is detailed in Table 1.

Table 1. Research design.

Group	Pretest	The integration of different learning strategies into ChatGPT instruction	Posttest
Experimental Group – ChatGPT natural science prompting instruction without using reflective prompting strategies	O1	X1	O2
Control Group – Worksheet tasks integrated into ChatGPTbased natural science instructional activities	O1	X2	O2

3.2 Research Participants

The participants in this study were fifth-grade students from an elementary school in Taichung City, with 26 and 24 learners in two classes, respectively. The two classes were divided into the Experimental Group, where prompting strategies were integrated into ChatGPT-based natural science instructional activities, and the Control Group, where worksheet tasks were integrated into ChatGPT-based natural science instructional activities. Each group was divided into six small groups, each consisting of three to four students. In total, there were 50 research subjects in this study. The teaching duration for this study was once a week for two weeks, with two classes in the first week and one class in the second week, each lasting 40 min for a total of 120 min.

Before the instructional activities, the researchers explained the course format to ensure that students understood how to participate in the lessons. Different learning strategy interventions were implemented during the instructional activities, including "prompting strategy integration into ChatGPT-based natural science instructional activities" and "worksheet task integration into ChatGPT-based natural science instructional activities." In the experimental group, researchers and class teachers guided students in using both prompting strategy and worksheet websites. In the control group, students used worksheets only. Post-instructional tests were conducted immediately after the activities for data collection.

Experimental Group. Integration of prompting strategies into ChatGPT-based natural science instructional activities. The learning tools utilized in the experimental group, which did not employ reflective prompting strategies, included the "Natural Science Prompting Usage Guide" website, natural science prompting template worksheets, modified natural science prompting template worksheets, and tablets. Prior to using the prompting strategy guide website, students were given 15 min for prompt creation. Subsequently, researchers guided students to use tablets and the website and engage in dialogue with ChatGPT to refine prompts and complete worksheets.

Control Group. Integration of worksheet tasks into ChatGPT-based natural science instructional activities. The learning tools utilized in the control group included natural science learning task booklets and tablets. Prior to using the ChatGPT tool, students were given 20 min to complete the learning task booklet, marking uncertain or unknown items. Researchers then guided students to use tablets and engage in dialogue with ChatGPT to complete the learning task booklet.

3.3 Research Tool

The research instruments used in this experiment were the "Natural Science Learning Achievement Test" and the "Natural Science Cognitive Load Scale". The details of each research tool are as follows:

Natural Science Learning Achievement Test. The natural science learning achievement questionnaire used in this study was jointly developed by the researchers and the original teaching teachers through multiple discussions and revisions. The test items were designed based on the actual teaching content. They included basic question types related to the third unit - composition and air reactions, such as knowledge-based and comprehension-based questions.

Additionally, the test included higher-order question types, such as application-based, analytical, and integrative questions. The natural science learning achievement test consisted of 47 questions with a total score of 100 points. The test was subjected to expert content validity, with three elementary school natural science teachers invited to review the test items and provide suggestions for content modification.

Natural Science Cognitive Load Scale. The natural science cognitive load scale used in this study was modified from Hwang, Yang, and Wang (2013), adapted from measurement scales proposed by Paas (1992) and Sweller, van Merriënboer, and Paas (1998), aiming to understand students' cognitive load during this natural science learning activity. The scale aimed to investigate whether there were significant differences in cognitive load between the prompting strategy integration into the ChatGPT-based natural science instructional group and the worksheet task integration into the ChatGPT-based natural science instructional group in different learning strategies. The natural science cognitive load scale adopted a Likert five-point rating scale, with 5 representing "strongly agree", 4 representing "agree", 3 representing "neutral", 2 representing "disagree", and 1 representing "strongly disagree". Participants were required to select the option that best matched their perceived feelings based on the content described in the items, with higher scores indicating heavier cognitive load in that dimension for the participants.

3.4 Data Processing and Analysis

This study primarily employs quantitative analysis as the research method, using the SPSS21 statistical software as the analytical tool. The quantitative data utilized include pre- and post-test data from the "Natural Science Learning Achievement Test" and the "Natural Science Cognitive Load Scale," conducting data-related analyses and tests to understand the differences in learning achievement and cognitive load between the experimental and control groups.

Natural Science Learning Achievement Test. To eliminate the influence of initial behavioral differences between the control and experimental groups, a one-way analysis of covariance (ANCOVA) is conducted. Before performing ANCOVA, the homogeneity assumption of regression slopes for the pre- and post-test scores of the two groups must be tested. If the significance value is greater than 0.05, it indicates that the data meet the prerequisite assumption for ANCOVA: homogeneity of regression coefficients within groups. Therefore, subsequent ANCOVA analysis can be conducted. In this study, the pre-test scores of learners in the "First Natural Science Segment Test" at the school serve as covariates, with the two different "learning strategies" as independent variables, exploring the results of the dependent variable "Natural Science Learning Achievement Test" scores. Additionally, Scheffe's post hoc multiple comparison method is utilized to analyze the data.

Natural Science Cognitive Load Scale. Based on the data collected from the Natural Science Cognitive Load Scale, a one-way analysis of variance (ANOVA) is employed, with "different learning strategy instructional activity groups" as the independent variable and the "Natural Science Cognitive Load Scale" as the dependent variable. This aims to examine the differences in natural science cognitive load between the two groups of learners after instructional experiments. Regarding reliability, according to the questionnaire reliability derived from Hwang, Yang, and Wang (2013), the Cronbach's α values for questionnaire reliability are 0.86 and 0.85, falling within an acceptable range.

4 Result

4.1 Analysis of Pre-and Post-test Scores on Natural Science Learning Achievement

The total score of the Natural Science Learning Achievement Test is 100 points. In the pre-test, as presented in Table 2, the mean score for the group where the problem-posing strategy was integrated into ChatGPT natural science teaching was 88.73, with a standard deviation of 7.94; for the group where worksheet tasks were integrated into ChatGPT natural science teaching, the mean score was 90.45, with a standard deviation of 9.45. In the post-test, the mean score for the problem-posing strategy integrated group was 72.36, with a standard deviation of 7.77; for the worksheet task integrated group, the mean score was 69.68, with a standard deviation 6.70.

Table 2. Descriptive pre- and post-test statistics for the Natural Science Learning Achievement Test with different learning strategies integrated into ChatGPT problem-posing teaching.

Learning Strategies	Number of Students	Pretest		Posttest	
		Mean	Standard Deviation	Mean	Standard Deviation
Problem-posing strategy integrated ChatGPT natural science teaching group	26	88.73	7.94	72.36	7.77
Worksheet task integrated ChatGPT natural science teaching group	24	90.45	9.45	69.68	6.70

From Table 2, it can be observed that in the pre-test scores, the pre-test scores of the group where the question-generation strategy is integrated into ChatGPT natural science teaching are slightly lower than those of the group where the worksheet task is integrated into ChatGPT natural science teaching. However, in the post-test, the group where the question-generation strategy is integrated into ChatGPT natural science teaching is higher than the group where the worksheet task is integrated into ChatGPT natural science teaching. A covariance analysis will be conducted below to examine whether the two groups have a significant difference in learning achievement.

4.2 Covariance Analysis of Natural Science Learning Achievement

Table 3. Post hoc multiple comparisons summary of covariance analysis of natural science learning achievement under different learning strategies.

Group	Compared group	mean difference	standard error	P	95% confidence interval	
					lower class boundary	upper class boundary
Test Group	control group	2.677	2.275	.504	-3.008	8.364

Based on Table 3, after posthoc multiple comparisons using the Scheffe method, it was found that the post-test scores of the experimental group (incorporating questionposing strategy into ChatGPT natural science teaching) were not significantly higher than those of the control group (incorporating worksheet task into ChatGPT natural science teaching).

4.3 Descriptive Statistics of the Natural Science Cognitive Load Scale

The aim of this study was to investigate whether there were significant differences in cognitive load among students when using different learning strategies integrated with ChatGPT question generation teaching. Therefore, this study employed one-way analysis of variance (ANOVA) to explore the Natural Science Cognitive Load Scale, which adopts a Likert five-point rating scale. Higher scores indicate heavier cognitive load in the respective dimension for participants. Descriptive statistics including the mean, standard deviation, standard error, and confidence intervals were computed for the Natural Science Cognitive Load Scale across different learning strategies.

The results revealed that in the Natural Science Cognitive Load Scale, the control group - Learning Sheet Task integrated with ChatGPT Natural Science Teaching Group had higher mean scores for mental load and mental effort compared to the experimental group - Question Generation Strategy integrated with ChatGPT Natural Science Teaching.

4.4 Analysis of Variance for the Natural Science Cognitive Load Scale

This study aims to investigate whether there were significant differences in cognitive load among students when using different learning strategies integrated with ChatGPT question generation teaching. Therefore, the researcher employed one-way analysis of variance (ANOVA), with "group of different learning strategies teaching activities" as the independent variable and "Natural Science Cognitive Load Scale" as the dependent variable, as shown in Table 4.

From Table 4, it can be observed that in the Natural Science Cognitive LoadScale, the F-value for the dimension of cognitive load is 4.225, with a significance of .018 ($p < .05$), reaching a significant level. This indicates a significant difference between groups, suggesting that students in the two groups exhibit different cognitive load performances in the Natural Science Cognitive Load Scale due to different learning strategies. However, in the dimension of mental effort in the Natural Science Cognitive Load Scale, the F-value is 2.811, with a significance of .067 ($p > .05$), not reaching a significant level. This implies that there is no significant difference between groups in terms of mental effort.

4.5 Discussion of Results on the Natural Science Cognitive Load Scale

In summary, there were significant differences observed in the overall dimension of cognitive load, specifically in the mental load aspect, when employing different learning strategies in natural science. However, no significant differences were found in the total dimension of mental effort, although the mean scores of the control group were

Table 4. Summary of One-Way ANOVA for Natural Science Cognitive Load Scale with Different Learning Strategies.

Cognitive load	Group	Within sum of squares, SSW	df	MS	F	p
Mental load	Between Groups	6.188	2	3.094	4.225	.018
Mental effort	Between Groups	4.904	2	2.452	2.811	.067

consistently higher than those of the experimental group. Based on these findings, the following inferences can be drawn: guided strategies help reduce cognitive load by systematically directing students, enabling them to engage with learning content without aimless pondering. This notion aligns with the results of Zhang (2023), which indicated lower psychological burden in the experimental group. Sung et al. (2019) suggested that using a guided questioning system for prompt strategy teaching can facilitate prompt-based instruction without increasing learners' external cognitive load, corroborating our study findings.

5 Conclusion

The integration of prompt strategies with ChatGPT teaching contributes to enhancing the natural science learning achievement of elementary school students without significantly increasing cognitive load. The integration of prompt strategies has a significant positive impact on improving the natural science learning achievement and reducing cognitive load of elementary school students. Introducing prompt strategies stimulates students' reasoning abilities and critical thinking, encouraging their active participation in the learning process. This strategy deepens students' understanding of natural science knowledge and enhances their problem-solving skills and creative thinking.

Incorporating prompt strategies into ChatGPT teaching provides students with a learning environment where they interact with artificial intelligence, sparking their interest and curiosity in learning. Through dialogue with ChatGPT, students can delve into scientific issues and receive timely feedback and guidance, aiding them in better understanding and applying what they have learned. Therefore, combining ChatGPT teaching with prompt strategies promotes students' autonomous learning and thinking, enhancing their learning achievement. This study further explores the integration of AIbased teaching strategies, aiming to continuously improve and optimize teaching practices in the future better to promote students' comprehensive development and learning outcomes.

References

1. Lin, K.M., Leng, L.W.: Using problem-posing as an assessment tool. In: 10th Asia-Pacific Conference on Giftedness, Singapore pp. 1–15, (2008)
2. Lukas, B., Benjamin, R. :Rethinking problem-posing situations: a review. Investig. Math. Learn. **13**(2), 59–76 (2021). https://doi.org/10.1080/19477503.2020.1841501

3. Akben, N.: Effects of the problem-posing approach on students' problem solving skills and metacognitive awareness in science education. Res. Sci. Educ. **50**, 1143–1165 (2020). https://doi.org/10.1007/s11165-018-9726-7
4. Lee, Y.H.: Embracing the ChatGPT wave in the education sector: insights from experimental teaching practices in Taiwan's frontline classrooms. ITHOME (2023). https://www.ithome.com.tw/news/157509
5. Casagrande, L.D.R., Caron–Ruffino, M., Rodrigues, R.A.P., Vendrúsculo, D.M.S., Takayanagui, A.M.M., Zago, M.M.F., Mendes, M.D.: Problem-posing in education: transformation of the practice of the health professional. Patient Educ. Couns. **33**(2), 161–167 (1998). ISSN 0738-3991. https://doi.org/10.1016/S0738-3991(97)000748.Holon (iq education intelligence unit. (2023, February 23). Artificial Intelligence in Education. 2023 Survey Insights. Holon IQ). https://www.holoniq.com/notes
6. Gill, S.S., Xu, M., Patros, P., Wu, H., Kaur, R., Kaur, K., Buyya, R.: Transformative effects of ChatGPT on modern education: emerging Era of AI Chatbots. Internet Things Cyber-Phys. Syst. **4**, 19–23 (2024)
7. Su, J., Yang, W.: Powerful or mediocre? Kindergarten teachers' perspectives on using ChatGPT in early childhood education, Interact. Learn. Environ. (2023). https://doi.org/10.1080/10494820.2023.2266490

Tutor-Bot: A Question-Answering Educational Robot Based on Deep Learning

Li-Chen Cheng[1] and Judy C. R. Tseng[2](✉)

[1] Department of Information and Finance Management, National Taipei University of Technology, Taipei City, Taiwan
[2] Department of Computer Science and Information Engineering, Chung Hua University, Hsinchu, Taiwan
judycrt@gmail.com

Abstract. In the context of the rapidly evolving fields of artificial intelligence and robotics, educational robots have emerged as pivotal tools in augmenting traditional teaching methodologies and fostering self-directed learning among students. In this study, an educational robot named Tutor-bot is designed and developed to enhance self-directed learning by employing deep learning technologies for real-time question-answering. The development of the Tutor-bot not only aims to improve students' learning effectiveness and motivation but also seeks to alleviate the teaching burdens of educators. Since traditional Q&A mechanisms have limitations in accuracy and responsiveness, Tutor-bot addresses the shortages by integrating deep learning and natural language processing techniques. From the systematic experimental results, this approach significantly improves the precision of question-answering, which could minimize students' learning disruptions, thereby fostering a conducive learning environment.

Keywords: Artificial Intelligence · Educational Robot · Question-Answering · Deep Learning

1 Introduction

Artificial intelligence and robotics have matured, prompting research into using robots in education to aid teaching and facilitate self-directed student learning. Robot-assisted learning integrates robots' interactive capabilities with educational content, improving knowledge dissemination [1, 2]. Previous studies have highlighted the effectiveness of this approach, fostering enjoyable and interactive learning experiences, particularly with affectionate robotic companions [1]. Robotics is a technology that can interact with people in a highly accepted mode. Robot-assisted learning is an approach that employs the interactive function embedded in robots with learning materials to deliver knowledge vividly. With flexible and interactive features, educational robots can accurately perform repetitive tasks, which are essential in various teaching and learning scenarios [2]. Many academic journals have reported that educational robots have gradually become an efficient tool to improve students' learning motivation and effectiveness [3].

Y.-P. Cheng et al. (Eds.): ICITL 2024, LNCS 14785, pp. 12–19, 2024.
https://doi.org/10.1007/978-3-031-65881-5_2

Recent attention has focused on the importance of self-directed learning skills for 21st-century human development [4]. Students adept in self-directed learning can navigate evolving knowledge landscapes, facilitating cross-border knowledge transfer [5]. However, challenges in self-directed learning often arise due to delays in problem-solving, leading to disruptions and decreased efficacy. Integrating robots as conversational partners in learning can offer timely guidance, enhancing students' self-directed learning experiences and outcomes.

Traditional Q&A matching methods use algorithms to find answers quickly, aiding educational robots in responding to student inquiries without teacher involvement autonomously. [6]. However, accuracy can improve; with rapid advancements in machine and deep learning, studies integrate deep learning in natural language processing [7, 8]. Studies have made notable progress in addressing fake news and misinformation identification, communist Q&A classification, and non-factual answer selection using deep learning technologies [9]. As Q&A matching falls under natural language processing, effective and precise application of deep learning in building Q&A mechanisms warrants further exploration.

Real-time answering of students' queries significantly enhances their self-directed learning efficacy [10, 11]. This study proposed a robot-assisted learning framework called "Tutor-bot," employing Q&A mechanisms for prompt query resolution. Tutor-bot integrates deep learning technologies into its Q&A matching system to enhance question-answering accuracy and reduce student frustration. Expectations include addressing teachers' absence in real-time problem-solving, easing their teaching workload, and boosting student learning outcomes.

2 Literature Review

In the following sections, we will discuss the research related to self-directed learning and Q&A matching.

2.1 Self-directed Learning

In the context of the burgeoning information age, learners must distill essential information from the ever-evolving landscape of knowledge and technologies. Self-directed learning was proposed between the 1900s and 1930s and refers to students' ability to exercise self-control during the learning process [12]. Students who have mastered the ability of self-directed learning can quickly transfer the knowledge they have learned to achieve cross-border learning [5]. Moreover, self-directed learning includes the following abilities: making decisions without instructions, deciding what to learn, listing learning outcomes, choosing and working on learning strategies, and evaluating learning outcomes [13].

2.2 Question-Answering

Recently, question-answering systems have found broad applications; industries utilized them for customer service to answer common queries [14], while they were extensively used in second language learning with high repetition, flexibility, and interactivity [15]. Scholars suggest incorporating natural language processing in chatbots for one-on-one guided problem-solving conversations between students and chatbots [16]. Traditional information retrieval of Q&A matching mechanisms often uses the text similarity approach. Algorithms commonly applied to convert sentences into characteristic vectors include Term Frequency-Inverse Document Frequency (TF-IDF), Word2vec [17] et.al. In recent years, machine learning and deep learning have been integrated into Q&A matching mechanisms [7, 18]. Given deep learning's exceptional accuracy, this study also utilized deep learning technologies to enhance the precision of question-answering.

3 Conceptual Framework and System Structure

This study introduces an educational robot called Tutor-bot, utilizing ASUS Zenbo as the learning device, to alleviate teachers' workload in addressing students' queries during self-directed learning. The proposed framework of Tutor-bot is shown in Fig. 1. Before students interact with Tutor-bot, teachers must create an "FAQ Database" using the "FAQ Management Module." Subsequently, teachers can employ the "Q&A Model Creation Module" to trigger the "Q&A Model Training Module," utilizing deep learning to form the "Q&A Model." During self-directed learning, students voice their queries to Tutor-bot, which leverages the "Voice Recognition Module" to convert voice messages to text format. The "Data Preprocessing Module" then converts text into characteristic vectors, and the "Answer Reasoning Module," employing deep learning, selects the most relevant vector from the "Q&A Model." Next, the "Answer Retrieval Module" fetches answers from the "FAQ Database" based on the vector, and the "Voice Synthesis Module" converts the answer into a voice message spoken by Tutor-bot to address students' questions.

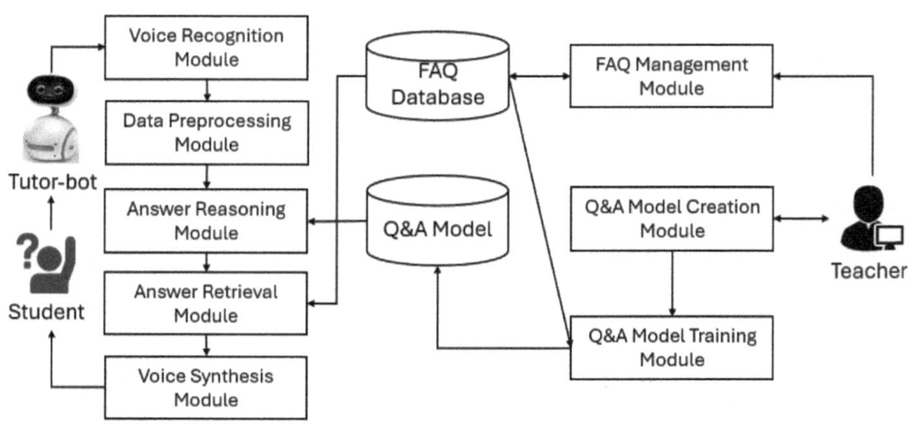

Fig. 1. The proposed framework of Tutor-bot.

To optimize question-answering accuracy and minimize students' frustration, Tutor-bot applied several deep learning technologies to build its Q&A matching mechanism, including the "Q&A model Training Module" and the "Answer Reasoning Module."

The following subsections will describe the traditional Q&A matching mechanism and the Q&A matching mechanism using deep learning in Tutur-bot, respectively.

3.1 Traditional Q&A Matching Mechanism

There are four pre-processing procedures in the traditional Q&A matching mechanism: word segmentation, stemming, stop word removal and characteristic vector generation. The characteristic vectors are a set of vectors composed of unique keywords from a document and their weightings, which can be indicated by the following equation:

$$\mathrm{VQi} = (\mathrm{T1}, \mathrm{Wi}, 1), (\mathrm{T2}, \mathrm{Wi}, 2), .., (\mathrm{Tj}, \mathrm{Wi}, \mathrm{j}), ..., (\mathrm{Tn}, \mathrm{Wi}, \mathrm{n}) \tag{1}$$

Qi: characteristic vectors of the *i*th question;
Tj: the keywords of the *j*th representative words;
Wi,j: the weighting of the *j*th keywords in the *i*th question;
n: the number of keywords.

When users ask a question, that question will also be converted into characteristic vectors following the same four procedures. Then, the similarity between these characteristic vectors and that in the "Q&A Model" will be calculated individually. At last, a question with the highest similarity relating to users' questions will be identified, and its corresponding answer in the "FAQ Database" will be provided.

Although many methods can be applied to calculate the similarity between two characteristic vectors, Cosine similarity is the most commonly used method. Based on the theory of Cosine similarity, the smaller the two measured angles, the more correlated the two measurements. In other words, it indicates the two questions have high similarity. The Cosine similarity is shown in the following equation:

$$\mathrm{Sim}(\mathrm{Q_i}, \mathrm{Q_j}) = \mathrm{Cos}(\mathrm{VQ_i}, \mathrm{VQ_j}) = \frac{\sum_{k=1}^{n} WikWjk}{\sqrt{\sum_{k=1}^{n} Wik2}\sqrt{\sum_{k=1}^{n} Wjk2}} \tag{2}$$

Q&A matching mechanism using deep learning in Tutor-bot.

The Q&A matching mechanism of Tutor-bot uses the Bidirectional Encoder Representations from Transformers (BERT) as the deep learning framework. BERT is a language-representative model proposed by Google in 2018 [19]. BERT is a bidirectional and unsupervised language representative model, training to be applied with a large number of unlabeled texts. BERT is a context-dependent embedding model that inputs all vocabulary in a sentence and uses deep learning to develop the contextual meaning of those words. As a result, it can provide different vocabulary vectors depending on the context. This research introduces a Q&A matching mechanism grounded on BERT, employing the BERT language model to facilitate the conversion of characteristic vectors and subsequent tasks. By preprocessing all questions and answers in the FAQ during the initial information processing phase, the development and training of a BERT-based Q&A matching mechanism can commence. We applied a Fine-Tuning BERT model before establishing the BERT-based Q&A matching module model. The training dataset must contain both positive and negative examples to train the BERT-based Fine-Tuning model to learn the correct and precise Q&A matching mechanism.

Because FAQs only include positive examples, negative examples will be generated by matching the questions with wrong answers. This study assigned each question with N wrong answers to generate negative examples and included all the positive and negative examples in the training samples. Positive examples will be labeled as one, while negative samples will be labeled as 0. In a training sample represented by VQ_i, VA_j, and t, VQ_i refers to the question, and VA_j refers to the answer. In addition, the t indicates the Q&A matching result, which is the label. If we assume m Q&A matchings in the FAQ, this method will generate $m*(N + 1)$ training samples.

When inputting all training samples (VQ_i, VA_j, t) one by one, VQ_i and VA_j are the input, and y is the output that will be generated. The loss function of the BERT-based pre-training model must be applied to calculate the differences between the current predictive result y and the correct result t to allow this model to automatically "learn" the determination of the correct label. It is necessary to set the percentage of the training samples to be extracted as the verification dataset. During each process, the model will be trained to determine the number of samples and the number of training sessions for the BERT-based model. The repeated training will allow automatic learning by going through the mentioned parameters, making the model make predictive results closer to the correct answers. This study applied the loss function of the BERT-based pre-training model and set the parameters, including the batches of data processing, the number of training times, and the percentage of the verification dataset. Next, this study has input the prepared training dataset into the deep learning model, which has been established in the previous section to perform repeated learning to complete the training of the Q&A matching mechanism.

The model processed with Fine-Tuning can be applied to generate predictive answers corresponding to students' questions. The questions (Q) posed by students will be converted to characteristic vectors (VQ) during the pre-processing phase. Subsequently, all the answers to VQ and FAQ will be matched with characteristic vectors (VAj), and then they will be input into the trained model for predictive answers. Ultimately, the model will generate a probability of getting label one as the correct answer and label 0 as the wrong answer.

4 Results

To evaluate the performance of Tutor-bot in question-answering, some experiments have been conducted to compare the traditional Q&A matching mechanism and the Q&A matching mechanism of Tutor-bot in terms of precision rate, recall rate, F1 measure, and execution time. The publicly accessible SciQ dataset containing Q&A related to the scientific fields is conducted in this study. The SciQ dataset has 12,679 positive and 38,037 negative examples, later divided into a training set with 11769 matchings and a testing set with 1000 matchings to evaluate the two Q&A matching mechanisms.

This study has applied the precision rate (P), recall rate (R), F1 measure (F), and execution time (T) to evaluate the performance of the model. The equations of precision rate, recall rate, and F1 measure are as follows:

$$\text{Precision rate} : \mathrm{P} = (\mathrm{TP}/(\mathrm{TP} + \mathrm{FP})) \tag{3}$$

$$\text{Recall rate} : \text{R} = (\text{TP} / (\text{TP} + \text{FN})) \tag{4}$$

$$\text{F1 measure} : F = (2 * \text{P} * \text{R} / (\text{P} + \text{R})) \tag{5}$$

The outcomes of the experiment, as presented in Table 1, reveal that the accuracy of the conventional Q&A matching module falls below 60%, whereas the accuracy for the BERT-based Q&A matching module exceeds 90%. These findings indicate that BERT constitutes a significantly more effective instrument for natural language processing applications. Although the traditional Q&A matching module exhibits a recall rate surpassing 90%, suggesting it can identify correct answers for most queries, its precision rate is 58%. This low precision rate implies that the responses it generates often fail to accurately address the students' inquiries. In contrast, the BERT-based deep learning Q&A matching module demonstrates the capability to produce accurate answers that align with users' questions, thereby effectively aiding in problem resolution.

Table 1. BERT-based deep learning Q&A matching module

	Precision	Recall	F1
Traditional Q&A matching module	0.5889	0.9205	0.71827
BERT-based Q&A matching module	0.9153	0.9153	0.94053

The F1 score of the conventional Q&A matching module exceeds 70%, reflecting a balance between its precision and recall rates. This module is adept at executing straightforward Q&A matching tasks and can furnish responses to a vast array of questions. Nevertheless, there is a notable need for enhancement in its precision, which currently falls below 60%. In contrast, the F1 score for the BERT-based deep learning Q&A matching module surpasses 90%, showcasing superior precision and recall metrics performance. This module employs text-based data from Google for extensive pre-training over time, enabling a nuanced understanding of user inquiries and producing solutions that effectively address a broad spectrum of issues.

5 Discussion and Conclusions

With guidance and support given by teachers, students are motivated to develop plans to achieve their learning outcomes [20]. A study has indicated that teachers should be the key partners for students in self-directed learning, suggesting that teachers play essential roles in self-directed learning. This study has developed an educational robot, Tutor-bot, based on deep learning. The tutor-bot acts as a teacher to provide guidance and support during self-directed learning and answer students' questions in real time. This study has compared the traditional Q&A matching mechanism and the Q&A matching mechanism based on deep learning.

The traditional Q&A matching module can generate answers corresponding to most questions based on the experimental results. However, its poor accuracy will result in providing irrelevant answers, which should not be applied to solving students' questions. As a result, its application as an assistant robot will be significantly reduced. The precision rate of the BERT-based deep learning Q&A matching module is as high as over 90%, indicating its effectiveness in the application of natural language processing.

This study successfully conducted systematic experiments to evaluate the performance of the deep learning-based Q&A matching mechanism. In the future, Tutor-bot will be applied in field learning to evaluate its effects on students' learning outcomes. We believe that its application can reduce the effort teachers have to make during after-school tutoring because the assistant robots can act as teachers to answer students' questions. At the same time, students can perform self-directed learning without disruption. When students have questions, they can directly ask the natural language processing implanted robots to automatically provide appropriate answers instead of searching them online. With this application, students can minimize the time spent searching for answers online. It can also make the learning process more enjoyable, increasing their effectiveness in self-directed learning.

To further improve the accuracy of Tutor-bot in question-answering, a user feedback mechanism should be introduced. With this feedback mechanism, students can give scores corresponding to the answers provided by the Tutor-bot based on users' satisfaction. This mechanism can collect users' feedback and then combine deep learning with enhanced reinforcement learning and machine learning to adjust the accuracy of the Q&A matching mechanisms. As a result, the tutor-bot can gradually improve its accuracy in question-answering through this user-robot interaction, meeting students' expectations better. Undoubtedly, artificial intelligence-related technologies have more in-depth applications in education and endless potential research purposes. The next generations should continue to make efforts in this research field.

Funding. This work was supported by the National Science and Technology Council, Taiwan, under 111–2410-H-027–011-MY3 and NSTC 112–2410-H-216–002.

References

1. Dorouka, P., Papadakis, S., Kalogiannakis, M.: Tablets and apps for promoting robotics, mathematics STEM education, and literacy in early childhood education. Int. J. Mobile Learn. Organ. **14**(2), 255–274 (2020)
2. Chang, C.Y., Hwang, G.J., Chou, Y.L., Xu, Z.Y., Jen, H.J.: Effects of robot-assisted digital storytelling on hospitalized children's communication during the COVID-19 pandemic. Educ. Technol. Res. Dev. **71**(3), 793–805 (2023)
3. Liang, J.C., Hwang, G.J.: A robot-based digital storytelling approach to enhancing EFL learners' multimodal storytelling ability and narrative engagement. Comput. Educ. **201**, 104827 (2023)
4. Alsancak Sirakaya, D., Ozdemir, S.: The effect of a flipped classroom model on academic achievement, self-directed learning readiness, motivation and retention. Malays. Online J. Educ. Technol. **6**(1), 76–91 (2018)
5. Boyer, N., Kelly, M.: Breaking the institutional mold: Blended Instruction, self-direction, and multi-level adult education. Int. J. Self-Directed Learn. **2**(1), 1–17 (2005)
6. Wu, J.W., Tsou, Y.H., Chiou, C.K., Tseng, J.C.: Development of a ubiquitous virtual tutoring assistant system. In: EdMedia+ Innovate Learning, 2007: Association for the Advancement of Computing in Education (AACE), pp. 1577–1585 (2007)

7. Tan, M., Santos, C.D., Xiang B., Zhou, B.: Lstm-based deep learning models for non-factoid answer selection, arXiv preprint arXiv:1511.04108 (2015)
8. Chen, K., Cheng, L.C., Ye, M.Y., Wang, J.H.: A graph neural network approach to detect original review spammers of astroturfing campaigns. Electron. Commer. Res. Appl. **62**, 101326 (2023)
9. Cheng, L.C., Wu, Y.T., Chao, C.T., Wang, J.H.: Detecting fake reviewers from the social context with a graph neural network method. Decis. Support Syst. **179**, 114150 (2024)
10. Mohrweis, L.C., Shinham, K.M.: Enhancing students' learning: instant feedback cards. Am. J. Bus. Educ. **8**(1), 63–70 (2015)
11. Nutbrown, S., Higgins, C., Beesley, S.: Measuring the impact of high-quality instant feedback on learning. Pract. Res. Higher Educ. **10**(1), 130–139 (2016)
12. Song, L., Hill, J.R.: A conceptual model for understanding self-directed learning in online environments. J. Interact. Online Learn. **6**(1), 27–42 (2007)
13. Khalid, M., Bashir, S., Amin, H.: Relationship between self-directed learning (SDL) and academic achievement of university students: a case of online distance learning and traditional universities. Bull. Educ. Res. **42**(2), 131–148 (2020)
14. Hwang, G.J., Wu, C.H., Tseng, J.C., Huang, I.: Development of a ubiquitous learning platform based on a real-time help-seeking mechanism. Br. J. Edu. Technol. **42**(6), 992–1002 (2011)
15. Chang, C.W., Lee, J.H., Chao, P.Y., Wang, C.Y., Chen, G.D.: Exploring the possibility of using humanoid robots as instructional tools for teaching a second language in primary school. J. Educ. Technol. Soc. **13**(2), 13–24 (2010)
16. Paladines, J., Ramírez, J.: An intelligent tutoring system for procedural training with natural language interaction. CSEDU **2**, 307–314 (2019)
17. Church, K.W.: Word2Vec. Nat. Lang. Eng. **23**(1), 155–162 (2017)
18. Pan, Y., Qiu, Z., Welt, C.: A framework for merging and ranking of answers in DeepQA. IBM Res. Dev **56**, 3–4 (2012)
19. Devlin, J., Chang, M.-W., Lee, K., Toutanova, K.: Bert: pre-training of deep bidirectional transformers for language understanding, arXiv preprint arXiv:1810.04805 (2018)
20. Dornan, J., Hadfield, B.M., Boshuizen, H., Scherpbier, A.: How can medical students learn in a self-directed way in the clinical environment? Design-based research. Med. Educ. **39**(4), 356–364 (2005)

Capacity for the Usage of Disruptive Technologies in Higher Education

Kai Pata[1](✉), Terje Väljataga[1], Mairi Matrov[1], Katrin Karu[1], Águeda Gómez-Cambroneroai[2], Rubén García-Vida[2], Inmaculada Remolar[2], and Katerina Theodoridou[3]

[1] Tallinn University, Narva Road 25, 10120 Tallinn, Estonia
kai.pata@tlu.ee
[2] Universitat Jaume I, Comunitat Valenciana, Castello de La Plana, Spain
[3] Center for Social Innovation, Rigenia 62, Nikosia, Cyprus

Abstract. This paper describes screening the capacity of tertiary education institutions in integrating practice-based e-learning with disruptive learning technologies. Within the scope of the H2020 project eDiploma, a self-evaluation questionnaire was developed and carried out in 6 project partner countries. The sample incorporated responses from educators, students and technical personnel from 146 tertiary education institutions. We aimed to identify the institutional, learning- and teaching-related, and personal components that differed in countries significantly, as well as the components that contributed to these differences. The discriminant analysis was used. The findings revealed that all countries are still on the low capacity level for integrating disruptive technologies to e-learning on a large scale. Infrastructural capacity in the countries did not differ significantly, but institutional norms and regulations, practices for teaching, and in attitudes and values diverged the countries. These critical elements may be used to develop the capacities in institutions to support the disruptive technology uptake.

Keywords: Capacity · Disruptive learning technologies · Practice-based learning

1 Introduction

The tertiary education is having the transition towards the larger use of new disruptive immersive and AI technologies (DT). This trend is driven by the digital transformation of the enterprises, and the learning industry. Generation Z students are calling for more flexible and accessible online learning environments [1–3]. This urgency is further amplified by the evolving job market, necessitating an alignment of educational content with industry needs, a challenge currently being addressed by researchers [4–6]. In this paper we introduce the research done in the H2020 project eDiploma preliminary phase, to identify the capacity of tertiary education institutions to move towards DT in practice-based e-learning. The paper sets the goal to find the critical points in the transition to teach with disruptive technologies (DT) in the partner countries of the project. The research questions are: RQ1: What is the overall capacity level of institutions in countries to perform practice-based e-learning with DT? RQ2: What components distinguish the institutional capacity to use DT in elearning in countries?

Y.-P. Cheng et al. (Eds.): ICITL 2024, LNCS 14785, pp. 20–29, 2024.
https://doi.org/10.1007/978-3-031-65881-5_3

2 Disruptive Technologies

Currently, artificial intelligence, and immersive learning technologies of augmented, virtual and extended reality have started to disrupt our understanding of the new opportunities in practice-based e-learning. In recent years "digital disruption" has been an emerging concept [7]. The term "disruptive technology" (DT) was coined by C. Christensen [8], who used the term in the context of disruptive innovation theory in business. Being criticized by many scholars [9], this understanding of DT is not best suited for ethics because of its theory-laden conceptualisation [10]. According to Cambridge dictionary, to disrupt means "to prevent something, especially a system, process, or event, from continuing as usual or as expected". Thus, disruption is usually perceived as a negative occurrence triggered by outside factors [11]. Schuelke-Leech [12] makes a distinction based on the depth and scope of the disruption and classifies disruption as 1) first-order (local market disruptions, certain domains are the only ones experiencing change, while society as a whole is not affected; ethical issues and values are domain specific); 2) second-order (systematic disruptions at societal scale, technologies' capacity to alter society and individuals). It is believed that some technologies are able to trigger profound changes and disrupt existing structures and norms, others not. The transfer of the traditional tertiary education system to deliver courses in elearning, has started to disrupt learning the ways that are not yet deeply explored. There is the need to see the effects of the disruptions taking place at the tertiary educational system level. This disruption will have to move towards new institutional infrastructures and choice-making for the technologies, norms and regulations that would create new processes around digital learning resource development and storage, as well as the AI data flows. There is a need for sustainable approaches for acquiring technical competence and gaining access to expensive technologies in the universities from external entities. The flexible enough development of digital learning resources and the training approaches for the staff in the rapid digital transformation must be found. The uptake of DT in practice-based learning requires also revising the personal attitudes and values.

3 Capacity to Teach with Disruptive Technologies

In this paper we use the capacity concept defined by Baser & Morgan [13] through several collective and individual capabilities in the systems. According to [13] capacity is an emerging attribute (state) in social ecosystems, a result of interaction, and it encompasses a complex combination of attitudes, resources, strategies, and skills both tangible and not tangible that allows to master the change. Digital capacity building is not just about adopting new technologies. It is a complex process and also includes the change of organizational culture, processes, and experiences to leverage these technologies effectively and sustainably to improve organization's efficiency, value, and innovation in response to an increasingly digital world. The synthesis of the literature [1, 14, 15] reveals a consensus among the models of organization´s digital transformation regarding several key convergences: 1) necessity of digital assets and integrating digital technologies thoroughly to enhance not only operational efficiency but also the educational experience and strategic planning within organizations 2) modify and adapt existing organizational and educational structures and methodologies 3) involving key stakeholders, particularly educators in the context of academic settings, in the digital transformation process. The components of tertiary education institutions digital transformation to conduct practical teaching with disruptive technologies, are proposed as following: infrastructure, leadership, collaboration, professional development, teaching practices, competences and attitudes.

4 Research Context

The study was carried out in the context of eDiploma project (Electronic, Didactive and Innovative Platform based on Multimedia Assets) (HORIZON-CL2–2021-TRANSFORMATIONS-01) that will examine the current e-learning ecosystems by analyzing the usefulness of DT (Virtual Reality, Augmented Reality, Artificial Intelligence or Chatbots) to support education and training systems, specifically in practical distance learning; co-create methodology to determine which technologies are the most suitable for dealing with different types of educational methodologies; develop online platform that will integrate artificial intelligence, virtual and augmented reality, interactive technologies and gamification techniques. eDiploma will explore the weaknesses of the current e-learning by studying the potential of DT applied to e-learning.

5 Method

A web-based survey was conducted to understand the capacity and main gaps of educational institutions to perform e-learning with DT.

Sample. In each region of project partners (Spain, Bulgaria, Estonia, Italy, Hungary, Cyprus) higher and higher vocational, and vocational education providers were contacted. It was planned to access: 10 lecturers; 20 students from the institution who have experiences with some forms of group-learning or practice-based learning spread so that different areas students would respond; 3–5 experts or technical support specialists. The responses were collected from experts (N = 96), about 30% of the expected sample, the educators (N = 351) about 29% of the expected sample, and the students (N = 516) about 29% of the expected sample. In Estonia responses were collected from 3 vocational schools and 6 HEIs, in Bulgaria from 3 HEIs, in Cyprus from 3 HEIs, in Hungary from 1 vocational school and 5 HEIs, in Spain from 28 high schools, 41 vocational schools, 47 HEIs, in Italy from 4 HEIs and 5 social enterprises. Proportionally, in web-based surveys the reached sample size is at the acceptable level (above 25%), but the generalizability of the data is limited.

Survey instruments. Three surveys were developed to view the capacity from the perspectives of technology experts, educators and students. The survey questions were formulated to the respondents similarly, but the questions were not identical. Some survey sections about infrastructure were answered only by experts. The survey structure:

1. General data
2. The capacity elements to teach with DT:

Tools, software and infrastructures - opportunities and constraints from national and institutional infrastructures and tools that promote applying DT. Agendas, norms, rules and regulations and roles, funding - constraints and support from national or institutional practices, norms, regulations, curricula that promote applying DT: Agendas, strategies; Roles and responsibilities; Regulations, policies; Incentives; Funding.

Community - collective development of the capacity, embeddedness of sociocultural elements, teaching practices, the value constraints of the professional community, alignment to learners' expectations: Teaching and Learning practices; Alignment to students; Social capital building; Communities of practice; Support; Training.

Personal level - values, attitudes, experiences, competencies related to DT: Competencies; Values, beliefs and attitudes; Intentions/ goals, impact.

Most of the survey items were presented at Likert scale (Strongly disagree -1; Somewhat disagree - 2; Neither agree nor disagree - 3; Somewhat agree - 4; Strongly agree). The instrument was directly tested out with the whole sample due to the tense time limits of the study. The instrument scales were validated with reliability analysis as presented in Table 1.

Table 1. Chronbach alpha values for the capacity instrument scales.

Sample	Infrastructure	Regulative	Teaching practice	Competences	Experiences	Attitudes	Values
Expert	.96	.97	.96	.96	.92	.92	.69
Educator	.95	.93	.97	.94	.89	.92	.66
Student	.72	.75	.95	.94	.88	.91	.65

Data collection and analytical procedures. The ethical agreements were asked from the partner universities. The online surveys were conducted in the national language. The combined datasets for specialists, educators and students' perspectives were formed from all the received data. We analyzed the dataset considering the capacity dimensions we have built into the survey instruments. We ran the descriptive data analyses for all the survey items, ANOVA analyses were performed to identify the mean values and significant differences between respondents' perspectives and country perspectives. For the space limits the descriptive data table of full survey is not presented and we explain the general trends in data. The discriminant analyses were performed to differentiate the countries' capacity perspectives on survey components' items.

6 Results

6.1 Overview of the Capacity for Using Disruptive Technologies in Institutions

The ability to perform transition to new learning technologies depends on the capacity that is available at the governmental or organizational level (technology, tools and infrastructures, norms, regulations), community level (teaching practices) and personal level (competences, attitudes and values). For comparative overview of the countries' capacity level in tertiary institutions to use DT for practice based learning, the overall compound values for the sample countries were calculated (see Fig. 1). It appeared that the capacity at Community component level was the weakest, and ranked lowest in all countries. The findings generally revealed that all countries are still on the low capacity level for integrating DT to practice based e-learning on a large scale. Of the countries, Hungary had the lowest compound values for the capacity constructs.

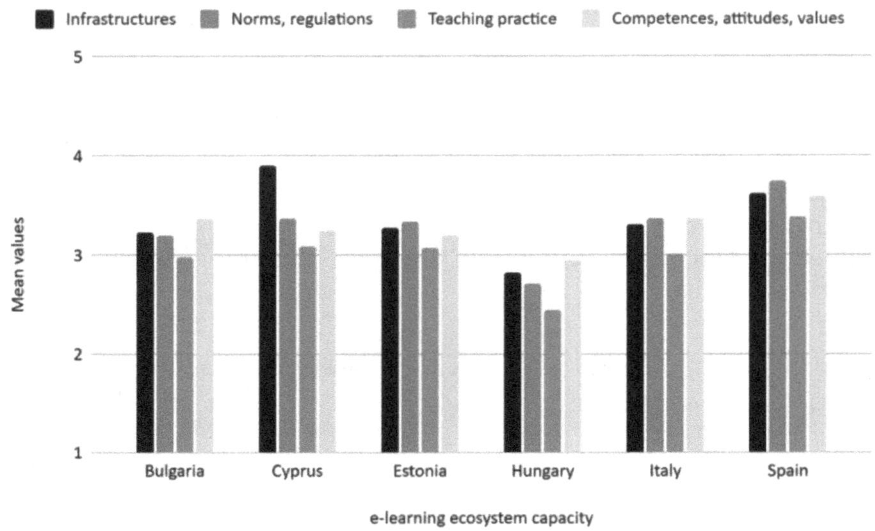

Fig. 1. The comparison of the capacities to use DT in partner countries (Strongly disagree -1; Somewhat disagree - 2; Neither agree nor disagree - 3; Somewhat agree - 4; Strongly agree).

6.2 Infrastructure and Tools Capacity for Learning with Disruptive Technologies

The institutions in sample countries have infrastructures for e-learning (LMS, video-conferencing, repositories) and technology sharing processes, but some gaps exist in centralized provision and availability in specific countries. The availability of robots for learning and teaching is rather limited in all the countries. It is common that the institutions have 1–3 VR headsets, a slightly different situation is in Spain, in which 10–20 sets are common. Availability of AI empowered feedback, chatbots in LMS systems partially available in Italy and Spain. Yet, there is lower availability of DT for the teaching process and general readiness for using Metaverse for learning purposes. While Internet connection speed for metaverse and processors of computers of students fit for metaverse are mostly available in all countries, processors of computers of lecturers fit for metaverse are less available in Bulgaria, Hungary, Italy. Using the discriminant analysis we could not discover significant functions that would define infrastructural capacity differences in the countries.

6.3 The Regulative Capacity to Use Disruptive Technologies

In explored countries and institutions there is no clear transition plan, and institutional strategy yet to move towards extensive e-learning mode in higher education. This is accompanied with a rather low level of involvement of educators and students to the technology decision making process in the institutions. Also there is a lack of incentive policies in countries to promote e-learning. The digital capacity of institutions has country specific gaps in having specific coordination units for technology training, coordination of edtech, infrastructure and tools. There is a flexibility in learning process planning for bringing in new technologies, the educators have the freedom to test and use new tools and teaching forms in the teaching process. Industrial technologies are mostly not well accessible in the teaching process in most of the countries except Spain, and technology sharing norms and practices across the university borders such as in internship are rather not developed. The countries have digital capacity at the normative level. They have insufficient availability of budgets for acquiring technologies.

Discriminant analysis revealed one significant function about normative institutional capacity (F1 (56% of the variance), Wilks lambda $= 0.006$, df $= 140$, $p < 0.021$). F1 $= 2.1$ institutions have departments that coordinate training and mentoring + 2.1 institutions provide incentives to study digital competence of lecturers + 1.53 institutions promote digitalization of teaching and learning with specific guidelines + 1.87 lecturers have full freedom to choose e-learning tools and technologies + + 0.91 lecturers are invited to suggest innovative technologies to the supply management + 1.2 there is sufficiently flexible learning process planning to grab innovative technology opportunities to lessons + 1.1 lecturers are encouraged to use their own spaces and internet for teaching + 1.0 lecturers are promoted towards OER + 1.0 lecturers follow health and safety guidelines. These function components are indicators of managing rather the lecturers competences but being quite bottom-up in enabling teachers' technology choices for lessons. Estonia represents this type of normative institutional capacity the most.

6.4 The Teaching Capacity to Use Disruptive Technologies

Regarding different e-learning teaching modes, teaching and learning in distant courses asynchronously; synchronous teaching and learning in video-conference lessons, blended lessons with synchronous or asynchronous online learning and hybrid learning, where some students attend online and others face-to-face are practiced in all countries. Using DT in lessons is rather modest. AR and VR experiences at courses as well as lessons with robots as course activities are rather not practiced in any of the countries. Using DT in the classroom can be seen to some extent in Spain. In addition to Spain, also in Estonia online simulations and games as course activities can be witnessed. Sharing e-teaching responsibilities hardly existed in any of the countries. Co-teaching with other lecturers in online sessions or students to co-support other students is seldom practiced in countries. There is a need to rely on students' competence when lecturers conduct technical lessons. Readiness to use technology innovations, such as searching for new technologies to be used in the classroom, or students suggesting new technologies to lecturers; or learners to test out new technologies in lessons, competence to adapt online scenarios to meet students' needs is mainly not visible specifically in Hungary. Teachers and students in all the countries prefer to use the same technology they are comfortable with. Need for support is rather prevalent in all the countries, especially to develop more complex learning resources in metaverse and in using DT. The need for technical and educational support to develop e-learning courses seems to be more required in Hungary. Staff in Cyprus and Spain have the need for technical assistance to set up lessons with technologies, and teachers in Spain claimed more the need for technical assistance during the lessons with technologies.

The Discriminant analysis with the learning capacity components revealed two functions that significantly differentiate the countries (F1 (56% of variance), Wilks lambda $= 0.57$, df $= 230$, $p < 0.001$; F (20% variance), Wilks lambda $= 0.21$, df $= 180$, $p < 0.001$). F1 $= 0.60$ there is a dedicated time slot for sharing technology experiences at institutions + 0.54 they have attended trainings where student/teacher roles were tested with technology + 0.79 they are teaching innovative technologies in their trainings + 0.48 they conduct co-teaching at lessons + 0.53 there is organized co-production with external clients in lessons + 0.52 they provide students with social timeslots at e-learning lessons. F1 function components indicate the profile of lecturers who themselves teach the technologies and share experiences with their colleagues about technologies. Spain, Italy and Cyprus represent this type of teaching capacity, whereas these teaching profiles are least apparent in Hungary. F2 $= 0.46$ have attended technology trainings that mainly focus on technology functionalities + 0.38 have learnt technology usage from developing technologies by themselves + 0,38 attend experience sharing events about technologies + 0.41 are conducting role-based and game based collaborative e-learning practices + 0.42 need educational technology support for developing metaverse learning resources. F2 function represents lecturers as self-learners about the innovation and highlights the collaboration driven practices they tend to use with students. Estonia and Bulgaria represent this type of teaching capacity.

6.5 The Personal Level Capacity to Use Disruptive Technologies

The personal level competences among lecturers and students to use DT are not equal in the sample countries, and are rather at lower level. The knowledgeability of the DT values is lower in the countries where the competences are lower. Estonian and Hungarian personal level capacity is lower than in other countries. There is a common understanding that using these technologies is cost effective and also requires training efforts and normative changes in institutions. There is generally still an optimistic view of the positive impacts of DT, and not a very high concern level. Lecturers do not have competences to develop learning scenarios, learning resources for DT and personalizing learning with it or adopting learning situations in most of the countries, the highest are competencies in Spain. Students are incompetent in participation in lessons with DT in Estonia, in other countries the mean values reached beyond average. Lecturers' knowledge of the potentials of DT was estimated the lowest in Estonia and Cyprus, in Spain the respondents were most knowledgeable. Students' knowledge of the pros and cons of DT was estimated the lowest in Estonia, in other countries the mean values reached beyond average. Knowing the learning effects and threats of the DT, and the sustainability issues was estimated low in Estonia, Cyprus and Hungary, whereas in Spain, Italy and Bulgaria the respondents were more knowledgeable. All the respondent samples in countries agreed that introducing DT in classes requires too much resources (time, money, energy consumption, natural resources etc.). In Estonia and Cyprus the respondents rather shared the belief that using DT in learning would not be more cost-effective. Introducing DT in classes requires too much staff training. Requiring the needs for changes in norms and regulations to implement DT were estimated at low levels in Estonia and Hungary, whereas in other countries the normative needs were estimated above average mean values. Recognising the educational institutions' role in estimating the learning potentials, threats, sustainability and health and wellbeing issues of DT was estimated lowest in Cyprus. Hungary also had lower mean value about estimating the sustainability concerns of DT. All the partners agreed that DT should be brought to educational process if they bring additional value to learning process, they also shared the belief that DT may advance human learning abilities, develop students' competences for digitized jobs, and there is no harm to be seen for the diversity of learning practices if DT are implemented. Most of the sample countries except Hungary had the high opinion that DT may increase resilience in the educational sector and may promote ecosystem sustainability and promoting students' learning results and advancing social and collaborative dimension.

The discriminant analysis indicated that two functions significantly determine the distribution of the country cases based on the personal capacity. Function 1 (44% of the variance) Wilks lambda $= 0.47$, df $= 140$, $p < .001$; F2 (26% of the variance), Wilks lambda $= 0.64$, df $= 108$, $p < 0.01$. Function 1 $= 0.58$ lecturers have sufficient competences for adopting learning scenarios with DT to special needs $+ 0.46$ lecturers have sufficient knowledge of the learning effects of DT $+ 0.32$ using DT promotes students learning results - 0.63 using DT does not threaten the diversity of learning practices. F1 relates with the positive perception of the effects of DT, seeing these as the enriching practices to the other learning practices. This optimistic view characterizes most the Spanish respondents and least the Estonian respondents. Function 2 $= 0.50$ using DT in classes advances social and collaborative dimension of learning $+ 0.45$ lecturers have sufficient knowledge of the sustainability issues of DT in education $+$ 0.42 institutions must evaluate the learning potential and threats of DT - 0.65 introducing DT in class requires too much resources (time, money, energy consumption, natural resources) - 0.42 using DT in learning promotes ecosystem sustainability. F2 may be associated with the controversial understandings related with the sustainability concerns and threats of DT. This more concerned view represents Estonian respondents.

7 Discussion

The findings generally revealed that all countries are still on the low capacity level for integrating DT to practice based e-learning on a large scale. Using the discriminant analysis we could not discover significant functions and capacity items that would define infrastructural capacity differences in the countries. The countries differed significantly on specifying institutional regulations on coordinating training and mentoring; providing incentives to study digital competence for lecturers; promoting digitalization into teaching and learning with guidelines; having dedicated time slots for sharing technology experiences at institutions, providing lectures freedom, flexibility and choice for selecting their learning environments; having lecturers who practiced teaching innovative technologies in their trainings; having lectures who attended trainings where student/teacher roles were tested with technology, having lecturers who had organized co-production with external clients in lessons. At personal level the recognition that introducing DT in class requires too much resources (time, money, energy consumption, natural resources); demands for institutions evaluating the learning potential and threats of DT in choosing the technologies; and the personal beliefs that using DT does not threaten the diversity of learning practices, and social learning were notable items discriminating countries' capacity. These general findings of critical elements may be used to develop the capacities in tertiary education institutions to support the disruptive technology uptake.

Acknowledgments. Research supported by the e-DIPLOMA, project number 101061424, funded by the European Union. Views and opinions expressed are, however, those of the authors only and do not necessarily reflect those of the European Union or the European Research Executive Agency (REA). Neither the European Union nor the granting authority can be held responsible for them.

Disclosure of Interests. The authors have no competing interests to declare that are relevant to the content of this article.

References

1. Mohamed Hashim, M.A., Tlemsani, I., Matthews, R.: Higher education strategy in digital transformation. Educ. Inf. Technol. **27**(3), 3171–3195 (2021). https://doi.org/10.1007/s10639-021-10739-1
2. Van der Vorst, C.: Higher Education turnaround supporting digital transformation. In Proceedings of Economics and Finance Conferences (No. 12413357). International Institute of Social and Economic Sciences (2021)
3. Mospan, N.V.: Trends in emergency higher education digital transformation during the COVID-19 pandemic. J. Univ. Teach. Learn. Pract. **20**(1) (2023)
4. Grigorescu, A., Zamfir, A.M., Sigurdarson, H.T., Lazarczyk Carlson, E.: Skill needs among European workers in knowledge production and transfer occupations. Electronics **11**(18), 2927 (2022)
5. Goulart, V.G., Liboni, L.B., Cezarino, L.O.: Balancing skills in the digital transformation era: The future of jobs and the role of higher education. Ind. High. Educ. **36**(2), 118–127 (2022)
6. Adedoyin, O.B., Soykan, E.: Covid-19 pandemic and online learning: the challenges and opportunities. Interact. Learn. Environ. **31**(2), 863–875 (2023)
7. Skog, D.A., Wimelius, H., Sandberg, J.: Digital disruption. Bus. Inf. Syst. Eng. **60**(5), 431–437 (2018)
8. Christensen, C.M.: The Innovator's Dilemma: The Revolutionary Book that Will Change the Way You Do. Business. Harvard Business School Press, Boston (1997)
9. Tellis, G.J.: Disruptive Technology or Visionary Leadership? The Journal of Product Innovation Management 23, 34–38 (2006). Utterback, J.M., Acee, H.J.: Disruptive technologies: an expanded view. Int. J. Innov. Manage. **9**(1), 1–17 (2005)

10. Hopster, J.: The ethics of disruptive technologies: towards a general framework. In: de Paz Santana, J.F., de la Iglesia, D.H. (eds.) New Trends in Disruptive Technologies, Tech Ethics and Artificial Intelligence. Advances in Intelligent Systems and Computing. Springer (2022)
11. Boucher, P., Bentzen, N., Laţici, T., Madiega, T., Schmertzing, L., Szczepanski, M.: Disruption by technology: impacts on politics, economics and society. Eur. Parliam. Res. Serv. PE652.079 (2020). https://www.europarl.europa.eu/stoa/en/document/EPRSIDA(2020)652079
12. Schuelke-Leech, B.: A model for understanding the orders of magnitude of disruptive technologies. Technol. Forecast. Soc. Chang. **129**, 261–274 (2018)
13. Baser, H, Morgan, P.: Capacity, Change and Performance. Study Report. Discussion Paper No.59B. European Centre for Development Policy Management: Maastricht, The Netherlands (2008)
14. Verhoef, P.C., et al.: Digital transformation: a multidisciplinary reflection and research agenda. J. Bus. Res. **122**, 889–901 (2021)
15. Quaicoe, J.S., Ogunyemi, A., Bauters, M.: School-based digital innovation challenges and way forward conversations about digital transformation in education. Educ. Sci. **13**(4), 344 (2023). https://doi.org/10.3390/educsci13040344

Enhancing ChatGPT in POE Inquiry Learning for STEM Education to Improve Critical Thinking Skills

Pin-Hui Li[1], Kinshuk[2], and Yueh-Min Huang[1](✉)

[1] Department of Engineering Science, National Cheng Kung University, Tainan City, Taiwan
huang@mail.ncku.edu.tw

[2] College of Information, University of North Texas, Denton, USA
kinshuk@unt.edu

Abstract. The importance of integrating inquiry-based strategies into STEM activities lies in creating a challenging and engaging teaching environment that promotes active learning among students. This educational setting not only sparks students' interest in learning but also enhances their critical thinking skills and practical application abilities. Inquiry-based strategies encourage students to learn through independent exploration and problem-solving processes, enabling them to actively participate and learn in activities, thereby cultivating critical thinking. However, to ensure that students effectively achieve these objectives and do not give up or withdraw due to the difficulty and challenge, appropriate guidance and feedback are necessary. The development of ChatGPT-based Inquiry Learning Assistant (InquiryGPT) in this study represents the integration of technology into education. InquiryGPT will provide constraints and dialogue during students' participation in inquiry-based STEM activities, aiming to prevent students from overly relying on ChatGPT without engaging in critical thinking. This study examined the effectiveness of InquiryGPT based on the Technology Acceptance Model (TAM) and investigated the differences in its impact on students compared to traditional ChatGPT. This research will contribute to a better understanding of the influence of new technology-enhanced educational tools on students' learning processes and provide valuable insights and guidance for future educational technology development.

Keywords: Inquiry-based learning · ChatGPT · critical thinking skills · Technology Acceptance Model (TAM)

1 Introduction

In today's society, the importance of STEM (Science, Technology, Engineering, and Mathematics) education is increasingly emphasized as a key pathway to nurturing future leaders and innovators. Emphasizing students' active involvement, inquiry-based learning focuses on fostering students' curiosity and thirst for knowledge compared to traditional lecture-based teaching [1]. Inquiry-based learning is not merely a teaching method

Y.-P. Cheng et al. (Eds.): ICITL 2024, LNCS 14785, pp. 30–39, 2024.
https://doi.org/10.1007/978-3-031-65881-5_4

but also an educational philosophy aimed at fostering students' comprehensive development. It cultivates students' critical thinking and problem-solving skills [2]. Additionally, inquiry-based learning promotes interdisciplinary learning. When addressing real-world problems, students need to integrate knowledge and skills from various disciplines. Such interdisciplinary learning enables them to gain a more comprehensive understanding of problems and fosters creativity. In summary, cultivating students' inquiry spirit and problem-solving abilities is crucial, and inquiry-based learning is one effective approach to achieving this goal.

The importance of critical thinking for students is self-evident. In today's era of information explosion, students need to possess good critical thinking skills to cope with complex challenges [3]. Inquiry-based learning not only imparts knowledge but, more importantly, cultivates students' critical thinking skills [4]. In inquiry-based learning, students are encouraged to think and question, emphasizing their active participation through processes such as posing questions, seeking in-formation, analyzing data, and proposing solutions. This exploratory learning environment nurtures students to consider the multifaceted aspects of problems, thereby stimulating their critical thinking [5, 6].

In the current digital and technologically advanced era, the entry of artificial intelligence technologies such as ChatGPT into the field of education has opened up new teaching methods and learning experiences. The intervention of this technology brings many new opportunities and challenges to education [7, 8]. In inquiry-based learning, traditional teaching methods often make it difficult for teachers to attend to each student individually, personalized guidance and feedback. In such situations, the intervention of ChatGPT can serve as an effective means to address this deficiency. However, if students can easily obtain answers through ChatGPT, they may not question the answers provided by ChatGPT and reduce their motivation for independent inquiry [9]. Therefore, to fully utilize the advantages of ChatGPT and prevent students from overly relying on it, this study developed the ChatGPT-based Inquiry Learning Assistant (InquiryGPT), specifically targeting inquiry-based activities in STEM. It standardizes students' correct use of ChatGPT and encourages them to solve problems through their own efforts and thinking.

To examine the effectiveness of the developed InquiryGPT in this study, the Technology Acceptance Model (TAM) [10] utilized to investigate the impact of students' perception of usefulness and ease of use regarding the intervention of InquiryGPT compared to traditional ChatGPT in inquiry-based STEM activities. Subsequently, the study aimed to delve into the differences in the impact of InquiryGPT and traditional ChatGPT on students in inquiry-based STEM activities. The following research questions:

1. In inquiry-based STEM activities, is there a difference in students' technological acceptance between using InquiryGPT and traditional ChatGPT?
2. In inquiry-based STEM activities, compared to unrestricted use of traditional ChatGPT, can the adoption of InquiryGPT enhance students' critical thinking abilities?

2 Related Work

2.1 Inquiry-Based Learning in STEM

In inquiry-based learning, students are no longer passive recipients of knowledge but actively engage in the learning process. They continuously pose questions, make discoveries, and conduct experiments, constructing knowledge and understanding through analysis and interpretation. The inquiry model proposed by White and Gunstone [11], known as Predict-Observe-Explain (POE), provides a framework to encourage students' reasoning of scientific concepts. Hong, Hwang, Liu, Ho and Chen [12] explicitly outlined the design process of each stage of POE in their study: (1) Teachers pose questions to stimulate students' predictive abilities(predict). (2) If students cannot answer the questions, the system provides opportunities for observation or reading relevant information, prompting students to rethink and attempt to answer the questions(observe). (3) If students remain puzzled after observation and reading, the system provides explanations of the answers to help them establish correct understanding. This inquiry-based learning model fosters students' critical thinking and problem-solving skills, leading to a deeper grasp of knowledge(explain).

2.2 Critical Thinking Ability in Inquiry-Based Learning

Inquiry-based learning encourages students to evaluate different perspectives, evidence, and solutions, and make reasoned judgments. Students need to analyze and compare information from various sources, assess their credibility and effectiveness, and make decisions based on these evaluations. This ability cultivates students' critical thinking about information, enabling them to make wise choices. Such capacity is not only crucial in academic domains but also a key skill needed for problem-solving and decision-making in real-life situations. Many studies emphasize the importance of critical thinking. For instance, Wale and Bishaw [5] explored the impact of inquiry-based learning on students' critical thinking abilities, revealing that inquiry-based teaching is recommended as a means to enhance students' critical thinking skills because this approach strengthens students' skills in explanation, analysis, evaluation, reasoning, interpretation, and self-regulation, which are core skills of critical thinking.

2.3 ChatGPT

ChatGPT not only provides a platform for communication but also serves as a guide. Through conversations with students, it sparks their curiosity, guides them to explore deeper questions, and encourages them to engage in critical thinking. Through dialogue with ChatGPT, students learn to question, analyze, and evaluate different perspectives, thereby expanding their thinking and enhancing their critical thinking skills. More importantly, ChatGPT, rather than just providing answers, guides students to contemplate the essence of questions through conversation, thereby elevating their level of critical thinking.

Overall, ChatGPT is highly suitable for use in inquiry-based learning both in terms of its technological capabilities and characteristics. However, it is important to note that overreliance on ChatGPT may have negative effects on students' learning [13, 14]. Teachers and educators guiding students in using ChatGPT should encourage them not only to rely on the answers provided by ChatGPT but also to engage in independent thinking, analysis, and discussion through interaction with ChatGPT. Furthermore, teachers can design inquiry-based learning tasks that require students to actively participate in the process of using ChatGPT such as posing deeper questions, verifying the answers provided by ChatGPT, and comparing different perspectives. Such activities can help students build a deeper understanding of knowledge and develop their analytical and critical thinking abilities. In conclusion, ChatGPT plays a significant role as a powerful auxiliary tool in inquiry-based learning. However, students should remain vigilant when using ChatGPT, actively engaging in the process of thinking and discussing, to derive greater learning outcomes.

2.4 Technology Acceptance Model (TAM)

Before introducing new technological systems, it is crucial to measure using technology acceptance model, is a theoretical model widely used in the field of technology adoption, which assesses users' acceptance and willingness to use new technology systems[10, 15]. By evaluating users' perceived ease of use and perceived usefulness of new technology systems, TAM helps us understand users' attitudes and intentions towards the system. Therefore, this study chooses TAM as the theoretical framework to evaluate whether students' perceived ease of use and perceived usefulness of InquiryGPT differ from traditional ChatGPT. By comparing the applications of InquiryGPT and traditional ChatGPT in inquiry-based STEM activities.

3 ChatGPT-Based Inquiry Learning Assistant (InquiryGPT)

Inquiry-based learning tasks centered around students often present challenges, as students typically require guidance to engage and complete them successfully. To address the immediate difficulties encountered by learners in inquiry-based learning, this study integrates ChatGPT and the POE (Predict, Observe, Explain) inquiry-based learning framework, developing an intelligent assistant suitable for such learning. This tool utilizes the large-scale language model ChatGPT to answer students' queries and regulates their questioning during operation to ensure they remain in the inquiry phase, thus preventing overreliance on ChatGPT. All operations are carried out through Apple's built-in app - Shortcut. The following will elaborate on the detailed operational workflow.

3.1 The Design of ChatGPT-Based Inquiry Learning Assistant

In the first stage - Predict, students are encouraged to contemplate potential answers when facing a problem, which helps stimulate their autonomous thinking ability. To prevent students from overly relying on ChatGPT to obtain answers directly, InquiryGPT employs measures to restrict students' questioning methods. Specifically, as indicated by the red box in Fig. 1, students are initially required to pose questions along with their presumed answers to the questions. Subsequently, students' responses are transformed into new question forms, as depicted by the blue box in Fig. 2. InquiryGPT automatically inputs these new questions into ChatGPT and retrieves their answers. This process helps students consider problems from different perspectives and learn to apply their knowledge to solve them.

Fig. 1. InquiryGPT restricts students' questioning.

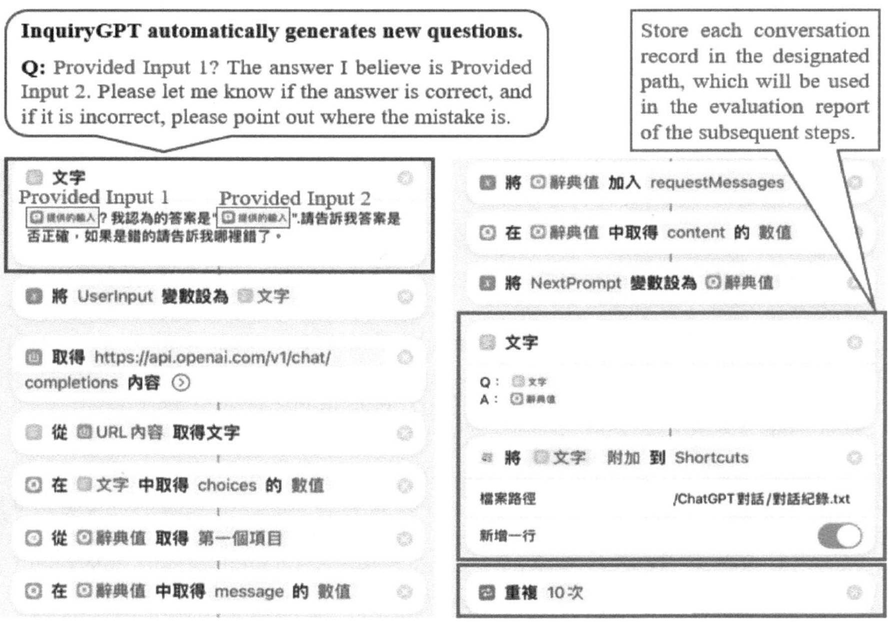

Fig. 2. Forming new questions for dialogue with ChatGPT and archiving the conversation.

In the second stage - Observe, after reading InquiryGPT's initial response, students begin hands-on implementation to address the problem posed by the teacher. It's important to note that InquiryGPT is not limited to a single conversation. If students have questions about ChatGPT's response or encounter new issues during the implementation process, they can continue the conversation. This step aims to train students' critical thinking skills because ChatGPT is not always correct, and students cannot simply trust its answers but need to converse with it to clarify concepts. InquiryGPT's system default is to conduct 10 conversations, as indicated by the green box in Fig. 2. Finally, InquiryGPT will save each question-and-answer record as a conversation log file, as shown by the red box in Fig 2.

The key to this process is to help students deepen their understanding of knowledge through practice and teach them how to continuously think and question during practice rather than blindly accepting answers. Through multiple conversations with InquiryGPT, students have the opportunity to continually examine and validate their ideas, thus cultivating their critical thinking abilities. Additionally, saving each conversation record not only helps students review and summarize the learning process but also serves as reference material for their further learning and exploration. This learning approach, which combines practice, discussion, and recording, contributes to the comprehensive development of students' cognitive abilities and learning skills.

3.2 The Implementation of InquiryGPT

InquiryGPT is a tool specifically designed for students engaged in inquiry-based learning. Figure 3 illustrates the usage process of InquiryGPT, clearly depicting the interaction between learners and the tool. This study aims to highlight the features and advantages of InquiryGPT as a new type of learning tool, which holds significant importance and wide-ranging application prospects. Through in-depth research into its functions and impacts, we can better understand its role in the field of education, providing new insights and methods for educational reform and innovation.

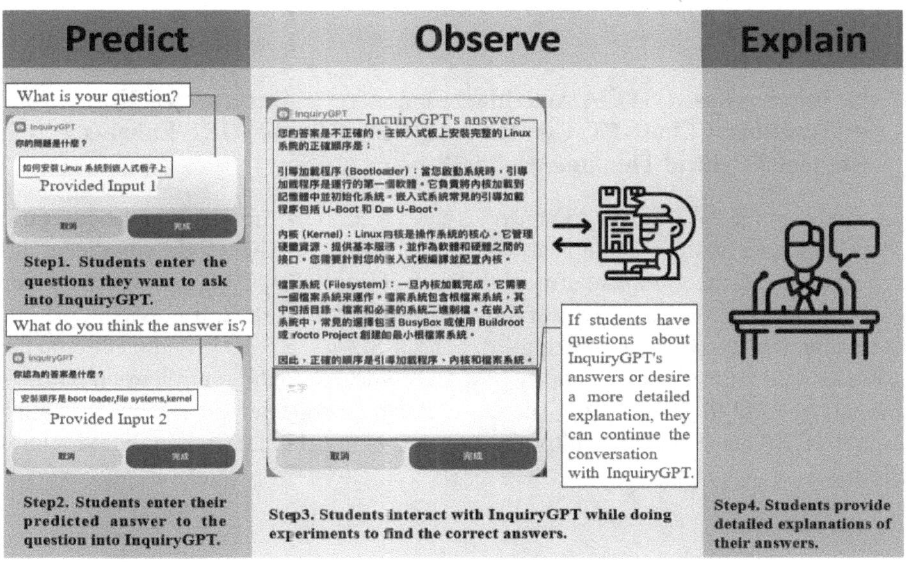

Fig. 3. The process of students using InquiryGPT.

4 Results

4.1 In Inquiry-Based STEM Activities, is There a Difference in Students' Technological Acceptance Between Using InquiryGPT and Traditional ChatGPT?

This study employed independent sample t-tests to analyze whether there was a difference in students' acceptance of the new technology. The analysis results are shown in Table 1. There were no significant differences between the experimental group and the control group in perceived usefulness ($t = 0.516$, $p > 0.05$) and perceived ease of use ($t = 0.457$, $p > 0.05$). From the mean scores, it can be observed that the scores of the two groups are quite close. Therefore, it can be concluded that there was no significant difference in the acceptance of InquiryGPT in the experimental group compared to the acceptance of ChatGPT in the control group.

Table 1. Independent Sample T-test Analysis Results of Technology Acceptance

	Group	Mean	SD	*t*	*p*	Effect size
perceived usefulness (PU)	EG	15.2	1.62	0.516	0.608	0.131
	CG	15.4	1.82			
perceived ease of use (PEU)	EG	15.4	1.47	0.457	0.649	0.116
	CG	15.5	1.84			

4.2 In Inquiry-Based STEM Activities, Compared to Unrestricted Use of Traditional ChatGPT, Can the Adoption of InquiryGPT Enhance Students' Critical Thinking Abilities?

This study utilized ANCOVA to analyze students' critical thinking, with descriptive results presented in Table 2 and analysis results in Table 3. There were significant differences between the groups in critical thinking ability ($F = 55.92$, $p < 0.001$). Upon observing the mean scores of critical thinking post-test in Table 2, it is evident that the experimental group (Critical thinking: $M = 12.3$, $SD = 2.87$) had significantly higher mean scores in critical thinking ability post-test compared to the control group (Critical thinking: $M = 11.9$, $SD = 3.16$). Therefore, it can be concluded that the intervention of InquiryGPT helps students cultivate critical thinking skills in inquiry-based STEM activities.

Table 2. Descriptive Results of critical Thinking Skills

	EG (N = 31)				CG (N = 31)			
	Pre-test		Post-test		Pre-test		Post-test	
	M	SD	M	SD	M	SD	M	SD
Critical thinking	11.2	3.43	12.3	2.87	11.4	2.79	11.9	3.16

Table 3. ANCOVA results for critical Thinking Skills

Variable	SS	df	Mean Square	F	*p*	Partial η^2
Critical thinking	371.9	1	371.9	55.92	$< 0.001^{***}$	0.517

Note. ** p < .01, *** p < .001

5 Discussion

To guide students through inquiry-based STEM activities, this study combined the inquiry-based learning strategy based on POE and the learning assistant developed using ChatGPT (InquiryGPT). Through this combination, we aim to provide students with sufficient opportunities for autonomous learning while offering necessary guidance and support. Students' acceptance of InquiryGPT through TAM, help under-stand students' attitudes and willingness to use this learning assistant, evaluating their perceived ease of use and perceived usefulness of InquiryGPT.

Furthermore, we explore the impact of this activity on students' critical thinking abilities through observing and analyzing their performance in inquiry-based STEM activities. By comparing the performance of students using and not using In-quiryGPT in critical thinking ability, we can preliminarily evaluate the impact of this learning assistant on students.

Educational activities often adopt various technology-developed systems to more effectively assist students' learning processes. The emergence of ChatGPT injects new vitality into this trend, providing many educational technology systems with more development opportunities and challenges. Multiple studies have shown the benefits of ChatGPT in learning, and this study aim to confirm whether InquiryGPT is similarly effective. The research findings indicate that students' acceptance of InquiryGPT does not significantly differ from ChatGPT, strengthening the application prospects of InquiryGPT as a teaching tool and providing new possibilities for educational technology development.

While ChatGPT can provide quick answers and information, it may lead to students relying on the robot-provided answers, reducing their opportunities for independent thinking and reasoning. Because they are more inclined to accept the answers provided by the robot rather than conducting exploration and thinking on their own [14]. Therefore, when using ChatGPT, educators need to balance the relationship between robot assistance and students' autonomous thinking to ensure that students' higher-order thinking skills are appropriately cultivated and developed.

The goal of inquiry-based STEM activities is to cultivate students' critical thinking abilities. To prevent the use of ChatGPT from hindering student learning, this study expects students to follow the steps of inquiry and maintain skepticism towards ChatGPT by operating InquiryGPT actively. This allows students to maximize their learning from the inquiry task. According to the results from Tables 2 and 3, the developed InquiryGPT in this study can effectively enhance students' critical thinking abilities, thereby improving their learning outcomes in inquiry-based STEM activities.

6 Conclusion

InquiryGPT is an intelligent assistant developed specifically for students engaged in inquiry-based STEM activities, integrating the POE inquiry strategy, ChatGPT, and the iOS app Shortcut. Its aim is to foster students' critical thinking abilities. The POE strategy emphasizes the processes of prediction, observation, and explanation, encouraging students' active participation and cultivating their critical thinking and problem-solving skills. Meanwhile, ChatGPT provides students with quick and convenient access to information and communication channels, enabling them to acquire necessary knowledge promptly and engage in in-depth discussions and explorations. By combining these elements, InquiryGPT becomes a powerful tool that effectively guides students in conducting thorough exploration and learning. Compared to the unrestricted use of ChatGPT, InquiryGPT assists students in completing inquiry-based STEM tasks through proper guidance, thereby enhancing their understanding and application abilities of knowledge. This guided learning process not only helps students establish a deeper understanding but also fosters their critical thinking and problem-solving skills, laying a solid foundation for their future academic and professional careers.

References

1. Wilis, R., Prayitno, B.A., Sunarno, W., Anjirawaroj, S.: Improving students' metacognitive abilities and creative thinking skills through STEM-based in online learning. JPBI (Jurnal Pendidikan Biologi Indonesia) **9**, 90–102 (2023)
2. Putra, M., Rahman, A., Ilwandri, I., Suhayat, Y., Santosa, T.A., Putra, R., Aprilisia, S.: The effect of STEM-based REACT model on students' critical thinking skills: a meta-analysis study. LITERACY: Int. Sci. J. Soc. Educ. Hum. **2**, 207–217 (2023)
3. Facione, P.A.: Critical thinking: what it is and why it counts. Insight Assess. **1**, 1–23 (2011)
4. Alsaleh, N.J.: Teaching critical thinking skills: literature review. Turk. Online J. Educ. Technol.-TOJET **19**, 21–39 (2020)
5. Wale, B.D., Bishaw, K.S.: Effects of using inquiry-based learning on EFL students' critical thinking skills. Asian-Pac. J. Second Foreign Lang. Educ. **5**, 1–14 (2020)
6. Isdianti, M., Nasrudin, H., Erman, E.: The effectiveness of STEM based inquiry learning packages to improving students' critical thinking skill. J. Educ. Gifted Young Sci. **9**, 223–232 (2021)

7. Huang, Y.-M., Cheng, A.-Y., Wu, T.-T.: Analysis of learning behavior of human posture recognition in Maker Education. Front. Psychol. **13**, 868487 (2022)
8. Lee, H.-Y., Chen, P.-H., Wang, W.-S., Huang, Y.-M., Wu, T.-T.: Empowering ChatGPT with guidance mechanism in blended learning: effect of self-regulated learning, higher-order thinking skills, and knowledge construction. Int. J. Educ. Technol. High. Educ. **21**, 1–28 (2024)
9. Cooper, G.: Examining science education in chatgpt: an exploratory study of generative artificial intelligence. J. Sci. Educ. Technol. **32**, 444–452 (2023)
10. Scherer, R., Siddiq, F., Tondeur, J.: The technology acceptance model (TAM): a meta-analytic structural equation modeling approach to explaining teachers' adoption of digital technology in education. Comput. Educ. **128**, 13–35 (2019)
11. White, R., Gunstone, R.: Prediction-observation-explanation. Probing Underst. **4**, 44–64 (1992)
12. Hong, J.-C., Hwang, M.-Y., Liu, M.-C., Ho, H.-Y., Chen, Y.-L.: Using a "prediction–observation–explanation" inquiry model to enhance student interest and intention to continue science learning predicted by their Internet cognitive failure. Comput. Educ. **72**, 110–120 (2014)
13. Rahman, M.M., Watanobe, Y.: ChatGPT for education and research: opportunities, threats, and strategies. Appl. Sci. **13**, 5783 (2023)
14. Baidoo-Anu, D., Ansah, L.O.: Education in the era of generative artificial intelligence (AI): Understanding the potential benefits of ChatGPT in promoting teaching and learning. Journal of AI **7**, 52–62 (2023)
15. Davis, F.D.: Perceived usefulness, perceived ease of use, and user acceptance of information technology. MIS Q. 319–340 (1989)

Personalisation is not Guaranteed: The Challenges of Using Generative AI for Personalised Learning

Kristjan-Julius Laak[1(✉)], Rania Abdelghani[2], and Jaan Aru[2]

[1] Institute of Computer Science, University of Tartu, Tartu, Estonia
julius.laak@gmail.com

[2] INRIA Research Center, University of Bordeaux, Talence, France

Abstract. Personalised learning promises to free learners from the shackles of traditional one-size-fits-all classrooms and fulfil the potential of every child. Generative artificial intelligence (GenAI) is seen as the solution that will bring personalised learning to all learners. Here, we argue that GenAI may not only fall short of this expectation but also hinder the development of the competencies necessary to unlock learners' potential. Our first argument posits that although personalised learning aims to diversify instruction to meet the needs of individual learners, the indiscriminate use of GenAI risks homogenising learners' performance and creativity, limiting the discovery of their potential. We argue that effective use of GenAI requires curiosity, critical thinking, self-regulation and metacognition. Our second argument is that these skills are not enhanced by GenAI but rather might suffer from its unregulated use. Thus, while GenAI has considerable potential to enhance learning, learners will not reap these benefits by default. Instead, to make the most of the opportunities GenAI offers, the education system must invest more in developing human skills rather than technology.

Keywords: Personalised Learning · Generative Artificial Intelligence · Metacognition · Self-regulated Learning · Critical Thinking · Curiosity

1 Introduction

Personalised learning aspires to equip individual learners with high-quality education, flexibility, and choice to fulfil their potential [6, 19, 38]. Decades of work on intelligent tutoring systems have proven their potential for knowledge acquisition [39, 43] and supporting learners' self-regulated learning skills (SRL) [3, 5, 16, 34]. Yet, their development can take years because what makes them effective – guidance at step level while supporting multiple solution paths within a single problem – makes building them quite complex [4, 42]. The recent advent of generative artificial intelligence (GenAI) has come with the hope of lifting the limitations of bespoke adaptive learning systems and providing every child with a general personal tutor [26, 33, 46].

In the tutoring context, the traditional perspective of personalisation—understood as delivering tailored instruction according to students' needs [36, 43]—is carried over

Y.-P. Cheng et al. (Eds.): ICITL 2024, LNCS 14785, pp. 40–49, 2024.
https://doi.org/10.1007/978-3-031-65881-5_5

to generative AI technologies. In his blog post on how AI will save the world, the techno-optimist Marc Andreessen argues that Large Language Models (LLMs) like ChatGPT will accelerate human intelligence only if we let it become our tutor: "Every child will have an AI tutor that is infinitely patient, infinitely compassionate, infinitely knowledgeable, infinitely helpful. The AI tutor will be by each child's side every step of their development, helping them maximise their potential with the machine version of infinite love." Driven by similar enthusiasm, Edtech companies have been racing to add GenAI-based tutors to their products (e.g. Khanmigo) and create new GenAI products from scratch (e.g. Sizzle).

The conviction of the GenAI's potential to provide personal tutoring is widespread not only in the private sector but also in the scientific literature. For example, [25] suggest that "ChatGPT can be used for one-on-one tutoring by providing immediate feedback on pupil work. A student composing an essay can use ChatGPT to receive feedback on their grammar, sentence structure, and overall organisation." [33] present various ways in which ChatGPT can act as an intuitive tutor for all levels of education: suggesting learning resources, providing suggestions to improve writing, creating practical exercises and quizzes, providing explanations and step-by-step solutions to problems, etc. The approach of personal tutoring to improve learning outcomes stems from Benjamin Bloom's early works, which showed that students receiving one-on-one tutoring scored two standard deviations higher than students in traditional classroom settings [6]. Bloom's work is still a central justification for AI-based personalised learning, as demonstrated by [32]: "ChatGPT can potentially be used to provide a virtual intelligent tutoring service, in which students can ask questions and receive personalised responses and feedback. This personalised feedback-enabled iterative learning leads to significant learning gains, as demonstrated by the Two Sigma Effect".

These trends assume that learning improvement is achieved through personal tutoring and suggest that as every student can use GenAI, all students will reap the benefits. Here, we challenge these assumptions.

Our central thesis is that providing every child with personalised learning opportunities cannot be solved with technology and GenAI alone. Rather, for the GenAI tools to help push learners towards fulfilling their potential, it is crucial for the learners first to develop independent learning and thinking skills. These skills include strong cognitive and metacognitive abilities that could allow them to control and evaluate their learning while using GenAI. Crucially, as we will explain, these human factors might not be enhanced but might even be hindered by GenAI. In doing so, we start by redefining personalised learning as a process within the learner's mind, decoupling it from AI-based tutoring systems. Then, we present evidence of the homogenising effect GenAI has on performance, reducing the diversity between learners. We discuss the competencies required for modern personalised learning (e.g., metacognition) and argue that unregulated use of GenAI might hinder the development of these skills. Finally, we briefly describe strategies for reaping the benefits of GenAI.

2 Personalisation Within the Learner's Mind

The prevalent approach to personalised learning that underpins most intelligent tutoring systems focuses on optimising knowledge acquisition at learners' own pace [43]. In Benjamin Bloom's terms, the goal is to close the achievement gap between diverse groups of students by increasing variation in instruction and providing flexible learning time [15]. This approach fits the Bloomian optimisation problem that narrows personalised learning down to mastery learning in which students progress based on academic mastery, not as a function of time [6, 18, 24, 37]. The primary manifestation of this paradigm is the pursuit of tailoring lessons to individual learners, based on their varied requirements [25].

However, the epistemic approach of adaptive learning systems, which traces student knowledge as binary truth statements, is argued to be an oversimplification and misrepresentation of mastery learning, which hinders the development of personal abilities and traits necessary for a diverse and democratic society [15, 40]. In short, Bloom's personalised learning might not serve the purpose of K-12 education [22].

Precisely due to the mismatch with the goals of modern education, critical AI and education studies have questioned the need for personalised learning as a technological optimisation problem [23, 31, 40]. The personalisation needed focuses on the learning process and does not necessarily need to be AI-driven.

A more holistic, learning-centred understanding of personalised learning requires system-wide changes in policy, curriculum, school organisation, and teaching practices [19]. [27] identifies five components of such personalised learning: (1) the need for formative assessment that supports learning, (2) pedagogy that actively engages each student to fulfil their potential, (3) enabling curriculum choice with opportunities for enrichment and creativity, (4) listening to student needs in the school organisational level (e.g. providing resting areas), and (5) connecting schools with the local communities to extend learning beyond the classroom.

These aspects put the modern goals of schooling at the core of personalised learning, enable active knowledge construction within each child, and develop broader competencies such as SRL, complex problem-solving skills, critical thinking, social skills, emotional intelligence, etc. [29]. In other words, personalised learning is an active learning process within the learner's mind, and technology serves a supportive role for the teacher via record-keeping and analytical dashboards [24]. We argue that providing every child unregulated access to GenAI does not support this more holistic view of personalised learning.

3 Generative AI as a Global Homogeniser

Our first argument is that while personalised learning is about increasing the variation and heterogeneity of the learning approach based on the characteristics of the learner and researchers assume that GenAI will support increasing the variation, in reality, when used uncritically, GenAI will make students' performance and creative output more homogenous.

Accumulating evidence suggests that the distribution of gains from AI assistance depends on the learner's initial abilities. In a study with college-educated professionals who had to complete two occupation-specific writing tasks, such as press releases and delicate emails, participants who had access to Chat- GPT in the second task had substantially lower completion times and higher evaluator grades than the control group [28]. However, the productivity increase depended on participants' scores on the first task: the productivity increased for less qualified but not for highly qualified participants, making the outcomes more equal. Similarly, in a study with 758 strategy consultants who had to complete a series of complex, knowledge-intensive tasks closely resembling their daily activities, participants who had access to ChatGPT showed 40% higher quality results with tasks within the frontier of AI capabilities, with the most significant beneficiaries being the bottom-half-skill subjects whose productivity improved by 43% compared to the 17% increase of the top-half-skilled performers [11].

These results have been repeated in other domains, too. The introduction of GenAI-based conversational assistants to customer support agents increased the performance of junior agents by 34%, helping them to move more quickly down the experience curve [8]. At the same time, there was minimal impact on productivity and even a decrease in the quality of conversations of the more experienced agents, showing a highly uneven impact of AI assistance on productivity (see Fig. 1). In another study, when writers were allowed to use GenAI for idea creation, access to GenAI ideas substantially improved the creativity of stories written by less creative writers but had little effect on inherently creative writers [12].

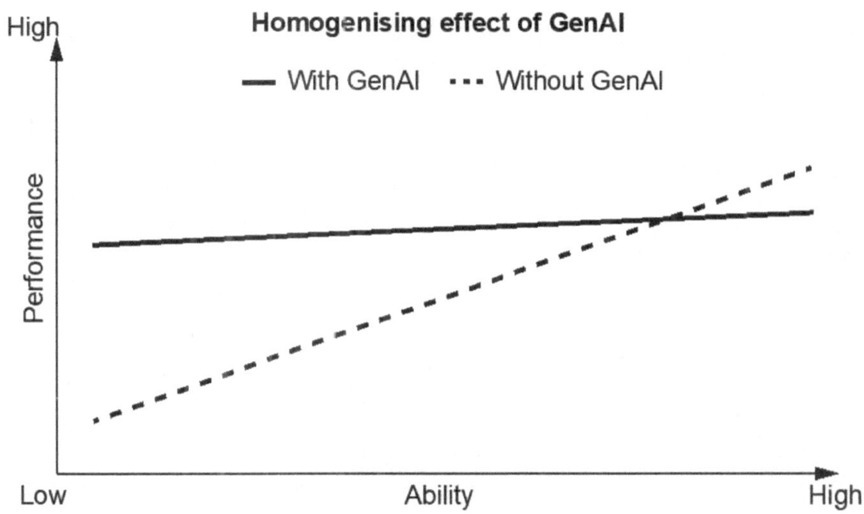

Fig. 1. The usage of generative artificial intelligence acts as a homogeniser of performance. People with low ability or initial performance are lifted closer to the output of high-performers while the latter has little to gain from using the tools.

While these results seem commendable, they are actually alarming as they reduce and do not increase the variability of the learning process. The usage of GenAI effectively equalises low and high performers, removing any disadvantage or advantage based on their initial ability. In other words, the effect of GenAI assistance might only benefit a proportion of the learners and get us further from the aspiration of opening up the potential of every child. The average learning outcomes become less unique and less diverse. The main reason for this pessimistic view is the evidence provided above: when different people give the prompts to GenAI, the results will be more similar compared to the case where these different students would try to solve the tasks independently.

In education, performance homogenisation could happen at three levels. First, horizontally: children within the same age group get more similar as the responses of GenAI will not much depend on the initial intrinsic variation of their abilities. Second, vertically: children of different ages become more similar because GenAI does not respond differently based on age. Third, culturally: children across the globe will become more similar as GenAI does not take into account the cultural background or specifics of the user (for instance, the response that GenAI gives to an Estonian or a French student is roughly the same and in both cases heavily influenced by the mostly English-language training data). In that regard, the unregulated use of GenAI might not help us get closer to the personalisation we aspire to achieve. Next, we argue that the exact skills we want children to develop in more holistic personalised learning settings are needed to effectively use the opportunities provided by GenAI.

4 (Meta)cognitive Factors Required for Personalised Learning

Many studies have shown that independent learning is driven by curiosity, which is enabled by providing children with cognitively engaging activities that offer options for discovery and surprises [9, 14]. Yet, GenAI tools are often explicitly designed to do the opposite: to offer rapid and explicit solutions while requiring minimal cognitive effort from the user. Despite children being avid learners, naturally yearning for new knowledge and skills, curiosity is suppressed through instruction that encourages performance over academic and intellectual exploration, as often happens when children attend school [20]. Enabling and supporting learners' curiosity should be at the heart of both human and AI tutors.

In addition, given the large amounts of training data and emergent properties, LLMs confidently answer even poorly formulated questions, potentially giving children the illusion that question-asking skills are no longer necessary. However, proper question-asking skills are needed for children to become independent, lifelong learners and should be explicitly trained and promoted [1, 2].

Lastly, we argue that learners must have SRL and metacognitive skills to effectively use GenAI tools for learning. Learners with SRL skills are actively engaged in a cyclic process of planning their learning, continuously monitoring their learning process, and reflecting on their learning approach and task outcomes [30, 44, 47, 48]. Metacognition, a component of SRL, refers to the ability to reflect on and control one's cognitive processes [7, 16]. Combined, these skills include self-monitoring (e.g., awareness of comprehension), planning and regulation (e.g., setting goals and adjusting learning strategies), and evaluation (e.g., judging the accuracy and effectiveness of one's thinking). Without those skills, GenAI could hinder learning. For instance, for learners to direct their writing process with GenAI, they must first be aware and able to describe what they are trying to say in the essay. Without elaborate input from the student, the essays will be more homogenous. Hence, learners need to be able to understand and express their aims when using these chatbots. In short, the effective use of GenAI depends on specific cognitive and metacognitive skills.

5 Does GenAI Support or Hinder These Skills?

One optimistic view about GenAI in education could be that the use of GenAI actually enhances curiosity, question-asking skills, SRL, and metacognition. However, our second key argument is that this scenario is unlikely: GenAI will not, by default, improve these skills. Rather, the unguided use of GenAI might hinder the development of these skills.

First, the unilaterally confident and fluent responses of GenAI models puts more, note less, pressure on human metacognitive skills. In their analysis, [21] describe a natural tendency of humans to learn and accumulate information from agents that are confident and knowledgeable. This distortion of human beliefs cannot be easily overcome with GenAI models that neither signal uncertainty (e.g. using "I think", "hmm", or "uh, oh" when talking) nor distinguish facts from fiction. The more certainty GenAI's output has, the more rapidly and with greater confidence people will adopt the (mis)information these models produce. This metacognitive bias leaves children to assume certainty where there is none, leading to difficulties correcting the information transmitted from GenAI to a child after the fact.

Second, GenAI-created misinformation is harder to detect by humans and detectors than semantically equivalent human-written misinformation [10]. In a study done in a prestigious business school, ChatGPT-aided students performed 28% worse compared to students who had to write the answers from scratch [17]. Failing to detect errors in the model's output was attributed to students' trust in ChatGPT answers, even when warned about the poor quality of these answers and the possible confirmation bias. As the author notes: "A correct use will not involve humans copying the output of these tools blindly," but that is precisely what the students did. These results indicate the essential role of critical thinking skills in evaluating and correcting GenAI output. Without existing skills, learners can do a considerably worse job when aided by GenAI than when working alone.

Third, despite studies investigating solving complex and ill-defined problems showing higher quality and originality of solutions when using ChatGPT [28, 41, 46], these studies also show higher self-efficacy of participants who used ChatGPT: learners approached the problems confidently and perceived the tasks as easier, requiring less mental effort [41]. However, the higher self-efficacy did not correlate with actual task performance and was associated with overestimating one's performance. This discrepancy between the feeling of self-efficacy and actual performance could be attributed to the Dunning-Kruger effect, stating that lower performers are often largely unaware of the deficiency of their expertise [13].

These examples already highlight a central problem with GenAI: while it might make it easier to arrive at a good (GenAI generated) output, these tools themselves do not train or enhance skills necessary for their effective use. Instead, GenAI adds additional complications. One such aspect is the metacognitive burden, meaning that when the learner (or employee) is working, they have to take more aspects into consideration due to GenAI. For instance, given that GenAI is prone to hallucinations, the learners need to focus more on fact-checking, which puts an additional demand on metacognitive skills. Learners could write better essays with GenAI, but a part of their time has to go into a critical assessment of the GenAI's output. Of course, there is a trade-off, as GenAI-written text comes faster, but the point is to illustrate that GenAI adds complications that were not so pronounced before.

6 What Can Be Done?

First, children need to be taught critical thinking. A recent survey of K-12 teachers indicates that without introducing the underlying mechanisms and discussing the meaningful usage of GenAI, pupils take the output of GenAI at face value [23]. Adding to that issue, more than half of the educators said they had made no changes to their teaching practices or regulated the usage of GenAI tools [23]. Second, before introducing pupils to technology, SRL and metacognition should be developed as early as possible [35]. Improving the human skills that are the basis for lifelong learning should be given priority: eliciting curiosity, training question-asking and metacognition are critical human capital investments required before children can benefit from using GenAI. Ultimately, we need teachers who can puzzle curious minds with tasks filled with uncertainty and surprises, a yet-to-seen characteristic in GenAI. Third, basic prompting techniques and mechanisms behind GenAI should be introduced to reduce the unnecessary burden and increase benefits. For example, chaining primitive prompts together could improve the quality of task outcomes and significantly enhance controllability and collaboration [45]. Lastly, researchers and developers should improve the explainability of the GenAI systems which would bring transparency to why GenAI chooses one or the other response.

7 Conclusion

One of the key applications of generative AI is considered to be the personalisation of learning. Learners with diverse backgrounds and skills are imagined to be instructed in a way that enhances their learning. While it is often assumed that GenAI will facilitate personalisation, we have presented arguments highlighting that this will not happen by default. The indiscriminate use of GenAI will not support personalisation. The first key problem is that if different learners all use GenAI roughly the same way, their output will be more homogeneous, not more diverse. The second problem is the false assumption that successful personalisation depends on AI. We have argued here that personalisation requires certain cognitive and metacognitive skills. Most importantly, it is debatable whether present-day GenAI tools support these skills. We have argued that these tools could hinder the development of these crucial skills. This does not mean that GenAI tools cannot be used. Rather, it shows that to take advantage of the opportunities offered by GenAI, we need to invest more in developing the human skills that will enable the successful use of GenAI in education.

Acknowledgements. This study was funded by the Estonian Research Council (grant number PSG728).

Disclosure of Interests. The authors have no competing interests to declare that are relevant to the content of this article.

References

1. Abdelghani, R., Oudeyer, P.Y., Law, E., de Vulpillières, C., Sauzéon, H.: Conversational agents for fostering curiosity-driven learning in children. Int. J. Hum. Comput. Stud. **167**, 102887 (2022)
2. Abdelghani, R., Wang, Y.H., Yuan, X., Wang, T., Lucas, P., Sauzéon, H., Oudeyer, P.Y.: GPT-3-driven pedagogical agents to train children's curious question-asking skills. Int. J. Artif. Intell. Educ. 1–36 (2023)
3. Aleven, V., Mclaren, B., Roll, I., Koedinger, K.: Toward meta-cognitive tutoring: a model of help seeking with a cognitive tutor. Int. J. Artif. Intell. Educ. **16**(2), 101–128 (2006)
4. Azevedo, R., et al.: Lessons learned and future directions of metatutor: leveraging multichannel data to scaffold self-regulated learning with an intelligent tutoring system. Front. Psychol. **13**, 813632 (2022)
5. Biswas, G., Leelawong, K., Schwartz, D., Vye, N., at Vanderbilt, T.T.A.G.: Learning by teaching: a new agent paradigm for educational software. Appl. Artif. Intell. **19**(3–4), 363–392 (2005)
6. Bloom, B.S.: The 2 sigma problem: the search for methods of group instruction as effective as one-to-one tutoring. Educ. Res. **13**(6), 4–16 (1984)
7. Brown, A.L.: The development of memory: knowing, knowing about knowing, and knowing how to know. Adv. Child Dev. Behav. **10**, 103–152 (1975)
8. Brynjolfsson, E., Li, D., Raymond, L.R.: Generative AI at work. Tech. rep., National Bureau of Economic Research (2023)
9. Ceha, J., Chhibber, N., Goh, J., McDonald, C., Oudeyer, P.Y., Kulić, D., Law, E.: Expression of curiosity in social robots: Design, perception, and effects on behaviour. In: Proceedings of the 2019 CHI conference on human factors in computing systems, pp. 1–12 (2019)
10. Chen, B., Zhu, X.: Integrating generative AI in knowledge building. Comput. Educ.: Artif. Intell. **5**, 100184 (2023)
11. Dell'Acqua, F., McFowland, E., Mollick, E.R., Lifshitz-Assaf, H., Kellogg, K., Ra- jendran, S., Krayer, L., Candelon, F., Lakhani, K.R.: Navigating the jagged techno- logical frontier: field experimental evidence of the effects of ai on knowledge worker productivity and quality. Harvard Business School Technology & Operations Mgt. Unit Working Paper (24-013) (2023)
12. Doshi, A.R., Hauser, O.: Generative artificial intelligence enhances creativity. Available at SSRN (2023)
13. Dunning, D.: The Dunning–Kruger effect: on being ignorant of one's own ignorance. In: Adv. Exp. Soc. Psychol. **44**, 247–296 (2011)
14. Gordon, G.: Social behaviour as an emergent property of embodied curiosity: a robotics perspective. Philos. Trans. R. Soc. B **374**(1771), 20180029 (2019)
15. Guskey, T.R.: Closing achievement gaps: revisiting Benjamin S. Bloom's "Learning for mastery". J. Adv. Acad. **19**(1), 8–31 (2007)
16. Hacker, D.J., Dunlosky, J., Graesser, A.C.: Handbook of metacognition in education (2009)
17. Hill, B.: Taking the help or going alone: ChatGPT and class assignments. HEC Paris Research Paper Forthcoming (2023)
18. Holmes, W., Tuomi, I.: State of the art and practice in AI in education. Eur. J. Educ. **57**(4), 542–570 (2022)
19. Hopkins, D.: Personalized learning in school age education (2010)
20. Jirout, J., Klahr, D.: Children's recognition of uncertainty and exploratory curiosity. In: Society for Research in Child Development conference, Denver, CO (2009)

21. Kidd, C., Birhane, A.: How Ai can distort human beliefs. Science **380**(6651), 1222–1223 (2023)
22. Laak, K.J., Aru, J.: AI and personalized learning: bridging the gap with modern educational goals (2024)
23. Laak, K.J., Aru, J.: Generative AI in K-12: opportunities for learning and utility for teachers (in print)
24. Lee, D.: How to personalize learning in K-12 schools: Five essential design features. Educational Technology pp. 12–17 (2014)
25. Limo, F.A.F., et al.: Personalized tutoring: Chatgpt as a virtual tutor for personalized learning experiences. Przestrzeń Społeczna (Social Space) **23**(1), 293–312 (2023)
26. Lo, C.K.: What is the impact of ChatGPT on education? A rapid review of the literature. Educ. Sci. **13**(4), 410 (2023)
27. Miliband, D.: Choice and voice in personalised learning. Schooling for tomorrow: Personalising education pp. 21–30 (2006)
28. Noy, S., Zhang, W.: Experimental evidence on the productivity effects of generative artificial intelligence. Science **381**(6654), 187–192 (2023)
29. OECD Learning compass 2030. https://www.oecd.org/education/2030- project/teaching-and-learning/learning/learning-compass-2030/. Last accessed 2023/05/14
30. Panadero, E.: A review of self-regulated learning: six models and four directions for research. Front. Psychol. **8**, 250270 (2017)
31. Pelletier, C.: Against personalised learning. Int. J. Artif. Intell. Educ. **34**(1), 111–115 (2024)
32. Qadir, J.: Engineering education in the era of ChatGPT: Promise and pitfalls of generative AI for education. In: 2023 IEEE Global Engineering Education Conference (EDUCON), pp. 1–9. IEEE (2023)
33. Rahman, M.M., Watanobe, Y.: ChatGPT for education and research: opportunities, threats, and strategies. Appl. Sci. **13**(9), 5783 (2023)
34. Roll, I., Aleven, V., McLaren, B.M., Koedinger, K.R.: Designing for metacognition—applying cognitive tutor principles to the tutoring of help seeking. Metacogn. Learn. **2**, 125–140 (2007)
35. Schunk, D., Berger, E.M., Hermes, H., Winkel, K., Fehr, E.: Teaching self-regulation. Nat. Human Behav. **6**(12), 1680–1690 (2022)
36. Shemshack, A., Spector, J.M.: A systematic literature review of personalized learning terms. Smart Learning Environ. **7**(1), 33 (2020)
37. Slavin, R.E., Karweit, N.L.: Effects of whole class, ability grouped, and individualized instruction on mathematics achievement. Am. Educ. Res. J. **22**(3), 351–367 (1985)
38. Smallwood, R.D.: A decision structure for teaching machines (1963)
39. Steenbergen-Hu, S., Cooper, H.: A meta-analysis of the effectiveness of intelligent tutoring systems on college students' academic learning. J. Educ. Psychol. **106**(2), 331 (2014)
40. Tuomi, I.: Beyond mastery: toward a broader understanding of AI in education. Int. J. Artif. Intell. Educ. 1–11 (2024)
41. Urban, M., Děchtěrenko, F., Lukavsky‘, J., Hrabalová, V., Svacha, F., Brom, C., Urban, K.: ChatGPT improves creative problem-solving performance in university students: an experimental study. Comput. Educ. 105031 (2024)
42. Waalkens, M., Aleven, V., Taatgen, N.: Does supporting multiple student strategies lead to greater learning and motivation? Investigating a source of complexity in the architecture of intelligent tutoring systems. Comput. Educ. **60**(1), 159–171 (2013)
43. Walkington, C., Bernacki, M.L.: Appraising research on personalized learning: definitions, theoretical alignment, advancements, and future directions (2020)
44. Winne, P.H.: Bootstrapping learner's self-regulated learning. Psychol. Test Assess. Model. **52**(4), 472 (2010)

45. Wu, T., Terry, M., Cai, C.J.: Ai chains: Transparent and controllable human-AI interaction by chaining large language model prompts. In: Proceedings of the 2022 CHI conference on human factors in computing systems, pp. 1–22 (2022)
46. Yilmaz, R., Yilmaz, F.G.K.: The effect of generative artificial intelligence (AI)-based tool use on students' computational thinking skills, programming self-efficacy and motivation. Comput. Educ.: Artif. Intell. **4**, 100147 (2023)
47. Zimmerman, B.J.: Becoming a self-regulated learner: which are the key subprocesses? Contemp. Educ. Psychol. **11**(4), 307–313 (1986)
48. Zimmerman, B.J.: Attaining self-regulation: A social cognitive perspective. In: Handbook of self-regulation, pp. 13–39. Elsevier (2000)

ChatGPT Assessment Design for Postgraduate Students

Komla Pillay(✉)

Department of Business Management, University of Johannesburg, Johannesburg, South Africa
komlap@uj.ac.za

Abstract. The use of artificial intelligence tools like ChatGPT in education has resulted in academics being unsure of whether student artefacts are their own. This study qualitatively surveyed fifty-three postgraduate students trying to determine how they use ChatGPT to assist them in their assessments. Feedback from the respondents indicated that ChatGPT has pros of being helpful or brainstorming and idea generation, it has cons of providing non-specific responses, unoriginal short responses, non-reputable sources and unable to provide meaningful examples. Based on the responses, the study proposes six guidelines that can assist academics design their assessments to encourage students to use innovative AI technologies. The six guidelines are (1) Design assessments to vary in format, (2) Design summative assessments to critique an AI tool response, (3) Design assessments to provide examples or work with case studies, (4) Design formative assessments to incorporate brainstorm ideas from AI tool, (5) Design assessment to provide proof of legitimate references, (6) Design assessments iteratively.

Keywords: ChatGPT · Assessment Design · guidelines · postgraduate students

1 Introduction and Background

COVID-19 resulted in academics rethinking the purpose of higher education systems. Online lectures were smooth and efficient to manage. While some changes, like moving lectures online, were relatively easy to manage, assessment posed a much bigger challenge. Assessment can take many forms, from essay assignments to written or oral exams. Software was used during this period to monitor what students were doing with regard to copying. Many of the efforts were not necessarily effective. Some academics were very harsh with prohibiting the use of Artificial Intelligence (AI) technologies like ChatGPT for assessments but could not enforce the prohibition.

Academic Institutions should have used the COVID-19 pandemic to relook at the role of higher education – is it just expecting students to regurgitate information or be critical thinkers? By incorporating the use of Artificial Intelligence (AI) technology, is there a way to facilitate a more modern thinking approach to learning. Rather than prohibiting the use of AI technology like ChatGPT, incorporate it into everyday learning. Employees in various fields are using such technologies to assist them do their jobs; why not incorporate such technologies into student assessment? We need to embrace such technologies in order to better prepare students for the modern working world.

Y.-P. Cheng et al. (Eds.): ICITL 2024, LNCS 14785, pp. 50–56, 2024.
https://doi.org/10.1007/978-3-031-65881-5_6

We need to try different types of assessments using AI technologies to determine which ones promote critical thinking. AI has proven to accomplish various tasks with ease, but its ability to demonstrate critical thinking is limited. AI can potentially only ruin higher education institutions if these institutions insist on trying to do things the "traditional" way. There needs to be more research in this field to determine what the future university will look like.

This study served to determine how postgraduate students use Artificial Intelligence (AI) to do their assignments. The research problem is that educational institutions are facing difficulty as students are increasingly using innovative technology to do their academic work. Educational institutions cannot always determine if students are doing their own work or are making use of other resources. In the current day and age, Educational Institutions cannot control the use of AI. This research aims to find out how students use AI, what the AI capabilities are in order to design assessments in a manner that ensures that students are achieving the learning outcomes of the module. This study answers the research question "How do Postgraduate students use AI technology to support their assessments?" The primary objective of the study was exploring how postgraduate students used AI to support their assessments, while the secondary objectives were: to determine what AI capabilities are in responding to an assessment; to investigate assessment types that can ensure student outcomes are met, even if AI technology is used to generate the assessment; and to determine the thinking and searching skills students need to produce a high quality assessment.

The remaining sections of the paper are structured as follows: In Sect. 2, the relevant literature is discussed. This includes an overview of ChatGPT and Assessments. The research method is presented in Sect. 3. The results and a detailed discussion are presented in Sect. 4. Section 5 concludes the paper.

2 Literature Review

2.1 ChatGPT

ChatGPT is an artificial intelligence application software that uses natural language processing to enable human like conversations with users [1]. Users of the software can ask questions and receive feedback in seconds. Users can also request the software to regenerate a response if the user is unsatisfied with the response. ChaptGPT is considered one of the most advanced AI software. Educators are finding it difficult to distinguish between work produced by students versus the software [2]. The versatility of ChatGPT extends from computational sums, essay writing to code generation [3]. The importance of critical thinking and discernment is extremely important to ensure students can identify AI biases and ensure that they can think for themselves [4]. The study conducted by Lin et al. [5] conclude that ChatGPT is beneficial to in assisting users to brainstorm and provide personalized services in various fields. The study also cautions about the possibility of academic users losing the originality of their work and also generate plagiarism issues with the content generated.

2.2 Assessments

Assessments are important in gauging if a student has grasped the expected learning outcomes of a module. Students are generally required to produce artefact namely a research report, written examination, software product amongst others. These produced artefacts are then assessed and it is determined if a student passes or fails. Historically, academic staff did not have the challenge of determining if the assessments were produced by the students themselves. Now, the extensive use of AI tools like ChatGPT have resulted in uncertainty of who the creators of the assessments are. Students integrity is being questioned. Academic staff require assistance in planning future assessments to ensure that academic integrity is in place. Many universities have invested in technology to attempt to determine if the work submitted by students are AI generated. Turnitin is one such program that is being used by universities. The AI tool space is seeing explosive innovation that makes it difficult to keep ahead and have systems in place to detect who produced the product [6].

According to [7], postgraduate students can use ChatGPT to help them develop their literature reviews, formulate ideas on certain topics, and draft research paper. It is also proposed that ChatGPT can foster their communication, and assist with content creation. This research suggests ways ChatGPT can be integrated in Postgraduate students lives, it does not confirm how ChatGPT is currently being used.

Some universities are working on their guidelines to support the use of ChatGPT while some are still finding ways to eliminate its use. Some of the university recommendation include using ChatGPT to generate content and have the student engage with what has been generated. This still needs to be tested over time in order to develop a set of best practice guidelines. This research can support the creation of the best practice guidelines as it is determining how students are using ChatGPT.

3 Method

The study employed a qualitative methodology, which supports the interpretative research paradigm by using qualitative methods to effectively address the study's question. According to [8], qualitative techniques allow the researcher to study selected issues in depth and detail what they identify while attempting to understand the categories of information that emerge from the data. The researcher was observing and not manipulating any behaviour of how students used AI tools. Data for the study was gathered from postgraduate students from various South African Higher Education Institution. An online survey was used to collect the data. The online survey was a cost-effective means of data collection. It was accessible as postgraduate students have access to the Internet on their campuses. Most students also have access to the Internet at their student residence. The study used snowball sampling. Students who were registered or completed postgraduate studies were eligible to participate. The planned sample size was 50 responses but the study gathered fifty-three (53) responses.

Data analysis included describing, organising, and compiling qualitative data. The study used descriptive statistics and thematic analysis of the surveys. The study contributes to academia by demonstrating how students are using AI tools to assist them with their academic studies. Having this information will provide the foundation for future assessment planning – assessment planning that ensures student are using AI tools to support their academic endeavours and not replace their learning. The findings are critical in helping to map the future of University assessment for Postgraduate students. The study has the ability to demonstrate how using technological innovation like AI can promote student learning and prepare students for the future.

Ethical clearance was be obtained from the Department of Business Management Ethics Committee at the University of Johannesburg. Consent to participate in the study was obtained from all respondents.

4 Results and Discussion

The biographic data confirmed all fifty-three respondents were postgraduate students. Forty-nine respondents were between 23 and 29 years of age. Four respondents were between 30 to 35 years of age.

Forty-seven respondents used ChatGPT, three respondents used Google Bard, two Perplexity AI and one used Copilot. All 100 % of respondents refined their input into the AI tool. Forty respondents refined their search more than 4 times, five refined their input search 3 times, seven refined their input search 2 times and one respondent only refined their input search1 time.

Forty-three respondents changed 50–70% of the request that was generated by the AI tool. Ten respondents changed less than 50%. Forty-two respondents were happy with the generated content. Two were unhappy with the generated content and eight respondents were unsure about the generated content. The word cloud below represents some of the reasons that the respondents gave about how they felt about the generated content. Apart from the words represented on the word cloud, some respondents felt that the content generated was not very substantial, just good words but the meaning was vague. They commented on the ideas being good but needed to be reworked, and also the content wording did not sound like them (Fig. 1).

Fig. 1. Word Cloud representing how Postgraduate Students felt about the generated content

No respondents felt that the generated content was good enough to submit even if plagiarism was not a concern. Six respondents also commented that their understanding of the question seems to differ from the AI tool. Forty-five respondents only used the AI tool to generate ideas to help start their assignment, with eight attempting to complete the given task using the AI tool. Some of the respondents indicated the reasons for only using the AI tool to generate ideas was that they were afraid of plagiarism, no sources referenced, the content seems to say the same things in different words, not new content in the different paragraphs and insufficient volume of content generated for postgraduate studies.

Well-designed assessments are key in determining whether student learning outcomes have been achieved [9]. The difference between formative and summative assessment is the time of the assessment and what the goals of the assessment are. Formative assessment assesses students' learning during the learning process with the aim to improve student learning and guide the teaching, whereas summative assessment assesses learning at the end of a module. Formative and summative assessment do not have separate assessment types, one assessment type can be categorized as both formative and summative [10].

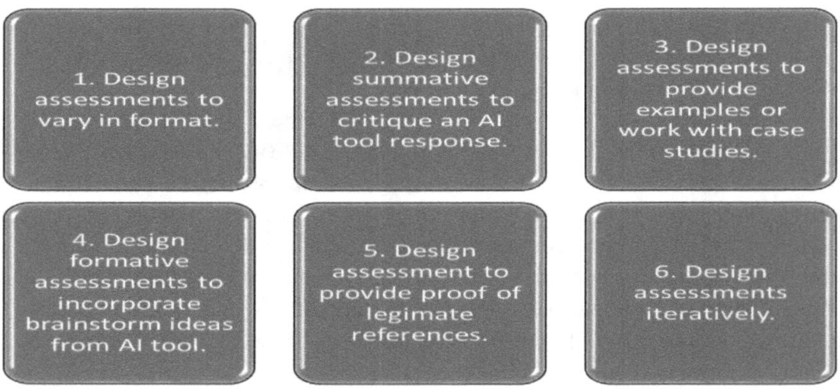

Fig. 2. Guidelines for ChatGPT Assessment Design

Figure 2 outlines the derived guidelines. Assessments can be designed as follows in order to ensure that postgraduate students achieve their learning outcomes while using AI tools like ChatGPT.

1. **Design assessments to vary in format**
   Students can be asked to deliver their assignments as a video or oral presentation, this will ensure that the students have adequately engaged with the assessment versus simply submitting something that was generated by AI.
2. **Design summative assessments to critique an AI tool response**
   As summative assessment, AI tools can be used to request a response to a query and then ask students to critique the response – this will promote critical thinking. Respondents indicated that they don't use the generated AI response as is, they make modifications or rerun the query – they are engaging with the response which indicates the higher order thinking skills are required.

Compare and critique the responses from 2 different AI tools – this also promotes critical thinking.

3. **Design assessments to provide examples or work with case studies**
Ask the student to quote personal experiences as the examples to support the content. Respondents indicated that ChatGPT was not good at providing suitable examples and cannot adequately work with existing cases.
4. **Design formative assessments to incorporate brainstorm ideas from AI tool**
For postgraduate students, it may be beneficial for the formative assessments to be designed integrating AI tools – many respondents mentioned that ChatGPT helped them brainstorm and generate ideas. These are foundational when undertaking formative assessments because academics require students to generate new ideas and question existing structures.
5. **Design assessment to provide proof of legitimate references**
Ensure legitimate sources are used in the reference list – this will ensure that students will go find original sources in order to cite in assignment.
6. **Design assessments iteratively**
Design assessments in iterations – one assessment feeds into another assessment. Part 1 of assessment requires to write down what was generated by the AI tool, part 2, student must show how that output was amended to make it their own.

5 Conclusion

This study conducted a qualitative survey to explore how postgraduate students used AI tools to support their assessments and to investigate assessment types that can ensure student outcomes are met with the use AI technology like ChatGPT. The paper presented the current challenge facing academics in determining if the artefacts produced for assessment are in fact the students own work. This study focused purely on postgraduate students at higher education institutions in South Africa. There is ongoing debate regarding the use of ChatGPT in education. This paper presents practical assessment design guidelines for academics to incorporate into their assessment design. Maintaining academic integrity is crucial to upholding institutional academic standards, academics can not ban the use of innovative technologies like ChatGPT, this has to be integrated into the academic process while still ensuring all institutional and student goals are ethically achieved.

This paper outlines six guidelines that academics can use to successfully incorporate ChatGPT into the assessment design. These six guidelines are, (1) Design assessments to vary in format, (2) Design summative assessments to critique an AI tool response, (3) Design assessments to provide examples or work with case studies, (4) Design formative assessments to incorporate brainstorm ideas from AI tool, (5) Design assessment to provide proof of legitimate references, (6) Design assessments iteratively.

Adopting these guidelines can assist postgraduate academics to better design their assessments achieve all student learning outcomes while incorporating innovative AI tools. Students should remain ahead of the technological curve by being encouraged to use the latest technological innovations like ChatGPT.

References

1. Reed, L.: ChatGPT for automated testing: From conversation to code. Sauce Labs (2022)
2. Rudolph, J., Tan, S., Tan, S.: ChatGPT: bullshit spewer or the end of traditional assessments in higher education? J. Appl. Learn. Teach. **6**(1) (2023)
3. Tung, L.: ChatGPT can write code . Now researchers say it's good at fixing bugs too. ZDNet (2023)
4. Kasneci, E., Sessler, K., Küchemann, S., Bannert, M., Dementieva, D.: ChatGPT for good? on opportunities and challenges of large language models for education. Learning and Individual Differences **103**, 102274 (2023). ISSN 1041-6080. https://doi.org/10.1016/j.lindif.2023.102274
5. Lin, S., Chung, H., Chung, F., Lan, Y.: Concerns about using ChatGPT in Education. In: Huang, Y.M., Rocha, T. (eds.) Innovative technologies and learning. ICITL 2023. Lecture Notes in Computer Science, vol. 14099. Springer, Cham (2023). https://doi.org/10.1007/978-3-031-40113-8_36
6. Mollick, E., Mollick, L.: New Modes of Learning Enabled by AI Chatbots: Three Methods and Assignments (2022). Available at SSRN: https://ssrn.com/abstract=4300783 or https://doi.org/10.2139/ssrn.4300783
7. Padhiyar, R., Modha, S.: Impact of the usage of ChatGPT on creativity among postgraduate student. Int. J. Sustain. Soc. Sci. (IJSSS) **2**, 83–92 (2024). https://doi.org/10.59890/ijsss.v2i1.1376
8. Terr Blanche, M., Durrheim, K., Painter, D.: Research in Practice: Applied Methods for Social Sciences, 2nd edn. UCT Press, Cape Town (2006)
9. Almond, R.G., Steinber, L.S., Mislevy, R.J.: Enhancing the design and delivery of assessment systems: a four-process architecture. In: Alter, A.L., Oppenheimer, D.M. (eds.) The Journal of Technology, Learning, and Assessment, p. 5 (2022)
10. Black, P., Wiliam, D.: Assessment and Classroom Learning. Assessment in Education: Principles, Policy & Practice **5**(1), 7–74 (1998). https://doi.org/10.1080/0969595980050102

Insights into Precision Education Through Multimodal Learning Analytics in STEM Education

Chia-Ju Lin[1], Margus Pedaste[2], and Yueh-Min Huang[1](✉)

[1] Department of Engineering Science, National Cheng Kung University, Tainan, Taiwan
huang@mail.ncku.edu.tw

[2] Institute of Education of the University of Tartu, Tartu, Estonia

Abstract. This study aims to explore the application of precision education in STEM education through multimodal learning analytics systems to enhance students' learning outcomes and knowledge construction behaviors. A quasi-experimental design was implemented, comprising a control group and two experimental groups, the latter of which utilized single-modal and multimodal learning analytics systems, respectively. The results demonstrated significant improvements in learning outcomes for students in the experimental groups compared to the control group, particularly for those using the multimodal learning analytics system. Moreover, the multimodal system was more effective in capturing students' learning behaviors and interactions, facilitating more effective teaching interventions and guidance. This study underscores the potential of multimodal learning analytics in precision education and its significant impact on improving the quality and outcomes of STEM education.

Keywords: STEM Education · Multimodal Learning Analytics · Precision Education

1 Introduction

STEM education aims to develop students' abilities to solve real-world problems through the integration of science, technology, engineering, and mathematics [1]. Numerous studies have indicated the positive impact of teamwork and interactive discussions on students' knowledge construction and learning engagement [2, 3]. However, due to the diversity of student backgrounds, traditional teaching methods often fail to meet the needs of all students, prompting the search for more effective teaching strategies [4, 5].

In response to this challenge, precision education has emerged as a solution [6]. The implementation of precision education has encouraged more educators to develop systems using data mining techniques to collect or extract students' learning behaviors or characteristics. These learning analytics systems focus on the students' learning process as a basis for decision-making or diagnosis, offering a more personalized, adaptive, and interactive educational environment to enhance learning outcomes [7, 8].

Y.-P. Cheng et al. (Eds.): ICITL 2024, LNCS 14785, pp. 57–63, 2024.
https://doi.org/10.1007/978-3-031-65881-5_7

The significance of precision education and the importance of multimodal learning analytics systems in teaching activities, especially in collaborative STEM activities where students' discussion interactions and physical changes are among the references for learning performance [9], are noteworthy. However, recent research on the practice of STEM education rarely establishes a multimodal learning analytics system based on image and voice features, let alone explores the differences in learners' motivation and knowledge construction behaviors after teachers intervene based on the diagnosis of different modal learning analytics systems [10]. To address these issues, this study aims to investigate the differences in learning performance and behaviors among student groups when teachers intervene based on the judgments from different learning analytics systems in STEM teaching activities. The research questions are as follows:

1. Are there differences in learning performance among different groups?
2. What are the differences in knowledge construction behaviors among different groups?

2 Literature Review

2.1 Multimodal Learning Analytics in Education

With the rapid development of artificial intelligence (AI) and educational technology, the education field is undergoing a significant transformation from traditional teaching models to data-driven personalized learning experiences [11, 12]. Precision education and multimodal learning analytics (MMLA) serve as key concepts, aiming to enhance learning outcomes and teaching quality by thoroughly analyzing learners' behaviors, interactions, and learning environments [13]. MMLA has been applied in a wide range of learning domains, from traditional classrooms to online learning environments and even hands-on activities [14]. The application of facial recognition and eye-tracking technology helps teachers adjust teaching strategies based on students' emotions and attention distribution [15]. MMLA offers a new perspective for implementing precision education and is expected to be increasingly applied in the education field as AI technology advances.

2.2 Knowledge Construction Behavior in Collaboration

In modern education, knowledge construction is regarded as a process achieved through the interaction, collaboration, and regulation among individuals and groups [16]. Collaborative learning emphasizes the importance of resolving problems through group interaction, facilitating the exchange of knowledge among students and sparking the generation of new concepts and information sharing [17]. Additionally, collaborative learning provides a platform for students to support and share viewpoints with each other, enhancing the depth and breadth of learning. Especially in the STEM field, future studies should focus on developing more automated and adaptive analysis and tracking tools to achieve precision education and deepen the understanding of the collaborative learning process [18].

3 Methodology

3.1 The Multimodal Learning Analytics System

In this study, we established two types of multimodal learning analytics platforms to assess the accuracy of learning behavior identification and the effectiveness of teaching interventions based on these identification results. These systems integrated three main technologies: facial expression analysis, gaze tracking technology, and voice recognition. Specifically, we used OpenFace 2.0 technology to track facial expressions and gaze direction [19] and Yolov7-tiny technology to determine students' gaze focus [20]. For voice data, we chose to use the Whisper voice recognition system developed by OpenAI for processing [21].

The learning analytics system for experimental group 1 utilized facial expression recognition and eye gaze tracking; experimental group 2, in addition to facial expressions and gaze, also added voice data, thereby establishing a more comprehensive multimodal learning analytics system. To ensure the system's effectiveness, we randomly selected some data segments of images and voice and invited two experts for coding. The Cohen's kappa for the coding of experimental group 1 with the two experts was 0.85, while the Cohen's kappa for the experimental group 2 reached 0.89, demonstrating our system's high consistency with expert coding in behavior identification, thereby proving its effectiveness and reliability.

In terms of coding for knowledge construction behavior, this study applied the social knowledge construction coding scheme by Wang, Fang and Gu [22], which is a modification of the IAM (Interactive Analysis Model). This coding scheme simplified the dimensions of the social level and distinguished learning-related behaviors through verb forms, including providing information (A1), requesting information (A2), responding to information (A3), agreeing (A4), negotiating (A5), discovering (A6), guiding (A7), and checking (A8). Additionally, there were two categories of behaviors unrelated to learning: social communication (S1) and behaviors unrelated to learning tasks (O1). The academic-related behaviors included providing or guiding information, requesting information or guidance, responding to information or guidance, agreeing with opinions or suggestions, negotiating with opinions or suggestions, discovering unclear content or information, leading task coordination or action, and checking the progress of learning tasks. Social communication-related behaviors referred to the rich expressions and informal chat interactions among group members. Behaviors unrelated to learning tasks, such as team members playing with phones or suggesting activities unrelated to learning.

3.2 Participants and Data Collection

A total of 32 high school students voluntarily participated. Students in each group were further randomly assigned into pairs for the learning activities. Consent for data collection was obtained from students and their parents before the study. Measurement tools included pre-tests and post-tests. The questionnaires were designed by professors with extensive teaching experience, and the Kuder-Richardson Formula 20 (KR-20) values for the pre-test and post-test questionnaires were 0.91 and 0.85, respectively, indicating high reliability. To understand the differences in learning behavior after teacher intervention, this study collected image data for experimental group 1 and both image and voice data for experimental group 2 as analysis data sources.

3.3 Experimental Procedure

The study organized a one-day hands-on collaborative workshop on educational robotics programming and practical applications, aimed at high school students with mostly no programming experience. Experimental group 1 used an image recognition learning analytics system, and experimental group 2 used a multimodal learning analytics system combining image recognition and voice recognition, while the control group did not use a learning analytics system. The experimental procedure as shown in Fig. 1. Through a pre-test, students' basic programming and logical abilities were assessed. Then, basic robot operations and applications were introduced, followed by collaborative tasks, including assembling educational robots, controlling robot movements, integrating motion and conditional judgment programs, and obstacle detection and avoidance tasks. The teaching content, difficulty, and instructors remained consistent for all groups, with the difference being that teachers provided timely intervention and guidance based on feedback from the learning analytics system in the experimental groups. After class, a post-test was conducted to understand students' learning outcomes.

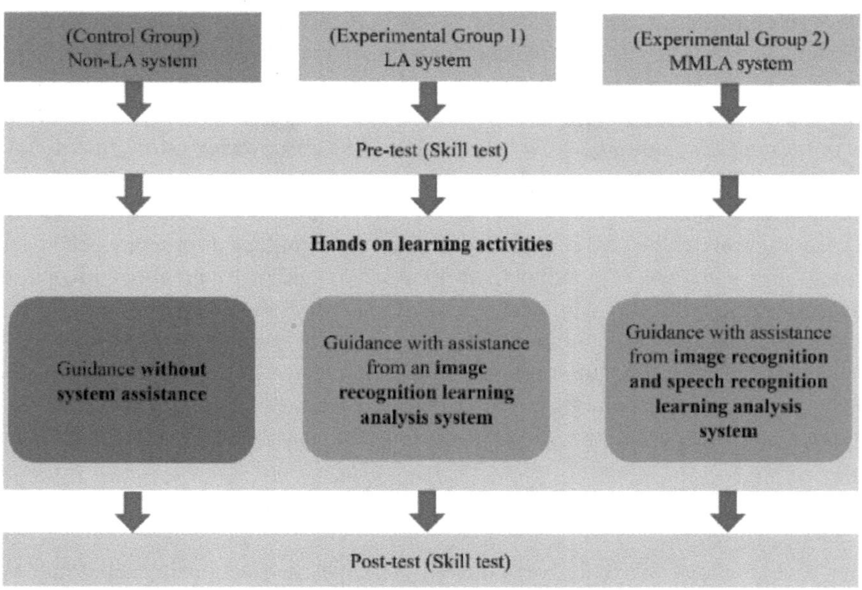

Fig. 1. Experimental procedure

4 Experimental Results

4.1 Learning Performance

The statistical analysis of the pre-test results showed no significant differences among the three groups ($F = 0.18, p > 0.05$), indicating no significant differences in their prior knowledge levels. The post-test results are shown in Table 1. The analysis of variance for the post-test scores revealed significant differences in learning outcomes among the three groups (F = 13.5, p < 0.001), indicating that the intervention of different learning analytics systems significantly affected students' learning outcomes. Further Post Hoc analysis revealed that compared to the control group, students in experimental groups 1 and 2 showed significant improvements in learning outcomes, with experimental group 2 showing the best learning outcomes compared to experimental group 1 and the control group. This indicates that teacher interventions based on the multimodal learning analytics system can more effectively enhance learning outcomes, further verifying the potential and benefits of multimodal learning analytics systems in the practice of precision education diagnosis.

Table 1. The results of the learning performance for the post-test.

Groups	N	M	SD	F	η2	Post hoc
Control Group	10	65.3	15.3	13.5***	0.258	(2) > (1) (3) > (1)
Experimental Group 1	12	72.4	13.2			
Experimental Group 2	10	83.6	11.0			

*** $p < 0.001$.

4.2 Learning Behavior

Research question 2 aimed to understand the differences in behavior among different groups. The learning behavior of the control group was coded by researchers through video observation, with a Cohen's kappa value of 0.88 (p < 0.01) for coding consistency, indicating high consistency in the coding process. Experimental groups 1 and 2 directly used the learning analytics system to automatically identify learning behaviors. In terms of behavior distribution as shown in Fig. 2, students in all three groups showed fewer behaviors related to agreeing (A4) and checking learning progress (A8), possibly because the learning tasks required active collaboration, leading students to seldom passively accept others' opinions and the task completion was intuitively reflected by the robot's actions, thus reducing the need for progress checks. The behavior distribution of the control group and experimental group 2 was more similar, especially in terms of negotiating opinions (A5). In terms of responding to information (A3) and agreeing with opinions (A4), multimodal data combining voice and image could more accurately determine students' collaborative interactions. Additionally, since students in the control group relied more on teachers' experiential guidance during the learning process, they exhibited a higher frequency of seeking information (A2) and more behaviors unrelated to the course (O1).

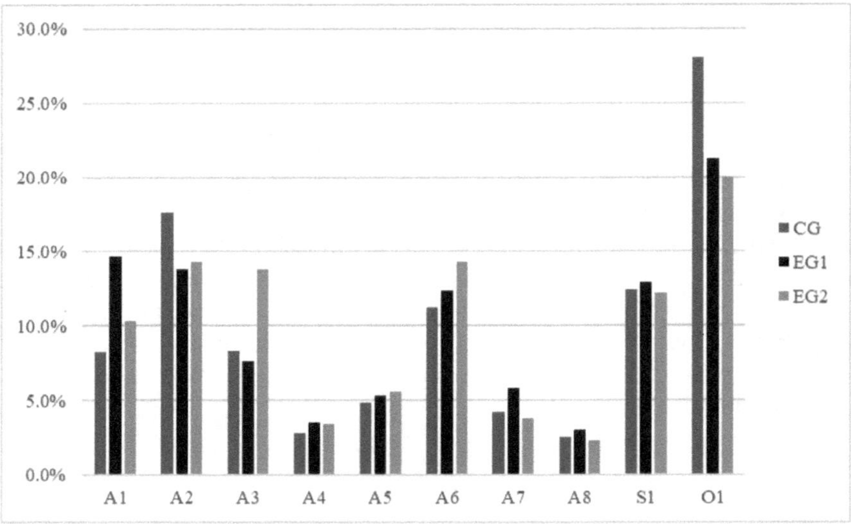

Fig. 2. Learning behavior bar chart.

5 Discussion and Conclusions

This study concludes that teaching interventions using learning analytics systems, especially multimodal learning analytics systems, can significantly improve students' learning outcomes. This provides empirical evidence for future teaching activities involving educational robot programming and practical applications and offers effective strategic directions for precision education. However, this study has some limitations, including restrictions on the sample size and the comprehensiveness of subjects. The widespread application of multimodal learning analytics systems should receive more attention in the future.

References

1. Huang, Y.-M., Wang, W.-S., Lee, H.-Y., Lin, C.-J., Wu, T.-T.: Empowering virtual reality with feedback and reflection in hands-on learning: Effect of learning engagement and higher-order thinking. J. Comp. Assis. Learn. (2024)
2. Wang, W.-S., Cheng, Y.-P., Lee, H.-Y., Lin, C.-J., Huang, Y.-M.: Impact of anxiety and confidence in virtual reality-mediated learning transferred to hands-on tasks. J. Comput. Assist. Learn. **39**, 1368–1381 (2023)
3. Wu, T.-T., Lin, C.-J., Pedaste, M., Huang, Y.-M.: The Effect of Chatbot Use on Students' Expectations and Achievement in STEM Flipped Learning Activities: A Pilot Study. In: Innovative Technologies and Learning, pp. 441–450. Springer Nature Switzerland (2023)

4. Lin, C.-J., Wu, T.-T., Wang, T.-H., Pedaste, M., Huang, Y.-M.: Exploring Student Discussion Topics in STEAM Hands-On Collaborative Activity. In: Innovative Technologies and Learning, pp. 13–21. Springer International Publishing (2022)
5. Lou, Y., Abrami, P.C., d'Apollonia, S.: Small group and individual learning with technology: a meta-analysis. Rev. Educ. Res. **71**, 449–521 (2001)
6. Lin, C.-J., Wang, W.-S., Lee, H.-Y, Huang, Y.-M., Wu, T.-T.: Recognitions of image and speech to improve learning diagnosis on STEM collaborative activity for precision education. Education and Information Technologies (2023)
7. Hwang, G.-J.: Definition, framework and research issues of smart learning environments - a context-aware ubiquitous learning perspective. Smart Learning Environments **1**, 4 (2014)
8. Xie, Y., Ke, F., Sharma, P.: The effect of peer feedback for blogging on college students' reflective learning processes. The Internet and Higher Education **11**, 18–25 (2008)
9. Ouyang, F., Dai, X., Chen, S.: Applying multimodal learning analytics to examine the immediate and delayed effects of instructor scaffoldings on small groups' collaborative programming. Int. J. STEM Edu. **9**, 45 (2022)
10. Wu, T.-T., Lee, H.-Y., Wang, W.-S., Lin, C.-J., Huang, Y.-M.: Leveraging computer vision for adaptive learning in STEM education: effect of engagement and self-efficacy. Int. J. Educ. Technol. High. Educ. **20**, 53 (2023)
11. Lee, H.-Y., Lin, C.-J., Wang, W.-S., Chang, W.-C., Huang, Y.-M.: Precision education via timely intervention in K-12 computer programming course to enhance programming skill and affective-domain learning objectives. Int. J. STEM Edu. **10**, 52 (2023)
12. Huang, A.Y.Q., Lu, O.H.T., Yang, S.J.H.: Effects of artificial Intelligence-Enabled personalized recommendations on learners' learning engagement, motivation, and outcomes in a flipped classroom. Comput. Educ. **194**, 104684 (2023)
13. Di Mitri, D., Schneider, J., Specht, M., Drachsler, H.: From signals to knowledge: a conceptual model for multimodal learning analytics. J. Comput. Assist. Learn. **34**, 338–349 (2018)
14. Giannakos, M.N., Sharma, K., Pappas, I.O., Kostakos, V., Velloso, E.: Multimodal data as a means to understand the learning experience. Int. J. Inf. Manage. **48**, 108–119 (2019)
15. Sharma, K., Giannakos, M.: Multimodal data capabilities for learning: what can multimodal data tell us about learning? Br. J. Edu. Technol. **51**, 1450–1484 (2020)
16. Beldarrain, Y.: Distance education trends: integrating new technologies to foster student interaction and collaboration. Distance Educ. **27**, 139–153 (2006)
17. Erkens, M., Bodemer, D.: Improving collaborative learning: guiding knowledge exchange through the provision of information about learning partners and learning contents. Comput. Educ. **128**, 452–472 (2019)
18. Ouyang, F., Xu, W., Cukurova, M.: An artificial intelligence-driven learning analytics method to examine the collaborative problem-solving process from the complex adaptive systems perspective. Int. J. Comput.-Support. Collab. Learn. **18**, 39–66 (2023)
19. Baltrusaitis, T., Zadeh, A., Lim, Y.C., Morency, L.P.: OpenFace 2.0: facial behavior analysis toolkit. In: 2018 13th IEEE International Conference on Automatic Face & Gesture Recognition (FG 2018), pp. 59–66 (2018)
20. Wang, C.-Y., Bochkovskiy, A., Liao, H.-Y.M.: YOLOv7: trainable bag-of-freebies sets new state-of-the-art for real-time object detectors, arXiv:2207.02696 (2022)
21. Radford, A., et al.: Robust Speech Recognition via Large-Scale Weak Supervision, arXiv: 2212.04356 (2022)
22. Wang, C., Fang, T., Gu, Y.: Learning performance and behavioral patterns of online collaborative learning: Impact of cognitive load and affordances of different multimedia. Comput. Educ. **143**, 103683 (2020)

Investigating the Acceptance of Large Language Model Technology on Nursing Interviews Among Nurse-Interns

Yen-Yu Huang[1], Chia-Ju Lin[2], and Ching-Min Chen[1](✉)

[1] Department of Nursing, College of Medicine, National Cheng Kung University, Tainan, Taiwan
chingmin@mail.ncku.edu.tw
[2] Department of Engineering Science, National Cheng Kung University, Tainan, Taiwan

Abstract. With the global healthcare landscape evolving, precision medicine has become pivotal, leveraging individual health data to tailor patient care and optimize resource use. However, the scarcity of registered nurses and the resultant increased workload pose challenges, including the risk of incomplete patient care records due to reliance on manual documentation during clinical interviews. To mitigate these issues, this research employs the ChatGPT mobile application to facilitate recording and collecting voice data, utilizing voice-to-text and LLM technologies. By conducting a Unified Theory of Acceptance and Use of Technology questionnaire survey among 25 nurse-interns, the study assesses the acceptance and impact of such technological applications in nursing practices. This study explores the integration of Large Language Models (LLMs) and Artificial Intelligence (AI) in addressing nursing shortages and enhancing precision medicine, aiming to improve the organization of nursing interview data, and provide empirical evidence for the benefits of LLM technology in nursing interviews, thereby offering recommendations for nursing education, enhancing patient care, and supporting the broader adoption of precision medicine strategies.

Keywords: Precision Medicine · Nursing Interview · Large Language Models

1 Introduction

Precision medicine is an emerging approach in clinical research and patient care that integrates patients' biological information with lifestyle, social, economic, cultural, and environmental factors [1]. By understanding a patient's health status and personalized information, and incorporating multimodal or multi-omics data from the patient, precision medicine aims to deeply understand diseases for precise treatments and to make the most suitable medical decisions for the patient [2]. Against this backdrop, nursing interviews, as a crucial tool for collecting personal information and health conditions of patients, play an indispensable role. Effective communication is essential for safe and effective care, and is critically important in establishing therapeutic relationships and developing individualized care plans [3].

Y.-P. Cheng et al. (Eds.): ICITL 2024, LNCS 14785, pp. 64–72, 2024.
https://doi.org/10.1007/978-3-031-65881-5_8

Nursing interviews are irreplaceable in patient assessment and care planning, yet today's healthcare systems face a critical issue of registered nurse shortages. Liu, Duan and Guo [4] highlighted that with the advent of an aging society, the demand for health services continues to grow. Given the high turnover rate of registered nurse who must work shifts and handle an increasing clinical workload, this underscores the shortage of care personnel [4]. In addition to their professional work, registered nurses often need to handle a large amount of administrative tasks, including completing nursing records, charting, and managing ward affairs. Registered nurses are unable to delegate these written records to others, leading to a situation where the immense workload becomes unmanageable, causing an increase in turnover rates. The scarcity of registered nurse not only leads to incomplete patient-related nursing records but also increases the likelihood of discrepancies in patient conditions during shift changes and handovers due to differences in record-keeping styles among registered nurse, thus increasing the probability of care issues [5]. Furthermore, Daouda, Hocine and Temime [6] also indicated that a shortage of registered nurse leads to increased feelings of fatigue and stress among the remaining staff, as well as reduced job satisfaction, leading to a decline in the quality and safety of care, and potentially increasing the risk of medication errors, falls, and infections among registered nurse.

Many nursing interview documents are still presented in narrative text form, lacking integration and focus. Thus, these nursing data are difficult to apply in clinical decision-making and biomonitoring in a timely manner [7]. To address this issue, the application of modern technology's speech-to-text features in various nursing records has reduced the inefficiency and low data accuracy of traditional manual recording methods, also alleviating the workload of registered nurse and improving the quality of patient care [5]. With the rapid progress of artificial intelligence (AI) and natural language processing (NLP) technologies, especially the emergence of large language models (LLMs), new possibilities have been opened for improving the processing of nursing interview data.

Despite the huge potential of LLM technologies in data processing and analysis, empirical research related to nursing interviews is still in its early stages. For instance, the use of LLM technology, such as ChatGPT, in nursing education can provide personalized learning experiences and promote collaborative learning techniques, and be applied in clinical scenario simulations to help registered nurse practice interacting with patients and hone their nursing skills, thereby enhancing their clinical practice capabilities. ChatGPT has been proven effective in diagnosing high-risk cases, assisting medical personnel in determining intensive care needs, and through further medical learning, improving accuracy in assessing other medical needs [8]. However, research on how to effectively integrate LLM technology into the nursing interview process is relatively scarce, especially on how such integration can improve nursing quality and efficiency, lacking concrete evidence. Under the premise of precision medicine, exploring the application and effectiveness of LLM technology in processing nursing interview data has significant theoretical and practical implications.

Therefore, this study aims to understand whether LLM technology can improve the efficiency and accuracy of nursing interview data processing, and thereby enhance nursing quality and patient care outcomes. The research question for this study is as follows:

Compared to traditional methods, how does the use of ChatGPT-assisted interview data processing as a facilitating condition for technology influence the relationships among the dimensions of technology acceptance, namely performance expectancy, effort expectancy, facilitating condition, self-efficacy, and behavioral intention, among nurse-interns?

2 Literature Review

2.1 The Contribution of Technology to Precision Medicine

In recent years, the contribution of technology to precision medicine has become a highlight in medical research and clinical practice, especially AI technology. In healthcare, its advantage lies in the ability to automatically screen and extract disease characteristics, holding great potential in analyzing a vast amount of medical information and disease assessment. Its applications range from early detection and diagnosis of diseases, predicting patient responses to various treatments, and formulating personalized medical plans, thereby providing more precise and appropriate treatments [9].

The integration of precision medicine with modern technology has transformed healthcare from a general approach applicable to all fields and patients into using big data to formulate personalized medical strategies, thereby achieving more accurate treatments and better outcomes. This has made a significant contribution to the healthcare sector. Especially for patients with rare diseases or symptoms, technological aids, such as through cloud data summaries or health records, help medical personnel predict disease risks and formulate treatment plans [10]. Therefore, technological aids like AI can more quickly and accurately obtain needed information, not only improving care quality for general patients but also providing more accurate treatment plans for rare diseases.

2.2 The Advantages of Technology Application in Nursing

Interviews have long been regarded as the best opportunity for registered nurse to establish partnerships with patients. They also encourage patients to participate in their care plans, understanding patient needs and self-awareness through conversations to provide more comprehensive and personalized care measures [11]. In terms of nursing education, students can make personal care recommendations and guidance through interviews during hospital internships, engaging in daily life conversations with patients to provide needed nursing information. Healthcare technology has been effectively integrated into the clinical routines of registered nurses. For instance, electronic health records can document extensive data, streamlining the clinical workflow for registered nurses and reducing the burden of manual documentation. Technology is also applied in infection prevention and control, assisting registered nurses in maintaining patient safety and the quality of care. In the hospital ward, having immediate access to patient conditions is indispensable for nursing staff; technology aids in the early detection of disease symptoms, patient management, and care. In the daily nursing activities of registered nurses, technology also supports the measurement of patients' clinical conditions, such as infections, imaging, physiological assessments, and temperature monitoring, enabling nursing staff to achieve maximum work efficiency in the shortest time [12].

In summary, interviews are an indispensable part of nursing care, allowing for a deeper understanding of patient information and potential needs. In nursing education, practical nurse students can enhance their knowledge and skills through interactions with patients.

2.3 Unified Theory of Acceptance and Use of Technology

Venkatesh, Morris, Davis and Davis [13] synthesized eight theoretical models, Theory of Reasoned Action (TRA), Theory of Planned Behavior (TPB), Technology Acceptance Model (TAM), the combination of the Technology Acceptance Model and the Theory of Planned Behavior (C-TAM-TPB), Model of PC Utilization (MPCU), Innovation Diffusion Theory (IDT), Motivational Model (MM), and Social Cognitive Theory (SCT), to propose the Unified Theory of Acceptance and Use of Technology (UTAUT). This theory outlines four key constructs that influence behavioral intention: Performance Expectancy, Effort Expectancy, Social Influence, and Facilitating Conditions. The definitions of the constructs used in this study's Unified Theory of Acceptance and Use of Technology are as follows:

1. Performance Expectancy (PE): The degree to which an individual believes that using the system will help them achieve gains in job performance. This construct encompasses five dimensions: Perceived Usefulness (from TAM/TAM2 and C-TAM-TPB), Extrinsic Motivation (MM), Job-Fit (MPCU), Relative Advantage (IDT), and Outcome Expectations (SCT).
2. Effort Expectancy (EE): The degree of ease associated with the use of the technology system, which refers to whether the technology has a user-friendly interface and can be easily operated. This includes Perceived Ease of Use (from TAM/TAM2), Complexity (MPCU), and Ease of Use (IDT).
3. Social Influence (SI): The degree to which an individual perceives that important others believe they should use the new system. It reflects the extent to which users' acceptance of new technology is influenced by others. Social Influence is divided into three sub-constructs: Subjective Norm (from TRA/TAM2/TPB/DPTB/C-TAM-TPB), Social Factors (MPCU), and Public Image (IDT).
4. Facilitating Conditions (FC): The degree to which an individual believes that an organizational and technical infrastructure exists to support the use of the system. It includes Perceived Behavioral Control (from TPB/DTPB/C-TAM-TPB), Facilitating Conditions (MPCU), and Compatibility (IDT).
5. Behavioral Intention (BI): Hill, Fishbein and Ajzen [14] defined BI as the degree of an individual's willingness to engage in a behavior, based on their subjective probability of the pros and cons of undertaking such behavior.

3 Methodology

3.1 Data Collection and Participant

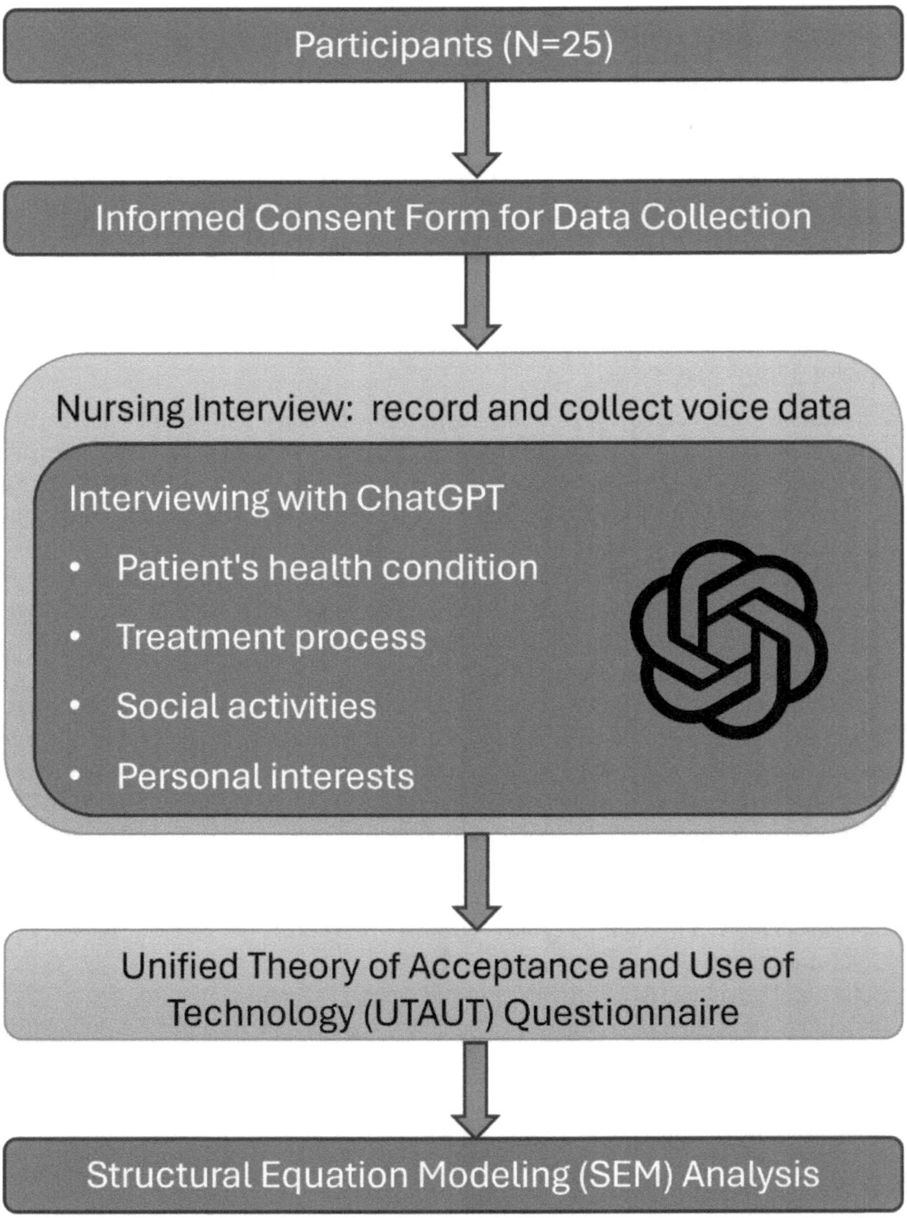

Fig. 1. Experimental design

This study aims to investigate the benefits and impacts of utilizing advanced technological tools, such as artificial intelligence-based large language models, to assist nurse-interns in interviews, with the goal of realizing the vision of precision medicine. We recruited 25 nurse-interns, aged between 21 to 23 years old. We adapted the Unified Theory of Acceptance and Use of Technology (UTAUT) questionnaire, as proposed by Pan and Gao [15] and Barchielli, Marullo, Bonciani and Vainieri [16], which measures the behavioral intention and acceptance levels of nurse-interns towards emerging technological applications. All items in the UTAUT questionnaire were measured using a Likert five-point scale, ranging from strongly disagree (score = 1) to strongly agree (score = 5). This program is an efficient, effective method of orienting new graduate nurses in their first work experience. Internships provide a highly realistic vehicle for smoothing the transition from nurse-intern to registered nurse and also promote recruitment and retention of qualified personnel.

3.2 Experimental Design

The experimental procedure is illustrated in Fig. 1. To understand the technology acceptance of nurse-interns using the LLM application tool - ChatGPT in the interview process, nurse-interns participating in this study were required to inform the interviewees about the purpose and use of collecting data with other applications before the interview and proceeded with the interview only after obtaining their consent. During the interview, the ChatGPT mobile application was used to record and collect voice data, involving the process of voice-to-text conversion and LLM processing. Generally, the aim was to understand the patient's health condition, treatment process, social activities, and personal interests. At the end of the experiment, nurse-interns completed the UTAUT questionnaire to understand the impact differences on technology application and acceptance.

4 Experimental Results

The results of the technology acceptance of nurse-interns using ChatGPT for interviews across various dimensions showed that the average score for PE was 12.9, for EE was 12.5, for FC was 13.6, for SE was 12.2, and for BI was 13.7. Subsequently, the reliability and convergent validity of the measurement model are presented in Table 1. Internal consistency was measured using Cronbach's alpha [17], indicating that all dimensions exceeded the threshold of 0.7, except for FC, which meets the acceptable reliability level, suggesting higher reliability. Furthermore, convergent validity was assessed through a combination of factor loadings, average variance extracted (AVE), and composite reliability (CR). The results in Table 1 show that factor loadings meet the standard suggested by Chen, Srinivasan, Elkasabany and Berenson [18] of being above 0.3; AVE meets the minimum standard suggested by Fornell and Larcker [17] of being above 0.36; and composite reliability (CR) meets the standard suggested by Fornell and Larcker [17] of being above 0.6. On the other hand, Fornell and Larcker [17] stated that if the square root of the AVE for each construct is greater than the correlation coefficients among constructs, and the correlation coefficients are less than 1, it indicates good discriminant validity. Therefore, Table 2 indicates that our questionnaire possesses good discriminant validity. Overall, the fit statistics for the structural model indicate that the model fits within acceptable standards (GFI = 0.99, SRMR = 0.094, RMSEA = 0.175).

This study employed Structural Equation Modeling (SEM) to examine the relationships among the constructs of the UTAUT model, with ChatGPT acting as a FC for nurse-interns in interviews. The results of the path analysis of the technology acceptance and use model are shown in Fig. 2, where only paths with significant relationships are labeled, with values representing z-scores. The results from Fig. 2 indicate that there are significant relationships between PE with EE, and SE, and between EE and SE. Additionally, our research model also confirmed that ChatGPT, as a FC for technology, significantly affects the BI of nurse-interns.

Table 1. Measurement model reliability and convergent validity

Constructs	Items	Factor loading	p	α	CR	AVE
Performance Expectancy	PE1	.687	<.001	0.878	0.886	0.721
	PE2	.562	<.001			
	PE3	.586	<.001			
Effort Expectancy	EE1	.793	<.001	0.851	0.857	0.669
	EE2	.666	<.001			
	EE3	.599	<.001			
Facilitating Condition	FC1	.385	<.001	0.646	0.661	0.388
	FC2	.312	<.001			
	FC3	.366	<.001			
Self-Efficacy	SE1	.764	<.001	0.898	0.921	0.793
	SE2	.837	<.001			
	SE3	.519	<.001			
Behavioral Intention	BI1	.497	<.001	0.761	0.812	0.564
	BI2	.338	<.001			
	BI3	.380	<.001			

5 Discussion and Conclusions

LLM technology, through the automation of processing and analyzing vast amounts of natural language data, aids in condensing lengthy documents, articles, or conversations into concise summaries. This is particularly beneficial when there is a need to quickly synthesize a large volume of text-related information, helping users grasp key points and providing faster and more accurate results. This study explores the technology acceptance level of nurse-interns toward using innovative technological tools such as large language model tools (ChatGPT) for interviews, including performance expectancy, effort

Table 2. Discriminant validity of measurement model

Constructs	PE	EE	FC	SE	BI
Performance Expectancy	**0.849**				
Effort Expectancy	0.839	**0.818**			
Facilitating Condition	0.443	0.631	**0.623**		
Self-Efficacy	0.474	0.581	0.427	**0.891**	
Behavioral Intention	0.540	0.559	0.412	0.416	**0.751**

Note. Off-diagonal elements are correlations among constructs. The bold fonts in the leading diagonals are the square roots of AVEs.

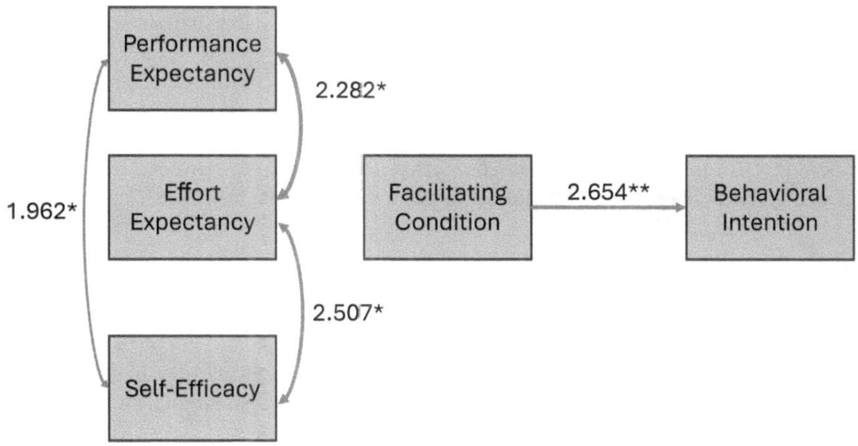

Fig. 2. Path analysis results of UTAUT

expectancy, facilitating condition, self-efficacy, and behavioral intention. Through the results of the UTAUT questionnaire, we sought to further understand the potential of ChatGPT in enhancing the efficiency and quality of interviews in nursing. The findings indicate that the behavioral intention of nurse-interns were significantly influenced by facilitating conditions, implying that the use of ChatGPT in nursing interviews will significantly encourage relevant personnel to accept technological interventions to assist their interview tasks. Although the relatively small sample size may impact the robustness and accuracy of the model, the research also confirmed the important role of technology in nursing interview strategies, which simultaneously will bring more positive benefits to the implementation of precision medicine measures and the formulation of treatment plans for patients. With the integration of generative AI and large language models into nursing, there is hope for significant improvements in patient care quality and greater advancements in the healthcare sector. Through this study, we aim to provide empirical evidence on the application of LLM technology in nursing interviews, offering direction for future nursing practice and education, and promoting the effective implementation of precision medicine strategies.

References

1. Fu, M.R., et al.: Precision health: a nursing perspective. Int. J. Nurs. Sci. **7**, 5–12 (2020)
2. MacEachern, S.J., Forkert, N.D.: Machine learning for precision medicine. Genome **64**, 416–425 (2020)
3. Larsen, R., Mangrio, E., Persson, K.: Interpersonal communication in transcultural nursing care in India: a descriptive qualitative study. J. Transcult. Nurs. **32**, 310–317 (2020)
4. Liu, Y., Duan, Y., Guo, M.: Turnover intention and its associated factors among nurses: a multi-center cross-sectional study. Frontiers in Public Health **11** (2023)
5. Hou, S.-Y., et al.: Code-switching automatic speech recognition for nursing record documentation: system development and evaluation. JMIR nursing **5**, e37562 (2022)
6. Daouda, O.S., Hocine, M.N., Temime, L.: Determinants of healthcare worker turnover in intensive care units: A micro-macro multilevel analysis. PLoS ONE **16**, e0251779 (2021)
7. Bakken, S., Hyun, S., Friedman, C., Johnson, S.B.: ISO reference terminology models for nursing: applicability for natural language processing of nursing narratives. Int. J. Med. Informatics **74**, 615–622 (2005)
8. Abujaber, A.A., Abd-Alrazaq, A., Al-Qudimat, A.R., Nashwan, A.J., AbuJaber, A.: A strengths, weaknesses, opportunities, and threats (SWOT) analysis of ChatGPT integration in nursing education: a narrative review. Cureus 15 (2023)
9. Chen, Z.-H., Lin, L., Wu, C.-F., Li, C.-F., Xu, R.-H., Sun, Y.: Artificial intelligence for assisting cancer diagnosis and treatment in the era of precision medicine. Cancer Commun. **41**, 1100–1115 (2021)
10. Quazi, S.: Artificial intelligence and machine learning in precision and genomic medicine. Med. Oncol. **39**, 120 (2022)
11. Adolphs, S., Brown, B., Carter, R., Crawford, P., Sahota, O.: Applying corpus linguistics in a health care context. Journal of applied linguistics 1 (2004)
12. Huang, F., Brouqui, P., Boudjema, S.: How does innovative technology impact nursing in infectious diseases and infection control? A scoping review. Nursing Open **8**, 2369–2384 (2021)
13. Venkatesh, V., Morris, M.G., Davis, G.B., Davis, F.D.: User acceptance of information technology: toward a unified view. MIS Q. **27**, 425–478 (2003)
14. Hill, R.J., Fishbein, M., Ajzen, I.: Belief, attitude, intention and behavior: an introduction to theory and research. Contemp. Sociol. **6**, 244 (1977)
15. Pan, M., Gao, W.: Determinants of the behavioral intention to use a mobile nursing application by nurses in China. BMC Health Serv. Res. **21**, 228 (2021)
16. Barchielli, C., Marullo, C., Bonciani, M., Vainieri, M.: Nurses and the acceptance of innovations in technology-intensive contexts: the need for tailored management strategies. BMC Health Serv. Res. **21**, 639 (2021)
17. Fornell, C., Larcker, D.F.: Evaluating structural equation models with unobservable variables and measurement error. J. Mark. Res. **18**, 39–50 (1981)
18. Chen, W., Srinivasan, S.R., Elkasabany, A., Berenson, G.S.: Cardiovascular risk factors clustering features of insulin resistance syndrome (Syndrome X) in a biracial (Black-White) population of children, adolescents, and young adults: the bogalusa heart study. Am. J. Epidemiol. **150**, 667–674 (1999)

Computational Thinking in Education

Effects of Computational Thinking and Collaborative Project-Based Learning on Student Attitudes Toward Learning: A Design and Implementation Study

Noviati Aning Rizki Mustika Sari[1], Anindya Prasisca Rena Zhetira Putri[1,2], Hong-Ren Chen[3], and Ting-Ting Wu[1](✉)

[1] National Yunlin University of Science and Technology, Yunlin 64002, Taiwan, Republic of China
ttwu@yuntech.edu.tw

[2] Faculty of Economics and Business, Universitas Muhammadiyah Semarang, Semarang 50273, Indonesia

[3] Department of Digital Content and Technology, National Taichung University of Education, Taichung 403, Taiwan

Abstract. This study examines the impact of integrating computational thinking (CT) into collaborative project-based learning (CPBL) approaches on undergraduate student attitudes toward learning in economics and business disciplines. Forty-seven students from a private university in Indonesia participated in a quasi-experimental design, with 23 students in the control group and 24 in the experimental group. Pretest and posttest scores for the Real-World Connection, Conceptual Connections, Applied Conceptual Understanding, and General Problem-Solving subscales were assessed using a modified Colorado Learning Attitude Science Survey (CLASS). Results indicated significant improvements in posttest scores for all subscales in the experimental group compared to the control group. Specifically, students in the experimental group demonstrated stronger perceptions of the relevance of course materials to real-world contexts, enhanced conceptual understanding, an improved ability to apply conceptual knowledge, and increased problem-solving skills. These findings suggest that integrating CT into CPBL approaches enriches students' learning experiences and prepares them for the dynamic challenges of the modern workforce. Educators are encouraged to consider the implications of these results and explore innovative pedagogical approaches that promote deeper learning and critical thinking skills among students.

Keywords: Computational Thinking · Collaborative Project-based Learning · Student Attitudes · Economics and Business Education · Design and Implementation

Y.-P. Cheng et al. (Eds.): ICITL 2024, LNCS 14785, pp. 75–83, 2024.
https://doi.org/10.1007/978-3-031-65881-5_9

1 Introduction

Economics and business graduates have been widely scrutinized and shown to be technically capable but without sufficiently broad skills in problem-solving and lifelong learning skills [1]. These skills are necessary for students, as there is an increasing demand for graduates who possess domain-specific knowledge and the ability to navigate complex problems using computational tools and collaborate effectively in diverse teams. However, traditional education has failed to incorporate such skills into curricula and teaching practice [2, 3].

Computational thinking (CT), defined by Wing, refers to a problem-solving approach that draws upon principles from computer science to formulate and solve real-world problems [4]. Its core components include decomposition, pattern recognition, abstraction, and algorithm design, all essential skills for navigating the complexities of today's data-rich business environments [5]. With the exponential growth of data and technological advancements, the ability to think computationally has become a requisite skill for economists and business professionals alike.

Furthermore, collaborative project-based learning (CPBL) has emerged as a pedagogical approach fostering student teamwork, communication, and critical thinking skills [6]. By engaging in authentic, real-world projects, students deepen their understanding of course concepts and develop crucial soft skills highly valued by employers [7]. In economics and business education, where interdisciplinary collaboration and problem-solving are paramount, CPBL offers a promising avenue for cultivating well-rounded graduates equipped to tackle complex challenges.

The integration of CT and CPBL aligns closely with the evolving needs of the workforce and the demands of the digital age. As the Association to Advance Collegiate Schools of Business (AACSB) emphasized, the ability to leverage technology and work effectively in teams is among the key skills that business schools should impart to their graduates [8]. By incorporating CT and CPBL into the curriculum, educators can better prepare students for modern business environments' dynamic and data-driven nature.

Given these considerations, this research explores the effectiveness of integrating CT and CPBL in undergraduate economics and business programs. By synthesizing insights from the latest literature and conducting empirical investigations, we seek to shed light on the design, implementation, and potential benefits associated with this pedagogical approach. Hence, this study poses the following research question: How do computational thinking and collaborative project-based learning impact student attitudes toward learning?

2 Literature Review

2.1 Computational Thinking (CT) and Collaborative Project-Based Learning (CPBL)

Recent literature emphasizes the pivotal role of computational thinking (CT) in shaping students' cognitive processes and problem-solving abilities. CT, as defined by Wing (2006), involves a systematic approach to problem-solving that draws upon concepts from computer science. Studies have shown that integrating CT into educational curricula enhances students' analytical skills and fosters their creativity and adaptability in addressing complex challenges [9]. Moreover, growing evidence suggests a positive relationship between CT and student attitudes toward learning. For instance, Bocconi et al. conducted a systematic review of curriculum practices and found that exposure to CT activities increased student engagement and enthusiasm for learning [5]. This suggests the importance of integrating CT into educational settings to cultivate a positive learning environment and enhance students' educational experiences.

Collaborative project-based learning (CPBL) has garnered significant attention in educational research for its potential to promote deeper learning, critical thinking, and teamwork skills among students. CPBL involves students working in groups to solve real-world problems or complete authentic projects, often spanning multiple disciplines [6]. Studies have highlighted various benefits associated with CPBL, including enhanced student engagement, motivation, and satisfaction with the learning process [10]. By immersing students in hands-on, experiential learning experiences, CPBL encourages active participation and fosters a sense of ownership over the learning process [11]. Furthermore, CPBL promotes the development of interpersonal skills such as communication, collaboration, and conflict resolution, which are essential for success in today's interconnected and dynamic workforce [12].

2.2 Attitudes

Understanding student attitudes toward learning is crucial for designing effective educational interventions and fostering positive learning experiences. Research indicates that student attitudes encompass various affective, cognitive, and behavioral components that influence their engagement, motivation, and achievement in academic contexts [13]. Positive attitudes toward learning are associated with greater persistence, effort, and enjoyment of the learning process, leading to improved academic performance and overall well-being [14]. Conversely, negative attitudes, such as apathy or disinterest, can impede learning outcomes and hinder students' ability to reach their full potential [15]. Therefore, exploring factors contributing to forming and modifying student attitudes toward learning is essential for educators seeking to enhance student engagement and academic success.

3 Methods

3.1 Participants

The subjects of this quasi-experimental study were 47 undergraduates enrolled in the faculty of economics and business at a private university in Indonesia. The participants were separated into two groups: the control group consisted of 23 students, and the experimental group comprised 24 students. Students in the control group utilized the CPBL approach. On the contrary, the experimental group engaged in an educational environment that incorporated CT combined with CPBL. Significantly, both cohorts were exposed to an online blended learning setting that incorporated components of online flipped learning. Furthermore, they were guided by a single instructor, maintaining uniformity in instructional approaches and content distribution throughout the experimental phases.

3.2 Experimental Procedure

In this quasi-experimental design lasting for seven weeks, each spanning a 50-min duration, a systematic procedure was followed to evaluate the impact of incorporating CT into CPBL strategies on student attitudes. Before the commencement of the experiment, both the control and experimental groups completed a pretest questionnaire assessing their attitudes toward online learning. Subsequently, students from both groups were organized into teams of four individuals. The experimental group of students participated in a 45-min online session to learn how to apply the CT paradigm to CPBL and were provided with instructions on specific activities to complete for each CT step.

Throughout the study, students engaged in an online flipped learning environment, accessing teaching materials distributed by the instructor via the school's learning management system. These materials were to be explored independently by students at their own pace, facilitating preparedness for online in-class activities. During online in-class sessions, the control group students participated in CPBL activities, while the experimental group students were exposed to a CT-enhanced CPBL approach. To ensure the integration of computational thinking, each group maintained a CT log, documenting detailed activities associated with CT steps. Every week, the instructor assigned small projects aligned with the designated topic, fostering practical application and critical thinking skills among the students. At the culmination of the experimental activities, students were tasked with submitting a final project and completing a posttest questionnaire assessing their attitudes toward online learning, enabling the comparison of pre- and post-intervention attitudes between the control and experimental groups. Figure 1 illustrates the experimental procedure details.

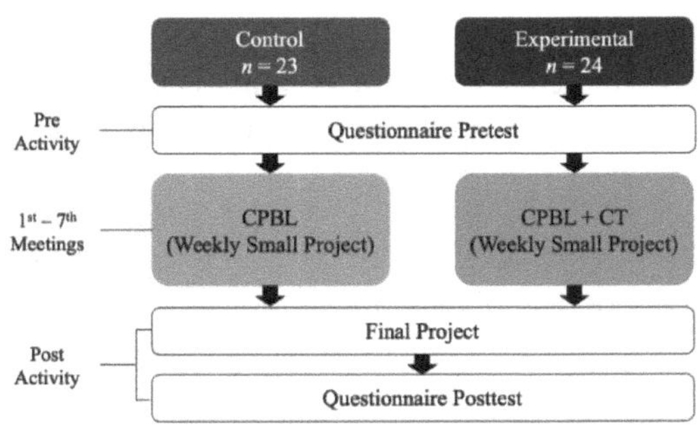

Fig. 1. Experimental procedure details.

3.3 Measurement

The evaluation of student attitudes toward learning adopted and modified the Colorado Learning Attitude Science Survey (CLASS) developed by Adams et al. [16]. The CLASS is used in this study as a reliable and valid tool to assess students' attitudes in the classroom. It provides valuable insights into their learning experience, which can help in developing targeted interventions and instructional strategies to improve learning outcomes. The questionnaire contained sixteen items, following the four subscales—Real-World Connection, Conceptual Connections, Applied Conceptual Understanding, and General Problem-Solving. The number of questions comprising each subscale varied. Specifically, Real-World Connection comprised four items: Conceptual Connections five, Applied Conceptual Understanding four, and General Problem-Solving three.

The Real-World Connection assesses the degree to which students consider the course materials pertinent and practical concerning real-life circumstances. The Conceptual Connections measure students' aptitude for establishing correlations or associations among various concepts or ideas covered in the course material. The emphasis of Applied Conceptual Understanding is on the ability of students to utilize their conceptual understanding to resolve problems or confront challenges in unique circumstances. The General Problem-Solving evaluates students' confidence in confronting scientific challenges or problems and their overall problem-solving abilities.

The results of the validity and reliability tests performed on the questionnaire were encouraging. The internal consistency of the subscales was assessed using Cronbach's alpha coefficients. The obtained values for all dimensions of Applied Conceptual Understanding ($\alpha = 0.858$), Real-World Connection ($\alpha = 0.842$), and General Problem-Solving ($\alpha = 0.848$) indicate a high level of reliability. Furthermore, to evaluate the construct validity of the instrument, correlation coefficients (r) were calculated. The results indicated statistically significant positive correlations ($p < 0.05$) between each subscale and student attitudes toward learning. The results highlighted the CLASS questionnaire's appropriateness and resilience as a tool for assessing student perspectives regarding the experimental procedures conducted in this research.

3.4 Data Analysis

Several crucial stages comprised the data analysis for this study, which aimed to determine how the integration of CT into CPBL strategies affected student attitudes toward learning. To commence, data were gathered using an online questionnaire survey distributed to participants prior to and subsequent to the intervention. Following that, to compare the pretest and posttest scores for student attitudes toward learning between the control and experimental groups while controlling for potential confounding variables, a one-way analysis of covariance (ANCOVA) was performed. In addition, descriptive statistics were calculated to summarize and compare the distribution of values for each variable of interest, which included means and standard deviations.

The homogeneity of variances between groups was also evaluated by conducting homogeneity tests on each subscale of the CLASS. The test results revealed that there were no statistically significant differences in variances between the control and experimental groups for the following subscales: Real-World Connection ($F = 0.715$, $p = 0.402$), Conceptual Connections ($F = 2.346$, $p = 0.133$), Applied Conceptual Understanding ($F = 0.059$, $p = 0.809$), and General Problem-Solving ($F = 2.612$, $p = 0.113$).

4 Results

4.1 Real-World Connection

The study findings unveiled a noteworthy difference in the Real-World Connection subscale between the experimental and control groups, as evidenced by a statistically significant F-value ($F = 34.127, p < 0.05$). The disparity is evident in Table 1, which presents the statistically elevated Real-World Connection scores of the experimental group (M = 4.17, SD = 0.381) compared to the control group (M = 3.39, SD = 0.499) on the same posttest. The results of this study indicate that individuals in the experimental group, who were simultaneously exposed to CT and CPBL, demonstrated a significantly higher level of confidence in the practicality and significance of course content than those in the control group.

Table 1. ANCOVA results for the Real-World Connection subscale.

Groups	Pretest		Posttest		Sum of Squares	F	p
	Mean	SD	Mean	SD			
Control	3.61	0.499	3.39	0.499	6.828	34.127	0.000*
Experimental	3.46	0.509	4.17	0.381			

*p < 0.05

4.2 Conceptual Connection

As shown in Table 2, the study results revealed significant differences between the experimental and control groups on the Conceptual Connections subscale. An F-value of 6.276 ($p < 0.05$) was obtained, suggesting that the experimental group demonstrated considerably more robust conceptual connections than the control group. The results indicate that the experimental group achieved significantly higher posttest scores (M = 4.00, SD = 0.417) on the Conceptual Connections subscale than the control group (M = 3.61, SD = 0.583). This finding emphasizes the positive impact of the intervention on students' capacity to establish connections among various concepts covered in the course material.

Table 2. ANCOVA results for the Conceptual Connections subscale.

Groups	Pretest		Posttest		Sum of Squares	F	p
	Mean	SD	Mean	SD			
Control	3.35	0.487	3.61	0.583	1.621	6.276	0.016*
Experimental	3.50	0.511	4.00	0.417			

*$p < 0.05$

4.3 Applied Conceptual Understanding

The research findings, which are presented in Table 3, demonstrate a significant statistical difference between the experimental and control groups on the Applied Conceptual Understanding subscale ($F = 9.128$, $p < 0.05$). In particular, the experimental group exhibited a statistically significant increase in posttest scores for the Applied Conceptual Understanding subscale (M = 4.17, SD = 0.482) compared to the control group (M = 3.65, SD = 0.647). The result highlights the efficacy of combining CT and CPBL in improving the capacity of students to implement theoretical understanding in real-world situations.

Table 3. ANCOVA results for the Applied Conceptual Understanding subscale.

Groups	Pretest		Posttest		Sum of Squares	*F*	*p*
	Mean	SD	Mean	SD			
Control	3.43	0.507	3.65	0.647	3.018	9.128	0.004*
Experimental	3.58	0.504	4.17	0.482			

*$p < 0.05$

4.4 General Problem-Solving

The results displayed in Table 4 demonstrate a statistically significant difference between the experimental and control groups for the General Problem-Solving subscale. This is supported by an F-value of 22.816 ($p < 0.05$). The experimental group exhibited significantly higher posttest scores on the General Problem-Solving subscale (M = 3.8986, SD = 0.46195) than the control group (M = 3.2569, SD = 0.65051). This finding indicates that individuals who participated in CT and CPBL approaches displayed considerably enhanced problem-solving abilities.

Table 4. ANCOVA results for the General Problem-Solving subscale.

Groups	Pretest		Posttest		Sum of Squares	*F*	*p*
	Mean	SD	Mean	SD			
Control	3.48	0.511	3.61	0.499	2.763	10.175	0.003*
Experimental	3.67	0.482	4.13	0.537			

*$p < 0.05$

5 Discussion

The results from this research emphasize the substantial advantages of incorporating CT into CPBL approaches for undergraduates majoring in economics and business. The discrepancies identified in the scores of Real-World Connection, Conceptual Connections, Applied Conceptual Understanding, and General Problem-Solving shed light on the effectiveness of this pedagogical approach in improving multiple facets of students' educational experiences. The findings presented in this study are consistent with prior research that underlines the significance of CT in fostering students' critical thinking, problem-solving abilities, and comprehension [9]. By facilitating significant associations between theoretical subjects and practical implementations, the incorporation of CT enhances students' educational encounters and promotes a more comprehensive and purposeful pedagogical stance.

Furthermore, incorporating CPBL enhances students' capacity to recognize interrelationships among various concepts and fosters their conceptual comprehension [10]. This approach fosters a more comprehensive and subtle comprehension of the subject matter, consequently augmenting the efficacy and profoundness of the students' educational journeys. Moreover, the observed improvements in student applied conceptual understanding and general problem-solving capabilities demonstrate the significant influence that CT-enhanced CPBL strategies can have in equipping students with the indispensable critical thinking and problem-solving skills required to succeed in diverse academic and professional settings. These results stress the significance of integrating CT into CPBL to equip students for the demands of the contemporary, interconnected, and ever-changing labor market.

6 Conclusion

The results of this research offer persuasive support for incorporating CT into CPBL approaches to enrich the educational experiences of undergraduates majoring in economics and business. The notable enhancements in student attitudes toward learning, as measured by the subscales of Real-World Connection, Conceptual Connections, Applied Conceptual Understanding, and General Problem-Solving, underscore the transformative capacity of this pedagogical approaches in cultivating a more profound comprehension, a more analytical mindset, and more effective problem-solving abilities among students. The implications of these findings for educators are significant, as they demonstrate the value of integrating CT into CPBL endeavors to enhance students' educational experiences and equip them with the necessary skills for the labor market of the 21st century.

Educators must, nevertheless, recognize the possible constraints of this research, including the particular setting in which it was carried out and the limited number of participants in the sample. Additionally, the long-term effects of CT-enhanced CPBL strategies on students' learning outcomes and attitudes toward learning require further investigation. However, by implementing innovative pedagogical approaches that combine CT and CPBL, teachers can equip students with the knowledge and abilities necessary to succeed in a progressively more intricate and interdependent world.

Acknowledgments. This research is partially supported by the National Science and Technology Council, Taiwan, ROC, under Grant No. MOST 110-2511-H-224-003-MY3 and MOST 111-2628-H-224-001-MY3.

Disclosure of Interests. None.

References

1. Hakim, R.R.C.: Are accounting graduates prepared for their careers? a comparison of employees' and employers' perceptions. Global Rev. Account. Fin. **7**, 1–17 (2016)
2. Oliver, B., Whelan, B., Hunt, L., Hammer, S.: Accounting graduates and the capabilities that count: Perceptions of graduates. employers and accounting academics in four Australian universities. J. Teach. Learn. Gradu. Employab. **2**, 2–27 (2011)
3. Van Romburgh, H., Van der Merwe, N.: University versus practice: A pilot study to identify skills shortages that exist in first-year trainee accountants in South Africa. Ind. High. Educ. **29**, 141–149 (2015)
4. Wing, J.M.: Computational thinking. Commun. ACM **49**, 33–35 (2006)
5. Bocconi, S., et al.: Reviewing computational thinking in compulsory education: State of play and practices from computing education (2022)
6. Johnson, D.W., Johnson, R.T., Smith, K.A.: Cooperative learning: Improving university instruction by basing practice on validated theory. J. Excelle. Univ. Teach. **25**, 1–26 (2014)
7. Prince, M.: Does active learning work? a review of the research. J. Eng. Educ. **93**, 223–231 (2004)
8. AACSB: Report of the AACSB International Alliance for Management Education Task Force (2006)
9. Grover, S., Pea, R.: Computational thinking in K–12: A review of the state of the field. Educ. Res. **42**, 38–43 (2013)
10. Bell, S.: Project-based learning for the 21st century: Skills for the future. The Clearing House **83**, 39–43 (2010)
11. Larmer, J., Mergendoller, J., Boss, S.: Setting the standard for project based learning. Ascd (2015)
12. Barron, B.J.S., et al.: Doing with understanding: Lessons from research on problem-and project-based learning. In: Learning through problem solving. pp. 271–311. Psychology Press (2014)
13. Martin, A.J., Dowson, M.: Interpersonal relationships, motivation, engagement, and achievement: Yields for theory, current issues, and educational practice. Rev. Educ. Res. **79**, 327–365 (2009)
14. Ainley, M., Hidi, S., Berndorff, D.: Interest, learning, and the psychological processes that mediate their relationship. J. Educ. Psychol. **94**, 545 (2002)
15. Schunk, D.H., Pintrich, P.R., Meece, J.L.: Motivation in education: Theory, research, and applications. (No Title) (2014)
16. Adams, W.K., et al.: New instrument for measuring student beliefs about physics and learning physics: The Colorado Learning Attitudes about Science Survey. Physical Review Special Topics - Physics Education Research 2 (2006). https://doi.org/10.1103/PhysRevSTPER.2.010101

Empowering Visual Programming and Motor Board Instruction in STEAM Education: Integrating Computational Thinking and Scaffolding Learning for Improving Learning Performance and Engagement of Students

Yu-Ping Cheng[1](✉), Andreja Istenič Starčič[2,3], and Jim-Min Lin[4]

[1] Department of Information Management, National Chi Nan University, Nantou County, Taiwan
yuping@mail.ncnu.edu.tw
[2] Faculty of Education, University of Primorska, Koper, Slovenia
[3] Faculty of Civil and Geodetic Engineering, University of Ljubljana, Ljubljana, Slovenia
[4] Department of Information Engineering and Computer Science, Feng Chia University, Taichung City, Taiwan
jimmy@fcu.edu.tw

Abstract. STEAM education can transform students' roles in traditional classrooms from passive to active through hands-on practice, but many students are prone to encounter difficulties in the interdisciplinary learning process, which affects the effectiveness of hands-on practice. In order to overcome the dilemma of STEAM education, scaffolded learning and computational thinking are considered effective instructional strategies. However, there are few studies exploring the educational implementation of integrating computational thinking with scaffolded learning in STEAM education. Therefore, this study uses a quasi-experimental design to conduct experimental activities in STEAM education and introduces the MakeCode platform and micro: bit motor board to explore the issues of this empirical study. According to the results, the experimental group was able to correctly use the MakeCode platform to code programs for practicing micro: bit motor board tasks. Not only did their learning performance significantly surpass that of the control group, but they also maintained higher engagement in terms of learning. Therefore, this study verifies that integrating computational thinking and scaffolding learning in STEAM education can significantly improve students' learning performance and engagement, thereby providing important educational implementation for the introduction of computational thinking and scaffolding learning in STEAM education.

Keywords: Computational Thinking · Scaffolding Learning · STEAM Education · Visual Programming · Learning Engagement

Y.-P. Cheng et al. (Eds.): ICITL 2024, LNCS 14785, pp. 84–94, 2024.
https://doi.org/10.1007/978-3-031-65881-5_10

1 Introduction

Benefiting from the development of information technology, teachers can incorporate multimedia or emerging technologies into the classroom, enabling students to acquire more knowledge and concepts while fostering greater engagement in classroom activities [1, 2]. Since traditional instructional methods only allow students to passively receive knowledge, it is challenging for them to engage actively in the learning process. If students lack opportunities for active learning in class, it may have a negative impact on their class participation and motivation to learn [3, 4]. According to Liu, Wang, Lei, Wang and Ren [2], teaching students in the classroom using digital learning methods can address many of the limitations of traditional teaching. Some studies also indicate that students can enhance learning efficiency through digital learning, emerging technologies, and multimedia teaching materials and resources. These approaches can help improve motivation for learning tasks and activities [5–7]. To enable students to take an "active" role in the classroom, STEM/STEAM education is considered a successful instruction strategy, allowing students to assume primary responsibility in learning activities [8]. STEM/STEAM is an interdisciplinary approach to education that integrates knowledge across disciplines to support students' practical interests. Some study has also indicated that the use of emerging technology or instruction strategy can have a positive impact on STEAM education, enabling students to demonstrate better learning performance through hands-on practice [9].

Although STEM/STEAM education has yielded positive results in hands-on practice, students often lack professional knowledge and concepts in the subject when learning new topics, leading to their inability to effectively apply the knowledge they have acquired to hands-on practice. To help students in obtaining better assistance or guidance when constructing knowledge, scaffolded learning is considered one of the effective instructional strategy [10]. Scaffolded learning offers students appropriate teaching aids and scaffolding materials tailored to topics and tasks, thereby aiding students in constructing knowledge and skills [11]. Kim, Belland, Lefler, Andreasen, Walker and Axelrod [12] emphasized that scaffolded learning can effectively help students develop STEM education abilities and provide the necessary support and guidance throughout the learning process.

On the other hand, CT is a problem-solving skill. When people encounter complex problems, they can systematically solve them through the core competence of CT [13]. A study has confirmed that students' use of visual programming can effectively develop and enhance CT skills [14]. Compared with traditional programming languages, visual programming has a lower learning threshold. It employs graphical building blocks to represent various components and concepts of a program, enabling novice programmers to write programs with greater confidence [15].

However, most research focuses on scaffolding learning and STEM education issues, with few studies exploring how to design scaffolding assistance through systematic thinking, especially in STEAM education, which remains largely unexplored. Students may become confused and encounter difficulties with learning tasks, finding it challenging to practice and solve problems using existing knowledge and skills [9]. To address these research limitations, this study concentrates on integrating CT with scaffolding learning, utilizing the core competence of CT to design corresponding scaffolds. This approach allows students to utilize CT skills to complete the steps of learning tasks through visual programming. Additionally, this study examines whether students can effectively enhance their learning performance and engagement in STEAM education through this method. Therefore, this study proposed the following two research questions:

1 Is the learning performance of the experimental group that integrates CT and scaffolded learning in STEAM education higher than that of the control group?
2 Is the learning engagement of the experimental group that integrates CT and scaffolded learning in STEAM education higher than that of the control group?

2 Literature Review

2.1 Computational Thinking and Core Competencies

In recent years, computational thinking (CT) has received great attention and recognition in the education and academic fields. Wing [16] pointed out that CT is not only a professional skill that computer scientists must possess, but also a basic quality that everyone must possess in the 21st century. CT is thought to represent the link between programming and thinking skills [17]. Although the concept of CT was proposed as early as the 20st century, its significance in the field of education has still not been specifically defined and described. To specifically define the term CT, Wing [16] proposed the meaning of CT ability in this paper, defining it as referring to the basic concepts of computer science that enable people to develop abilities to solve problems and design systems. Wei, Lin, Meng, Tan and Kong [18] stated that CT can serve as a method of problem-solving and innovation, and teachers can cultivate students' CT skills through appropriate teaching theories, strategies, and technological tools. CT has not only achieved great success and advantages in computer science and programming [15, 19], but also holds significant implications in educational issues and practical applications in non-computer science fields, such as English writing [20] and mathematical ability [21].

According to Anderson [13], CT is defined as a process that includes five main core competencies, namely Decomposition, Pattern Recognition, Abstraction, Algorithm Design and Evaluation, the interpretation of these competencies is as follows:

- Decomposition: Decompose the main and complex overall problem into smaller sub-problems.
- Pattern Recognition: Identify whether there are identical or repeated patterns in each sub-problem after decomposition, and find patterns or rules that are beneficial to solving the sub-problems.
- Abstraction: Generate an iterative model representing the problem based on patterns or rules corresponding to several sub-problems.
- Algorithm design: Design the algorithm of the iterative model in a systematic manner to design a solution to the overall problem.
- Evaluation: Ensure that the designed algorithm can effectively solve the overall problem.

Cheng, Lai, Chen, Wang, Huang and Wu [15] confirmed that combining the above five CT core competencies with appropriate instructional strategies and using a game-based learning platform can significantly improve students' CT skills. Brennan and

Resnick [22] considered that interactive media tools can help students practice CT concepts by developing basic principles and concepts of programming through graphical methods. Beginner programmers can use interactive media tools and visual programming languages to develop basic programming logic and concepts in computer science. Many studies have shown that common tools such as App Inventor, Scratch, Alice, or MakeCode help develop CT skills or abilities among beginners [23, 24]. Therefore, this study mainly utilizes the five core competencies of CT proposed by Anderson [13], namely decomposition, pattern recognition, abstraction, algorithm design, and evaluation, so that students can generate solutions through the above key core competencies.

2.2 Scaffolding Learning

Scaffolded learning is an instructional strategy that aims to support students in building their understanding and acquisition skills through a step-by-step process when learning new knowledge or skills [10]. Scaffolded learning is derived from the zone of proximal development (ZPD) proposed by Vygotsky and Cole [10]. As the name suggests, students can use appropriate teaching and assistance to enable them to complete learning tasks or teaching arrangements effectively develop competencies and skills. The concept of scaffolded learning originated from the scaffolding used on construction sites. Scaffolding is used as a temporary structure during the construction of a building to allow workers to work at height and is gradually dismantled after the building is completed. In the field of education, scaffolded learning refers to teachers or tutors providing students with the support and guidance they need to help them complete tasks or solve problems [11, 25]. The teaching implementation of the scaffolding method can be designed in an organized and systematic manner according to the needs of the students and the complexity of the tasks [5].

Scaffolded learning is also commonly utilized in cross-disciplinary STEM education. Effective hands-on learning in science, technology, engineering, and mathematics is facilitated with the aid of appropriate scaffolding [12]. Additionally, scaffolded learning enables students to receive suitable assistance through scaffolding during the practical process, thereby enhancing their effectiveness in STEM learning [12]. However, there are few studies in the field of STEAM education that explore how to design scaffolding assistance through systems thinking. Therefore, this study focuses on integrating CT with scaffolded learning, utilizing the core competencies of CT to design corresponding scaffolds, and verifying the impact of this method on students' STEAM education through empirical research.

3 Research Method

3.1 Integrating Computational Thinking and Scaffolding Learning into the MakeCode Platform

This study used the MakeCode platform developed by Microsoft, an educational programming tool designed to assist students and educators in learning and teaching programming concepts, particularly in areas such as the Internet of Things, robotics, and electronic circuit manufacturing. The platform offers a graphical interface that enables beginners and children to write programs easily through visual programming, without needing to deeply understand the syntax and structure of text-based programming languages.

This study designs teaching materials based on the Micro: bit motor board and uses scaffolded learning to create various program frameworks, such as light sensors, infrared reflective sensors, ultrasonic sensors, etc. Additionally, the researchers employed the five core competencies of CT. Learners can accomplish program functions according to the scaffolded program framework provided by the researcher and the five core competencies of CT. As shown in Fig. 1, researchers offer a scaffolded programming framework for each Micro: bit motor board. Students must employ the five core competencies of CT to decompose the problem step by step into several subproblems following task instructions (decomposition); recognize repeating rules and patterns in subproblems (pattern recognition); develop corresponding functions based on the identified patterns (abstraction); design algorithm to address the problem (algorithm design); and ensure the correctness of the algorithm (evaluation). Therefore, students can execute the corresponding functions based on the scaffolded program frameworks and the core competencies of CT (as shown in Fig. 2), and download their program to the Micro: bit motor board to test the correctness (as shown in Fig. 3).

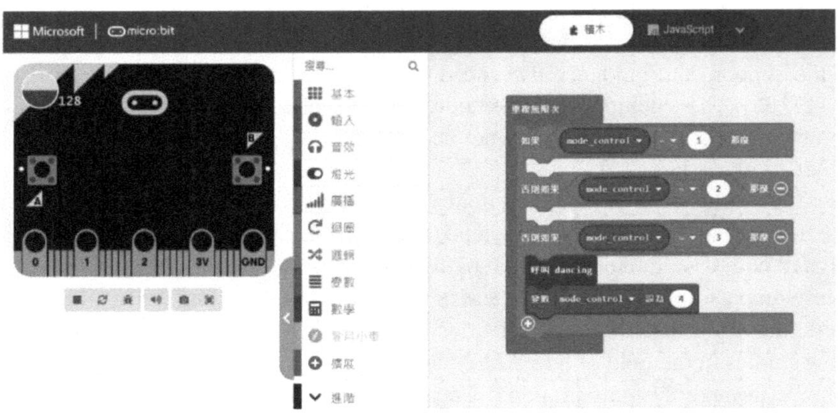

Fig. 1. Using the scaffolding program frameworks and core competencies of CT on the MadeCode platform.

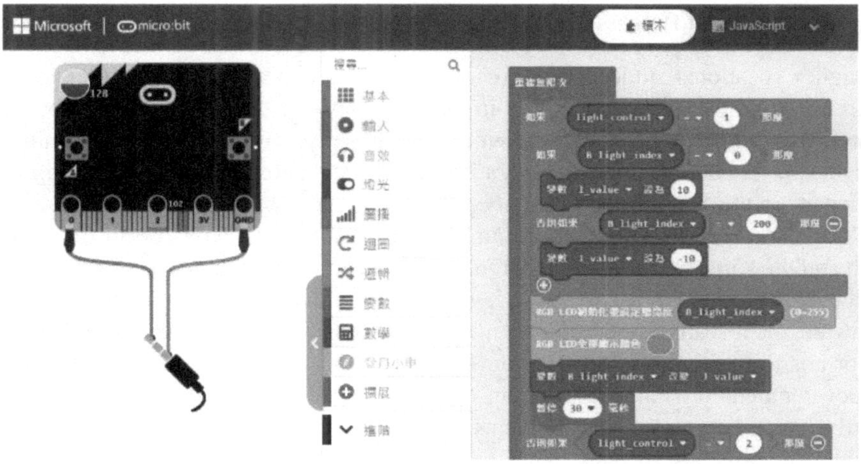

Fig. 2. Completing the scaffolding program frameworks through core competencies of CT.

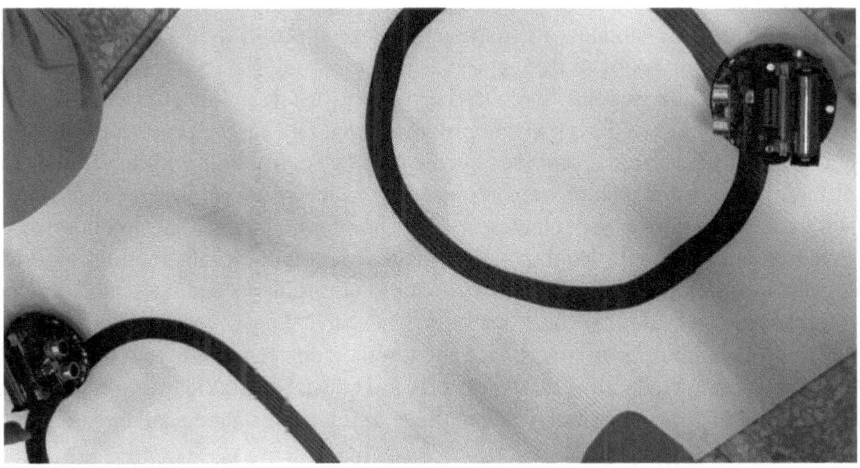

Fig. 3. Downloading the program to the Micro: bit motor board through the MakeCode platform to test the correctness of program.

3.2 Participants

This study recruited 42 students from a vocational high school in southern Taiwan, including 22 students in the experimental group and 20 students in the control group. The average age of the participants is 16–17 years old. As all participating students were under 18 years old, the researchers provided an informed consent form before the experiment, which included a detailed description of the experimental process and data collection procedures. All students were required to obtain consent from their parents and themselves before participating in the experiments. Finally, 42 valid informed consent forms were collected for this study.

3.3 Experimental Process

42 higher vocational students were recruited for this experimental activity, including 22 in the experimental group and 20 in the control group. All students participated in a three-week experimental activity, with three classes per week, totaling 450 min. All students must obtain parental authorization and consent before the experiment begins to participate in this experimental activity.

In the first class, the researchers introduce to all students the process of this experiment and the software and hardware tools that need to be used. In terms of software, all students are required to use MakeCode for programming and development. In terms of hardware, the researchers distribute a micro: bit motor board and toolkit. The micro: bit motor board used in this study was developed by iCshop. Since it supports the micro: bit development version, students can use the relevant hardware components on this board to design corresponding functions. After distributing the materials, the researcher conduct an online test (pre-test) via Google Forms to survey students' prior knowledge of programming and micro: bit.

After the pre-test, the researcher taught 8 lessons, totaling 400 min, to instruct all students in using the MakeCode platform and micro: bit motor board to code relevant program functions. 22 students for experimental group used the MakeCode platform and micro: bit motor board to design visual programming through integating CT and scaffolded learning. 20 students for control group only used the MakeCode platform and micro: bit motor board to design visual programming. During the process of the experimental group, the researcher provided corresponding scaffolding program frameworks for different lessons. Students were required to code program blocks corresponding to each task, using core competencies of CT. Therefore, students had to complete the relevant functions through decomposition, pattern recognition, abstraction, algorithm design, and evaluation in accordance with the task requirements and the scaffolding program framework provided by the researcher. Then, they can download their programs into the micro: bit motor board to practice and test their corresponding functions. Finally, the researcher conducted online test (post-test) and questionnaire (learning engagement) via Google Forms to explore and measure the learning performance and engagement of the two groups of students.

3.4 Instruments

This study designed pre-test and post-test to investigate whether students' learning performance in programming have been improved. In the pre-test and post-test, the researcher designed items related to visual programming, including conceptual items (such as loops, conditions, functions, etc.) and program application items (such as providing program blocks for confirmation the function of its program). There are 20 items in the pre-test and post-test, with a maximum score of 100 points. 42 pre-test and post-test were collected in this study.

This study refers to the engagement questionnaire proposed by Reeve and Tseng [26] and edited the corresponding items based on the experimental activities. The engagement questionnaire has a total of 17 items, which are divided into four different engagement dimensions, namely behavioral engagement, agentic engagement, cognitive engagement, and emotional engagement. In addition, we used a five-point Likert scale as the questionnaire measurement scale, in which strongly agree is 5 and strongly disagree is 1.

4 Results

This study aims to explore whether there are differences in the learning performance and engagement of two groups of students after implementing different experimental activities in STEAM education. The experimental group integrated CT and scaffolding learning and used the MakeCode platform and micro: bit motor board to conduct visual programming; the control group used the MakeCode platform and micro: bit motor board to conduct visual programming.

The mean and standard deviation of the experimental group are 42.73 and 8.96, and those for the control group are 35.75 and 9.49. In addition, this study used ANCOVA to further analyze whether the two groups met the homogeneity regression test. According to Table 1, the interaction between group and pretest did not reach significant differences ($F = 0.583, p > .05$).

Table 1. The within-group homogeneity regression test.

Source	SS	df	*F*	*p*
Pre-test	248.58	1	1.51	.266
Groups	873.78	1	5.313	.027
Groups*Pre-test	95.92	1	0.583	.450
Error	164.47	38		
Corrected Total	15840.48	41		

Table 2. The ANCOVA result of learning performance.

Group	N	Mean	SD	Adjusted Mean	SE	*F*	*p*	η^2
Experimental group	22	87.95	4.79	87.05	2.82	43.30^{***}	< 0.000	0.526
Control group	20	58.25	17.94	59.24	2.96			

Note: *** $p < 0.001$.

The post-test results of the two groups are shown in Table 2. The mean of the experimental group is 87.95 and the standard deviation is 4.79; the mean of the control group is 58.25 and the standard deviation is 17.94. After excluding the influence of the pre-test, the adjusted mean of the experimental group is 87.05 and the standard error is 2.82; the adjusted mean of the control group is 59.24 and the standard error is 2.96. The F value of the result is 43.30 ($p < 0.001$), the effect size is 0.526, and the two groups reached a significant difference. This means that the experimental group is able to successfully control and practice the functions of the micro: bit motor board in STEAM activities through the integration of CT and scaffolding learning, thereby effectively improving the students' learning performance in programming.

Table 3 shows the independent sample t test results of the learning engagement of the two groups of students. The mean of the experimental group is 4.34, with a standard deviation of 0.39; the mean of the control group is 3.79, with a standard deviation of 0.94, and the t value is 2.396 ($p < 0.05$). There is a significant difference between the two groups. This means that the experimental group maintains higher learning engagement through integrating CT with scaffolded learning. In addition, students actively use the MakeCode platform to code programs to control the micro: bit motor board, thereby practice the hands-on in STEAM education.

Table 3. The independent sample t test result of learning engagement.

Group	N	Mean	SD	t	p
Experimental group	22	4.34	0.39	2.396^*	< 0.05
Control group	20	3.79	0.94		

Note: $^* p < 0.05$.

5 Conclusion

This study mainly explores whether the integration of CT and scaffolded learning in STEAM education can effectively improve students' learning performance and engagement. In addition, this study uses the MakeCode platform to provide a scaffolding program framework, allowing students to use the five core competencies of CT to solve various scaffolding programming frameworks with systematic thinking, thereby meeting and completing the learning tasks provided by the researcher. To solve and verify the problems of this empirical study, this study recruited 42 students to conduct STEAM activities, and used quasi-experimental design for teaching, testing, questionnaire collection, and data analysis.

The result of the learning performance shows that the experimental group achieved better performance in STEAM activities through the integration of CT and scaffolding learning, and was able to correctly use the MakeCode platform to code programs to practice the task of micro: bit motor board. The result of the study on learning engagement shows that the experimental group was able to maintain a higher learning engagement in STEAM activities, and also actively participated in coding programs and trying out the functions of the micro: bit motor board in different learning tasks. Therefore, this study confirms that integrating CT and scaffolded learning in STEAM education can significantly enhance students' learning performance and engagement, thereby providing educational implication for introducing CT and scaffolded learning into STEAM education.

References

1. Cheng, Y.-P., Cheng, S.-C., Yang, M., Lin, J.-M., Huang, Y.-M.: Applying computational thinking and formative assessment to enhance the learning performance of students in virtual programming language. In: International Conference on Innovative Technologies and Learning, pp. 130–139. Springer (Year)
2. Liu, R., Wang, L., Lei, J., Wang, Q., Ren, Y.: Effects of an immersive virtual reality-based classroom on students' learning performance in science lessons. Br. J. Edu. Technol. **51**, 2034–2049 (2020)
3. Cheng, S.-C., Cheng, Y.-P., Huang, Y.-M.: Developing a learning pathway system through web-based mining technology to explore students' learning motivation and performance. Sustainability **15**, 6950 (2023)
4. Lee, H.-Y., Cheng, Y.-P., Wang, W.-S., Lin, C.-J., Huang, Y.-M.: Exploring the learning process and effectiveness of STEM education via learning behavior analysis and the interactive-constructive-active-passive framework. J. Edu. Comp. Res. **61**, 951–976 (2023)
5. Lin, Y.-C., Hou, H.-T.: Multi-dimensional evaluation of an educational board game using real-time diagnostic procedure scaffolding: analysis of learners' learning effectiveness, flow, anxiety, and emotion. Educ. Psychol. **43**, 874–894 (2023)
6. Önal, N., Çevik, K.K., Şenol, V.: The effect of SOS Table learning environment on mobile learning tools acceptance, motivation and mobile learning attitude in English language learning. Interact. Learn. Environ. **30**, 834–847 (2022)
7. Yin, J., Goh, T.-T., Yang, B., Xiaobin, Y.: Conversation technology with micro-learning: the impact of chatbot-based learning on students' learning motivation and performance. J. Edu. Comp. Res. **59**, 154–177 (2021)
8. Christensen, R., Knezek, G., Tyler-Wood, T.: Alignment of hands-on STEM engagement activities with positive STEM dispositions in secondary school students. J. Sci. Educ. Technol. **24**, 898–909 (2015)
9. Cheng, Y.-P., Lai, C.-F., Cheng, S.-C., Huang, Y.-M.: Using immersive virtual reality to explore the learning performance and cognitive load of students in STEAM electronic circuits learning. In: International Conference on Innovative Technologies and Learning, pp. 107–116. Springer (Year)
10. Vygotsky, L.S., Cole, M.: Mind in society: Development of higher psychological processes. Harvard university press (1978)
11. Lin, P.-C., Hou, H.-T., Chang, K.-E.: The development of a collaborative problem solving environment that integrates a scaffolding mind tool and simulation-based learning: an analysis of learners' performance and their cognitive process in discussion. Interact. Learn. Environ. **30**, 1273–1290 (2022)
12. Kim, N.J., Belland, B.R., Lefler, M., Andreasen, L., Walker, A., Axelrod, D.: Computer-based scaffolding targeting individual versus groups in problem-centered instruction for STEM education: Meta-analysis. Educ. Psychol. Rev. **32**, 415–461 (2020)
13. Anderson, N.D.: A call for computational thinking in undergraduate psychology. Psychol. Learn. Teach. **15**, 226–234 (2016)
14. Lye, S.Y., Koh, J.H.L.: Review on teaching and learning of computational thinking through programming: What is next for K-12? Comput. Hum. Behav. **41**, 51–61 (2014)

15. Cheng, Y.-P., Lai, C.-F., Chen, Y.-T., Wang, W.-S., Huang, Y.-M., Wu, T.-T.: Enhancing student's computational thinking skills with student-generated questions strategy in a game-based learning platform. Comput. Educ. **200**, 104794 (2023)
16. Wing, J.M.: Computational thinking. Commun. ACM **49**, 33–35 (2006)
17. Papert, S.: Children, computers, and powerful ideas. Harvester (1980)
18. Wei, X., Lin, L., Meng, N., Tan, W., Kong, S.-C.: The effectiveness of partial pair programming on elementary school students' computational thinking skills and self-efficacy. Comput. Educ. **160**, 104023 (2021)
19. Yilmaz, R., Yilmaz, F.G.K.: The effect of generative artificial intelligence (AI)-based tool use on students' computational thinking skills, programming self-efficacy and motivation. Comp. Edu. Artifi. Intellig. **4**, 100147 (2023)
20. Wu, T.-T., Silitonga, L.M., Murti, A.T.: Enhancing English writing and higher-order thinking skills through computational thinking. Computers & Education 105012 (2024)
21. Angraini, L.M., Yolanda, F., Muhammad, I.: Augmented reality: the improvement of computational thinking based on students' initial mathematical ability. Int. J. Instr. **16**, 1033–1054 (2023)
22. Brennan, K., Resnick, M.: New frameworks for studying and assessing the development of computational thinking. In: Proceedings of the 2012 annual meeting of the American educational research association, p. 25. Vancouver, Canada (Year)
23. Özmutlu, M., Atay, D., Erdoğan, B.: Collaboration and engagement based coding training to enhance children's computational thinking self-efficacy. Thinking Skills and Creativity **40**, 100833 (2021)
24. Zhao, L., Liu, X., Wang, C., Su, Y.-S.: Effect of different mind mapping approaches on primary school students' computational thinking skills during visual programming learning. Comput. Educ. **181**, 104445 (2022)
25. Lee, Y.-F., Lin, C.-J., Hwang, G.-J., Fu, Q.-K., Tseng, W.-H.: Effects of a mobile-based progressive peer-feedback scaffolding strategy on students' creative thinking performance, metacognitive awareness, and learning attitude. Interact. Learn. Environ. **31**, 2986–3002 (2023)
26. Reeve, J., Tseng, C.-M.: Agency as a fourth aspect of students' engagement during learning activities. Contemp. Educ. Psychol. **36**, 257–267 (2011)

Computational Thinking and Creative Programming Activities Enhance the Information Literacy of Freshmen

Hsin-Chin Chen[1](✉), Kan-Lin Hsueh[1], Yeong-Chyi Lee[1], and Jan-Pan Hwang[2]

[1] Office of Library and Information, Cheng Shiu University, Kaohsiung City, Taiwan
{0662,kanlin,yeongchyi}@gcloud.csu.edu.tw

[2] Department of Information Management, National Chin-Yi University of Technology, Taichung City, Taiwan
janpan@ncut.edu.tw

Abstract. This study proposes conducting an information literacy test for freshmen to assess their level of information literacy, serving as a reference for instructors. The test is grounded in the six major themes of information technology outlined in the curriculum guidelines of 12-year basic education, including: "System Platforms," "Data Representation, Processing, and Analysis," "Algorithms," "Programming," "Information Technology Applications," and "Information Technology and Human Society." The outcomes of the test can evaluate freshmen's information literacy, allowing students to gauge their own IT skills and further analyze their strengths and weaknesses across these six themes. The results will provide guidance for teaching instructors and learning students, offering supplementary materials to those with high proficiency, and enhancing their programming and writing skills through computational thinking and creative programming activities. Additionally, the study includes the administration of a computational thinking and programming skills certification, using pre-tests, post-tests, and surveys to understand the changes in students' learning outcomes.

Keywords: Computational thinking · Programming design · Learning outcomes

1 Introduction

In recent years, there has been rapid advancement in both hardware and software equipment in the field of information and technology. Information technology professionals are creating and applying vast amounts of information that far exceed previous expectations, thereby creating more value for humanity. Through deep exploration of information technologies such as artificial intelligence, computer vision, and deep learning, these valuable datasets can be utilized to improving the daily living environment of humans. Possessing strong information literacy is key to rapidly absorbing new knowledge and enhancing employability competitiveness. By means of practicing computational thinking is the first step to understand and solve complex problems more effectively and further promote information literacy [1, 2].

Y.-P. Cheng et al. (Eds.): ICITL 2024, LNCS 14785, pp. 95–105, 2024.
https://doi.org/10.1007/978-3-031-65881-5_11

To assess students' computational thinking and information literacy, most universities adopt the same set of standard specifications for different disciplines and use examination methods to ensure students meet certification standards [3]. Information technology involves the collection, application, transmission, and storage of digital information and falls under the scope of information communication technology. In recent years, some technological universities have begun to emphasize students' information literacy and are employing various methods to cultivate computational thinking capabilities. For example, technological universities may exempt credits through selecting specific hardware and software tests or offering information-related courses as mandatory. Simultaneously, these schools set information literacy as a graduation threshold.

This study aims to elucidate the importance of computational thinking and information literacy for students, discuss the establishment of information literacy thresholds in Taiwan higher education institutions, and explore how to shape students' information learning processes through data analysis and experimental design, as well as how Taiwanese higher education institutions should cultivate students' abilities in computational thinking and information technology.

Through this study, freshmen will be assessed based on the six dimensions outlined in the curriculum guidelines of 12-year basic education, analyzing students' strengths and weaknesses across these dimensions. By understanding and discussing the data, suitable courses and activities can be devised to enhance and cultivate students' interest and motivation in computational thinking and information literacy. In the global internet age, information technology has been regarded as a core competency in many advanced countries, listed as a compulsory subject. The main objective of this study is to cultivate and enhance computational thinking and programming skills for non-information field students. It encourages students in the information field to strengthen their learning, enhancing more competitive in-depth study and project production. The study execution plan and goals include: 1. Conducting freshmen information literacy tests; 2. Offering three-stage information courses on computational thinking and creative programming; 3. Conducting student evaluations of computational thinking and creative programming capabilities to quantify student learning outcomes; 4. Organizing teacher teaching communities, convening teaching research meetings, and improving programming teaching skills.

2 Related Studies

2.1 College Students' Information Literacy

Since colleges and universities have made information literacy a necessary curriculum, it is considered a way to cultivate information literacy among college students. In recent years, colleges and universities have opened many related courses and tests to cultivate students' information literacy [4, 5]. However, some freshmen lack a conducive environment during their study period, leading to a deficiency in information-related abilities, such as losing motivation and willingness to learn, students generally lose enthusiasm for learning information literacy. To understand and evaluate students' weaknesses and requirements for information literacy. Through the six-dimensional test conducted in this study, both students and the university can understand their respective needs. The teachers can further understand known weaknesses of students, plan future courses, and provide remedial teaching.

2.2 Computing Thinking

Computing thinking have become fundamental subjects for students, especially those in the electrical and information engineering disciplines, where they are listed as compulsory subjects. The importance of computing thinking for college students can be explored through several factors: (1) Decomposition: breaking down complex problems into smaller, more manageable parts. (2) Pattern Recognition: looking for similarities among and within problems. (3) Abstraction: focusing on the important information only and ignoring irrelevant detail. (4) Algorithms: developing a step-by-step solution to the problem, or the rules to follow to solve the problem. Computing thinking allows students to understand the principles and execution processes of computers, and further solve real-life problem [6, 7]. Meanwhile, computing thinking requires students to understand computer operation processes and become familiar with programming language structures. Through the learning process, students are trained in logical thinking and problem-solving skills. Advanced systems such as embedded systems, the Internet of Things (IoT), and artificial intelligence (AI) systems are developed based on computing thinking. However, during the process of computing thinking, these learning processes can lead students to feel frustrated with learning programming and reduce their motivation to learn without the use of pedagogical strategies and technologies in teaching computing thinking [8].

3 Research Method

The study aims to investigate the effectiveness of enhancing freshmen's information literacy through conducting a freshmen information literacy test, offering a three-stage "Computational Thinking and Creative Programming" information course, conducting a computational thinking and creative programming ability assessment, and organizing a teaching community for faculty members. The activities conducted are as follows:

3.1 Conducting a Freshmen Information Literacy Test

Based on the high school curriculum's six major topics in information technology, including "System Platform," "Data Representation, Processing, and Analysis," "Algorithms," "Programming," "Information Technology Applications," and "Information Technology and Human Society," a pool of 1,000 questions was established, from which 40 questions were randomly selected for the test. The test results are analyzed to: (1) categorize information literacy into four levels (A–D) to inform students of their own proficiency, and (2) analyze students' proficiency in the six major topics of information technology, providing teaching references for instructors and supplementary materials for students to strengthen their programming skills and proficiency.

3.2 Offering a Three-Stage "Computational Thinking and Creative Programming" Information Course

For non-information majors, including civil engineering, mechanical engineering, industrial management, architecture, business administration, international business, early childhood education, foreign languages, finance, leisure and recreation management, tourism, makeup and beauty, fashion, and catering, totaling 14 departments with approximately 1,400 students annually, guiding them through the three stages of "Computational Thinking and Creative Programming," "Programming Languages" or "Multimedia Production," and "Internet Applications." This curriculum continues throughout the four years of university education, allowing students to complete relevant digital technology micro-programs offered by various colleges to enhance their competitiveness in future employment or further education.

3.3 Conducting a Computational Thinking and Creative Programming Ability Assessment

Conducting a computational thinking and creative programming ability assessment: After completing the computational thinking and creative programming courses, students undergo an assessment to evaluate their proficiency. A total of 400 questions are prepared, and an information literacy assessment platform is established to provide pre-course assessments and post-course evaluations, analyzing the differences in pre- and post-course scores to investigate the impact of the curriculum implementation on learning outcomes.

3.4 Organizing a Teaching Community for Faculty Members

The Department of Computer Science convenes a teaching community comprising teaching faculty members, who regularly discuss learning objectives, teaching materials, teaching methods, and learning assessments at the beginning and end of each semester. Experts and scholars from both inside and outside the university are invited to give lectures to exchange experiences, thereby enhancing students' learning motivation and effectiveness.

In addition, this study designed computational thinking and creative programming course for freshmen and used teachers' guidance to improve students' learning effectiveness. The specific research purposes are as follows:

1. To design computational thinking and creative programming course, to investigate whether its learning effectiveness is better than before.
2. To design computational thinking and creative programming course, and to investigate whether the learning satisfaction of students can be improved.

4 Discussion

Through the analysis of the freshmen information literacy test, it was found that a total of 1,680 individuals were administered the test, with 1,521 candidates taking it and 159 candidates absent. The pass rate was 39%. The pass rates for each college are illustrated in Fig. 1, with the College of Management having a pass rate of 51%, the College of Engineering with 43%, and the College of Life and Creativity with 30%. The College of Management freshmen showed a significantly higher pass rate in the information literacy test compared to other colleges, with pass rates below 50% in other colleges. This disparity may be attributed to differences in professional disciplines, resulting in a superior information literacy level in the College of Management compared to other colleges.

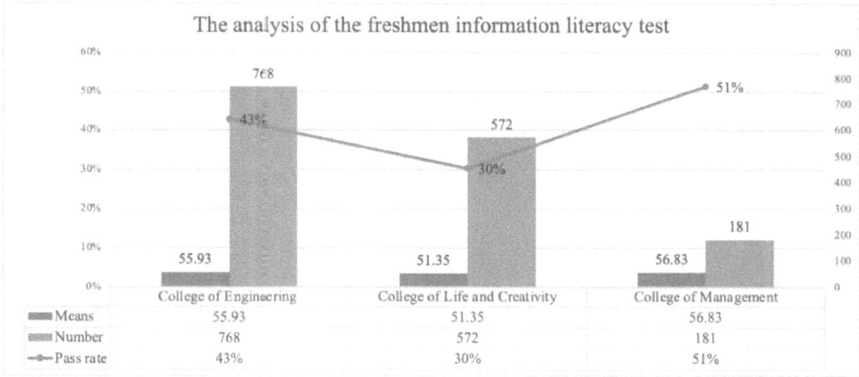

Fig. 1. The analysis of the freshmen information literacy test.

According to the research analysis, the percentage of correct responses for the six major dimensions is shown in Fig. 2. Information Technology and Human Society had a percentage of 68%, Information Technology Applications had 63%, Data Representation, Processing, and Analysis had 58%, Algorithms had 36%, and Programming had 46%. The percentage of correct responses for the six major dimensions indicates that Information Technology and Human Society performed the best, while Programming and Algorithms need further improvement. Additionally, the comparison of the percentage of correct responses for the six major dimensions across different colleges is shown in Table 1. The percentage for Information Technology and Human Society is higher compared to the other five dimensions, while Algorithms and Programming remain weaker dimensions across all colleges.

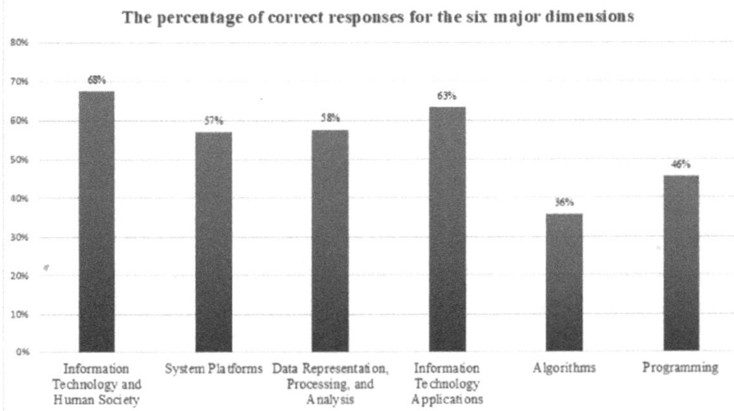

Fig. 2. The percentage of correct responses for the six major dimensions.

Table 1. The percentage of correct responses for the six major dimensions among colleges.

College	Information Technology and Human Society	System Platforms	Data Representation, Processing, and Analysis	Information Technology Applications	Algorithms	Programming
Business	70%	71%	61%	66%	35%	44%
Engineering	68%	59%	60%	64%	35%	47%
Life and Creativity	66%	49%	53%	60%	37%	44%

To implement the assessment of computational thinking and creative programming abilities for students, a total of 400 questions were prepared and a platform for information literacy testing was established. This included both pre-test and post-test to gauge students' information literacy. The difference in scores between pre- and post-tests was analyzed to investigate the impact of course implementation on learning outcomes. The pre-test comprised 40 multiple-choice questions with a maximum score of 100 points, while the post-test also consisted of 40 multiple-choice questions with a maximum score of 100 points. Both tests were designed by teachers specializing in programming courses and underwent evaluation by two experts for validity.

Additionally, a survey questionnaire was used to measure student learning conditions, satisfaction, and motivation regarding the "Computational Thinking and Creative Programming" course. The questionnaire consisted of 12 questions covering various aspects of the course, from instructional content and methods to learning environment and assessment. A Likert 5-point scale was employed for implementation.

To assess the feasibility of this programming course, analyses and discussions were conducted on pre-tests, post-tests, questionnaires, and interviews. Statistical analysis was performed using SPSS for Windows to evaluate student learning outcomes and examine their learning situations throughout the course. Finally, through the questionnaire, insights were gained into the applicability and satisfaction of students regarding learning programming through this method. Table 2 below presents the descriptive statistics of pre-test and post-test scores.

Table 2. The results of pre- and post-test.

Number		Means		Passing rate	
Pre-test	Post-test	Pre-test	Post-test	Pre-test	Post-test
758	932	42.85	59.44	17.5%	50.0%

From Table 2, it is evident that the average score of the post-test is close to 60 points, with a pass rate exceeding 50%. This indicates that students have achieved good learning outcomes in the programming teaching activities. Through the implementation of computational thinking and creative programming teaching activities, there is a noticeable narrowing of the learning gap, suggesting that students are willing to learn programming, and their grades are generally above the passing threshold. However, for students with lower willingness to learn, their test scores tend to be relatively lower.

Based on the questionnaire results as shown in Table 3, most students exhibit a higher level of affirmation regarding motivating factors for learning, indicating the success of the course in stimulating students' interest in programming, computer software applications, information technology security, and internet applications. Regarding the understanding of course content and acquisition of skills, most students also express positive responses, suggesting that students are not only interested in the course but have also successfully mastered the relevant knowledge and skills.

Table 3. Questionnaire result.

Question	Items	Percentage
1. The course content can arouse my motivation to learn programming	Strongly agree	37%
	Agree	35%
	Neutral	24%
	Disagree	2%
	Strongly disagree	2%
2. The course content can stimulate my motivation to learn about computer software applications	Strongly agree	37%
	Agree	36%
	Neutral	23%
	Disagree	2%
	Strongly disagree	2%

(*continued*)

Table 3. (*continued*)

Question	Items	Percentage
3. The course content can stimulate my motivation to learn about information technology security	Strongly agree	37%
	Agree	38%
	Neutral	23%
	Disagree	2%
	Strongly disagree	0%
4. The course content can stimulate my motivation to learn about Internet applications	Strongly agree	38%
	Agree	36%
	Neutral	23%
	Disagree	2%
	Strongly disagree	1%
5. Taking this course has enabled me to understand the concepts of information technology security and ethics	Strongly agree	38%
	Agree	40%
	Neutral	20%
	Disagree	1%
	Strongly disagree	0%
6. Taking this course has equipped me with the ability to use computer software to analyze data	Strongly agree	36%
	Agree	39%
	Neutral	22%
	Disagree	3%
	Strongly disagree	1%
7. Taking this course has enabled me to understand the principles of how the Internet works	Strongly agree	36%
	Agree	40%
	Neutral	22%
	Disagree	3%
	Strongly disagree	0%
8. Taking this course has equipped me with the ability to program at a basic level	Strongly agree	35%
	Agree	40%
	Neutral	21%
	Disagree	3%
	Strongly disagree	1%
9. I am satisfied with the curriculum arranged for this course	Strongly agree	40%
	Agree	37%

(*continued*)

Table 3. (*continued*)

Question	Items	Percentage
	Neutral	20%
	Disagree	2%
	Strongly disagree	1%
10. I am satisfied with the teaching methods of this course	Strongly agree	41%
	Agree	38%
	Neutral	19%
	Disagree	1%
	Strongly disagree	1%
11. I am satisfied with the teaching environment of this course	Strongly agree	42%
	Agree	38%
	Neutral	19%
	Disagree	1%
	Strongly disagree	0%
12. I am satisfied with the assessment methods used in this course	Strongly agree	40%
	Agree	38%
	Neutral	20%
	Disagree	1%
	Strongly disagree	0%

In terms of satisfaction with teaching arrangements, methods, environments, and assessments, over 75% of students selected "strongly agree" and "agree," reflecting that teaching design and implementation are effective and satisfactory from the students' perspective. Students also demonstrate a positive attitude towards further learning, with most students willing to invest more time and effort into acquiring new knowledge and skills, indicating a positive impact of the course on students' long-term learning paths.

Overall, the questionnaire demonstrates that students are generally satisfied with various aspects of the "Computational Thinking and Creative Programming" course. However, it also highlights the need to improve teaching explanation methods to help students better focus and reduce learning stress. Teachers and course designers should consider this feedback to optimize course structure and teaching methods, ensuring that all students can derive maximum benefit from the course [9–11].

Regarding the statistical data from the computational thinking questionnaire, we can conduct the following descriptive statistical analysis and discussion. In terms of learning motivation and satisfaction with course content, most students affirm that the course content enhances their motivation to learn programming, computer software applications, information technology security, and internet applications. For these areas, over 80% of students chose "strongly agree" or "agree." Students also hold positive views regarding the course's ability to help them understand information technology security and ethical concepts, analyze data, and comprehend the operation principles of the internet, as indicated in questions 5 to 7, with over 85% of students selecting "strongly agree" or "agree." In questions 9 to 12, over 85% of students express satisfaction with teaching content, methods, teaching environment, and assessment methods. In terms of learning attitude and desire for progress, over 80% of students indicate willingness to engage in more learning to promote personal progress, demonstrating a positive attitude towards continuous learning and self-improvement.

5 Conclusion

This study examines the information literacy of freshmen through an information capability test, analyzing it across six dimensions to assess the overall model's adequacy. Parameter estimation was conducted to understand the reinforcement needed for each dimension, aiming to evaluate their strengths and weaknesses. The results indicate that among the facets of information literacy, the dimension of information technology and humanities performs the best, while the dimensions of programming and algorithms require further enhancement. Based on the understanding of students' strengths and weaknesses in the six dimensions of information, the results serve as a basis for course offerings in various departments. Indeed, this approach provides a pathway for students to learn information literacy effectively. Therefore, universities can allow students to choose which information capabilities they need in the future or guide them in setting learning goals. Additionally, the results of pre- and post-tests and questionnaires demonstrate that besides effectively enhancing freshmen's information literacy, it is equally important to establish students' motivation and interest by implementing computational thinking and creative programming course.

References

1. Wing, J.M.: Computational thinking and thinking about computing. Phil. Trans. R. Soc. A: Math., Phys. Eng. Sci. **366**(1881), 3717–3725 (2008)
2. Selby, C., Woollard, J.: Computational thinking: the developing definition (2013)
3. Korucu, A.T., Gencturk, A.T., Gundogdu, M.M.: Examination of the computational thinking skills of students. J. Learn. Teach. Digit. Age **2**(1), 11–19 (2017)
4. Aharony, N., Gazit, T.: Students' information literacy self-efficacy: an exploratory study. J. Librariansh. Inf. Sci. **52**(1), 224–236 (2020)
5. Rieh, S.Y., et al.: Assessing college students' information literacy competencies using a librarian role-playing method. Libr. Inf. Sci. Res. **44**(1), 101143 (2022)
6. Li, Y., et al.: Computational thinking is more about thinking than computing. J. STEM Educ. Res. **3**, 1–18 (2020)
7. Li, Y., et al.: On computational thinking and STEM education. J. STEM Educ. Res. **3**, 147–166 (2020)
8. Angeli, C., Giannakos, M.: Computational thinking education: issues and challenges. Comput. Hum. Behav. **105**, 106185 (2020)
9. Tang, X., Yin, Y., Lin, Q., Hadad, R., Zhai, X.: Assessing computational thinking: a systematic review of empirical studies. Comput. Educ. **148**, 103798 (2020)

10. Tikva, C., Tambouris, E.: Mapping computational thinking through programming in K-12 education: a conceptual model based on a systematic literature Review. Comput. Educ. **162**, 104083 (2021)
11. Hooshyar, D., et al.: From gaming to computational thinking: an adaptive educational computer game-based learning approach. J. Educ. Comput. Res. **59**(3), 383–409 (2021). https://doi.org/10.1177/0735633120965919

Design and Framework of Learning Systems

Exploring Learning in Basic Logic Using Stored Log Data and Exam Data

David Jakobsen[1(✉)], Steinar Thorvaldsen[2,3], and Peter Øhrstrøm[1]

[1] Department of Communication and Psychology, Aalborg University, 9000 Aalborg, Denmark
{poe,davker}@ikp.aau.dk

[2] Department of Education, NLA University College, 5812 Bergen, Norway
steinar.thorvaldsen@uit.no

[3] Department of Education, UiT-the Arctic University of Norway, 9037 Tromsø, Norway

Abstract. This paper presents how the analysis of log data generated in the context of a basic logic course may be used in the evaluation of the students' learning during the course. It is shown how the analysis of the log data may give rise to rather detailed and profound knowledge on the learning challenges experienced by the students. In this way, we suggest that the systematic and detailed analysis of log data may lead to a more general approach to the evaluation of the learning during the courses in basic logic One important observation is that the log data shows to what extent the students are able to benefit from a longer response time and therefore to what extent they can make use of the tools available to them. This may provide an important understanding of the students' problems and challenges when working with basic logic.

Keywords: Log data from courses · learning analytics · learning tools · basic logic · syllogistics · propositional logic · validity of arguments · understanding basic logic

1 Introduction

A course in basic logic has been offered during 2023 to 2nd year students of communication at X University[1]. The course was taught at the A campus and B campus of X University. The focus of this course is the study of logical validity of arguments formulated in terms of elementary propositional logic and classical syllogistics.

Learning Analytics, as a discipline, is "the measurement, collection, analysis, and reporting of data about learners and their contexts, for purposes of understanding and optimizing learning and the environment in which it occurs" [1]. Learning logic falls under this category as well and it has earlier been demonstrated how the learning during a course of this kind can be evaluated based on the logged answers given by the students regarding the validity of arguments presented to them by the teaching system, Syllog

[1] We have anonymized the name of the university to protect the privacy of the participants in the study.

Y.-P. Cheng et al. (Eds.): ICITL 2024, LNCS 14785, pp. 109–119, 2024.
https://doi.org/10.1007/978-3-031-65881-5_12

and Proplog (see [3–6]). For each group of answers the score can be calculated as the fraction of arguments that have been evaluated correctly as valid or invalid. It has been shown that the students' scores are rather low, although it is possible to raise them a bit during the course. But why are the scores so relatively low, even after a traditional course in basic logic? The main purpose of this paper is to provide at least a partial answer to this question.

It is obvious that some students find the some of the topics and problems they are facing even in basic logic extremely difficult. Clearly, it is essential that the teacher understands the nature of the problems and challenges the students are facing. As we shall see, it appears that this kind of better understanding can be obtained through a systematic and detailed analysis of log data generated during the course. Specifically, we shall be interested in exploring the relation between learning and response time as the 'contextual evidence' [2] needed to shorten the inferential distance between claim and observation concerning the student learning.

In the following we shall discuss the course mentioned above and the use of stored log data generated from the student activities during the course. It will be demonstrated how important insights may be extracted from the analysis of the log data. It will be obvious how the procedure may give rise to a more general approach to the teacher's course evaluation.

2 Description of the Course

The course in Logic and Argumentation falls in the 2nd year of the education in communication at X University. The students are often surprised when they are introduced to symbolic logic, truth-tables and methods to prove validity etc. Apparently, they associate it mainly with what they encountered in high-school mathematics. One important ambition during the course is to demonstrate that basic logic is in fact closely related to crucial aspects of human communication in general.

144 students, 89 in A and 54 in B, took the course during the period from 6 September 2023 to 6 January 2024. The lectures and exercises were based on a textbook [7] along with various notes. The course covered the following topics: the history of logic, basic syllogistics and propositional logic, reasoning, formal ontology illustrated using Protégé. During a three-day exam at the end of the course the students had to answer a set of questions in writing individually. A part of that exam consisted in using an exam module to answer 10 unique syllogisms and 10 unique propositional arguments. The exam module makes use of two other modules developed for the course, Syllog and Prolog (presented in the sections below) (Fig. 1).

When working with the exam module, the student will get, 10 propositional (or 10 syllogistic) arguments to evaluate using the tools and methods taught in class. Having checked an argument for validity, clicking 'valid' or 'invalid', the student proceeds to the next and after 10 arguments 'submit' must be pressed (Fig. 2).

Any use of the exam module as well as any use of Syllog and Proplog during the course is logged anonymously.

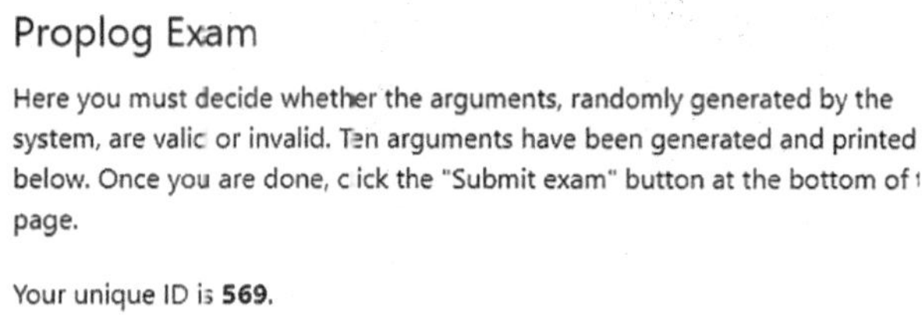

Fig. 1. The student is introduced to the exam and gets a unique ID which will be used when correcting the exam.

Fig. 2. The argument shown here is invalid since the conclusion does not follow from the premises. After evaluating the argument as valid or invalid the student proceeds to the next argument.

3 The Use of Syllog and Proplog During the Course

The teaching makes use of exercises from the two online tools developed for the teaching, Syllog[2] and Proplog[3]. The tools are constructed as games in which the students, when clicking 'new argument' will be presented with a new syllogism or propositional argument. The student must then decide whether the argument is valid or invalid and make use of the tools taught on the class and linked to at the website (Fig. 3).

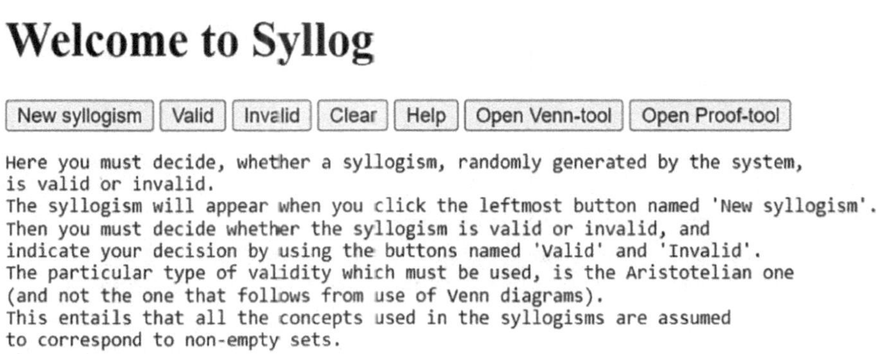

Fig. 3. The online tool 'Syllog' where the student must decide whether a given argument is 'valid' or 'invalid'.

---

[2] https://logic.aau.dk/syllog/webapp/.

[3] https://logic.aau.dk/proplog/applet/.

The students have been taught to evaluate the validity of Syllogisms by 1) transforming the syllogism into canonical form on the basis of which the student can decide whether it is syllogistic Fig. 1, 2, 3 or 4. When this is done it is possible, on the basis of lists constructed by medieval logicians using Aristotelean ideas (see [8]), to decide whether it is valid or invalid. If the student discovers that a syllogism is valid, she is taught to prove the validity by the online Proof tool. Here the student inserts the premises in the boxes which can only be correctly done after the student has transformed the syllogism into logical form. When the premises and the conclusion of the syllogism are inserted, she will be given a list containing the two premises and the negated conclusion. The task is now to derive a contradiction from these three propositions using the three logical rules, TRANS, MUT and EX, which may be presented as follows (Fig. 4):

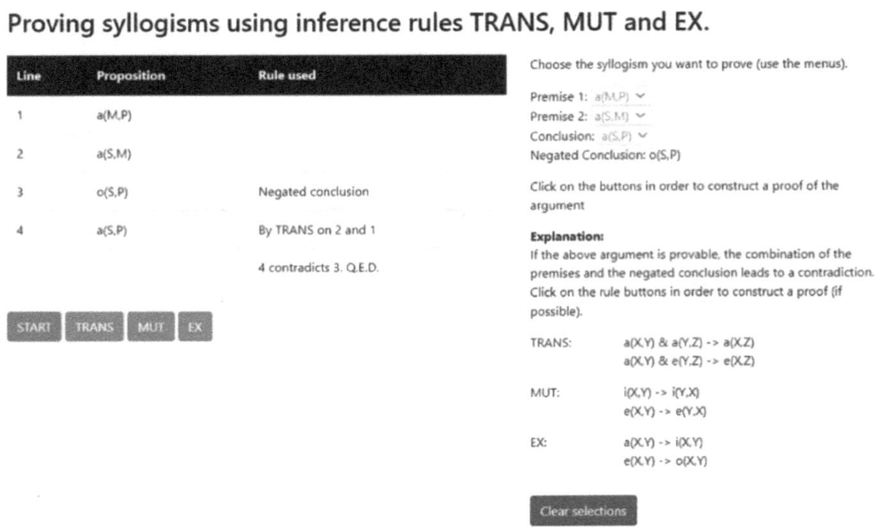

Fig. 4. The proof tool will guide the student into proving validity for syllogisms. In this case it is the Barbara syllogism from which a contradiction is derived of the negated conclusion by the use of the rule TRANS on 2 and 1.

In case the syllogism is invalid the student uses the Venn tool where she must demonstrate that it is possible to construct a Venn diagram setting (a model) in which the premises are true, but the conclusion is false (Fig. 5).

The students also work with Proplog. As with Syllog, they must decide on valid/invalid of the arguments presented, having some tools available from the course (Fig. 6).

The process of checking validity/invalidity of a propositional argument is quite different from what is done in case of syllogisms. Working with a propositional argument, the student will first have to transform it into logical form. Consider, for instance,

If Adam is at home, then Eve is not at home.
Adam is at home.
Therefore: Eve is not at home.

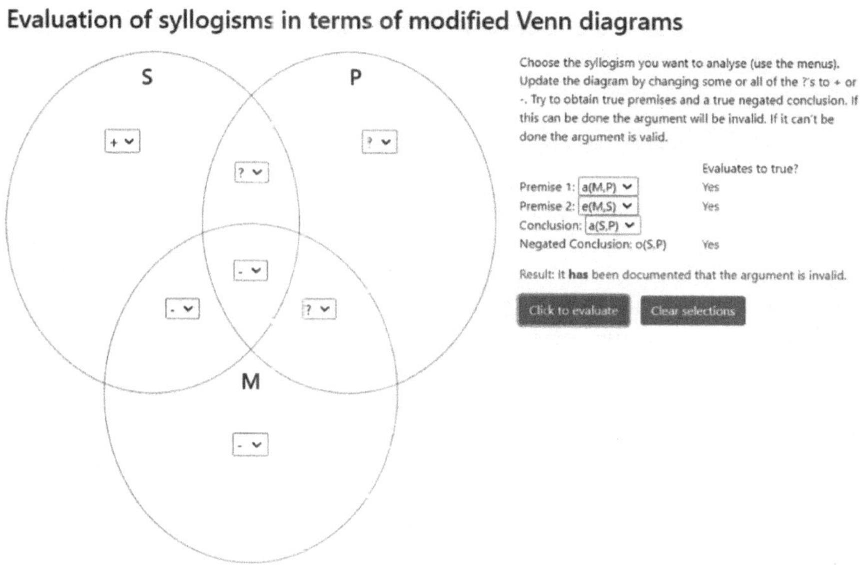

Fig. 5. A Venn diagram filled out to make premise 1 a(M,P) and 2 e(M,S) true, and also the negation of the conclusion true o(S,P) which demonstrates that the argument is invalid.

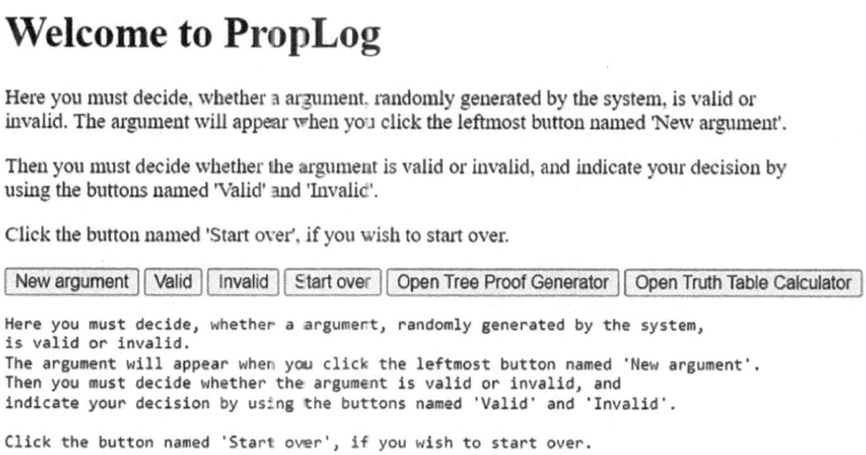

Fig. 6. The student clicks on 'New argument' and may then use the available tools.

This argument can be formalized using p (Adam is at home), and q (Eve is not at home), and put into the form: $p \rightarrow q, p \models q$. Following this transformation, a standard truth-table may be constructed to determine the validity of the argument. The student can here take various strategies. She can go all the way and demonstrate that it is a tautology, i.e., that the sequent $((p \rightarrow q \land p) \vdash q)$ is a tautology, or she can simply demonstrate in a truth-table that every time the premises are true the conclusion is also true. The general impression is that students are better at proving validity/invalidity for syllogisms than for classical propositional logic.

4 Log Data Stored During the Course

The system automatically logs the data of the students' use of Proplog and Syllog which also includes the exam module for both as well. Various data is logged. For Syllog we log the date and time and the time-lapse of the various answers given to the syllogisms (i.e. the response times). We also log the correct/incorrect score, whether the conclusions of the given syllogisms are true or false and finally we log the syllogistic Figs. 1, 2, 3 and 4, quantor (a,e,i,o), and term (S,M,P) of the syllogism.

For Proplog the data logged concerns date and time and time-lapse, the validity value (valid/invalid) of the argument, which number of the 32 included arguments it was and finally what rule was used to solve the argument (modus ponens, modus tollens, disjunction, not listed). The data is used for two overall goals. The first is to do research and improve the teaching based on research and also to make it possible to evaluate the student's progress during the course.

The results based on the log data from the whole course and exam period can be summarized in the following manner (Table 1):

Table 1. The results based on log data from the whole course period.

	Correct	Incorrect	Score
Syllog	1963	1242	0,61
Proplog	2468	2360	0,51

The data support strong statistical evidence against the presumption that tasks on syllogistics and propositional logics will be handled equally well (p-value < 0.001 by the X^2-test). As it has been observed in our earlier studies, the Syllog-score is higher than the Proplog-score. However, both scores are rather low. But why is this so? What is behind the numbers?

5 An Analysis of Students' Challenges in Syllogistic Logic

Again, we take all the log data together for the whole course period (Table 2).

The results show that the valid syllogisms are significantly easier to detect as such than the invalid syllogisms (p-value < 0.001 by the X^2-test).

The development in score during the first three minutes is shown in the following table and diagram (Table 3).

As pointed out in [2] response-time is a useful context evidence for cleaning data, which is also the case for getting a firmer grip on the log data for the answers. An obvious interpretation of the first short period in this table is that most of the answers

Table 2. General results based on log data from the use of Syllog.

Syllogisms	Correct	Incorrect	Score
Valid	1204	360	0,77
Invalid	755	886	0,46

Table 3. The Syllog score relative to the response time.

Response time	Answers	Score
0–2	1202	0,49
2–20	867	0,59
20–60	429	0,72
60–120	223	0,76
120–180	129	0,78

given within the first two seconds are based on simple guessing and not very much reflection and reasoning on the aspects and meaning of the arguments in question. As expected, based on how Syllog is constructed the score is close to 0,50.

After the first two seconds the score is increasing during the whole period with a slightly decreasing rate. This means that the users benefit from having more response time. It seems very likely that the users during the longer response time can make use of the tools (syllogistic proofs and Venn diagrams) that have been introduced during the course (Fig. 7).

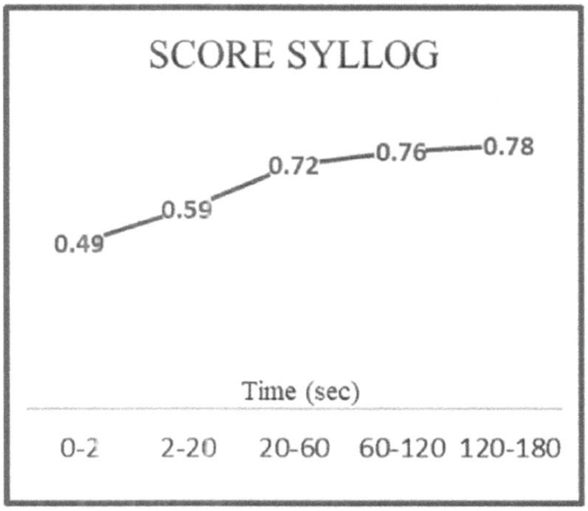

Fig. 7. The Syllog score relative to the response time.

6 An Analysis of Students' Challenges in Propositional Logic

A similar study can be carried out for propositional arguments (Table 4):

Table 4. General results based on log data from the use of Proplog.

Propositional arguments	Correct	Incorrect	Score
Valid	1856	619	0,75
Invalid	612	1741	0,26

It seems that in this case the invalid arguments are even harder to detect compared with valid ones (p-value < 0.001 by the X^2-test). In this case the difference is much more remarkable than in the case of syllogistics. It must be admitted that the score of the invalid propositional arguments (0,26) is surprisingly low. It would be interesting to learn more about reasons behind this.

The Proplog-system is designed with 16 valid and 16 invalid schemes of propositional argumentation. However, there is none of the 16 invalid propositional arguments which appear to give results that differ a lot from the others. It seems that the problem related to the invalid propositional arguments is general. The question the teachers should ask here is why so many (in fact a majority) of the students think that an argument like: $q \rightarrow \sim p, \sim p \models q$, is valid. In other words, why are so many students ready to accept the following as valid?

If Eve is at home, then Adam is not at home.
Adam is not at home.
Ergo: Eve is at home.

Could it be that many students simply don't see the difference between the above argument and the following argument?

If Eve is at home, then Adam is not at home.
Eve is at home.
Ergo: Adam is not at home.

The latter argument was correctly accepted as valid by the vast majority of the students. In fact, the score for the argument, $q \rightarrow \sim p, q \models \sim p$, was 0,88 during the course period.

What is behind this misunderstanding is apparently that it is rather easy in common discourse to jump from "if" to "if and only if", i.e., from a conditional to the corresponding biconditional (see [9]).

As in the Syllog case, it is interesting to look into the log data of the scores relative to the response times. The following table and diagram show how the score varies with the response time (Table 5).

The development in score relative to the response time from zero to three minutes is shown in Table 5 and in Fig. 8. It is evident that the scores after the first two seconds are almost constant. This means that the users in this case are unable to benefit from

Table 5. The Proplog score relative to the response time.

Response time	Answers	Score
0–2	2029	0,44
2–20	1840	0,55
20–60	531	0,55
60–120	130	0,62
120–180	60	0,57

having a longer response time. It seems that the majority of the students during the longer response time are unable to make proper use of the tools (mainly truth table analysis) that have been introduced during the course.

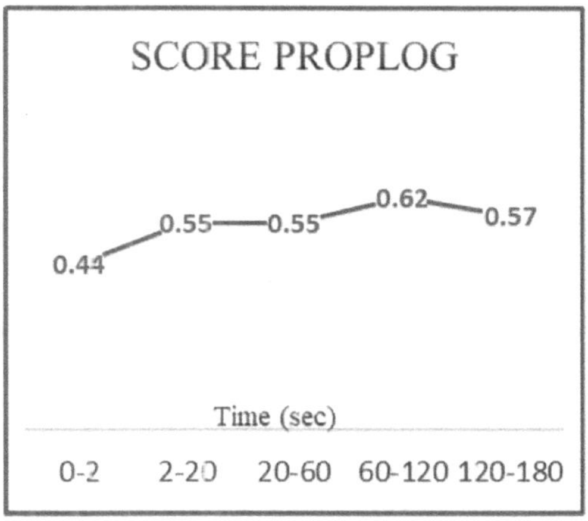

Fig. 8. The Proplog score relative to the response time.

In this respect the difference between the Syllog and Proplog cases are remarkable.

7 Analysis of Students' Results at Their Exam

It might be suspected that learning logic simply depends on some specific ability to handle abstract notions, symbolic representation etc. If so, there should be a strong correlation between the ability to handle any two branches of logic. For this reason, it might be interesting to compare the Syllog and Proplog marks at the exam, when the students were evaluated with a mark on a 5-point scale, with 5 as the best mark. The results are shown below (Fig. 9).

Nonparametric Correlation coefficient (Spearman's rho) is 0.54 (p-value < 0.001) between the Syllog and Proplog results. This is a moderate correlation [10, p. 746]. This result certainly does not exclude that there is a specific ability to handle logical

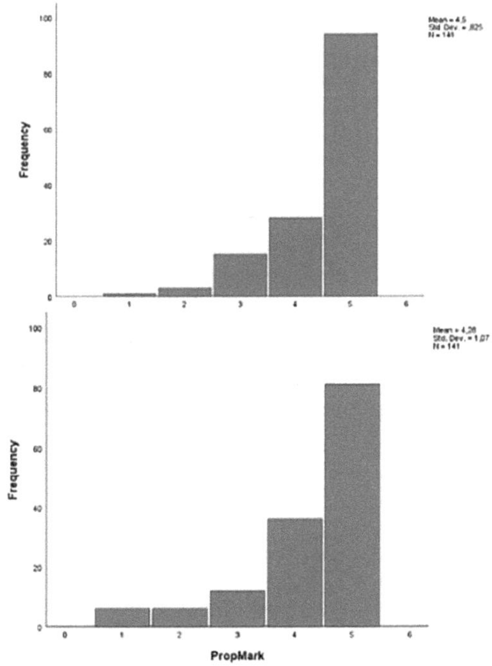

Fig. 9. Syllog and Prolog marks at the exam.

problems. On the other hand, logic learning may still depend on some combination of general logic ability, the quality of the courses and the energy invested in course work.

8 Conclusion and Perspectives

It is obvious from the above observations that teachers and others can extract a lot of useful information from a careful analysis of the stored log data. The following may be suggested based of the analysis of the log data from the use of Syllog and Proplog during the course:

- The students see it as more difficult to meet the requirements regarding propositional logic than the requirements regarding syllogistics.
- In both cases the invalid arguments are even harder to detect compared with valid ones.
- In average the students can benefit from having more response time when they work with syllogistic arguments. This indicates that the majority of the students in this case are able to use the available tools constructively.
- In average the students can't benefit from having more response time when they work with propositional arguments. This indicates that majority of the students in this case are unable to use the available tools constructively.
- The poor result in propositional logic appears to be related to many students' wrongful identification of the conditional ("if") and the biconditional ("if and only if").

The present study indicates that the teacher during the course should have invested more energy in showing the students how to use to tools designed to evaluate propositional arguments. In addition, the teacher should have focused more on the difference between the conditional and the biconditional. In general, it may be concluded that such observations of response times and other log data may guide the teacher in locating the topics that ought to be more emphasized or adjusted when the course is offered again.

References

1. Long, P.D., Siemens, G.: Penetrating the Fog: analytics in learning and education. Edacause Rev. **46**(5), 31–40 (2011)
2. Oranje, A., Gorin, J., Jia, Y., Kerr, D.: Collecting, analyzing and interpreting response time: eye-tracking and log data. In: Ercikan, K., Pellegrino, J.W. (eds.) Validation of Score Meaning For the Next Generation of Assessments: The use of response processes, pp. 39–51. Routledge, New York (2019)
3. Øhrstrøm, P., Sandborg-Petersen, U., Thorvaldsen, S., Ploug, T.: Teaching logic through web-based and gamified quizzing of formal arguments. In: Hernández-Leo, D., Ley, T., Klamma, R., Harrer, A. (eds.) Scaling up Learning for Sustained Impact, pp. 410–423. Springer Berlin Heidelberg, Berlin, Heidelberg (2013). https://doi.org/10.1007/978-3-642-40814-4_32
4. Øhrstrøm, P., Sandborg-Petersen, U., Thorvaldsen, S., Ploug, T.: Teaching syllogistics through gamification and interactive proofs. In: Conole, G., Klobučar, T., Rensing, C., Konert, J., Lavoué, E. (eds.) Design for Teaching and Learning in a Networked World: 10th European Conference on Technology Enhanced Learning, EC-TEL 2015, Toledo, Spain, September 15-18, 2015, Proceedings, pp. 609–612. Springer International Publishing, Cham (2015). https://doi.org/10.1007/978-3-319-24258-3_70
5. Øhrstrøm, P., Thorvaldsen, S., Sandborg-Petersen, U., Ploug, T.: Teaching propositional and syllogistic logic using e-learning tools. In: Rønningsbakk, L., Wu, T.-T., Sandnes, F.E., Huang, Y.-M. (eds.) ICITL 2019. LNCS, vol. 11937, pp. 854–864. Springer, Cham (2019). https://doi.org/10.1007/978-3-030-35343-8_89
6. Øhrstrøm, P., Thorvaldsen, S., Jakobsen, D.: Learning analytics based on streamed log data from a course in logic. In: Huang, Y.-M., Rocha, T. (eds.). Innovative Technologies and Learning, Proceedings: ICITL 2023, Lecture Notes in Computer Science, vol. 14099, pp. 430–440. Springer (2023)
7. Øhrstrøm, P., Ploug, T., Jakobsen, D.: Logisk set, 2nd edn. Metaphysica, Aalborg (2019)
8. Parry, W., Hacker, E.: Aristotelian Logic. State University of New York Press (1991)
9. Cohen, L., Manion, L., Morrison, K.: Research Methods in Education, 8th edn. Routledge, London (2018)
10. Horn, L.R.: From if to iff: conditional perfection as pragmatic strengthening. J. Pragmat. **32**, 289–326 (2000)

Sequence Analysis as a Tool for Visualizing Students' Patterns of Taking Tests in Interactive E-Book Environment

Yaroslav Opanasenko(✉), Margus Pedaste, and Leo A. Siiman

Institute of Education, University of Tartu, Tartu, Estonia
yaroslav.opanasenko@ut.ee

Abstract. This study investigates the use of sequence analysis as a tool to visualize and analyze students' patterns of test-taking within interactive E-Book environments. With the growing incorporation of multimedia and interactive elements in educational materials, understanding how students engage with these features, especially tests, is crucial for both improving learning experiences and providing educators with insights into the learning process. Through sequence analysis of log data from an Estonian E-Book Opiq, the research identifies distinct patterns in how students with varying levels of procedural mathematical competence approach tests in E-Books. The analysis focuses on students' interactions with tests, categorizing them based on their procedural math competence and examining the types of tests (multiple choice or open response questions) they took. The findings reveal differences in test-taking strategies and outcomes between students of high and low procedural math competence, highlighting the potential of sequence analysis not only as a research tool but also as a means for educators to gain a deeper understanding of student engagement and learning processes. By integrating sequence analysis into digital learning environments, educators could access valuable insights to tailor and enhance the educational experience.

Keywords: E-Book · interaction patterns · sequence analysis

1 Introduction

Interactive elements of E-Book have been a topic of discussion in numerous studies among recent years [8, 13, 14]. While multimedia elements have been under skepticism of some researchers because of distracting learning of students [2, 9], late studies show that these elements can expand and improve students' learning experiences with the condition of correct design [3]. The development of such design should be based both on the students' or teacher's feedback [7] and studying interaction patterns using log-data [17]. However, most of the studies are focused on the multimedia elements of interactive E-Books environments while opportunities for testing might be out of the scope. Opportunities for practicing and immediately receiving feedback might be useful not only for students to engage them in improving their result [21], but also for teachers to better understand the nature of the process of interaction with E-Books [11]. Detailed

Y.-P. Cheng et al. (Eds.): ICITL 2024, LNCS 14785, pp. 120–128, 2024.
https://doi.org/10.1007/978-3-031-65881-5_13

information about the process of test-taking, including the sequences of actions and the results, can enrich the teachers' vision of the learning process, providing them with insights of how to make it more engaging or effective. Therefore, finding the potential ways visualizing of the process of test-taking in interactive E-Books is set as the aim of this study.

Research questions:

1. How sequence analysis can be used as a visualization tool for analyzing patterns of taking tests in interactive E-Books?

2 Literature Review

2.1 Interactive E-Books as an Environment for Testing Students' Knowledge

Although the testing process in E-Books environment is usually behind the scope of research, its positive role in the interaction process has been widely studied. Interactive E-books have been proven to improve early reading and writing skills, indicating the effectiveness of including interactive exercises and tests in e-learning materials for young learners [7]. Software testing techniques have been applied to efficiently manage programming exercises on e-learning platforms, enhancing the support for tutors and the learning experience for students [18]. The use of interactive images in e-assessment systems has shown to improve the assessment process by allowing students to interact with graphical objects, which can help prevent cheating and enhance the evaluation of knowledge and skills [5]. Interactive E-Books not only enrich the learning experience but also generate vast amounts of log-data that can provide deep insights into the process of interaction with tests.

Log-data has been proven as one of the richest sources of information, being appropriate for analyzing both test-taking process and interaction with E-Books. Nakao & Oomachi [16] explored the development of an estimation method using track logs in the programming learning process for students ranging from elementary school to university. They found that students with more "run" or "execute" actions achieved their goals in a shorter period, indicating that log analysis is a useful method for evaluating programming learning. Mouri et al. [15] proposed a method to analyze interaction patterns from digital textbooks' log data, finding three student types: poorly motivated, efficient, and diligent. This study suggests that analyzing interaction patterns can contribute to the improvement of learning and teaching. Wang et al. [20] introduced ProcData, an R package for process data analysis, highlighting its utility in enhancing educational assessment accuracy by utilizing rich information contained in response processes. Zoanetti & Griffin [22] discussed a methodology for analyzing log-file data from students' interactions with computer-based problem-solving tasks, emphasizing its role in scoring complex **sequences** of process data. Andrews & Zhang [1] described a lightweight formal method for checking test results through log file analysis, suggesting its competitiveness with other unit testing procedures.

Log-data together with educational data mining (EDM) methods seems to be promising source for understanding and improving the teaching and learning process. However, due to the little experience of applying it in analyzing interaction with E-Books, it appears there is a need for further exploration into new methods for log-data analysis and its result integration into pedagogical strategies. In our study sequence analysis has been chosen as a potential method of visualizing the process of test-taking in interactive E-Books.

2.2 Sequence Analysis in the Educational Science

Sequence analysis is a categorical longitudinal modeling procedure with a holistic approach that allows the inclusion of the whole trajectories of a set of objects, stating all states of interaction experienced within a specific timeframe, to create categorical sequences and usually produce a product of a typology or clustering classification [19]. In the last two decades, sequence analysis has seen many successful applications in the social sciences [12].

The utilization of learning sequences and sequence analysis in Educational Data Mining (EDM) and Learning Analytics (LA) presents several advantages, including the capability to uncover sequential patterns of interaction within data, recognize these patterns as specific learning behaviors, tactics, or strategies, and integrate time-based structures into behavioral analysis [13]. While many studies focus on identifying these patterns as indicative of learning process [4, 7, 8, 10], a subset of research advances further by leveraging the identified patterns for classifying learners and predicting outcomes. Some of the studies propose potential interventions [6, 20]. For example, Wang et al. [20] suggest an early warning system to alert educators about students employing tactics that might result in underperformance, or automated tools designed to predict when a learner is at risk of hitting a stumbling block. Hurtig et al. [6] provide a solution as an interactive dashboard for teachers presenting results of analysis. The application of sequence analysis shows that it can be useful in many areas of analyzing educational log-data. By applying it to analyze interaction patterns of test-taking process in interactive E-Books we plan to expand the experience of its usage by gaining insights not only for teachers, but also for researchers by enriching the understanding of potential results of applying sequence analysis as EDM method.

3 Methodology

3.1 Data Collection

Opiq E-Book enables the collection of operational log data detailing students' interactions, which can be considered as an advantage compared to the textbooks. These records of learning activities can be useful for analyzing the learning processes of students. Our study uses data collected within the Estonian project DigiEfekt dedicated to the study of how and whether the use of digital learning materials in different ways predicts learning outcomes. The log data were gathered during the academic year 2021–2022 from DLE (Digital learning environment) Opiq. Opiq usage log data provide detailed information about every action made by the student during interaction with E-Books; in this study, we focused on the type of the test (multiple choice or open response questions), number of questions in each test, timing of students' answers, correctness of the result. Students' IDs have been used to relate gathered information to the level of procedural mathematical competence of respondents. Among all the data, 11 students with a higher level of procedural mathematical competence (more than 80%) and 8 students with lower level of procedural mathematical competence (less than 70%) have been chosen for comparison. The information about procedural mathematical competence has also been gathered with the DigiEfekt project. Two tests from the paragraph «Sine and cosine of an acute angle in a right triangle» of the 9th-grade mathematics textbook has been chosen for further analysis (Fig. 1). The first test consists of 8 multiple choice questions (students must choose between 4 options in every question). The second test consists of 4 exercises with 8 open response answers needed.

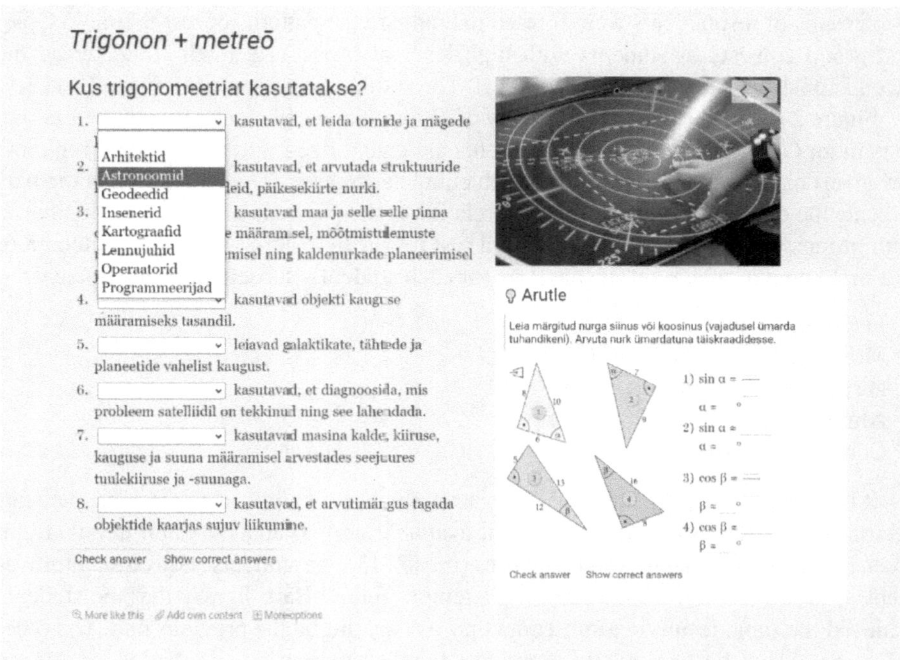

Fig. 1. Multiple choice and open responce exercises from the Opiq paragraph

3.2 Methods of Analysis

The TraMineR 2.2.7 package for R was used for sequence analysis: filtering data log file on the interaction traces with tests in Opiq, creating sequences from data log files, computing distances between sequences with optimal matching algorithm and visualizing results. The first step involves preparing the dataset for analysis including filtering the operational log data from Opiq to focus on the interaction traces related to the tests chosen according to the available sample of students with different level of procedural mathematical competence. The filtering process ensures that only relevant data are considered, removing any noise. Using the TraMineR package (version 2.2.7) for R, sequences are created from the filtered log data. Each sequence represents the chronological order of interactions a student has with the Opiq platform. The next phase involves computing distances between sequences using the optimal matching algorithm. This algorithm quantifies the dissimilarity between sequences, considering the number and types of operations required to transform one sequence into another. By calculating these distances, the similarity of learning behaviors among students can be accessed, providing a basis for grouping similar interaction patterns.

4 Results

Two groups of respondents were formed to compare the patterns of test-taking in Opiq: first group consists of students with high level of procedural math competence, the second consists of students with low level. The results are presented in Figs. 2 and 3.

Figure 2 shows the relative frequency of different types of results for students taking tests in an Opiq environment. The students are categorized into two groups (high and low level) based on their procedural math competence level. The colors within the bars indicate the outcome of the test attempt relative to the previous attempt. The first bar in both groups (Bar 1) represents the initial test result. Its color signifies the outcome of that first attempt, which set the baseline for each student's subsequent performance:

- Incorrect result (0%)
- Mostly incorrect result (1–49%)
- Partly correct result (50–89%)
- Almost correct result (90–99%)
- Correct result (100%)

It is worth mentioning that TraMiner currently doesn't allow us to mark the percentage of related frequency, which makes it available only to analyze main trends. Light green bars indicate that on subsequent tries (tries 2–13), the students showed an improvement in their results from the previous attempt. Yellow Bars signify that the students achieved the same result on a subsequent try as they did on the previous one. The other colors represent the final result of the test for that attempt if it is the last one taken by the student. As no red or blue bars are present beyond the first attempt, it indicates that all students from both competency levels eventually achieved a level of success by improving their results throughout their tries.

Distinct interaction patterns are visible between the two groups:

- The first group primarily shows light green bars, suggesting that these students frequently improved their results with each attempt.
- The second group shows a more mixed pattern of light green and yellow bars, indicating a combination of improvement and consistency in their results over the tries.
- While the first attempt (bar 1) for both groups can be bad, partly correct, or almost correct, the first group achieved the correct result firstly by the third attempt (bar 3), as we can observe the first dark green bar. In the case of the second group the correct result was not achieved until the seventh attempt (bar 7).

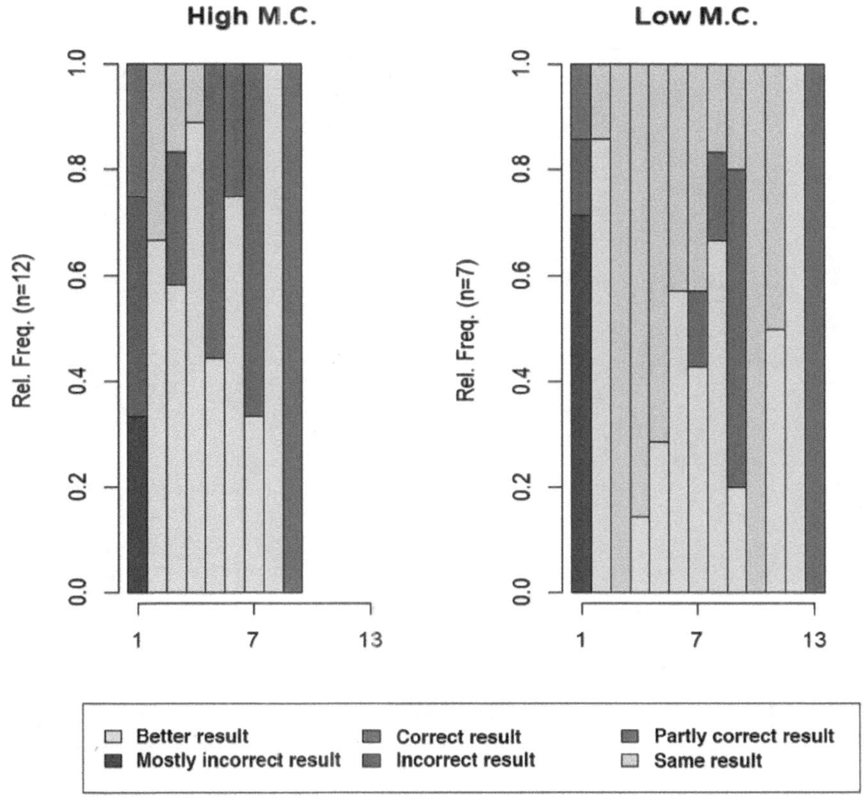

Fig. 2. Students' patterns of taking tests, multiple choice questions X-axis – attempt number; Y-axis – frequency

Figure 3 shows the visualization of students' patterns of taking tests with open response questions. Since not all the students with low level of procedural math competence have taken all the 4 exercises in the test, each exercise has been studied separately. As could be seen from the graph, students with high level of procedural math competence achieve a correct result by the 4th attempt as earliest as indicated by the presence of the dark green color. Following the correct result, students predominantly show improvements (light green) than maintaining same results (yellow). The rare occurrence of yellow bars (same results) among scores shows that students stall at a high-performance level, possibly reflecting on the previous mistakes. Resets are unique for the first group, which could be considered as a strategy to achieve the correct result from the first try without additional improvements needed. Students finished the test only 2 times without achieving the highest result: one session ended after 3 tries with almost correct result and the second example could be seen on the 6th bar indicating incorrect result as the final. As with the open response questions test, almost all the students with high level of procedural mathematical competence succeeded in achieving the correct result when one of the respondents has done it from the first try.

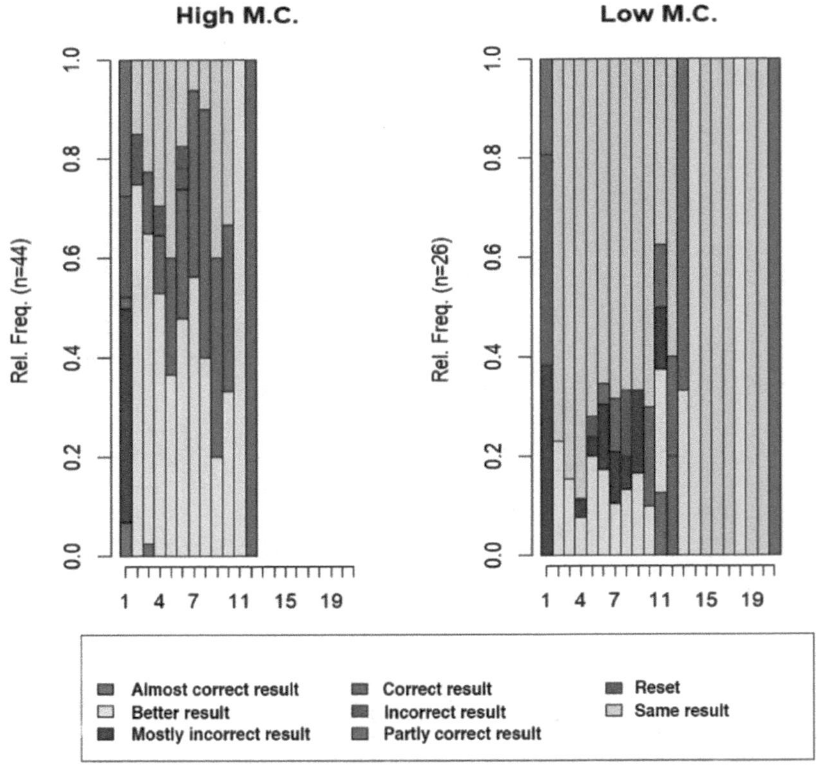

Fig. 3. Students' patterns of taking tests, open response questions X-axis – attempt number; Y-axis – frequency

Almost all the students with low level of procedural mathematical competence have done at least 3 tries to improve their result (except the one who finished the test at the 4th try with bad result). On the attempts from the 4th to the 10th the frequency of bad incorrect results begins to increase, which may imply growing frustration or difficulty with the content. Improvements (light green) are still present but less frequent.

5 Discussion

Sequence analysis potential isn't limited to the results presented in this study: it has already been applied to derive interaction patterns with different chapters of the workbooks in Opiq [17]. Through sequence analysis, it's possible to identify periods of high activity and engagement with E-Books, patterns of sessions inherent to different groups of students, most typical transitions between different types of interaction etc. These results might be valuable not only for teachers and students, but also for content-developers to create an environment that can increase students' motivation and engagement. By bringing sequence analysis into the hands of educators, the hidden students' interaction patterns with digital content can be discovered. This transition from research to practice could empower teachers with direct, actionable insights, enabling them to adjust the learning experience in real-time, based on empirical evidence of student engagement and performance. For students, visualization of their learning paths may foster self-regulation and metacognitive awareness, while content developers could leverage these insights to design more engaging and rich E-Book experiences. However, the realization of sequence analysis as a practical tool should be supported not only by studies, but also by technical solutions to break the barriers between EDM tools and teachers. The complexity of current sequence analysis software, usually requiring programming skills, underscores the need for more accessible, user-friendly platforms that can be integrated into digital learning environments. Further research should focus on developing such tools, with an emphasis on intuitive interfaces that require minimal statistical or technical knowledge to use. AI tools might have promising potential to solve these problems.

There is also a need to understand how teachers and students interpret and act upon the data presented by sequence analysis: the educational outcomes of these interventions remain to be seen. The reasons behind the learning patterns uncovered by sequence analysis require deeper investigation—what educational, cognitive, or social factors contribute to these behaviors? Understanding these underlying mechanisms is essential for designing interventions that effectively support learning and engagement in digital spaces. Current results indicate a decline in performance for some students, possibly due to demotivation or cognitive overload. Other students have been showing consistent improvement of the result, which might be explained both by internal motivation and good decisions in test design. All these hypotheses should be studied withing more complex studies, including not only log-data analysis, but also interviews with teachers and students to enrich the understanding of the interaction with E-Books.

Acknowledgements. This research has been partly supported by the DIGIVARA5 project "The effect of using digital learning materials for learning and teaching in the context of Estonian basic school (1.05.2020–30.04.2023)" financed by the Ministry of Education and Research in Estonia.

References

1. Andrews, J.H., Yingjun, Z.: General test result checking with log file analysis. IEEE Trans. Softw. Eng. **29**(7), 634–643 (2003)
2. Chiu, T.K.: Introducing electronic textbooks as daily-use technology in schools: a topdown adoption process. Br. J. Edu. Technol. **48**(2), 524–537 (2017)
3. Çırakoğlu, N., Toksoy, S.E., Reisoğlu, İ: Designing, developing, and evaluating an interactive e-book based on the predict-observe-explain (POE) method. J. Form Des. Learn. **6**, 95–112 (2022)
4. Gomez, M.J., Ruipérez-Valiente, R., Martinez, P., Kim, Y.: Exploring the affordances of sequence mining in educational games. In: Eighth International Conference on Technological Ecosystems for Enhancing Multiculturality. ACM, Salamanca Spain, pp. 648–654 (2021)
5. Gusev, M., Ristov, S., Armenski, G., Gushev, P., Velkoski, G., E-Assessment with interactive images. In: 2014 IEEE Global Engineering Education Conference (EDUCON), pp. 484–491 (2014)

6. Hurtig, N., Hollingsworth, J., Scrivner O.: Visualization of students' solutions as a sequential network. In: 2022 IEEE Global Engineering Education Conference (EDUCON), pp. 1189–1194 (2022)
7. Janawati, D., Pradnyana, P., Darmayanti, N.: Developing Interactive E-Book for Early Reading-Writing Stage at Class I Elementary School. Jurnal Pendidikan, Pedagogia (2021)
8. Kuromiya, H., Majumdar, R., Miyabe, G., et al.: E-book-based learning activity during COVID-19: engagement behaviors and perceptions of Japanese junior-high school students. RPTEL **17**, 12 (2022)
9. Lee, H.J., Messom, C., Yau, K.L.A.: Can an electronic textbooks be part of K-12 education? Challenges, technological solutions and open issues. Turkish Online J. Educ. Technol. **12**(1), 32–44 (2013)
10. Li, S., Zheng, J., Lajoie, S.: Temporal structures and sequential patterns of self-regulated learning behaviors in problem solving with an intelligent tutoring system. Educ. Technol. Soc. **25**, 1–14 (2022)
11. Li, X., Xia, Q., Chu, S.K.W., Yang, Y.: Using gamification to facilitate students' self-regulation in e-learning: a case study on students' l2 english learning. Sustainability **14**(12), 7008 (2022)
12. Liao, T.F., et al.: Sequence analysis: Its past, present, and future. Soc. Sci. Res. **107**, 102772 (2022)
13. Lim, J., Whitehead, G.E., Choi, Y.: Interactive e-book reading vs. paper-based reading: comparing the effects of different mediums on middle school students' reading comprehension. System **97**, 102434 (2021)
14. Merkle, A.C., Ferrell, L.K., Ferrell, O.C., Hair, J.: Evaluating e-book effectiveness and the impact on student engagement. J. Mark. Educ. **44**(1), 54–71 (2022)
15. Mouri, K., Ren, Z., Uosaki, N., Yin, C.: Analyzing learning patterns based on log data from digital textbooks. Int. J. Distance Educ. Technol. **17**(1), 1–14 (2019). https://doi.org/10.4018/IJDET.2019010101
16. Nakao, M., Oomachi, Y.: Characterization of studying process of using student log analysis on software programming. In: Proceedings of the 9th International Conference on Applied Computing & Information Technology (2022)
17. Opanasenko, Y., Pedaste, M., Siiman, L.A.: Students' Patterns of interaction with e-books in Estonian basic schools: a sequence analysis study. In: Huang, YM., Rocha, T. (eds.) Innovative Technologies and Learning. ICITL 2023. Lecture Notes in Computer Science, vol 14099 (2023)
18. Schwieren, J., Vossen, G., Westerkamp, P.: Using software testing techniques for efficient handling of programming exercises in an e-learning platform. Electron. J. e-Learn. **4**, 87–94 (2006)
19. Tan, T.K., Samavedham, L.: The learning process matter: a sequence analysis perspective of examining procrastination using learning management system. Comput. Educ. Open **3**(April), 100112 (2022)
20. Wang, Y., Li, T., Geng, C., Wang, Y.: Evaluating student learning effect based on process mining. In: Florez, H., Leon, M., Diaz-Nafria, J.M., Belli, S. (eds.) ICAI 2019. CCIS, vol. 1051, pp. 59–72. Springer, Cham (2019). https://doi.org/10.1007/978-3-030-32475-9_5
21. Yan, Z., Xiao, Y., Sin, K.-F., Yang, L., Guo, W.-Y.: Formative assessment practices in special school classrooms with the support of e-books: a case study. Front. Educ. **6**, 674869 (2021)
22. Zoanetti N., Griffin, P.: Log-file data as indicators for problem-solving processes. Educ. Res. Innov. 177–191 (2017)

Exploring Collaborative Learning Constructs in the Metaverse: A Pilot Study

Zoe Ruo-Yu Li[1], Cheng-Huan Chen[2](✉), and Yong-Cih Yang[3]

[1] University College London, London WC1E 6BT, UK
[2] National Tsing Hua University, Hsinchu 300044, Taiwan, Republic of China
polarchen.nthu@gmail.com
[3] National Taiwan University of Science and Technology, Taipei 106335, Taiwan, Republic of China

Abstract. Metaverse, specifically defined and previously known as virtual worlds, has recently gained wide attention from the public to education. Prior literature has validated this immersive virtual reality (VR) on facilitating students' problem-solving, communication, and collaboration. However, many challenges including learning outcomes may result from the scarcity of investigation in collaborative learning activities. Accordingly, this study adopted the repertory grid (RG) technique to identify the collaborative learning constructs in the virtual worlds; we also assessed the RG procedure and modified the constructs for subsequent studies. During the process, six experts from academics and schools were recruited to design activity planners for construct elicitation. After completing the RG survey by the other 6 participants, the consistency results revealed a moderate correlation between two participants both possessing higher related experiences. Most importantly, based on the participants' feedback, this study successfully streamlined the RG flow and determined a 24-construct grid for the upcoming research.

Keywords: metaverse · virtual world · immersive VR · collaborative learning · repertory grid

1 Introduction

The metaverse, as an epidemic word after Meta launched its virtual reality (VR) product in 2019, seems like a "future expectation" for the educational field. Nevertheless, the associated technology, namely virtual worlds, has been integrated into schools for over two decades [1, 2]. Virtual worlds can be a supporting platform of immersive VR (iVR), which refers to a 3D virtual environment in which users wear VR headsets or head-mounted displays to interact with each other with their own avatars [3, 4].

Y.-P. Cheng et al. (Eds.): ICITL 2024, LNCS 14785, pp. 129–135, 2024.
https://doi.org/10.1007/978-3-031-65881-5_14

According to the prior literature on collaborative learning, the virtual worlds significantly improved students' visual communication, problem-solving, and learning engagement [5–7]. However, due to the rapid technological advancement, the learning modes and strategies in virtual worlds for iVR are different from those in non-immersive VR, such as desktop VR. In other words, rare studies investigate what key activities, materials, and instruction in the virtual world can successfully facilitate students' collaboration. Consequently, this gap may cause multiple challenges, such as learning gains, audio communication, and socializing [8, 9].

Given that practical examples and studies of virtual worlds for iVR are scarce, Kelly's repertory grid (RG) is adopted in this study to answer this question. The RG technique was originally proposed by Kelly in 1955 based on the theory of personal construct psychology [10, 11]. Specifically, the repertory gird allows researchers to extract abstract cognitive concepts through a series of construct elicitation [12–14]. Thus, it is an optimal method to identify the latent constructs and build the cognitive model.

In light of this, our current project aims to discover the cognitive constructs of collaborative learning in the virtual world of iVR, using the RG survey. As a pilot investigation, this study attempted to confirm the feasibility of the RG process for collaborative learning of iVR, and adjust the initial constructs for the foundation of further RG survey and experimental research.

2 Method

In order to achieve the research goal, this study employed the repertory grid (RG) technique. Based on the comparison study [15], this study also used the contrast method appropriate for the activity planner contrast. In terms of the participants, six experts whose backgrounds related to iVR curriculum design and iVR teaching experience were invited from both academics and schools in Taiwan.

To illustrate, the whole RG process referred to the study [11], was as follows (see Fig. 1): the researchers first outlined the relevant literature and sent it to the experts for their reference on activity planner design. After receiving the planners, the researchers interviewed each expert online to elicit the constructs regarding collaborative learning in the virtual worlds of iVR. Next, an online RG questionnaire was built based on the expert's constructs. This study then recruited 6 participants to complete the RG survey, and ultimately assessed the consistency and collected data.

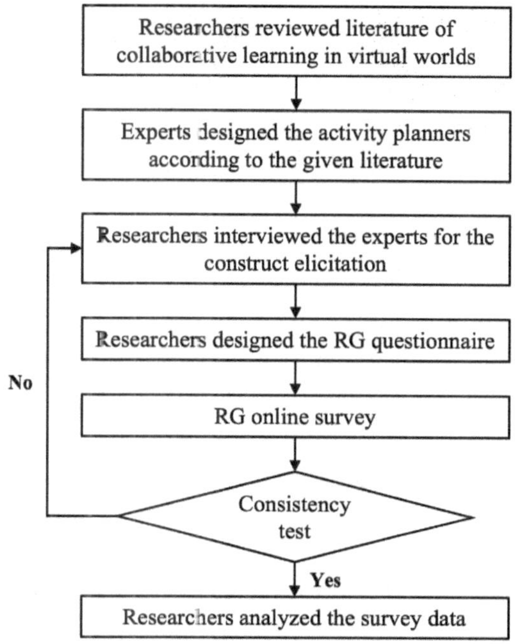

Fig. 1. The proposed procedure in this study.

3 Results

This study received data from all the six participants. The participants consisted of 4 females and 2 males, consisting of undergraduates, graduates, and a research assistant holding a master's degree. On average, most of the online questionnaires were completed from 55 min to 1 h and 10 min. Specifically, for the first part of the repertory grid (RG) survey, it mostly took the participants 15 to 20 min to evaluate the first activity planner and gradually decreased to 10 to 15 min for the following planners; on the other hand, the participants finished the second part of impact assessment in about 1.5 min. In addition, one participant filled up the answers in around 20 min, whose answers were different from the others; thus, we discarded this data before the correlation analysis. Overall, the time spent provided a reliable reference for the researchers to determine the appropriate length of the subsequent RG survey.

Since this pilot study aimed to discover the questionnaire's weight consistency and latent problems, this study performed Pearson's correlation to achieve our objective. The correlation data from the remaining five participants was demonstrated in Table 1. To illustrate, based on the correlation strength in a study [16] shown in Table 2, only P1 and P5 moderately correlated with each other ($r = .58, p < .01$). Apart from the data between P2 and P4, along with P3 and P4, the rest of the participants presented weak correlation ($r_{s1s2} = .31, p < .001$; $r_{s1s3} = .18, p < .05$; $r_{s2s3} = .22, p < .001$; $r_{s1s4} = .2, p < .05$; $r_{s2s5} = .29, p < .001$; $r_{s3s5} = .18, p < .05$; $r_{s4s5} = .23, p < .01$).

Table 1. Pearson's correlation results.

Variable	M	SD	1	2	3	4
1. P1	2.36	1.68				
2. P2	2.51	1.39	.31***			
			[.15, .45]			
3. P3	2.25	1.76	.18*	.22***		
			[.01, .33]	[.05, .37]		
4. P4	2.51	0.70	.20*	−.04	.00	
			[.03, .35]	[−.21, .13]	[−.16, .17]	
5. P5	2.48	1.56	.58***	.29***	.18*	.23**
			[.45, .68]	[.13, .44]	[.02, .34]	[.07, .38]

Note. Values in square brackets indicate the 95% confidence interval for each correlation. * $p <$ .05. ** $p < .01$. *** $p < .001$.

Table 2. The strength of correlation coefficients.

Absolute value	Correlation
−1	Perfect
0.70–0.99	Strong
0.40–0.69	Moderate
0.01–0.39	Weak
−0.00	Zero

Note. Modified from "Statistics without maths for psychology," by C. P. Dancey and J. Reidy, 2020, *Pearson Education Limited*, p. 304.

After the initial discussion with the six participants, the researchers modified several constructs and improved the questionnaire instruction. We amended some words in c2, c3, c4, c5, c16, c19, c20, and c23, and their contrast constructs to minimize semantic ambiguities in the construct meanings. Furthermore, given the participants reflected they were confused about when to scale with a score of 3 using the 5-point scale, we clearly defined it in the subsequent questionnaire instruction. For example, "Score 3 is marked when you cannot find or are unsure whether to attribute either a similar or contrast construct in the evaluated planner," this statement was added to the instruction. Finally, the updated RG for collaborative learning in the virtual world was determined, as indicated in Table 3.

Table 3. Repertory grid for the following study.

Constructs	Activity Planners						Constructs
	1	2	3	4	5	6	
c1 Student groups have interactive learning							c1′ Students study by themselves within the group/there is no interactive learning between groups
c2 Students discuss in the virtual world							c2′ Students do not discuss in the virtual world
c3 Students discuss outside the virtual world							c3′ Students do not discuss outside the virtual world
c4 Peers in the group assess each other/offer feedback							c4′ Peers in the group do not assess each other/offer feedback
c5 Peers between the groups assess each other/offer feedback							c5′ Peers between the groups do not assess each other/offer feedback
c6 Teacher provide constructive materials to students							c6′ Students create constructive materials by themselves
c7 Teacher guidance outside the virtual world							c7′ Self-study activities outside the virtual world
c8 Teacher arouses students' motivation							c8′ Students directly experience learning context
c9 Teacher-limited scope/specified topic							c9′ Student-chosen topic
c10 Teacher instruct VR operation							c10′ Teacher does not instruct VR operation
c11 Teacher asks questions during the activity							c11′ Teacher do not ask questions during the activity
c12 Teacher highlights the key points							c12′ Teacher does not highlight the key points
c13 Teacher gives grades/feedback							c13′ Teacher does not give grades/feedback
c14 Students observe and explore in the virtual world							c14′ Students do not observe and explore in the virtual world
c15 Students solve problems/complete tasks in the virtual world							c15′ Students do not solve problems/complete tasks in the virtual world
c16 Students verbally explain/report learning content							c16′ Students do not verbally explain/report learning content
c17 Students follow standards to create materials							c17′ Students freely create materials

(continued)

Table 3. (*continued*)

Constructs	Activity Planners						Constructs
	1	2	3	4	5	6	
c18 Students adjust their co-work during the activities							c18′ Students do not adjust their co-work during the activities
c19 Students make final presentations in the virtual world							c19′ Students do not make final presentations in the virtual world
c20 Students present final results in the real world							c20′ Students do not present final results in the real world
c21 With virtual avatar							c21′ Without virtual avatar
c22 Scenes in the virtual world show prompts							c22′ Scenes in the virtual world do not show prompts
c23 Students can do activities in different scenes/attractions within the virtual world							c23′ Students can only do activities in the same scene/attraction within the virtual world
c24 Learning sheets outside the virtual world							c24′ Learning sheets inside the virtual world

4 Discussion and Conclusion

This pilot study attempted to evaluate and improve the repertory grid (RG) for the subsequent investigation for collaborative learning constructs in virtual worlds of iVR. The result enabled us to preferably estimate the survey's total duration and streamline the research procedure. Despite the pilot results failing the consistency test, this research considered the correlation coefficient between participant P1 and participant P5 to be higher than the others due to more experience in the related topic. In other words, it might be derived from the fact that other participants did not obtain master's degrees and had relative limited associated background knowledge. Nevertheless, their opinions were valuable for developing the following RG questionnaire for iVR. We modified our constructs to be more understandable according to the suggestions from these participants and finally built the RG framework. This grid comprising 24 constructs will then be delivered to the same group of interviewed experts for our upcoming research, exploring the key constructs of collaborative learning in the metaverse.

Acknowledgments. This study was funded by the Research Project for Emerging Young Scholars under Grant NSTC 112-2628-H-468-001 from the 2030 Cross-Generation Young Scholars Program of the National Science and Technology Council, Taiwan, R.O.C.

Disclosure of Interests. The authors have no competing interests to declare that are relevant to the content of this article.

References

1. Ahn, S., Heo, Y.: The principles and practices of college writing education using the metaverse. Korean J. Gen. Educ. **17**(1), 63–76 (2023)
2. Bailey, F., Moar, M.: The vertex project: Children creating and populating 3D virtual worlds. J. Art Des. Educ. **20**(1), 19–30 (2001)
3. Monahan, T., McArdle, G., Bertolotto, M.: Virtual reality for collaborative e-learning. Comput. Educ. **50**(4), 1339–1353 (2008)
4. Slater, M., Sanchez-Vives, M.V.: Enhancing our lives with immersive virtual reality. Front. Robot. AI **3**, 1–47 (2016)
5. Dirin, A., Nieminen, M., Laine, T.H., Nieminen, L., Ghalebani, L.: Emotional contagion in collaborative virtual reality learning experiences: An eSports approach. Educ. Inf. Technol. **28**(11), 15317–15363 (2023)
6. Han, H.C., Hung, L.: Virtual technology in an art classroom. Int. J. Arts Educ. **19**(1), 47–67 (2021)
7. Yeh, Y.-L., Lan, Y.-J., Lin, Y.-T., R.: Gender-related differences in collaborative learning in a 3D virtual reality environment by elementary school students. J. Educ. Technol. Soc. **21**(4), 204–216 (2018)
8. Makransky, G., Andreasen, N.K., Baceviciute, S., Mayer, R.E.: Immersive virtual reality increases liking but not learning with a science simulation and generative learning strategies promote learning in immersive virtual reality. J. Educ. Psychol. **113**(4), 719–735 (2021)
9. Prasolova-Førland, E., McCallum, S., Estrada, J.G.: Collaborative learning in VR for cross-disciplinary distributed student teams. In: Proc. 2021 IEEE Conf. Virtual Real. 3D User Interfaces Abstr. Workshops (VRW), pp. 320–325 (2021)
10. Latta, G.F., Swigger, K.: Validation of the repertory grid for use in modeling knowledge. J. Am. Soc. Inf. Sci. **43**(2), 115–129 (1992)
11. Phythian, G.J., King, M.: Developing an expert support system for tender enquiry evaluation: A case study. Eur. J. Oper. Res. **56**(1), 15–29 (1992)
12. Chu, H.-C., Hwang, G.-J., Tsai, C.-C.: A knowledge engineering approach to developing mindtools for context-aware ubiquitous learning. Comput. Educ. **54**(1), 289–297 (2010)
13. D'Ambrosio, D.: Conceptualizing metadata via repertory grids: exploring a method for the development of domain-specific systems for knowledge organization. Knowl. Organ. **34**(1), 41–57 (2007)
14. Gray, D.E.: Facilitating management learning: developing critical reflection through reflective tools. Manag. Learn. **38**(5), 495–517 (2007)
15. Neimeyer, G.J., Bowman, J.Z., Saferstein, J.: The effects of elicitation techniques on repertory grid outcomes: difference, opposite, and contrast methods. J. Construct. Psychol. **18**(3), 237–252 (2005)
16. Dancey, C.P., Reidy, J.: Statistics without maths for psychology, 8th edn. Pearson Education Limited, Harlow, England (2020)

A Study on the Current Situation, Problems and Needs Assessment for Development of Adaptive Digital Technology System for Testing Information and Communication Technology Competency and Digital Literacy Skills for Teacher and Administrator

Charuni Samat[1](✉), Pinyarat Singha[2], Suchat Wattanachai[3], Pornsawan Vongtathum[1], Issara Kanjug[4], and Sumalee Chaijaroen[4]

[1] Division of Computer Education, Faculty of Education, Khon Kaen University, Khon Kaen, Thailand
scharu@kku.ac.th

[2] Nakhon Phanom Primary Educational Service Area Office 1, Nakhon Phanom, Thailand

[3] Division of Surgery, Faculty of Veterinary Medicine, Khon Kaen University, Khon Kaen, Thailand

[4] Division of Educational Technology, Faculty of Education, Khon Kaen University, Khon Kaen, Thailand

Abstract. This research aims to: (1) examine the current situation, problems, and essential needs for developing an adaptive digital technology system for testing Information and Communication Technology (ICT) competency and digital literacy skills among teachers; and (2) study the current situation, problems, and essential needs for developing a similar system for school administrators. The sample group consisted of 303 individuals from primary education schools in the northeastern region, including 192 teachers and 111 school administrators, selected through simple random sampling. The research methodology employed was survey research, which gathered both quantitative and qualitative data. The findings revealed that: For teachers (N = 192), the current assessment of their own development in ICT competency and digital literacy skills indicated significant issues ($\overline{x} = 3.84$, SD = 0.77) and high essential needs ($\overline{x} = 3.96$, SD = 0.72). Their self-assessment for professional competence enhancement also showed substantial issues ($\overline{x} = 3.88$, SD = 0.74) and very high needs ($\overline{x} = 4.08$, SD = 0.67). For school administrators (N = 111), the self-assessment regarding their development in ICT competency and digital literacy skills highlighted major issues ($\overline{x} = 4.02$, SD = 0.81) and the highest level of essential needs ($\overline{x} = 4.27$, SD = 0.68). Their self-assessment for professional competence enhancement also indicated significant issues ($\overline{x} = 4.04$, SD = 0.82) and the highest needs ($\overline{x} = 4.27$, SD = 0.63).

Keywords: The Current Situation Problems · Needs Assessment · Adaptive Digital Technology System · Digital Literacy Skills

Y.-P. Cheng et al. (Eds.): ICITL 2024, LNCS 14785, pp. 136–146, 2024.
https://doi.org/10.1007/978-3-031-65881-5_15

1 Introduction

The teaching profession, a field distinguished by its intellectual engagement and unique community service, faces significant challenges in both the quantity and quality of professionals, markedly affecting educational standards. Presently, global advancements in 'Disruptive Technology' necessitate the urgent adaptation and development of new skills to remain competitive by 2030. Such technological shifts profoundly influence socio-economic landscapes. This has a profound impact on the social and economic context. Occupations and human resources are being replaced by digital technologies, particularly artificial intelligence and robotics. High-speed, high-efficiency communication technology affects lifestyle patterns and the dissemination of information, knowledge, and misinformation, leading to incorrect decisions due to a lack of critical thinking skills. Thus, education is significantly affected by the current digital technology shift, leading the world fully into the 'Education Disruption". The technological changes that are rapidly approaching a critical turning point also pose significant challenges [1].

Research on developing ICT competencies and digital literacy among teachers and school administrators highlights key issues in basic education. Budget constraints often hinder infrastructure purchases and maintenance, resulting in slow internet access and insufficient equipment. There is a shortage of ICT-skilled personnel relative to the number of teachers. Many teachers lack computer skills and struggle to create and use digital learning media effectively. More support from the Ministry of Education is needed, including budgets for ICT and digital technology and personnel with ICT and digital literacy skills to enhance learning management and foster positive attitudes towards diverse digital presentation formats [2]. From the problems mentioned above, it shows that the condition of schools still needs self-development in terms of information and communication technology competencies and digital literacy skills, but the current form of development is through training for self-development, and after training, very few are monitored and networked for sustainable professional development.

Additionally, standards related to information and communication technology competencies and digital literacy skills are defined from the standards of information and communication technology for educational personnel by the International Society for Technology in Education: ISTE, UNESCO's standards for educational personnel, the Commission on Information and Communications Technology (NICS) standards for teachers, and the professional standards by the Teachers' Council Regulations, regarding innovations and information and communication technology in education, and basic education office competencies related to educational innovations and information and communication technology, which include standards of knowledge of educational innovations and technology, promoting quality learning, technology and information, problem analysis from the use of innovations and information, learning resources and networks, and the design, creation, application, evaluation, and improvement with competency, being able to select, design, create, and improve innovations to enhance good learning, develop technology and information to foster good learning, and seek various learning resources to promote student learning [3–6] and the standards of the Ministry of Higher Education, Science, Research and Innovation (MHESRI) and the International Computer Driving License (ICDL) in developing digital literacy skills, which is a standard test for computer skills, which the conceptual framework mentioned above will be used as a basis for synthesizing the conceptual framework to create standards for information and communication technology competencies and digital literacy skills that match the context of teachers and educational administrators in Thailand.

Previous research has highlighted the need to enhance teachers' and educational administrators' competencies to meet international standards. This requires both digital lessons and adaptive competency testing. Current exams focus mainly on content and cognitive domains, but there is a need for skill-based assessments that simulate real-life scenarios. Future research will develop exams that assess practical skills, provide feedback for improvement, and support self-monitoring and development through online practice. These exams will use Item Response Theory (IRT) and adaptive testing, aiming to create a database of ICT competencies and digital literacy skills that meet international standards. By integrating modern technology with educational testing, this approach seeks to enhance teachers' and administrators' skills, ensuring their performance aligns with school requirements and maximizes benefits for learners.

This research aims to develop digital technology to enhance education by examining the current situation, problems, and necessary needs to create an adaptive digital technology system. This system will assess the information and communication technology (ICT) competencies and digital literacy skills of teachers and school administrators, which includes the key parts: Studying the current situation, problems, and needs of teachers and school administrators and Using these findings to develop competency frameworks for ICT and digital literacy skills, next step to Designing competency tests for these skills, including exam questions and a test database, Creating a high-quality digital technology system with an effective user manual, and Providing guidelines for developing a digital technology system to improve professional competency standards and the integration of modern technology into learning management, addressing societal changes. This concise approach will aid in advancing professional competencies and adapting to evolving educational technology needs.

2 Literature Review

2.1 Educational Context Under the Basic Education Commission

Detailed Overview. The Office of the Basic Education Commission, a pivotal department within the Ministry of Education, governs a vast network comprising 62 Secondary Education Area Offices and 183 Primary Education Area Offices, which collectively supervise over 29,500 schools. These institutions are instrumental in implementing and enhancing basic educational frameworks throughout the region [7]. Schools under the jurisdiction of the Office of the Basic Education Commission are educational institutions that provide a basic education system. This includes a minimum of twelve years of education before higher education, starting with nine years of mandatory education beginning at age seven until the student reaches sixteen, unless they pass the ninth year of mandatory education earlier. The objectives and principles are guided by the National Education Act, B.E. 2542 [7], Sect. 6, which states, "The management of education must aim to develop Thais into well-rounded human beings physically, mentally, intellectually, knowledgeable, and morally. They must possess ethics and cultural norms for living peacefully with others." Sect. 7 emphasizes, "The learning process should instill a correct understanding of political and administrative systems under a democratic regime headed by the Monarchy, promoting and preserving rights, duties, freedom, respect for the law, equality, and human dignity It should cultivate pride in Thai identity, protect national and common interests, and encourage the advancement of religion, arts, national culture, sports, local and Thai wisdom, as well as universal knowledge, while conserving natural resources and the environment. The capabilities to engage in careers, be self-reliant, show initiative, be curious, and engage in continuous self-learning are also important." Sect. 8 outlines the educational principles as follows: 1) Education is lifelong learning for all citizens, 2) The community should participate in education management, 3) Content and learning processes should be continuously developed".

Educational Management Approach of the Office of the Basic Education Commission. The National Education Act, B.E. 2542 [7], stipulates that the educational management approach must adhere to the principle that all learners are capable of learning and self-development, and that learners are of utmost importance. The educational process must promote natural and potential development, emphasizing knowledge, morality, learning processes, and integration appropriate to each educational level as follows:

1. Knowledge about oneself and one's relationship with society, including family, community, nation, and the global community, as well as knowledge about the history of Thai society and the political governance system under a democratic regime with the King as Head of State.
2. Knowledge and skills in science and technology, including understanding and experience in managing, maintaining, and utilizing natural resources and the environment sustainably.
3. Knowledge about religion, arts, culture, sports, Thai wisdom, and the application of local wisdom.
4. Knowledge and skills in mathematics and languages, focusing on the correct use of the Thai language.
5. Knowledge and skills necessary for a profession and living happily.

Role of Schools under the Office of the Basic Education Commission in Educational Management. The National Education Act, B.E. 2542 [7] outlines the roles of schools in educational management as follows:

1. Tailor content and activities to align with the interests and aptitudes of learners, taking into account individual differences.
2. Train skills, thinking processes, management, confrontation of situations, and application of knowledge to prevent and solve problems.
3. Organize activities that allow students to learn from real experiences, practice performing tasks effectively, foster a love for reading, and inspire continuous curiosity and learning.
4. Conduct teaching by integrating various knowledge areas in a balanced proportion, and embed morals, good values, and desirable characteristics in all subjects.
5. Support and enable teachers to create a learning environment and provide the necessary resources to facilitate learning and comprehensive understanding, including using research as part of the learning process. In this regard, both educators and

learners may learn simultaneously from educational materials and various scientific resources.

6. Facilitate learning at any time and place, coordinating cooperation with parents, guardians, and community members to jointly develop students according to their potential.
7. Assess students by considering their development, behavior, observation of learning behavior, participation in activities, and tests, integrated within the teaching process appropriate for each level and educational format.

2.2 ICT Competency and Digital Literacy in Education: A Focus on Educators and Administrators Expanded Analysis

This section delves into the crucial competencies in information and communication technology (ICT) and digital literacy required by teachers and administrators to effectively incorporate technology into educational practices. The literature has been updated to include recent studies reflecting the latest trends and challenges in integrating digital tools in education. This update is crucial for understanding the dynamic landscape of digital literacy and its impact on educational efficacy [2–5, 8–13]. The details are as follows:

Competencies in Information and Communication Technology and Digital Literacy Skills for Teachers (DICT Competencies for Teachers), consisting of 6 competencies:

1. Competence in using basic digital information technology refers to the ability to understand information and digital technologies, use computers, basic application software, internet, networks, and network resources.
2. Competence in the legal, ethical, and safe use of digital information technology refers to the ability to comply with laws related to the use of digital information technology, adhere to ethical and professional codes in the use of digital information technology, and maintain data and information security.
3. Competencies in the use of digital information technology to prepare and design learning management refers to the ability to use digital technology to find resources and media, as well as tools suitable for learning, design activities that promote higher-level thinking using digital technology, use digital technology to develop learning media or innovations, and use digital technology to improve learning strategies to accommodate diverse learner needs.
4. Competencies in the use of digital information technology in learning management refers to the ability to use digital technology to create interactions, communicate, and discuss student ideas, present learning activities or tasks, collect media and learning resources, promote students to summarize and generate their own knowledge, supervise and monitor, and reflect on learning outcomes.
5. Competence in using digital information technology to measure and evaluate learning outcomes refers to the ability to use digital technology to design diverse assessments, collect and analyze data to determine student learning outcomes, and choose methods of presenting assessment results and reflecting on student learning.
6. Competence in the use of digital information technology for professional development refers to the ability to use digital technology for exchanging experiences, creating

professional learning communities (PLC), and using it for continuous professional development research.

Competencies in Information and Communication Technology and Digital Literacy Skills for Educational Administrators (DICT Competencies for Educational Administrators), consisting of 5 competencies:

1. Competence in using basic digital information technology as previously described.
2. Competence in the legal, ethical, and safe use of digital information technology as previously described.
3. Competence in using digital technology to prepare effective school management systems and structures refers to the ability to use digital technology to find resources and media suitable for school management, create digital technology plans and projects to support a digital work culture, and use digital technology to oversee, monitor, and improve management strategies.
4. Competencies in using digital technology in human resource management and performance assessment in schools refers to the ability to use digital resources to manage personnel, develop and train staff, assess performance, and develop innovations for school administration.
5. Competence in the use of digital information technology for professional development as previously described.

3 Purposes

To study the current conditions, problems, and necessary requirements for developing an adaptive digital technology system for testing the information and communication technology competencies and digital literacy skills of teachers.

To study the current conditions, problems, and necessary requirements for developing an adaptive digital technology system for testing the information and communication technology competencies and digital literacy skills of educational administrators.

4 Method and Result

4.1 Scope of Research

This study employs a structured survey approach focusing on: the current status, problems, and essential needs related to information technology and communication competencies and digital literacy skills of school administrators.

4.2 Target Group of the Study

The sample comprises 303 participants from the Office of Primary Education in the Northeastern region, including 192 teachers and 111 administrators, selected through simple random sampling.

4.3 Research Design

This research is survey research that collects both quantitative and qualitative data.

4.4 Research Instruments

Developed a structured survey to explore the current condition, problems, and necessary requirements related to the information and communication technology competencies and digital literacy skills of teachers.

Similarly, a survey was structured for assessing the same parameters among school administrators.

4.5 Data Collection and Analysis

1. Reviewed relevant literature, concepts, and existing research to ensure the comprehensive design of the survey.
2. Constructed and refined the survey instruments through expert reviews to ensure validity and reliability.
3. Piloted the survey among a small group of educators to test the clarity and effectiveness of the questions.
4. Launched an online version of the survey.
5. Distributed the survey via multiple channels, including social media and official communications, to ensure a wide participant response.

4.6 Research Results

The analysis of responses from 192 teachers highlighted significant needs for developing an adapted digital technology system for testing competency in information and communication technology and digital literacy skills of teachers. It was found that, as show in Table 1.

From Table 1, self-evaluation of information technology competency development. And communication and teachers' digital literacy skills include (1) the current problem, found that the overall level is at a high level ($\overline{x} = 3.84$, SD = 0.77). The competency with the highest mean value is the competency in using digital information technology correctly. According to the law, ethics, code of conduct and safety were at a high level ($\overline{x} = 4.20$, SD = 0.76) (2) Necessities were found to be overall at a high level ($\overline{x} = 3.96$, SD = 0.72). Competencies with an average. The highest is the competency in using digital information technology legally, ethically, ethically, and safely at the highest level ($\overline{x} = 4.26$, SD = 0.69).

The analysis of responses from 111 school administrators highlighted significant needs for developing an adapted digital technology system for testing competency in information and communication technology and digital literacy skills of school administrators that similarly underscored the urgency and necessity for such developments in administrative capacities. It was found that, as shown in Table 2.

From Table 2, the self-evaluation of the development of information and communication technology competency and digital literacy skills of school administrators includes (1) the current state of the problem, found that overall it is at a high level ($\overline{x} = 4.02$, SD = 0.81) The competency with the highest mean value is the competency in using digital information technology legally, ethically, ethically, and safely at a high level ($\overline{x} = 4.32$, SD = 0.89) (2) Necessities, overall, are At the highest level ($\overline{x} = 4.27$, SD =

Table 1. Self-evaluation of information technology competency development and communication and digital literacy skills of teachers

Competency/Issue	The Current Situation Problems			Needs		
	$\overline{x}$	S.D	Meaning	$\overline{x}$	S.D	Meaning
1. Competence in using basic digital information technology	3.77	0.77	Very	3.96	0.71	Very
2. Competence in the use of digital information technology that is legal, ethical, ethical and safe	4.20	0.79	Very	4.26	0.69	Very Much
3. Competencies in the use of digital information technology to prepare and design learning management	3.85	0.75	Very	3.93	0.72	Very
4. Competencies in the use of digital information technology in learning management	3.71	0.78	Very	3.85	0.75	Very
5. Competence in using digital information technology to measure and evaluate learning outcomes	3.71	0.78	Very	3.83	0.76	Very
6. Competence in the use of digital information technology for professional development	3.81	0.73	Very	3.92	0.71	Very
Result	**3.84**	**0.77**	**Very**	**3.96**	**0.72**	**Very**

0.68), the competency with the highest mean value was the competency in using digital information technology legally, ethically, ethically and safely at the highest level ($\overline{x}$ = 4.54, SD = 0.57).

4.7 Statistical Analysis

To gain deeper insights from the survey data, we employed basic inferential statistics, including mean, standard deviation, and percentages. These methods helped identify significant differences and relationships within the data, providing a robust foundation for our findings and conclusions.

Table 2. Self-evaluation of the development of information and communication technology competencies and digital literacy skills of school administrators

Competency/Issue	The Current Situation Problems			Needs		
	x̄	S.D.	Meaning	x̄	S.D.	Meaning
1. Competence in using basic digital information technology	3.84	0.80	Very	4.24	0.67	Very Much
2. Competence in the use of digital information technology that is legal, ethical, ethical and safe	4.32	0.89	Very Much	4.54	0.57	Very Much
3. Competent in the use of digital technology in preparing effective school management systems and structures	4.03	0.76	Very	4.25	0.67	Very Much
4. Competencies in the use of digital technology in human resource management and performance assessment in schools	3.97	0.78	Very	4.15	0.75	Very
5. Competence in the use of digital information technology for professional development	3.94	0.80	Very	4.20	0.75	Very
Result	**4.02**	**0.81**	**Very**	**4.27**	**0.68**	**Very Much**

5 Conclusions

Our study identified significant gaps in ICT competencies and digital literacy among teachers, particularly in the legal and ethical use of digital technologies ($\bar{x} = 4.20$, SD $= 0.76$). This highlights an urgent need for structured training programs that emphasize ethical standards and digital safety, reflecting a high demand for such competencies ($\bar{x} = 4.26$, SD $= 0.69$). Self-assessment results indicate that current professional competencies are at a high level overall ($\bar{x} = 3.88$, SD $= 0.74$), with the highest scores in promoting and supporting learning management ($\bar{x} = 3.93$, SD $= 0.75$). The necessity for these competencies is also rated high ($\bar{x} = 4.08$, SD $= 0.67$), again with the highest need in promoting and supporting learning management ($\bar{x} = 4.09$, SD $= 0.68$).

The results highlight significant challenges faced by school administrators in adopting ICT solutions, especially in managing digital infrastructure responsibly and ethically (highest issue $\bar{x} = 4.32$, SD $= 0.89$). There is a critical need for policies supporting continuous professional development and infrastructure enhancement to foster secure and effective technology use in education (highest need $\bar{x} = 4.54$, SD $= 0.57$). The self-assessment for raising professional competencies shows that the current problem is generally high ($\overline{x} = 4.04$, SD = 0.82), with the highest average in facility management ($\overline{x} = 4.14$, SD = 0.84). Overall necessities are also at the highest level ($\overline{x} = 4.27$, SD = 0.63), with the highest average again in facility management ($\overline{x} = 4.33$, SD = 0.67).

The main issue in educational technology is the lack of readiness among teachers and administrators. Teachers often lack the necessary skills to use media and information technology effectively. Therefore, developing teachers' skills should be prioritized over materials, equipment, and budget constraints [3, 12–14]. The Ministry of Education's 11th Educational Development Plan (2012–2016) highlighted several challenges in basic educational institutions. These include an overemphasis on developing materials and equipment rather than integrating technology into teaching, outdated and poor-quality media, and a shortage of personnel skilled in using educational technology. Additionally, there is a lack of modern and sufficient equipment, making self-study and research difficult for teachers and students. Teachers and school administrators also lack essential ICT and digital literacy skills necessary for effective learning management, a need exacerbated by the COVID-19 pandemic and ongoing economic challenges.

References

1. Kiratikon, K., et al.: Digital World and Transformation of Future Education and Technology. Kasetsart University, Bangkok (2023)
2. Samat, C., Wattanachai, S., Vongtathum, P., Kanjug, I., Chaijaroen, S.: Development of learning innovations that promote ICT competencies for teachers and school administrators in small schools in Northeastern Thailand. Educational Technology Development Fund, Ministry of Education (2019)
3. Commission on Information and Communications Technology Commission on Information and Communications Technology, National ICT Competency Standard (NICS) for Teachers. http://www.ncc.gov.ph/nics/files/NICS-Teachers.pdf. Accessed 27 Feb 2022
4. Office of the Basic Education Commission. http://www.obec.go.th. Accessed 01 Nov 2021
5. International Society for Technology in Education (ISTE). National Education Technology Standard (NETS) and Performance Indicators for Teachers. http://www.iste.org/standards/standards for-teachers. Accessed 27 Feb 2022
6. UNESCO, Strategy framework for promoting ICT literacy in the Asia-Pacific region (2018). http://www2.unescobkk.org/elib/publicationsX188/promotinglCTliteracy.pdf
7. Office of the National Education Commission: The National Education Act. Prig Wan Communication, Ltd., Bangkok (1999)
8. Teachers' Council. The Royal Gazette, vol. 137, Special Part 109, pp. 10–14 (2020)
9. Digital Economy and Society Ministry, National Digital Committee for Economy and Society. Digital competency framework for Thai citizens, Bangkok (2018)
10. European Commission. https://joint-research-centre.ec.europa.eu/digcomp_en. Accessed 21 Feb 2022
11. North Carolina Department of Public Instruction. California ICT Digital Literacy Assessments and Curriculum Framework. http://www.ictliteracy.info/rf.pdf/. Accessed 27 Feb 2022
12. Jangsook, S., Songleknok, S.: Guidelines for the Development of ICT Usage Skills of Teachers in Outstanding Schools of Sub-district Under the Office of Secondary Education Area 23. Praewa Kalasin Journal of Kalasin University (2017)

13. Komolwanich, S., Sonsupee, S.: Digital Leadership of School Administrator Affecting Teacher Competency for 21 Century Under the Secondary Educational Service Area Office 23. KKU Research Journal of Humanities and Social Sciences (Graduate Studies), vol. 9, no. 2 (2021)
14. Suksaard, P., Longpradit, P.: Digital competency needs in times of crisis for school administrators and physical education teachers in the Western Provinces of Thailand. Integr. Soc. Sci. J. **10**(1), (2023)

Pedagogies to Innovative Technologies and Learning

On Portfolio Assessment, Group Work, and Quasi-Anonymization: What Structural Information Do Anonymized Reports Reveal?

Frode Eika Sandnes(✉)

Oslo Metropolitan University, 0130 Oslo, Norway
frodes@oslomet.no

Abstract. With traditional summative exams students' identities are often hidden from the examiners. However, achieving anonymity can be challenging with portfolio and coursework-based assessments. This study was motivated by a discussion of whether students should, or can, be anonymized in courses with portfolio assessments, especially if the teacher is both actively involved in the students' learning process and the assessment. With portfolios the student will work on a set of projects throughout a course and submit the final product for assessment. One may argue that as the teacher gains familiarity with students' work throughout the semester it is challenging to achieve true anonymity even if the final submissions are technically anonymized. To provide empirical evidence of this an experiment was designed to assess the degree of simplicity to which non-anonymous coursework submitted for formative evaluation can be matched with anonymized coursework submitted for the final summative evaluation. The experiment was also designed to assess whether it was possible to automatically detect student group structures based solely on the reports. The results based on 1098 reports show that students' writings could be successfully matched across versions, while it was only possible to partially detect group structures. Implications of this work is that conscious decisions need to be taken about the quality of the student-teacher dialogue quality versus the need for anonymous assessments.

Keywords: Portfolio assessment · formative assessment · anonymization · privacy · group work

1 Introduction

Portfolio assessment is an alternative to traditional exams with several benefits. A portfolio is typically established by a student while learning throughout the semester, while an exam is usually held during a limited time interval on one day. Portfolios shifts the pressure, anxiety, and stress of performing on a given day to working on the course throughout the semester. Moreover, portfolios can help change the emphasis from rote memorization to learning by doing. Portfolios can also make it easier to operationalize individualized assignments and project work, making the learning more motivating for the student and grading less mundane for teachers. Portfolios facilitate formative evaluation, allowing

Y.-P. Cheng et al. (Eds.): ICITL 2024, LNCS 14785, pp. 149–158, 2024.
https://doi.org/10.1007/978-3-031-65881-5_16

students to get feedback about their progress throughout the learning process to make corrections and adjustments. Finally, portfolios can facilitate socio-cultural learning if students are encouraged to work on tasks together in groups.

1.1 Anonymization or Quasi-Anonymization

The identity of students can be hidden from the examiners with traditional exams to avoid bias. For instance, a teacher may have subjective impressions of students' performance affecting the grading. Also, examiners that have not taught the course may be biased by factors such as gender or cultural affiliation clues in the students' name [1]. Also, anonymized exam papers are also easier to handle with external examiners from a privacy perspective.

This study is addressing the anonymity of students with portfolio assessments. There are certain situations where students' anonymity can be guaranteed, namely, if the portfolios are assessed by someone who did not teach the course, or if the teacher serving as examiner has no insight about the students' projects. However, when harvesting the benefits of portfolios, the teacher should be in dialogue with the students throughout the learning process and provide formative feedback on the work. However, the teacher will undeniably accumulate insight and knowledge about the students. It is naïve to believe that all this insight will be forgotten or "reset" by the time of assessment.

It is the author's experience that students and administrators often request assessments to be technically anonymized. In the author's country, anonymization rights are protected through legislation. This study therefore explored whether true anonymization is practically possible with certain forms of portfolios. If it turns out that anonymization is compromised, one could argue that flagging an examination as anonymous is misleading students.

1.2 Group Structures

This study also explores the challenge of collecting student group information in situations where students work together in groups. Information about groups is needed if a component of a portfolio comprises group work so that the contributing students can be credited.

The author's experiences with current educational technologies shows that the functionality for supporting group work submissions seems like an afterthought often hidden behind awkward user interface mechanisms. Typically, the students are automatically placed into groups, set into groups by the teacher, or students choose their own group composition.

This study documents a particular variation of group work where individually written reports are based on group work. For this mode it is also important to know the group structures to assess the overall contribution of the group members. Unfortunately, the mechanisms in the submission systems do not support this portfolio variation since each student submits individual reports for the group work. To overcome this challenge, the students are asked to declare their other group members on the reports using their student id numbers. This scheme can be anonymized if some anonymous candidate numbers are used instead, however, these numbers will then have to be shared with the other students in the group. However, this study explores if it is possible to extract information about group structures implicitly from anonymous portfolios.

1.3 This Study

The following two hypotheses were therefore formulated:

- H1: We can find the identity of an anonymized student that authored a final report if we know the students' identity for a draft version of the report.
- H2: We can identify which students worked together in a group based on the contents of the reports.

This paper is organized as follows. Related work is reviewed in the next section. This is followed by a description of the method, a presentation of the results and the discussion. Finally, a set of concluding remarks is provided.

2 Background

According to Brennan [2] there has been an active debate about the role of anonymization in higher education assessment of student work. Brennan argues that more empirical insight is needed. As pointed out by Lopez-Agudo and colleagues [3] the teachers in many countries and contexts often also serve as the assessor, with the possible entanglement of the two roles (see also [4]). Most of the studies discuss teachers as assessors, but some also addressed student peer-assessment and effects of anonymity [5, 6].

As pointed out by O'Flynn-Magee and Clauson [7] discussions related to assessment exist in a climate with inconsistent assessment practices across courses and teachers, unrealistic grade expectations among students and patterns of inflated grades. Kim and Helms [8] point to the many studies claiming effects of bias in grading when a teacher resumes the role of assessor. They suggested that such bias can be reduced by anonymization or the use of external assessors that are not involved in the teaching.

Rotsaert et al. [9] discussed the tension between bias prevention with anonymization and how anonymization hinders two-way interaction that can be important to the learning process. They argue for a mixed approach where students start with anonymized grades (as scaffolding) and move to non-anonymous assessment as trust is established.

Several other voices argue that anonymization can reduce bias caused by unrelated information such as previous performance, students' gender, and students' cultural affiliation. For instance, through a meta-analysis of an array of studies Malouff and Thorsteinsson [10] documented bias in grading. In another study, Malouff and colleagues [11] conducted a controlled study to see whether a "good" and "poor" presentation influenced the subsequent assessment of an independent writing. They found a strong "halo effect" where the presentation affected how the subsequent writing was assessed. Consequently, the authors are advocates for anonymization. Similarly, Burgess and Greaves [12] observed bias connected to the cultural affiliation of students.

Several studies document findings suggesting that anonymization has no or little effect on bias. For instance, in an experiment of blinded vs non-blinded assessment Bygren [13] observed no gender effects, although very small positive effects of immigrant names in favor of the students were seen. Also, Birch et al. [14] were unable to detect biases caused by gender and observed that the assessors only relied on the content alone. They concluded that anonymization may be unnecessary in higher education. Lopez-Agudo and colleagues [3] explored if tutor-tutee relationships influence grading. They detected only a very small positive effect in favor of tutees. Results pointing in the direction of no bias effects of "reputation information" in terms of previous performance were also reported by Batten et al. [15].

Also, Pitt and Winstone [16] were unable to observe any effects of gender and ethnicity on grading when comparing anonymous versus non-anonymous assessment. They also observed no differences in perceptions among students subjected to anonymous versus non-anonymous assessment. The authors argue against anonymization as it may reduce the potential and opportunities for learning as anonymization negatively affects the quality of the dialogue between the students and the teacher.

Often assessment is associated with traditional summative exams, but in this study the assessments are based on portfolios, which are common in subjects requiring reflection [17]. Richardson [18] uses the general term coursework and thus describes assessment as either based on coursework conducted during a course, exams conducted after the course, or mixed assessments-based coursework and exams. Richardson points out that coursework-based assessment may easily lead to higher grades compared to exams. Coursework assessment may also reduce the negative effect of large class sizes. However, it is argued that coursework is more vulnerable to cheating. Richardson points out collusion, plagiarism, and contract cheating though "bespoke essays" as challenges.

Vogl and Pekrun [19] argue that students' feelings related to assessment can affect motivation, learning behavior and therefore also the assessment outcome. Negative feelings range from anxiety, frustration, and shape to more positive feelings of hope, pride, and achievement. They argue that assessment should be rigged to minimize the impact of anxiety or hopelessness that can be a hindrance for some students. Portfolio assessment as used in this study is one such mechanism that is intended to reduce anxiety as several studies have linked exams/texts with anxiety [20]. This work builds on the author's previous work on anonymous linking of research data [21] and approximate linking of student records [22].

3 Method

An experiment was designed to assess to what degree of simplicity versions can be automatically matched, and student group structures can be automatically detected, solely from text contents.

3.1 Material

This study is based on the draft and final portfolios of an undergraduate class of 250 students comprising 1098 reports ranging from 1000 to 3000 words. Each portfolio comprised three individually written reports. The first report was based on an individual project on a self-chosen topic, the second individually written report documents group work on a given topic, and the third individually written report documents group work on a topic selected by each group. The workload of the three projects were distributed throughout the semester and the students were encouraged to submit a draft report for formative feedback which they could take into consideration when revising the texts and preparing the final version for assessment. The teacher was available for individual and group supervision throughout the semester for help with the coursework.

Throughout the semester 69.6%, 56.5%, and 65.4% of the students submitted the optional draft version of the three reports, respectively, for formative feedback. Only 224 of 250 students submitted the final obligatory portfolio for summative assessment. All the reports were submitted in pdf-format. The identities of the students and the groups were known.

3.2 Analysis

An analysis tool was written in JavaScript using the pdf.js, filesaver.js, and community edition Sheet.js libraries. First, the text contents of the pdf-files were extracted. Each project set was analyzed separately.

The former and final reports were matched by comparing their respective dice scores [22] of the word-bigrams and selecting the pairs with the highest score. The word bigrams for a report were created by splitting the text into words (tokens) and treating each consecutive word pair as a bigram. Next, only a unique copy of each bigram was kept. The aggregated statistics were computed by comparing the automatic match to the ground truth.

Group matching was conducted by comparing the reports in each set (former and final). The approach involved identifying groups based on the five reports with the highest word-bigram dice score above 10% similarity. Next, aggregated statistics were computed, namely the percentage of correctly detected groups, partially detected groups, completely incorrect groups.

4 Results

4.1 Version Similarity (H1)

Table 1 summarizes the results of the version matching experiment. The table shows that the matching accuracy is high and above 95% in all instances. Only one incorrect match was made for the 3rd set of reports. The remaining cases were undetected.

Table 1. Version matching statistics.

	Correct	Incorrect	Undetected
1st (individual free)	96.8%	0.0%	3.2%
2nd (group fixed)	98.4%	0.0%	1.6%
3rd (group free)	97.9%	0.7%	1.4%

Figure 1 shows the similarity of all the report pairs for all students who submitted both reports. Each curve shows the project pair similarities for each project. A similarity of 0% means no similarity while a similarity of 100% indicates identical reports. The horizontal axis shows the percentage points of the submissions (the distribution) sorted in increasing order of similarity). The use of percentage distributions allows the three data series to overlap as they contain different data points.

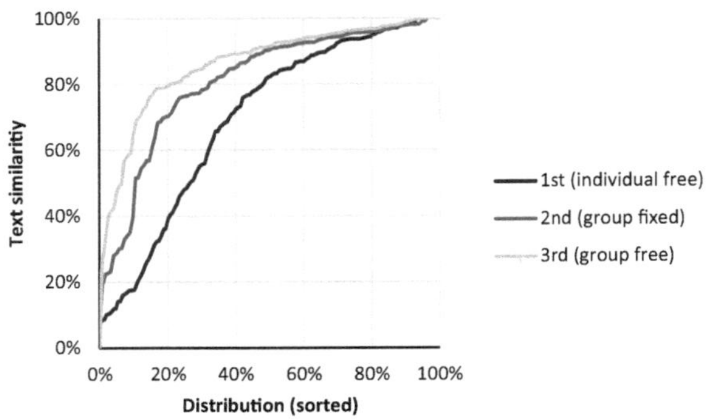

Fig. 1. Similarity of the report distribution.

The chart shows that 50% of the reports have similarities of 80% or more, 80% of the report pairs have a similarity of 40% or more, and only 10% of the reports or less have a similarity of 20% or less.

Figure 1 reveals that the height of the three curves appears to be related to their recency, namely the most recent (3rd) the highest, followed by the second recent (2nd) and the first (1st) at the bottom. To further quantify these differences the mean similarity for each distribution was computed and plotted (see Fig. 2).

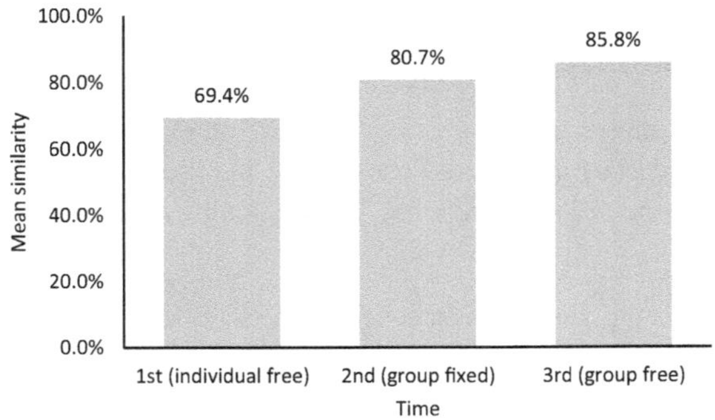

Fig. 2. Mean similarity for report distributions from least recent to most recent.

4.2 Group Identification (H2)

Figure 3 shows the results of the group identification experiment. The results show that only a small fraction of reports was successfully recognized, a somewhat larger fraction was partially detected, and a large fraction was completely incorrect.

The fraction of correct recognitions was larger for the two formative sets compared to the two final sets. Also, the fraction of successfully identified groups is larger for the third set of reports documenting a self-selected topic compared to the second set of reports documenting a pre-assigned topic.

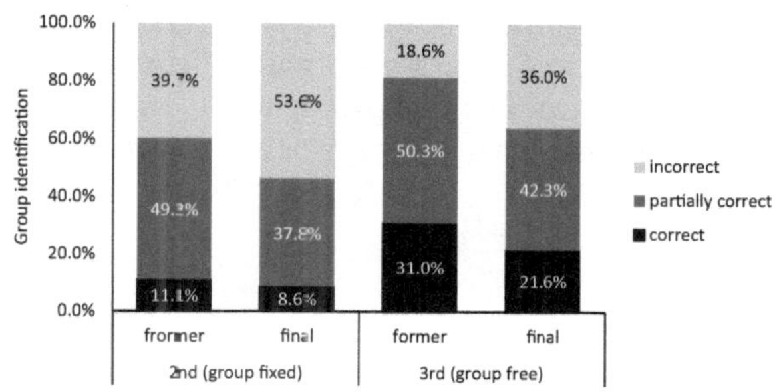

Fig. 3. Group identification statistics.

5 Discussion

5.1 Version Similarity (H1)

The results of the former-final version matching similarity revealed that more than 95% of the reports could be successfully matched based on the text contents alone. An investigation of the few anomalous cases helps provide explanations; on a few occasions the students only provided a very brief outline in the draft report as opposed to the complete text in the final report. Also, some students decided to start from scratch and redo the assignment based on the feedback. There was also one case where a student submitted the draft report but not the final report (incorrectly matched).

The results also seem to suggest that the differences between versions are related to time as differences were larger if the duration between the former and final version were larger. One explanation for this is that given more time, the student also has more opportunities to adjust and fine-tune and polish the reports, while less time permits fewer amendments. Still, the reduction in similarity caused by the time-factor does not seem to notably affect the ability to match versions.

Overall, the findings give support to H1, namely that a draft version of a report can be successfully matched with a final revised version of a report without knowing the identity of the student.

Implications of this result are that if the students' identities are known for one version of the reports (typically the draft), the identities of the students can be automatically inferred for anonymous revised versions of the reports. Therefore, one may argue that flagging an assessment as anonymous indeed is misleading students as one is only achieving quasi-anonymization. This is particularly problematic if students believe they are anonymous. One could also argue that it is important for students to gain a basic understanding of privacy and develop their ability to assess their privacy in various situations. It seems thus relevant to discuss this dilemma with students.

One possible solution is to ensure that both versions of a report are anonymous. Although versions can still be successfully matched, the identity of the students will remain unknown. However, this would mean that the teacher needs to be at a further distance from the student to prevent gaining detailed insight into what the students are working on.

Anonymity can also be ensured if the assessors are different from the teacher. Then, the teacher can be even more involved in supporting the students with their work. However, using separate assessors may not necessarily be a practical alternative as it requires additional resources.

5.2 Group Identification (H2)

The results of the group identification showed that it was challenging to extract the groups using text similarity. One explanation for the higher group recognition rates for former versus final versions could be that the set of submissions are generally smaller with the former set compared to the larger final sets. Hence, the group matching with fewer submissions has fewer ambiguous cases compared to the larger final set leading to more ambiguities.

Next, the notable difference between the second and third report sets could be explained by the context. The second report set was based on a given pre-assigned topic, while the third report set was based on a free topic chosen by the groups. Hence, the reports with the third assignment would be more varied and diverse compared to the second assignment. Consequently, it was probably easier to distinguish between the diverse set of reports clustered around group work, compared to the less diverse reports on the same topic with more overlap across groups. Still, even the individual topics in the third project did not provide sufficient unique information for group structures to be accurately detected.

The results therefore give no support to H2; the hypothesis that groups can be detected based on the report similarity was therefore rejected.

Implications for this finding is that if group information is needed during assessment, explicit information about group structures need to be provided in some manner. As demonstrated by several practical implementations, such group information can be provided without revealing the students' identities.

5.3 Limitations

Portfolio schemes can be realized in many ways. This study is based on one specific implementation of portfolio assessment and the results do not necessarily generalize to other forms of portfolio assessment. Only a very rudimentary text-similarity based group identification scheme was used and this is reflected in the results. It is thus possible that a more sophisticated group detection algorithm may give more accurate results.

6 Conclusions

A simple experiment was conducted to assess whether a former and final report can be successfully matched and whether group structures can be extracted from the same reports. The results showed that the version could be successfully matched, but group information could not. The implication of this work is that student anonymity cannot be guaranteed if their identities are known from one of these versions. Therefore, flagging such assessments as anonymous is misleading. Possible compromises therefore include choosing a misleading practice with quasi-anonymization, employing non-anonymous assessment with possible negative student perceptions of grading bias, ensuring that both former and final reports are anonymous with longer distance between teachers and the student, or separating the assessor role from the teaching role at the cost of additional resources.

References

1. Eika, E., Sandnes, F.E.: Starstruck by journal prestige and citation counts? On students' bias and perceptions of trustworthiness according to clues in publication references. Scientometrics **127**(11), 6363–6390 (2022)
2. Brennan, D.J.: University student anonymity in the summative assessment of written work. High. Educ. Res. Dev. **27**(1), 43–54 (2008)
3. Lopez-Agudo, L.A., Marcenaro-Gutierrez, O.D., Molina-Marfil, J.A.: School tutoring and academic performance: a too close relationship? Stud. Educ. Eval. **66**, 100903 (2020)
4. Sasanguie, D., Elen, J., Clarebout, G., Noortgate, W.V.D., Vandenabeele, J., De Fraine, B.: Disentangling instructional roles: the case of teaching and summative assessment. Stud. High. Educ. **36**(8), 897–910 (2011)
5. Vanderhoven, E., Raes, A., Montrieux, H., Rotsaert, T., Schellens, T.: What if pupils can assess their peers anonymously? a quasi-experimental study. Computers & Education **81**, 123–132 (2015)
6. Tong, Y., Schunn, C.D., Wang, H.: Why increasing the number of raters only helps sometimes: Reliability and validity of peer assessment across tasks of different complexity. Stud. Educ. Eval. **76**, 101233 (2023)
7. O'Flynn-Magee, K., Clauson, M.: Uncovering nurse educators' beliefs and values about grading academic papers: Guidelines for best practices. J. Nurs. Educ. **52**(9), 492–499 (2013)
8. Kim, D.G., Helms, M.M.: Assessing faculty bias in rating embedded assurance of learning assignments. J. Edu. Bus. **91**(3), 159–165 (2016)
9. Rotsaert, T., Panadero, E., Schellens, T.: Anonymity as an instructional scaffold in peer assessment: its effects on peer feedback quality and evolution in students' perceptions about peer assessment skills. Eur. J. Psychol. Educ. **33**, 75–99 (2018)
10. Malouff, J.M., Thorsteinsson, E.B.: Bias in grading: A meta-analysis of experimental research findings. Aust. J. Educ. **60**(3), 245–256 (2016)
11. Malouff, J.M., Emmerton, A.J., Schutte, N.S.: The risk of a halo bias as a reason to keep students anonymous during grading. Teach. Psychol. **40**(3), 233–237 (2013)

12. Burgess, S., Greaves, E.: Test scores, subjective assessment, and stereotyping of ethnic minorities. J. Law Econ. **31**(3), 535–576 (2013)
13. Bygren, M.: Biased grades? changes in grading after a blinding of examinations reform. Assess. Eval. High. Educ. **45**(2), 292–303 (2020)
14. Birch, P., Batten, J., Batey, J.: The influence of student gender on the assessment of undergraduate student work. Assess. Eval. High. Educ. **41**(7), 1065–1080 (2016)
15. Batten, J., Batey, J., Shafe, L., Gubby, L., Birch, P.: The influence of reputation information on the assessment of undergraduate student work. Assess. Eval. High. Educ. **38**(4), 417–435 (2013)
16. Pitt, E., Winstone, N.: The impact of anonymous marking on students' perceptions of fairness, feedback and relationships with lecturers. Assess. Eval. High. Educ. **43**(7), 1183–1193 (2018)
17. Forenc, K.M., Eriksson, F.M., Malhotra, B.: Medical Students' perspectives on an assessment of reflective portfolios. Adv. Medical educ. Pract. 463–464 (2020)
18. Richardson, J.T.: Coursework versus examinations in end-of-module assessment: a literature review. Assess. Eval. High. Educ. **40**(3), 439–455 (2015)
19. Vogl, E., Pekrun, R.: Emotions that matter to achievement: Student feelings about assessment. In: Handbook of human and social conditions in assessment, pp. 111–128. Routledge (2016)
20. Brandmo, C., Bråten, I., Schewe, O.: Social and personal predictors of test anxiety among Norwegian secondary and postsecondary students. Soc. Psychol. Educ. **22**, 43–61 (2019)
21. Sandnes, F.E.: HIDE: short IDs for robust and anonymous linking of users across multiple sessions in small HCI experiments. In: Extended Abstracts of the 2021 CHI Conference on Human Factors in Computing Systems, pp. 1–6 (2021)
22. Sandnes, F.E.: FLINK: An Educator's Tool for Linking Inaccurate Student Records. In: International Conference on Innovative Technologies and Learning, pp. 143–152. Springer Nature Switzerland, Cham (2023)

Developing Reading Literacy with Digital Texts

Nursulu Shaimerdenova[1], Gulbarshin Baigunissova[2], Zhanargul Beisembayeva[2], Assel Amrenova[2](✉), Akzhan Abdykhalykova[2], Aygul Tadjibaeva[2], Rustam Shadiev[3], Narzikul Shadiev[4], Mirzaali Fayziev[4], and Natalya Turkenova[5]

[1] AlFarabi Kazakh National University, 777, Almaty 050064, Kazakhstan
[2] L.N. Gumilyov Eurasian National University, Astana 01000, Kazakhstan
baigunissovagi@enu.kz, assel.s.a14@gmail.com
[3] Zhejiang University, Hangzhou 310058, Zhejiang Province, China
[4] Uzbekistan-Finland Pedagogical Institute, Samarkand 140100, Uzbekistan
[5] Zhetysu University, Taldykorgan 040009, Kazakhstan

Abstract. The article examines the influence of digital sources (texts) on the development of reading literacy among students. By reading literacy, the authors of this study consider the reader's ability to understand, evaluate and reflect on text, as well as use text ideas in everyday life. The purpose of this work is to determine the impact of reading digital texts on the level of reading literacy of Kazakhstani youth. To achieve this goal, the study was conducted on what texts students read from the university website and other Internet sources, and how this reading affects their reading literacy. In the process of studying the issue, observations were made of the peculiarities of students' work with digital text, and a sociological survey was conducted among students of the L.N. Gumilyov Eurasian National University (Kazakhstan, Astana), as well as subsequent analysis of the data obtained. The choice of the target audience was determined by the relevance of the study - in their professional are, university teachers are often faced with a low level of reading literacy among students, which creates the need to work to improve their reading literacy.

Keywords: teaching · reading literacy · digital text

1 Introduction

As an outcome of centuries of evolution, the modern world citizens have now become a progressive multilingual society. According to scientific studies, there is a less percentage of monolingual individuals and the number is dropping every year due to the mix of cultures and globalization. Kazakhstan, as one of many countries where representatives of many ethnicities live, has accepted the usage of three languages: Kazakh as the state language, Russian language can also be used in state organizations and local self-government institutions, whereas English is the language applied for international communication and business. English, dominating the intercultural, international relations, is taught all around the globe and yearly more and more people are adopting it as their first or second foreign language.

Y.-P. Cheng et al. (Eds.): ICITL 2024, LNCS 14785, pp. 159–166, 2024.
https://doi.org/10.1007/978-3-031-65881-5_17

There are certain steps to learning a language and it requires the effort to master a language on a good level. Literacy is often defined as an ability to read and write. Students become literate when they acquire knowledge, skills, and inclinations to successfully comprehend and apply language for learning and communicating both inside and outside of school, as well as for engaging in society. Literacy aids learners for listening to, perusing, speaking, writing, and creating spoken, print, visual, and digital texts, as well as employing and altering language in a variety of circumstances. Reading literacy was defined in PISA [1, p. 231–249] as the capacity to comprehend, utilize, evaluate, and reflect on texts, as well as the willingness to engage with them in order to attain one's own goals and partake in society. Simply described, reading is the cornerstone for all the learning and it is one of four main skills that must be acquired in the process of language learning. Reading ability is essential for obtaining work or pursuing education. Reading skill is vital in facilitating a country's growth. Students' reading proficiency is critical for showcasing their abilities in other academic areas. Based on research, if an individual's reading abilities are poor, it might cause issues in studying various subjects. Reading can extend the learners' horizons, making them more receptive to new experiences and knowledge.

The aim of this study is to analyze the impact of digital text on the level of reading literacy. Reading ability cannot form the reading literacy by itself, reading comprehension, readiness to critically analyze the text and other aspects play a fairly big role. Recent studies and observations of how a modern student perceives information reveal that digital tools for reading, electronic textbooks, blogs and websites are getting more relevant in terms of convenience than regular physical materials. We, as human beings adapt to the needs and demands of the era they are living in and right now, as the digital technologies are evolving, our abilities, skills and necessities are also changing alongside with the changes. This led us to the realization that progress-tracking and change-documenting is crucial for the improvements in the education and specifically in attempting to reach the reading fluency are much needed.

2 Methodology of the Research

2.1 Design

This research used the quantitative research approach using a cross-sectional survey for data collection. For this purpose, the research survey was conducted online (accessed by the URL link) and the instrument applied for it was an anonymous questionnaire that was developed to clarify the youth's perception of reading literacy.

2.2 Participants

The survey participants were composed of bachelor students of Eurasian National University and practicing English language teachers. Besides, it was essential to establish that the participants were well-informed of the aim of the survey. The students are from the 1-year bachelor's multilingual group of non-linguistic specialties – "tourism" and "restaurant and hotel business", age category of the respondents is 17–25.

2.3 Instrument

A brief questionnaire was developed based on the literature review. As the participants were students who study in English and English language teachers, it was decided the best to conduct a survey in English. Questions of different types were offered – open and closed types, with multiple choice of answers and several answers from several options.

Students were given a questionnaire consisting of 14 questions including multiple-choice questions and general questions to reveal their awareness of reading literacy.

2.4 Data Collection

The study used a questionnaire designed to answer the research question of how beneficial multilingualism is. The list of participants consisted of bachelor students of L. N. Gumilyov Eurasian National University and practicing English language teachers. As the questionnaire was conducted online using Google Forms, the link was sent to group chats with the participants. Recipients were requested to complete the questionnaire and were pre-informed that participation in the study was voluntary and that they were under no obligation to participate.

2.5 Data Analysis

Using Data from the Google Forms, descriptive statistics and independent sample t-tests, the data was analyzed. The descriptive statistics were used for overall mean scores of the different investigated variables. The independent sample t-tests were used to determine the overall attitude of students and teachers towards reading.

3 Results and Discussion

The first result of our study was related to the need to identify students' knowledge about reading literacy. The option that got most votes (85%) was "the ability to understand, use, evaluate, and reflect on texts, as well as being prepared to engage with them in order to achieve one's own goals". The purpose here was to define 'reading literacy' and test whether survey participants knew this term (it was taken from the PISA exam framework). The results show that the majority knows the meaning of reading literacy.

Reading, as a language skill, is very important both for students and for teachers. The survey also showed a growing passion for reading among Kazakhstani youth: 90% of respondents admitted that they enjoy reading. Figure 1 illustrates the reading speed of survey participants. It can be concluded that fair amount of them have a slightly below average (40%) and average (40%) reading speed. Some exclusions were also noted: 10%, who read 300–350 words and another 10% of those who read more than 350 words per minute.

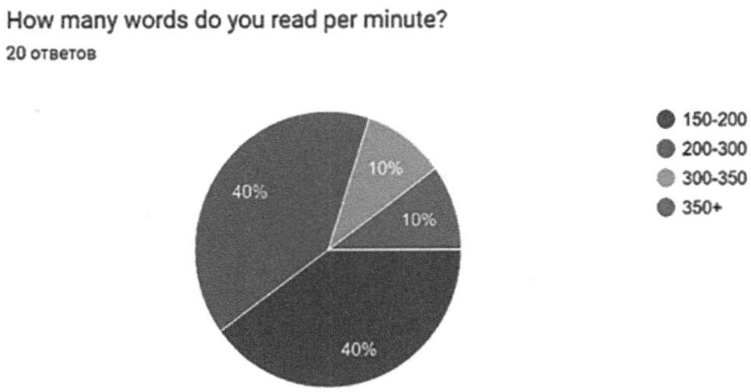

Fig. 1. The reading speed

There are many types of texts and the preferences can be seen below in Fig. 2. Most of the reacts were collected by the option "website articles" (45%) and it can be justified by the fact that we call the current time "a digital era". Second most chosen type of test was "tables/ diagrams/ graphs" which is known for having less text and providing information by a scheme. Novels and newspaper articles share the same result of 30%. This conveys how different the picks of repliers are.

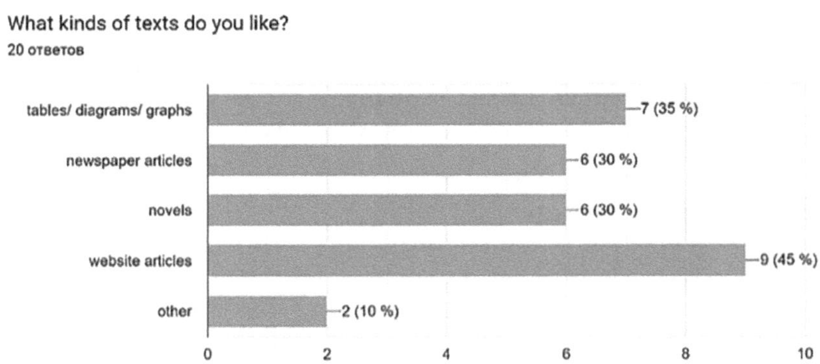

Fig. 2. Text preferences

Figures 3 and 4 demonstrate how often the digital texts are used and what types of digital texts are applied the most. Half of the repliers exposed that they utilize digital tools when they read. 30% denoted that they sometimes use digital tools and 15% revealed that they do not use any digital tools. Among the specific types of digital tools E-Library and Online Dictionary were revealed to be the most popular, both gaining 35%. ReadWriteThink (15%) and Good Reader (10%) also seem to be used quiet often. Figure 3 and 4 can be seen below.

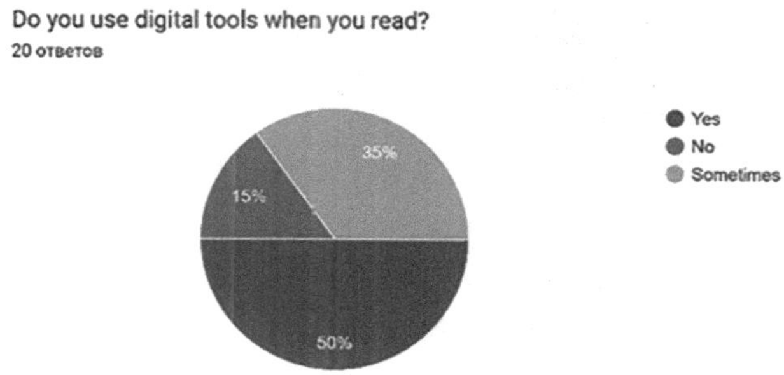

Fig. 3. The usage of digital tools

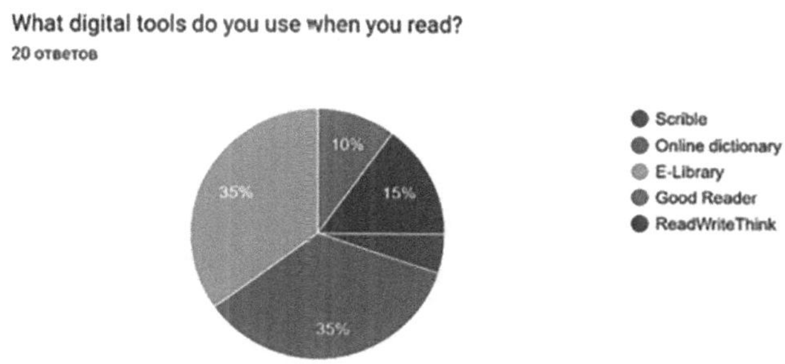

Fig. 4. Digital texts

The survey showed that the university's website is used by 75% of respondents and the rest (25%) are said to be the practicing English language teachers from another educational organizations, who also took part in the research survey.

The responses given in Chart 5 reveal the most frequently used sections of L. N. Gumilyov Eurasian National University website. As expected, results inform us that Platonus section of the website is used the most (70%). Another top answer (45%) unveils the actuality of "Student life section" as it is regularly visited by ENU students. The other sections as "ENU news" (35%), "Notifications poll" and "Science section" (30%) gathered approximately similar amounts of votes. It should be pinpointed that "Vacancies" section ended up being the least visited of all (15%) (Fig. 5).

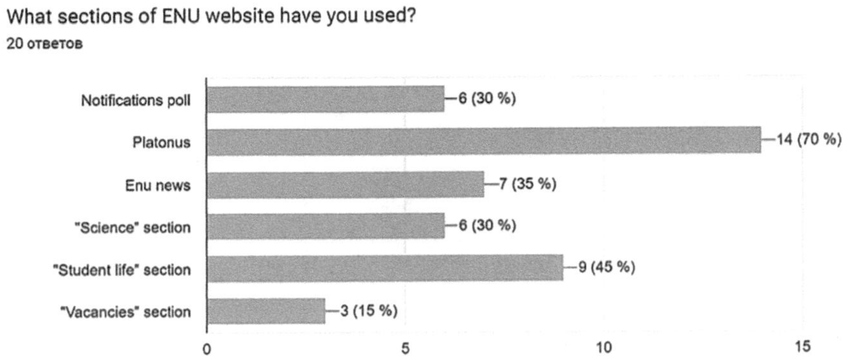

Fig. 5. The most frequently used sections of ENU website

We assume the reason for this is that most of the participants are bachelor students and this particular section is of no need for them yet.

Based on the survey results demonstrated above, this section discusses the research findings. The results show that the students of L.N. Gumilyov university and English language teachers who took part in this survey are generally familiar with the term "Reading literacy". The collected answers ensure us that reading is more than existent in youth's life whether if it's for academic or personal purposes.

As it has been mentioned, the respondents were exposed to have an average and close-to-average reading speed. According to the research done by Brysbaert M., the average reading speed is different for when learners read silently (sometimes referred to as "reading inward") – 238 wpm, and when reading aloud this number is significantly lower – 183 words per min. Skilled readers were observed to read more than 300 words per minute. Survey participants likely read silently most of the times, which means that the gathered numbers are not low, but there is definitely a way for improvement [2].

Reading is a complicated process, consisting of identification of text and absorption of the meaning of the written words and this skill is a complex one, which corresponds with the other three skills. There are a plenty of factors that affect the development of a learner's reading literacy. As PISA monitors and assesses the achievements of students in reading, mathematics and science, some scholars also explored the correlation between these subjects for a deeper overview. Interesting results were collected in the study by Koyuncu, İ. And Fırat T. – reading literacy affects the scientific performance more than it affects the mathematical performance of students [3, p. 263–275].

Students that have dedicated some time in their daily lives for reading, those who read classics, fictional literature, science fiction books or any other texts to their liking foster the interest for reading and it is often associated with them better performing academically. The results of our research show that the repliers also read and do it willingly, not only for studies, but also for enjoyment. Experienced readers were reported to need less strict instruction and just need a guide from a teacher. A practicing teacher commented on the importance of showing genuine interest in students' learning and engaging them in activities, promoting their understanding can be effective to improve their reading skills without putting extra pressure on them [4].

For the best outcome, in any problem question both ups and downs need to be examined. Linnakyla conducted a comparative study based on PISA's indication of Swedish and Finnish students as 'best readers' among the OECD countries. The findings showed that the likelihood of being a poor achiever is substantially influenced by gender and a variety of sociocultural factors, as well as students' personal attributes, perspectives, and behaviors within and out of school.

Replies of our survey participants also declared that they use the digital tools while reading and the most used one is E-library, which enables web-users to access, read and download e-books from the Internet. López-Escribano expands on the impact of e-books on the reading efficiency of young learners. When selected and used properly, the study reports, e-books can contribute to the development of reading and comprehension skills to the same extent, and sometimes even more than the actual print books that we're all used to at this point [5, p. 65].

PISA allows nations to evaluate how multiple layers of factors differ across countries, allowing particular countries to discover features of their systems that appear to benefit students in general and those that may be less helpful [6, p.3]. The research survey has been conducted with the same purpose – to identify the state of the reading literacy among Kazakhstani youth and find ways to improve it [7].

R. Rintaningrum's work focuses on the reading culture of Indonesian people and the results exhibited that reading literacy is able to transform the way people think and act [8, p. 3–23]. What and how one reads can, in fact, contribute to certain alteration in his/her character and it can easily be observed in real life as well. Reading was proven to cultivate imagination and critical thinking, that's why reading must be nurtured in young people. Statistically, Canada is the country with most readers in the world, scoring 66%, while Spain follows in the second place with 50% [9, p.10–13]. Kazakhstan has a way to go and hopefully, the number of readers in our country also make it to the top-reader countries' list.

In the digital age the reading habits vastly differ from those documented decades ago. That's why it is important to consider the peculiarities of today's youth's reading preferences. O. Shatunova did an international study including Russia, the U.S. and the Czech Republic to identify how and why the preferences and interests of young people changed over the years, which proceeded to put fantasy on the pedestal in recent years [10, p. 62–73]. K. Shulman's "Reading for Life" inspects the benefits of reading on young people's health, both physical and mental, which is also a fascinating topic that captured our attention [11, p. 4–13]. Keeping these in mind, more in-depth research on this matter can be conducted in the future.

4 Conclusions

Reading literacy has always been in high demand and this study explored factors that can affect one's acquisition of reading skill. Since ancient times, people have been gaining knowledge through reading and observing changes in reading, in reading habits, in readers' preferences and for reading purposes give us the opportunity to understand how humans are developing in society.

In the prospect of our further research, we propose to consider the issues of the development of reading literacy and the potential of e-reading as a means for the reading proficiency enhancement. It has been established, that Kazakhstani youth is aware of reading literacy and has every possibility of expanding the number of readers in our country as they read different types of texts and have the capacity to improve their reading skills with a little to no help from outside (teacher's guidance is always needed). The theoretical relevance of the study relies with the current globalization process and the rising number of multilingual individuals. Data, collected with the research survey showed the inclusivity of the results, proving that multi-linguals are, indeed, different from the monolinguals in so many areas. Responses have been taken into consideration further in practice and the changes have been applied in the guidance to completion of the reading tasks, the digital tools are recommended to implementation. This study can be expanded more by the deeper research and by studying the reading literacy of multilingual societies of adults – the college groups, which, we assume, will give more diverse opinions and scientific opportunities to researchers.

References

1. Linnakyla¨, P., Malin, A., Taube, K.: Factors behind low reading literacy achievement. Scandinavian J. Edu. Res. **48**, 231–249 (2004). https://doi.org/10.1080/00313830410001695718
2. Brysbaert, M.: How many words do we read per minute? A review and meta-analysis of reading rate. J. Mem. Lang. **109**, 104047 (2019). https://doi.org/10.1016/j.jml.2019.104047
3. Koyuncu, İ., Fırat, T.: Investigating Reading Literacy in PISA 2018 Assessment. IEJEE **13**, 263–275 (2021). https://doi.org/10.26822/iejee.2021.189
4. Rojas-Torres, L., Ordóñez, G., Calvo, K.: Teacher and Student Practices Associated with Performance in the PISA Reading Literacy Evaluation. Front. Educ. 6 (2021). https://doi.org/10.3389/feduc.2021.658973
5. López-Escribano, C., Valverde-Montesino, S., García-Ortega, V.: The impact of E-book reading on young children's emergent literacy skills: an analytical review. IJERPH **18**, 6510 (2021). https://doi.org/10.3390/ijerph18126510
6. Perkins, R.: Reading Literacy in PISA 2009. eprint Limited, Dublin (2011)
7. Literacy in reading of Kazakh youth. Survey, https://forms.gle/UkRrhAVdo9SLCwEAA. Last accessed 05 December 2023
8. Rintaningrum, R.: Explaining the Important Contribution of Reading Literacy to the Country's Generations: Indonesian's Perspectives (2019)
9. Baigunissova, G.: Developing academic speaking and writing skills of university students by means of stylistic devices and expressive means under Muller's method, https://www.webofscience.com/wos/woscc/full-record/WOS:000545005700103. Last accessed 20 October 2023
10. Shatunova, O., Bozhkova, G., Tarman, B., Shastina, E.: Transforming the reading preferences of today's youth in the digital age: intercultural dialog. J. Ethn. Cult. Stud. **8**, 62–73 (2021). https://doi.org/10.29333/ejecs/347
11. Trabucchi, S., Shulman, K.: Reading for Life: The Impact of Youth Literacy on Health Outcomes. https://teacher.scholastic.com/education/researchpdf/topic_paper/ReadforLife.pdf. Last accessed 10 December 2023

Exploring the Relationship Between Collaborative Learning Factors and Perceived Learning

Hua-Xu Zhong[1], Chin-Feng Lai[1], Shang-Hsuan Ku[2], and Jui-Hung Chang[3](✉)

[1] Department of Engineering Science, National Cheng Kung University, 1, University Rd., Tainan 701, Taiwan, R.O.C.

[2] Department of Computer Science and Information Engineering, National Cheng Kung University, 1, University Rd., Tainan 701, Taiwan, R.O.C.

[3] Computer and Network Center, and Department of Computer Science and Information Engineering, National Cheng Kung University, Tainan, Taiwan, R.O.C.

changrh@ncku.edu.tw

Abstract. Online courses or distance learning often exhibit lower levels of teacher-student interaction and participation. The success of student collaborative learning in this context depends on various tangible and intangible factors. Therefore, this study explores online collaborative learning and its impact on academic outcomes by examining factors such as learning engagement, collaborative learning, and computer anxiety. This study, conducted at a national university in southern Taiwan, involved 67 participants from the Department of Information Engineering. Findings reveal a significant negative influence of computer anxiety on perceived learning. Additionally, a positive correlation is found between learning engagement and perceived learning, emphasizing the importance of an engaging online environment. The study emphasizes the need to overcome these challenges for a more effective learning experience. Understanding these nuances is crucial for tailored, effective collaborative learning strategies in online education.

Keywords: collaborative learning · programming course · learning engagement

1 Introduction

Distance learning generally produces low teacher-student interaction [1–3]. In contrast, computer-supported collaborative learning (CSCL) enhances interactions among students [4], and collaborative processes [5], addressing crucial educational concerns Some research indicates that collaborative learning plays a pivotal role in aiding students in programming tasks, contributing to their programming learning [6], and perceived satisfaction [7]. Additionally, collaborative learning in an online setting facilitates the co-construction of knowledge among students [4], and promotes teamwork [3] highlighting its significance in the educational landscape. Nevertheless, the implementation of collaborative learning by teachers remains essential for students to effectively grasp programming courses.

Y.-P. Cheng et al. (Eds.): ICITL 2024, LNCS 14785, pp. 167–174, 2024.
https://doi.org/10.1007/978-3-031-65881-5_18

In the realm of online education, the success of collaborative learning for students hinges on a multitude of both tangible and intangible attributes, with the appropriate use of technology being paramount. Several studies have primarily employed the Technology Acceptance Model (TAM) to scrutinize learners' behavioral intentions [8–10], explored Computer-Supported Collaborative Learning (CSCL) research models [11], delved into collaborative learning under the umbrella of social media [12–14], and considered Expectation-Confirmation Theory (ECT) [15, 16]. However, extensive research has been conducted on exploring the potential factors of collaborative learning, and many have proven instrumental in the effectiveness of collaborative learning. Few have directed attention to the ultimate goal of distance education, which is to enhance learners' learning performance and achievement. Recognizing this gap is crucial, as it prompts a holistic evaluation of collaborative learning in the context of remote courses, thereby paving the way for a more comprehensive understanding of its impact on learners' academic outcomes.

The impact of collaborative learning in online courses is intricately woven with the interplay of various features and functionalities, which may determine the factors influencing it alongside other elements. Previous empirical research has highlighted potential factors affecting online courses, including learning engagement [17, 18], computer anxiety [19, 20], and factors related to collaborative learning [11, 19]. The learning environment involves students' active participation, interaction, focused attention, and positive responses to course content [21, 22]. Successful collaborative learning necessitates teachers to design suitable tasks, support learning, and encourage active student engagement in interactions [21]. The collaborative process of student participation and interaction significantly influences the ultimate learning content produced [22].

Learning engagement plays a crucial role in online courses, affecting student interactions and the influence of other factors [11, 14, 23]. Specifically, students may experience anxiety due to unfamiliarity with computer operations or uncertainty about digital tools [24, 25], which can serve as barriers hindering their participation in online courses. In the online environment, collaboration and interaction among students are paramount for knowledge construction and sharing [16]. Collaborative learning, facilitated through online learning platforms, integrates a variety of learning activities and provides teachers with an opportunity to employ different instructional models to enhance students' learning abilities and teamwork skills [26].

Given this context, to address the research gap, this study applies various factors to assess online collaborative learning and evaluate learners' academic outcomes. Beyond examining learning engagement, the effectiveness of collaborative learning and computer anxiety is explored, aiding in understanding the learning situations of students engaged in online collaborative learning. The study develops a research model to analyze these relationships comprehensively. Therefore, in navigating the complexities of students' experiences in online collaborative learning, this research seeks to explore the roles of learning engagement, collaborative learning, and computer anxiety. The aim is to provide a nuanced understanding of the dynamics influencing the effectiveness of online collaborative learning and its impact on learners' academic achievements. This multifaceted approach contributes to a more holistic evaluation of the intricate interplay of factors shaping the online collaborative learning environment.

2 Research Hypothesis

Collaborative learning extends beyond the mere utilization of social interaction to enhance students' cognitive abilities. It includes the integration of emotional aspects to foster student engagement and collective accomplishment of learning objectives [27–29]. In addition, some studies indicated that collaborative learning positively impact learning engagement [28, 30]. Not only does collaborative learning encourage participation and the acquisition of additional resources and information through group discussions, but it also utilizes interaction to elevate students' academic performance [30].

Therefore, the following hypotheses are proposed:

H1a: Collaborative learning positively affects cognitive engagement.
H1b: Collaborative learning positively affects emotional engagement.
H1c: Collaborative learning positively affects behavior engagement.

Computer anxiety is characterized as a learning process involving computer technology that induces negative emotions and cognitive challenges [31]. However, it's noteworthy that computer anxiety can have adverse effects on learning engagement with educational applications [32]. Specifically, when students encounter technical barriers in the learning process, it can trigger computer anxiety and negative emotions, thereby hindering effective learning [33].

Many studies have investigated how learning engagement (e.g., cognitive, affective, behavioral) significantly impacts students' perceived learning [34–36]. For instance, a study by Buil, Catalán and Martínez [34] explored the use of business simulation games in teaching marketing courses, revealing that cognitive engagement and emotional engagement positively influenced students' perceived learning. In a MOOC learning environment, Lan and Hew [35] found a positive correlation between learning engagement and students' perceived learning outcomes.

Therefore, the following hypotheses are proposed:

H2a: Computer anxiety negatively affects perceived learning.
H3a: Cognitive engagement positively affects perceived learning.
H3b: Emotional engagement positively affects perceived learning.
H3c: Behavior engagement positively affects perceived learning.

3 Research Method

3.1 Sample

This study enrolled 67 participants in the Department of Information Engineering at a national university in southern Taiwan. It is noteworthy that all students were afforded the option to either actively partake or abstain from the survey.

3.2 Research Instrument

This research employed a variety of questionnaires to execute the survey, utilizing a five-point Likert scale that ranged from 1 (strongly disagree) to 5 (strongly agree). To measure cognitive engagement (4 items), emotional engagement (6 items), and behavior engagement (4 items) with a total of 14 questionnaire items [37, 38]. In addition, the survey encompassed perceived learning with 13 items [39], drawing inspiration from previous studies. To evaluate the participants' computer anxiety, five items were incorporated, referencing established works [24, 25]. This comprehensive approach ensured a nuanced exploration of various dimensions, including cognitive, emotional, and behavioral engagement, as well as perceived learning and computer anxiety.

3.3 Research Model Reliability

In order to ascertain the reliability and validity of the study model, several rigorous tests were employed, ensuring robustness and credibility. The model was subjected to three key assessments: Cronbach's Alpha Value: The model was deemed reliable if the Cronbach's alpha value exceeded 0.7. Factor Loading Value and CR Value: A high level of reliability and internal consistency was confirmed if both the factor loading value and the Composite Reliability (CR) value surpassed 0.7. AVE Value: The Average Variance Extracted (AVE) value needed to exceed 0.5 for each variable, indicating satisfactory discriminant validity.

To evaluate validity, the Fornell-Larcker method [40] was employed. This method involved verifying that the square root of the AVE for each variable surpassed the correlation coefficients with other variables. The analysis unequivocally demonstrated that the AVEs for all variables surpassed the correlation coefficients with other variables, affirming the discriminant validity of the model.

4 Results

For this investigation, we employed SmartPLS 3 software to iteratively apply the bootstrap sampling technique with 5000 samples. This was done to assess the hypotheses and derive the corresponding t-values, which are presented in Tables 1 below.

Table 1. Hypothesis results.

Hypothesis	Path	Path coefficient (β)	t-Statistics	Results
H1a	Collaborative learning - >Cognitive engagement	0.17	0.89	Rejection
H1b	Collaborative learning - >Emotional engagement	0.18	0.96	Rejection
H1c	Collaborative learning - >Behavior engagement	0.22	1.31	Rejection
H2a	**Computer anxiety - >Perceived learning**	**−0.16**	**2.24***	**Acceptance**
H3a	**Cognitive engagement - >Perceived learning**	**0.27**	**2.92****	**Acceptance**
H3b	**Emotional engagement - >Perceived learning**	**0.50**	**5.09*****	**Acceptance**
H3c	Behavior engagement - > Perceived learning	0.17	1.91	Rejection

*$p < .05$; t > 1.96, **$p < .01$; t > 2.57, *** $p < .001$; t > 3.29.

In this study, it was found that students with a computer anxiety negatively influenced perceived learning ($\beta = -.16$, t = 2.24, $p < .05$), supporting the validity of hypothesis

H3b. However, the results indicated that cognitive engagement ($\beta = .27$, $t = 2.92$, $p < .01$) and emotional engagement ($\beta = .50$, $t = 5.09$, $p < .001$) have a positive impact on perceived learning, validating hypotheses 2a and 2b. The remaining hypotheses were not supported.

5 Discussion and Conclusions

The main aim of this study is to explore the relationships among online collaborative learning, students' collaborative learning, learning engagement, computer anxiety, and perceived learning. We focus on these factors because they play a pivotal role in understanding the dynamics of online collaborative learning. The findings of the research indicate that computer anxiety has a significantly negative impact on perceived learning. This result aligns with the study conducted by Wilfong [33], indicating that computer anxiety arising from technical obstacles can potentially hinder effective student learning. As the complexity of the online collaborative learning experience increases, students may encounter greater obstacles in extracting the necessary insights and competencies from the curriculum. The more challenging and demanding students find online collaborative learning courses, the more difficult it becomes for them to perceive the knowledge and skills required for learning in the course. Navigating through the intricacies of collaborative learning in an online setting can pose obstacles that hinder students' ability to extract the necessary insights and competencies from the curriculum. Overcoming these challenges is crucial for fostering a more effective and enriching learning experience in online collaborative environments. Furthermore, the research results indicate a significant positive impact of learning engagement on perceived learning. This finding aligns with numerous studies that consistently demonstrate the beneficial influence of learning engagement on perceived learning [34–36]. Active participation in the learning process emerges as a key factor contributing positively to students' perception of the knowledge and skills acquired, highlighting the importance of fostering an engaging and participatory online learning environment. Finally, the research results indicate that collaborative learning does not have a positive impact on learning engagement. This observation may vary based on the type of student participation and interaction [23]. Specifically, when students transition from social-emotional interaction to cognitive interaction, collaborative learning in this context may not positively influence any aspect (cognitive, emotional, behavioral engagement). Students may focus on cognitive and emotional engagement to actively participate in the course, deriving perceived benefits and insights from their involvement. In essence, students might prefer engaging in collaborative learning through existing team structures, optimizing their participation with fewer resources while enhancing their overall engagement in the course. Understanding the nuances of different student engagement types is crucial for tailoring effective collaborative learning strategies that cater to the diverse dynamics of online education.

References

1. Yazgan, Ç.Ü.: Attitudes and interaction practices towards distance education during the pandemic. Educ. Inf. Technol. **27**, 5349–5364 (2022). https://doi.org/10.1007/s10639-021-10843-2
2. Tulaskar, R., Turunen, M.: What students want? experiences, challenges, and engagement during emergency remote learning amidst COVID-19 crisis. Educ. Inf. Technol. **27**, 551–587 (2022). https://doi.org/10.1007/s10639-021-10747-1
3. Sjølie, E., Espenes, T.C., Buø, R.: Social interaction and agency in self-organizing student teams during their transition from face-to-face to online learning. Comput. Educ. **189**, 104580 (2022)
4. De Backer, L., Van Keer, H., De Smedt, F., Merchie, E., Valcke, M.: Identifying regulation profiles during computer-supported collaborative learning and examining their relation with students' performance, motivation, and self-efficacy for learning. Comput. Educ. **179**, 104421 (2022)
5. Borge, M., Aldemir, T., Xia, Y.: How teams learn to regulate collaborative processes with technological support. Educ. Technol. Res. Dev. **70**, 1–30 (2022). https://doi.org/10.1007/s11423-022-10103-1
6. Lai, X., Wong, G.K.W.: Collaborative versus individual problem solving in computational thinking through programming: a meta-analysis. Br. J. Educ. Technol. **53**, 150–170 (2022)
7. Hernández-Sellés, N., Muñoz-Carril, P.-C., González-Sanmamed, M.: Interaction in computer supported collaborative learning: an analysis of the implementation phase. Int. J. Educ. Technol. High. Educ. **17**, 1–13 (2020). https://doi.org/10.1186/s41239-020-00202-5
8. Yadegaridehkordi, E., Shuib, L., Nilashi, M., Asadi, S.: Decision to adopt online collaborative learning tools in higher education: a case of top Malaysian universities. Educ. Inf. Technol. **24**, 79–102 (2019). https://doi.org/10.1007/s10639-018-9761-z
9. Boruzie, P.K., Kolog, E.A., Afful-Dazie, E., Egala, S.B.: Social network for collaborative learning: what are the determining factors? Univ. Access Inf. Soc. 1–15 (2022). https://doi.org/10.1007/s10209-022-00942-3
10. Al-Adwan, A.S., Li, N., Al-Adwan, A., Abbasi, G.A., Albelbisi, N.A., Habibi, A.: Extending the technology acceptance model (TAM) to Predict University Students' intentions to use metaverse-based learning platforms. Educ. Inf. Technol. **28**, 15381–15413 (2023). https://doi.org/10.1007/s10639-023-11816-3
11. Muñoz-Carril, P.-C., Hernández-Sellés, N., Fuentes-Abeledo, E.-J., González-Sanmamed, M.: Factors influencing students' perceived impact of learning and satisfaction in computer supported collaborative learning. Comput. Educ. **174**, 104310 (2021)
12. Liu, S., Zaigham, G.H.K., Rashid, R.M., Bilal, A.: Social media-based collaborative learning effects on student performance/learner performance with moderating role of academic self-efficacy. Front. Psychol. **13**, 903919 (2022)
13. Sabah, N.M.: The impact of social media-based collaborative learning environments on students' use outcomes in higher education. Int. J. Human-Comput. Interact. **39**, 667–689 (2023)
14. Ansari, J.A.N., Khan, N.A.: Exploring the role of social media in collaborative learning the new domain of learning. Smart Learn. Environ. **7**, 1–16 (2020). https://doi.org/10.1186/s40561-020-00118-7
15. Cheng, X., Bao, Y., Yang, B., Chen, S., Zuo, Y., Siponen, M.: Investigating students' satisfaction with online collaborative learning during the COVID-19 period: an expectation-confirmation model. Group Decis. Negot. **32**, 749–778 (2023). https://doi.org/10.1007/s10726-023-09829-x

16. Luo, M.M., Chea, S.: Wiki use for knowledge integration and learning: a three tier conceptualization. Comput. Educ. **154**, 103920 (2020)
17. Li, L., Zhang, R., Piper, A.M.: Predictors of student engagement and perceived learning in emergency online education amidst COVID-19: a community of inquiry perspective. Comput. Human Behav. Rep. **12**, 100326 (2023)
18. Lu, K., Pang, F., Shadiev, R.: Understanding college students' continuous usage intention of asynchronous online courses through extended technology acceptance model. Educ. Inf. Technol. **28**, 9747–9765 (2023). https://doi.org/10.1007/s10639-023-11591-1
19. Magen-Nagar, N., Shonfeld, M.: The impact of an online collaborative learning program on students' attitude towards technology. Interact. Learn. Environ. **26**, 621–637 (2018)
20. Lakhal, S., Khechine, H.: Technological factors of students' persistence in online courses in higher education: the moderating role of gender, age and prior online course experience. Educ. Inf. Technol. **26**, 3347–3373 (2021). https://doi.org/10.1007/s10639-020-10407-w
21. Vuopala, E., Hyvönen, P., Järvelä, S.: Interaction forms in successful collaborative learning in virtual learning environments. Act. Learn. High. Educ. **17**, 25–38 (2016)
22. Yücel, Ü.A., Usluel, Y.K. Knowledge building and the quantity, content and quality of the interaction and participation of students in an online collaborative learning environment. Comput. Educ. **97**, 31–48 (2016)
23. Isohätälä, J., Näykki, P., Järvelä, S.: Cognitive and socio-emotional interaction in collaborative learning: exploring fluctuations in students' participation. Scand. J. Educ. Res. **64**, 831–851 (2020)
24. Chu, P.C., Spires, E.E.: Validating the computer anxiety rating scale: effects of cognitive style and computer courses on computer anxiety. Comput. Hum. Behav. **7**, 7–21 (1991)
25. Heinssen, R.K., Glass, C.R., Knight, L.A.: Assessing computer anxiety: development and validation of the computer anxiety rating scale. Comput. Hum. Behav. **3**, 49–59 (1987)
26. Wen, L.: Influence of emotional interaction on learners' knowledge construction in online collaboration mode. Int. J. Emerg. Technol. Lear. (iJET) **17**, 76–92 (2022)
27. Kreijns, K., Kirschner, P.A., Jochems, W.: Identifying the pitfalls for social interaction in computer-supported collaborative learning environments: a review of the research. Comput. Hum. Behav. **19**, 335–353 (2003)
28. Blasco-Arcas, L., Buil, I., Hernández-Ortega, B., Sese, F.J.: Using clickers in class. The role of interactivity, active collaborative learning and engagement in learning performance. Comput. Educ. **62**, 102–110 (2013)
29. Zheng, L., Yang, J., Cheng, W., Huang, R.: Emerging approaches for supporting easy, engaged and effective collaborative learning. J. King Saud Univ. Comput. Inf. Sci. **26**, 11–16 (2014)
30. Qureshi, M.A., Khaskheli, A., Qureshi, J.A., Raza, S.A., Yousufi, S.Q.: Factors affecting students' learning performance through collaborative learning and engagement. Interact. Learn. Environ. **31**, 2371–2391 (2023)
31. Bozionelos, N.: Computer anxiety: relationship with computer experience and prevalence. Comput. Hum. Behav. **17**, 213–224 (2001)
32. Lee, J.-C., Xiong, L.N.: Investigation of the relationships among educational application (APP) quality, computer anxiety and student engagement. Online Inf. Rev. **46**, 182–203 (2021)
33. Wilfong, J.D.: Computer anxiety and anger: the impact of computer use, computer experience, and self-efficacy beliefs. Comput. Hum. Behav. **22**, 1001–1011 (2006)
34. Buil, I., Catalán, S., Martínez, E.: Engagement in business simulation games: a self-system model of motivational development. Br. J. Edu. Technol. **51**, 297–311 (2020)
35. Lan, M., Hew, K.F.: Examining learning engagement in MOOCs: a self-determination theoretical perspective using mixed method. Int. J. Educ. Technol. High. Educ. **17**, 1–24 (2020). https://doi.org/10.1186/s41239-020-0179-5
36. Chan, S., Lin, C., Chau, P., Takemura, N., Fung, J.: Evaluating online learning engagement of nursing students. Nurse Educ. Today **104**, 104985 (2021)

37. Wang, M.-T., Fredricks, J.A., Ye, F., Hofkens, T.L., Linn, J.S.: The math and science engagement scales: scale development, validation, and psychometric properties. Learn. Instr. **43**, 16–26 (2016)
38. Reeve, J.: How students create motivationally supportive learning environments for themselves: the concept of agentic engagement. J. Educ. Psychol. **105**, 579–595 (2013)
39. Tiwari, S.R., Nafees, L., Krishnan, O.: Simulation as a pedagogical tool: measurement of impact on perceived effective learning. Int. J. Manag. Educ. **12**, 260–270 (2014)
40. Fornell, C., Larcker, D.F.: Evaluating structural equation models with unobservable variables and measurement error. J. Mark. Res. **18**, 39–50 (1981)

Artificial Intelligence Literacy to Enhance Teacher Critical Thinking

Michele Della Ventura(✉)

Department of Music Technology, Music Academy Studio Musica, Treviso, Italy
micheledellaventura.mdv@gmail.com

Abstract. Nowadays the teacher must be open to the transformation of the socio-educational context in which he/she works and, consequently, must develop new skills, including those linked to the use of Information and Communication Technologies equipped with Artificial Intelligence, which favor new inclusive learning/teaching paths. In these paths the teacher must consider the intertwining of very important variables such as: the styles and strategies with which teachers teach and students learn; the interaction context in which learning takes place (learning environment); the interpersonal dynamics that develop between teachers and students. This paper is intended as a guide for the teacher, to help him/her to overcome prejudices/stereotypes towards new technologies in order to create an innovative teaching activity through a learning process that allows all students (even students with specific learning disorders) to build knowledge and skills that can then be transformed into competences. The most important challenge that this paper has taken into consideration is to ensure that the teacher understands and appreciates new technologies and the fact that they can enhance the student's experience, making him/her an active protagonist of the learning process.

Keywords: active teaching · artificial intelligence tool · constructivism · inclusive teaching · Information and Communication Technologies

1 Introduction

Information society, e-society, Information and Communication Technologies (ICT) and artificial intelligence are some of the salient features that characterize contemporary society, often defined as a knowledge society: information as a building block of society is no longer sufficient and "knowledge" it is determined by the intertwining of information, experience and the ability to use information in the appropriate context. The knowledge society requires a substantial change in the social organization of knowledge and the ability of schools to adapt to ever new contexts through a transformation of the conditions of teaching and learning. Teachers must act as innovators by rethinking all the aspects involved in their educational practice [1] because the student finds himself immersed in multiple communication and learning flows, exposed to very diversified experiences, based on heterogeneous codes and languages, which require the ability to acquire, in addition to skills, new criteria for choosing and managing knowledge [2]. The teacher

Y.-P. Cheng et al. (Eds.): ICITL 2024, LNCS 14785, pp. 175–184, 2024.
https://doi.org/10.1007/978-3-031-65881-5_19

therefore becomes an important and strategic point of reference in the discovery and valorization of skills and a guide to the exploration and construction of knowledge through inclusive teaching open to discussion and exchange with students, where everyone is protagonist and not simple spectator in the face of the cognitive processes in progress [3]. The role of the teacher is therefore transforming on the basis of some innovative elements: circulating knowledge (widespread knowledge and the role of electronic media), new skills (planning, etc.), new teaching methods (such as those proposed by the use of ICT), new processes of the mind (in contradiction to traditional learning methods, based on linearity and written culture), new spaces and dimensions in which to develop relationships and teaching [4].

The quality and innovation of teaching become strategic priorities within the learning process and the teacher must take into account the transformations of the education-society relationship based on the social and cultural changes also (and perhaps, above all) determined by ICT and artificial intelligence, which have a profound impact on ways of relating and communicating and therefore on lifestyles [5]. The teacher must therefore be able to design and develop a teaching/learning process that makes the most of the opportunities offered by new technologies.

However, it should be highlighted the persistence of critical issues and resistance to teaching innovation on the part of many teachers who are afraid of losing the meaning of the contents of their discipline and direct contact with students, and are unable to find the right balance between traditional teaching and that which makes use of the innovations offered by constantly evolving technological means.

This paper aims to be a tool for reflection, aimed at teachers, on the concept of ideal modus-operandi in order not to demonize new technologies and artificial intelligence but, on the contrary, to consider them an opportunity that must be increasingly known and used to improve the teaching/learning process and create an inclusive learning environment capable of enhancing the learning, cognitive and emotional potential of each student. Emphasis is placed on the ability of new technologies to enhance active learning by focusing on the centrality of the learner through reflective, experiential and transformative learning models.

The structure of this paper has been organized as follows. Section 2 focuses on identifying pedagogical principles that can help teachers design new teaching methods. This is followed (Sect. 3) by a description of the teaching alternatives that the teacher faces in order to design an effective learning environment. Section 4 presents the analyses of some technologies in order to understand how to identify in a technology the characteristics useful for teaching activities. Finally, in Sect. 5 the paper ends with concluding remarks on the current issues.

2 Are There New Teaching Methods?

Within the learning process, regardless of the teaching discipline, not only the activation of a positive educational relationship plays a fundamental role, through which the cognitive-affective processes linked to learning and to study, but also the teaching action aimed at enhancing motivation for learning [6]. In this case the experience becomes the fulcrum of a teaching action which must stimulate in the student the desire and need to know and discover new things. The teacher, however, finds himself facing increasingly heterogeneous classes from the learning point of view and must therefore implement all those actions which, also thanks to ICT, can help all students to achieve common objectives. The presence of students with "Special Educational Needs" (SEN) or "Specific Learning Disorder" (SLD) such as dyslexia requires the teacher to use *active teaching methodologies* that allow the creation of inclusive training courses that increasingly respond to inclinations personal aspects of the students, with the aim of enhancing the peculiar aspects of each individual's personality [7, 8].

In this statement it is possible to find the principles of constructivism, an orientation according to which reality cannot be considered as something objective and independent of the person who experiences it, because it is the person who creates, builds, invents everything he/she wants to understand about what surrounds him/her. Reality cannot be considered independently of the observer, since it is the observer who gives it meaning by actively participating in its connotation [9].

The principles of constructivism can already be identified in Dewey who claimed that "every individual has grown and will always have to grow, in a social medium. His responses become intelligent or make sense, simply because he lives and acts in a medium of shared meanings and values" [10].

Constructivist learning is perhaps the most general of the various teaching models, the one that brings them all together, and Bruner suggests that the aim of constructivist teaching is to help the student develop the use of the tools of doing: this should be the operational criterion on which learning techniques are based [11].

Vygotsky is another important figure for constructivism. He maintains that words assume a functional equivalence: that is, they do not correspond to an identity of concepts and meaning [12]. Meanings must be negotiated through a continuous and mutual work of interpretation. For Vygotsky, true learning is achieved through a variety of processes activated by the person when, interacting with the peer group, in his own environment, he learns the use of resolution strategies that he does not yet possess, but which he already internalizes [12].

In this perspective, knowledge is seen as a social product that arises from the interaction between different actors and tools, such as new information and communication technologies equipped with artificial intelligence. Therefore, it is possible to see how constructivism allies itself with new technologies, both as a means to lighten the workload and to introduce new ways of learning. It is precisely the new learning methods that the teacher must discover how to implement in order to improve the teaching action in an inclusive perspective: "*a path towards the unlimited growth of learning and participation of all*" [13]. From this it emerges that the teacher's attention must be directed towards the spaces of educational action, the tools and methodologies that can create opportunities for participation and improve the experience of the students' learning process in general (talented and less talented students, dyslexic and non-dyslexic students) [14]. The inclusive dimension will therefore be played on the teacher's ability to create an adequate learning environment.

3 The Teaching Dilemma

In order to learn effectively it is necessary to have a series of tools and teaching activities that offer the possibility of learning and, even more, that offer the stimuli to encourage learning, all clearly related to the needs of each student. The learning environment should in fact create a level of consciousness and awareness that allows each individual student to have an active role and live a teaching experience that makes them feel competent and effective. Creating motivation must be the first step in designing the learning process. Motivation to achieve certain objectives is fundamental: without motivation the student is not able to feel emotions.

An optimal and inclusive learning environment must provide students with the resources and stimuli necessary to explore, experiment and learn in a meaningful way. In an inclusive learning environment, diversity must be exploited as precious resources, as an opportunity for enrichment for all, and teaching activities must not be seen as "at risk" but on the contrary "enhanced": dyslexic students and those more talented people must feel challenged by the learning environment, whose key principles must be the acceptance and valorization of diversity, the consideration of others and the valorization of everyone, in a positive and respectful atmosphere that encourages active participation and expression of different opinions, collaborative working, and promoting change [15].

A constructivist learning environment should: give emphasis to the construction of knowledge and not its production; avoid excessive simplifications by representing the complex nature of the real world; present authentic tasks (contextualize rather than abstract); offer multiple representations of reality; nourish reflective practices; allow the construction of knowledge dependent on the context and content; promote inclusion and therefore the cooperative construction of knowledge, through social negotiation.

New technologies also equipped with Artificial Intelligence (AI) can be powerful allies in offering dynamic educational experiences. AI acts as a powerful support tool, expanding the capabilities of educators and improving the learning experience of students. Pedagogy plays a crucial role in AI-enhanced education. Artificial intelligence, while powerful, is only a means to an end. Its positive impact and its true value in education strictly depend on how it is integrated and used. In this context, pedagogy becomes essential.

Through theories and practices, pedagogy offers a fundamental framework for using AI effectively and responsibly in education. The integration of AI in the educational sector is configured as a symbiosis: the technology acts in support of the pedagogical skills of teachers, who remain the indispensable pillars of the educational process. While AI offers innovative tools, the wisdom, empathy and creativity of the teacher guide its application, ensuring that education remains a deeply human experience, enriched and expanded by the advent of new technologies.

There is, therefore, no learning environment, but rather many possible learning environments as responses to the innumerable variables that are able to influence the teaching-learning process and as a response to the certainly more important variable represented by the individual student, by his learning and cognitive styles. It is up to the teacher to design the optimal environment based on the class group.

The choice of the technologies to be used cannot ignore all the considerations set out above and must take into consideration a very important aspect: teachers find themselves witnesses, not always adequately aware of the great change induced by new technologies and AI. For this reason, it is important to educate teachers first, in order to guarantee an effective teaching action for all students, who are the most direct witnesses of this change. And this can be done not from outside but, as far as possible, from within the media: not education to, but education in the media. The teacher must learn to look at the school from the point of view of new technologies and must not look at the new technologies from the perspective of the school. This leads to very important indications for the teacher: the need to adapt to the logic of improvisation, not as an alternative but as a possibility to actualize thought (a thought, therefore, that cannot be bound by a rigid idea of educational planning); the possibility of welcoming and valuing the relationship between extracurricular and intracognitive student identities. The concept of improvisation could create confusion in a delicate context such as the one just described. It must be considered from two different points of view. On the one hand, it should not be understood in the sense of the teacher who arrives unprepared and "improvises", but on the contrary corresponds to the behavior of the expert teacher who is able to draw from a vast repertoire of scripts and procedures at his disposal to offer an instant and effective response to the problem at hand [16, 17]. The expert teacher is an experimenter, a mediator between the context, with respect to which he/she has a very fine sensitivity, and his/her vast methodological knowledge. He/she acts through trial and error, developing a particular intuition [18, 19] which allows him/her to have a broad vision and predictive [20]. On the other hand, the teacher must take into consideration that in order to do this he/she must have an effective and flexible learning environment which can never be the result of improvisation It must be designed with great attention and awareness, because the students' experience will be characterized by the meaning of what they will do and experience in it.

4 An Approach to Teacher Technology Development

Based on the considerations expressed in the previous paragraph, the learning environment must be understood by the teacher as an "inclusive action space" where students and teachers interact; a place of cognitive as well as affective, emotional, interpersonal and social experiences; a place where learning is not simply understood as the acquisition of knowledge, where the teacher transmits knowledge to the student, but where an active and constructive process is established and implemented.

Currently the new technologies place the teacher in front of two different and contrasting panoramas:

- technologies designed and created through the analysis of teaching, and
- teaching designed and created through the analysis of technologies.

The technologies designed and created through the analysis of teaching represent a static situation, in which the teacher has specific tools at his disposal that can be used (in different ways) for the teaching action. The strengths of these applications are [21]: accessibility, which allows every student to use these tools at any time; the reuse of contents/activities for future work; easy review of content/activities already created; the possibility of creating interactive content/activities; the possibility of developing collaborative activities that facilitate active learning. As regards the weaknesses, it is necessary to highlight how these applications can be part of a learning environment but they are not very flexible regarding the emotional (and therefore motivational) aspect, because they present tools that (even if developed after having considered a wide spectrum of different situations) generalize the demands of active learning and are poorly adapted to the lifestyles that students have based on new information and communication technologies.

However, the teacher's research must not be limited to these tools, but must look at the entire panorama of new technologies, in order to identify those most useful to the class group to achieve the objectives of the teaching activity.

The learning environment should be functional, friendly and pleasant. To be functional, it must respond to the methodological and cultural premises and learning objectives, making the most of the specific characteristics of the tools used. To be enjoyable, it must take into account the reactions and preferences of the learner, encouraging their involvement and motivation. To be friendly it must take into account pre-existing habits and skills, preferring simple solutions to unnecessarily complicated ones and also taking into account the emotional component (and not just the rational one) of the learning processes.

Technologies must be appropriately selected and part of the learning environment in order to make it welcoming and stimulating for all students involved, even for those with cognitive difficulties.

From what has been said above it emerges that the concept of learning environment has a necessary and immediate relationship with the student: the student's performance increases if he/she is put in a position to be able to have an experience according to an acquisition method that brings him/her closer to the world (also technological) that surrounds him/her and in which reality lives. A reality that today sees Artificial Intelligence in the foreground.

4.1 An Overview of Student Technologies

The spread of artificial intelligence tools in education could really bring a digital revolution in classrooms through the transformation of teaching methodologies. Artificial intelligence can represent an engine for educational inclusion, for the personalization of both teaching and learning. Many technologies designed and created through the analysis of teaching have artificial intelligence algorithms that allow the needs of each individual student to be analyzed and segmented, who become unique, individual and with specific needs for the AI. It is still a sterile use of technologies. In a context of progressive increase in students with SEN or SLD it is essential to offer tools tailored to different learning styles. The solution can and must be found outside of applications designed specifically for teaching. In a constructivist context, it is not sufficient for an AI application to read a text or a response to the dyslexic student, or to create a concept map based on a written text. Hence the need to make the teacher more aware of the possibilities that different applications offer to help the student learn according to his/her lifestyle.

A first observation can therefore be made to Social Media (SM) which have become an integral part of students' lives. In addition to serving as communication platforms, these platforms connect common interests, thus strengthening relationships between students through online contacts. There are many social networks, each with different characteristics. It is up to each teacher to seek them out, inhabit them and analyze them in order to identify the useful characteristics for each class group.

WhatsApp with its instant messaging functions (which encourage immediate interaction between students and teachers, eliminating the delays associated with traditional communication methods) can enhance the learning process by encouraging collaboration (through group chat), sharing multimedia resources (texts, images, videos, audio) and active learning [5]. The possibility of receiving voice messages and therefore listening to the voice of another student or the teacher: strengthens the emotional aspect of communication and e-educational experience; favors the dyslexic student who can listen several times a message and better memorize information/ concepts, without having to read them; to develop listening skills and improve the acquisition of specific technical terminology or the pronunciation of words (or expressions) in a foreign language (a significant aid for the dyslexic student for whom the foreign language presents an insurmountable barrier).

Twitter (known as "X" since 2023) allows anyone to share short text messages (called tweets) that also contain an image. What may seem to be a limitation of MS in reality is the quality that distinguishes it: few characters stimulate creativity because it forces thought to be essential, teach pondering not only every word, but also every semicolon, and to give importance also the spaces, allowing each student to develop synthesis skills. This helps the dyslexic student on the one hand in reading (because he doesn't have to read long texts and doesn't get tired) and on the other it allows him/her to take advantage of his/her strength which is the ability to summarize. In general, it helps all students, even those with high academic performance, who must learn to communicate with a simple, effective language that is understandable by all [22]. The introduction of the hashtag (word preceded by the # symbol) to a message becomes an important resource for instantly identifying all the main tweets relating to a certain topic, facilitating data collection on specific topics [23]. The choice of hashtags also represents an important activity because it helps the student to develop the capacity for abstraction, identifying the words that could increase the number of people interested in the information in a message. This choice can be the result of an individual activity (by the individual student) or even the result of a group activity.

Another interesting SM for teaching is Instagram, a tool that is both camera and social media. It is an application that allows the possibility to take photographs, apply special filters that resemble analogue prints and share them in real time. It is possible to add captions, comments and hashtags to the photographs. These characteristics make it attractive, from an educational point of view, for dyslexic students: they prefer tools that facilitate visual memory (images, diagrams, maps, photographs) then multimedia materials in which images, graphs and key words are inserted. This allows them to quickly connect different concepts and construct a reasoned speech [24]. On Instagram the emotional component is therefore greater than on Twitter, as well as on other social networks.

The use of SM can therefore be considered in line with the constructivist approach with regard to various aspects: the production of forms of collaborative knowledge (technological dimension), the activation of teaching and learning processes (cognitive dimension), the development of social responsibility skills (ethical dimension of self-disclosure and the boundary between public and private space).

4.2 An Overview of the Future Technologies

The central theme of AI is its ability to select data to arrive at an answer that is more responsive to reality or the problem posed [25], Practical and already existing examples are the algorithms for generating mental and cognitive maps, automated text or subtitle transcription, and the more recent ChatGPT (Generative Pre-trained Transformer). It is a conversational bot (created by the OpenAI company) with an extraordinary capacity for linguistic argumentation which opens up to multiple implications: of a technical-scientific nature, of a methodological nature, of a philosophical nature. One of teachers' biggest concerns is that the use of artificial intelligence could reduce students' critical thinking. But in this case, it is necessary to draw teachers' attention to other points of view, useful for an effective learning process: artificial intelligence tools can be used for activities that require students to analyze and evaluate information from a text (created by ChatGPT), synthesize new ideas, engaging in debates and discussions (collaborative activity) to correct/modify the text. The fact that ChatGPT responses are often imprecise can become the subject of a critical thinking exercise. The teacher might lead students to try to trip ChatGPT (to make mistakes), or to rate its answer the way a teacher would rate a student's answer.

It is therefore a question of verifying the reality of AI as it presents itself, verifying its development without prejudice and trying to identify the guidelines within which to orient the development of educational research and teaching action. ChatGPT and similar tools based on artificial intelligence are now part of society and collective life, so it is important to teach students the strengths and weaknesses of these systems, to be able to work alongside them.

It is up to the teachers to guide the students in this new world.

5 Conclusions

It is undeniable that the extraordinary, unpredictable and very rapid changes in society require new and more advanced educational approaches, certainly incorporating new technologies and artificial intelligence. This requires the teacher to acquire new skills, which do not only correspond to knowledge, know-how and attitudes, but to the ability to mobilize different cognitive resources to cope with a certain type of educational situation, in some cases of difficulty and discomfort (just think of students with specific learning disabilities), which require "deciding in uncertainty and acting urgently", to achieve the educational objectives of all students.

On the basis of what has been outlined so far, it is possible to state that the scenario described, with all the limitations of the case, suggests at least the opportunity to continue to investigate to what extent new technologies (supported by artificial intelligence) can be useful for implementation of inclusive learning processes.

As mentioned, the theoretical perspectives which are today clear points of reference for the teacher who thinks about an inclusive educational and social system, offer an extremely fruitful background for reflecting on the potential that ICT offers in the teaching-learning process. This opens the way for certain improvements in the ability to understand and implement training practices, so as to intentionally and systematically overcome barriers or obstacles to learning and to ensure the effective participation of each and every one by giving everyone the opportunity to be proud of their own achievements.

Today, technologies offer the opportunity to respect the individuality of the student who learns in an independent, but at the same time engaging space within a stimulating learning community. The teacher becomes a facilitator of learning processes and can therefore be more proficient in personalizing each student's teaching strategies.

References

1. Ellis, W.J.R., Blamire, R., Van Assche, Frans: Innovative technologies for an engaging classroom (iTEC). In: Van Assche, F., Anido-Rifón, L., Griffiths, D., Lewin, C., McNicol, S. (eds.) Re-engineering the Uptake of ICT in Schools, pp. 1–15. Springer, Cham (2015). https://doi.org/10.1007/978-3-319-19366-3_1
2. Alosaimi, M.: The role of knowledge management approaches for enhancing and supporting education. Business administration. Université Panthéon-Sorbonne, Paris I (2016)
3. Besozzi, E.: Il processo di socializzazione nella società moderna e contemporanea. In: Ribolzi, L. (a cura di), Formare gli insegnanti. Lineamenti di sociologia dell'educazione, Carocci, Roma, pp. 23–47 (2002)
4. Besozzi, E.: Società, cultura, educazione, Roma, Carocci (2006)
5. Della Ventura, M.: Creating inspiring learning environments by means of digital technologies: a case study of the effectiveness of whatsapp in music education. EAI Endorsed Trans. e-Learning (J.) **4**, 1–9 (2017)
6. Hanson, R., Shapiro, S., Hutton-Thamm, E., Hagerty, M.R., Sullivan, K.P.: Learning to learn from positive experiences. J. Posit. Psychol. **18**(1), 142–153 (2023)
7. Della Ventura, M.: Compensatory skill: the dyslexia's key to functionally integrate strategies and technologies. In: Uden, L., Liberona, D. (eds.) LTEC 2022. Communications in Computer and Information Science, vol. 1595, pp. 153–163. Springer, Cham (2022). https://doi.org/10.1007/978-3-031-08890-2_12
8. Jia, L., Tan, R., Santi, M.: Teachers' understanding of inclusive education: comparing perspectives in China and Italy. Asia Pacific J. Educ. **44**, 1–13 (2022). https://doi.org/10.1080/02188791.2022.2066628
9. Hayes, R.L., Oppenheim, R.: Constructivism: reality is what you make it. In: Sexton, T.L., Griffin, B.L. (eds.) Constructivist Thinking in Counseling Practice, Research, and Training, pp. 19–40. Teachers College Press (1997)
10. Dewey, J.: Democracy and Education, An Introduction to the philosophy of education (1916)
11. Bruner, J.S.: La mente a più dimensioni. Ed. Laterza, Roma Bari (2003)
12. Vygotsky, L.S.: Thought and Language. MIT Press, Cambridge (1962)
13. Booth, T., Ainscow, M.: L Index per l'inclusione. Erickson (2008)
14. Calvani, A., Vivanet, G.: Tecnologie per apprendere: quale il ruolo dell'Evidence Based Education? J. Educ. Cult. Psychol. Stud. **10**, 83–112 (2014). https://doi.org/10.7358/ecps-2014-010-calv
15. Kanter, A.S., Damiani, M.L., Ferri, B.A.: The right to inclusive education under international law: following Italy's Lead. J. Int. Special Needs Educ. **17**(1), 21–32 (2015)
16. Ellis, R.: Teaching and research: options in grammar teaching. TESOL Q. **32**(1), 39–60 (1998)

17. Sawyer, R.K.: Creative teaching: collaborative discussion as disciplined improvisation. Educ. Res. **2**, 12–20 (2004)
18. Santi, M., Zorzi, E.: Verso la società del jazz? L'improvvisazione come "capabilty" nell'educazione inclusiva. Rivista Italiana di Educazione Speciale per l'Inclusione, pp. 13–32 (2020)
19. Eisner, E.: Two visions of education. Teach. Coll. Rec. **95**(4), 542–554 (2005)
20. Gagnon, R.: L'improvisation théâtrale au service de l'expression oral et écrite et so insegnament. Revue Suisse de sciences de l'éducation **33**(2), 251–265 (2011)
21. Adamoli, M., Masiero, J., Meneghetti, C.: Media Education, Analisi critica e buone pratiche. Libreriauniversitaria (2020)
22. Della Ventura, M.: Twitter as a Music Education Tool To Enhance The Learning Process: Conversation Analysis. In: Deng, L., Ma, W., Fong, C. (eds.) New Media for Educational Change: Effect on Learning and Reflection on Practice, pp. 81–88. Springer, People's Republic of China (2018). https://doi.org/10.1007/978-981-10-8896-4_7
23. Java, A., Song, X., Finin, T., Tseng, B.: Why we twitter: understanding micro-blogging usage and communities. Paper Presented at the Proceedings of the 9th WebKDD and 1st SNA-KDD 2007 Workshop on Web Mining and Social Network Analysis (2007)
24. Della Ventura, M.: Between research and action: the generative sense of technology. In: Rønningsbakk, Lisbet, Ting-Ting, Wu., Sandnes, Frode Eika, Huang, Yueh-Min. (eds.) ICITL 2019. LNCS, vol. 11937, pp. 754–763. Springer, Cham (2019). https://doi.org/10.1007/978-3-030-35343-8_78
25. Rainsberger, L.: Explanation: what is new and different about AI? In: Rainsberger, L. (ed.) AI - The New Intelligence in Sales: Tools, Applications and Potentials of Artificial Intelligence, pp. 1–16. Springer, Fachmedien (2022). https://doi.org/10.1007/978-3-658-38251-3_1

ERP Logs and Its Use for Process Mining Student Learning Purposes

Radim Dolak(✉), Tomas Barcak, and Michal Halaska

School of Business Administration in Karvina, Silesian University in Opava, 733 40, Karvina, Czechia

{dolak,barcak,halaska}@opf.slu.cz

Abstract. This paper deals with the possibility of using ERP logs for Process mining student learning purposes. The basic idea is that event logs from ERP systems are essential for Process Mining, as they provide the data necessary to gain insights into business processes. The availability of data in the form of event logs is crucial for the application of Process Mining techniques, enabling the discovery and analysis of business processes. Process Mining has been applied to manufacturing or logistic processes, with a focus on extraction, correlation, and abstraction of event data. Process Mining techniques offer valuable opportunities for organizations to analyze, monitor, and improve their real processes. However, challenges exist in extracting event logs from ERP systems, as the concept of business activity may be missing, making it difficult to use different tools on the same dataset. As part of this contribution, literature research in the given area will be carried out first and then a case study from the teaching will be presented.

Keywords: ERP logs · Process Mining · learning purposes

1 Introduction

An Enterprise Resource Planning (ERP) system as a data source for Process Mining research can have certain benefits. These systems integrate core company functions such as accounting, human resources, procurement, logistics, or manufacturing. We assume there is an important potential for using ERP logs for Process Mining analysis, especially for students in a field of study called Managerial Informatics. The main aim of this paper is to provide an overview of published basic research and case studies about using ERP logs Process Mining analysis as a practical study benefit.

The fundamental premise is that event logs from ERP systems are critical to Process Mining since they offer the information required to understand company processes. The capacity to uncover and analyze business processes through the application of Process Mining techniques is dependent on the availability of data in the form of event logs. Manufacturing and logistical operations have benefited from the application of Process Mining, which focuses on the extraction, correlation, and abstraction of event data. Process mining approaches present organizations with significant potential to examine, track, and enhance their actual processes.

Y.-P. Cheng et al. (Eds.): ICITL 2024, LNCS 14785, pp. 185–192, 2024.
https://doi.org/10.1007/978-3-031-65881-5_20

2 Literature Overview

The subsequent subchapters, such as ERP systems and student learning case studies, Process Mining and business processes, and Extraction of event logs from ERP systems, will make up the literature overview.

2.1 ERP Systems and Students Learning Case Studies

In the realm of Managerial Informatics, the integration of Enterprise Resource Planning (ERP) courses for students holds significant promise in preparing future professionals to navigate the complexities of modern business environments. The literature offers valuable insights into the design and implementation of ERP courses, shedding light on various aspects that can enhance the learning experience for students of Managerial Informatics.

The integration of ERP education into university curricula has the potential to enhance students' understanding of business processes, improve their problem-solving abilities, and prepare them for real-world challenges in organizations that utilize ERP systems. Alharbi [4] deals with highlights the positive impact of ERP systems on students' learning and understanding, aligning with the task of utilizing ERP logs for student learning. The case study was performed at the University of Jeddah, Saudi Arabia. There was a one-semester graduate course that was used to teach and assess the suggested framework. A survey was used to inferentially evaluate the course design, and the findings showed that the suggested framework improved students' learning outcomes. The assessment's findings confirm that employing open-source ERP systems in conjunction with experiential learning can result in better learning outcomes. The study by Nisula and Pekkola [12] provides valuable insights into the use of ERP-based business learning environments as a boundary infrastructure, offering a holistic approach to learning that aligns with the multidimensional nature of managerial informatics. This approach can be instrumental in providing students with a comprehensive understanding of ERP systems within the context of managerial informatics, bridging the gap between theoretical knowledge and practical application. Furthermore, the study by delves into the challenges associated with introducing ERP concepts to IT students using an experiential learning approach, emphasizing the need for a nuanced understanding of the learning process in the context of ERP education [5]. This insight is particularly relevant for designing ERP courses that resonate with students pursuing managerial informatics, as it underscores the importance of addressing the unique learning requirements of this specialized field.

2.2 Process Mining and Business Processes

Process mining is a valuable technique for gaining insights into business processes by analyzing event logs [6]. Event logs, such as those from ERP systems, serve as the foundation for process mining [8]. Furthermore, the use of process mining to analyze configuration logs for discovering configuration workflows based on user experiences demonstrates the versatility of this technique [15]. Additionally, process mining has been applied to analyze manufacturing processes based on event logs obtained from manufacturing execution systems, showcasing its applicability across various domains [7]. This paper demonstrated the utility of process mining in analyzing production planning in a global manufacturing company, emphasizing its ability to investigate variations and deviations from expected workflows. Yurtay [16] wrote the paper Process Mining in Manufacturing: A Literature Review. Process Mining has been applied also to the analysis of business processes in the banking and financial domain, as indicated by sources [10] and [13].

2.3 Extraction of Event Logs from ERP Systems

The main idea of business process mining is to extract the execution of business processes preserved in event logs, which are available in information systems like Enterprise Resource Planning (ERP) systems. This extraction facilitates the direct construction of business process models, comparison with existing models, and the enhancement of business processes. The researchers have suggested methods to handle the difficulties related to convergence, divergence, and the volume and structure of the data. The extraction of event logs from ERP systems is a crucial step for a variety of analyses. The goal of these methods is to make it possible to extract trustworthy event logs for process mining and business activity tracking. The extraction of event logs from ERP systems is crucial for process mining, as it allows for the discovery of knowledge based on the execution of activities within business processes [3]. Extracting event logs from ERP systems for process mining poses several challenges. Simovic et al. [14] highlighted that the resulting log may suffer from convergence and divergence issues when extracting event logs from ERP systems, leading to unreliable or confusing performance diagnostics [6, 14] also emphasized the challenges in extracting event logs from ERP systems, particularly the size and structure of the data, as well as the deficiencies related to convergence and divergence issues [6]. Classic process mining techniques typically require linear event logs as input, which may not align with the multi-dimensional relational databases used by ERP systems [11]. Despite these challenges, process mining techniques aim to extract knowledge from event logs to discover, monitor, and improve real processes [1, 2].

3 Case Study from the University Course About ERP

Students of Managerial Informatics are learning about the fundamental ideas and framework of integrated business information systems (ERP) in the course "Business Information Systems – ERP". This course covers particular solutions based on SAP, Oracle, K2, and MS Dynamics 365 Business Central systems.

3.1 K2 ERP System for Student Learning Purposes

The K2 ERP system is a comprehensive information system designed to manage various aspects of a business. It includes everything, including sales, financial, and managerial analysis, as well as manufacturing and inventory management. The K2 information system makes it possible to use the workflow to record and manage both simple processes, such as mail records or minutes of meetings, as well as to manage operational processes - such as invoicing, holidays, or production requirements. The operating system behaves according to the company's clearly defined ISO and proceeds with the processes only if all ISO-defined tasks are fulfilled.

We have started with the pre-implementation meetings between our university and company K2 covered the following topics:

- Extent of involvement of ERP system K2 in teaching
- Draft timetable
- Extent of responsibility for individual phases of implementation, roles of individual team members including system supplier
- Consultation with IT administrator and solution of system requirements for ERP K2
- Preparation of technological background at the university– installation of servers, accesses, etc.

The final technical decision was to implement an ERP system K2 with sample data for students on the faculty virtual server in collaboration with the distributor of the K2 ERP system. Working with an ERP system in a classroom setting, where students evaluate the functionality of the system, is completely different from working in a traditional production setting. Users in a production facility work for a certain company in a single database, interacting with one another through their activities. This cannot be resolved in the same manner as a teaching demonstration. Each student must use the same data in their database while working in the learning environment, according to the requirements outlined in the system. This entails duplicating the database containing the sample data and creating access for every user concurrently.

Finally, each student can use their account to try working with an information system based on sample data and create business process scenarios. We believe that the fully functional system will be used in instruction going forward, which will help students become more knowledgeable about ERP systems. Within the work, teaching examples for a basic orientation to the system have been built. In reality, using ERP systems is challenging since most users are only familiar with a small portion of the system; thorough training and a working understanding of the specific problems businesses face are necessary to become familiar with the ERP system. It is advisable to plan additional K2 system demos in the future so that the fundamental orientation can be expanded.

Another benefit is the partnership with K2 company, which allows students to participate in professional practice. The field of managerial informatics is included in the professional study programs of our university with a focus on real-world experience that meets employer demands. These needs of the modern education program are partially met by the opportunity to complete a practical internship at K2 company and by the practical teaching of ERP systems during university classes.

3.2 Process Mining Analysis in Disco for Student Learning Purposes

Accurate information on the working user's approach to resolving the practical tasks associated with using the ERP system can be obtained by tracking their activities in the ERP K2 system. We have tested tracking for teacher accounts, but we intend to attempt it with student accounts as well. We can obtain the following data structure by logging user activities in ERP system K2:

- Timestamp
- Action
- Startup Count
- Module identifier in K2
- Special K2 treatment
- Identifier of the action performed in K2
- Tracked action name
- Applications
- User

From the point of Process Mining analysis is for us the most important only some specific data structure. We can see a transformed activity log from ERP system K2 in the following Table 1.

Table 1. Activity Logs from ERP system K2

Date and time	Action	Module in K2	User
01.02.2024, 09:49:10	Distribution	TDeliveryOrderDM	1
01.02.2024, 09:50:23	Distribution items	TDeliveryOrderItemDM	1
01.02.2024, 09:51:27	Distribution items	TDeliveryOrderItemDM	1
01.02.2024, 09:52:29	Distribution items	TDeliveryOrderItemDM	1
01.02.2024, 09:54:28	Packing slips	TDeliveryNoteDM	1
01.02.2024, 09:56:25	Scheduled deliveries	TDeliveryPlanDM	1
01.02.2024, 09:58:26	Transport lines	TDeliveryLineDM	1
02.02.2024, 07:45:15	Confirmation Delivery	TDeliveryConfirmationDM	1

Source: ERP system K2

The acquired event log can then be imported into the Process Mining tool. In our case, we have used the university license for the Disco tool. Disco is a Process Mining tool developed by Fluxicon [9]. Company Fluxicon provides licenses for software Disco free of charge to students and research staff members of partner universities. We can see an example of process visualization in the following Fig. 1.

Source: Disco Process Mining tool

The main advantages of using logs from the ERP system for Process Mining during the tutorials and university courses are potentially as follows:

- students get a comprehensive overview of business processes and can reflect on any shortcomings of these processes,
- it is possible to use the generated logging data from the ERP system for the study purposes of other courses within the university teaching, such as Business Process Management or Modeling and Simulation,

Fig. 1. Example of Process map in Disco

- develop critical student thinking and problem-solving skills by identifying areas for improvement or optimization within a process,
- the teacher can compare the work speed and progress of individual students within the processing of the same assigned tasks for all students.

4 Conclusion

ERP courses in Managerial Informatics can significantly prepare students for modern business environments. The integration of ERP education into university curricula can enhance students' understanding of business processes, and problem-solving abilities, and prepare them for real-world challenges.

Studies have shown that using open-source ERP systems and experiential learning can improve learning outcomes. ERP-based business learning environments can bridge the gap between theoretical knowledge and practical application. However, challenges such as introducing ERP concepts to IT students using an experiential learning approach need to be addressed. Therefore, designing ERP courses that resonate with students pursuing managerial informatics is crucial.

It should be possible to gain benefits from using ERP system logs for Process Mining analysis in teaching university courses. Students can receive a thorough understanding of corporate procedures and can consider any inadequacies in these procedures. The logging data created by the ERP system can be utilized for the objectives of other university courses, such as Modeling and Simulation and Business Process Management.

Further research will aim to determine the possibilities of application in these above-mentioned courses. We assume that there is potential from the point of view of using process maps in order to encourage students to adopt a system thinking approach by considering how individual processes interact together, how to monitor real workflows, or how to develop critical student thinking and problem-solving skills by identifying areas for improvement or optimization within a process.

Acknowledgments. "This paper was supported by the Ministry of Education, Youth and Sports Czech Republic within the Institutional Support for Long-term Development of a Research Organization in 2024".

Disclosure of Interests. The authors have no competing interests to declare that are relevant to the content of this article.

References

1. Aalst, W.M.P.: Process mining. In: Liu, L., Özsu, M. (eds.) Encyclopedia of Database Systems, pp. 1–3. Springer, New York (2016). https://doi.org/10.1007/978-1-4899-7993-3_1477-2
2. Aalst, W.M.P.: Process mining manifesto. In: Daniel, F., Barkaoui, K., Dustdar, S. (eds.) Business Process Management Workshops. LNCS, vol. 99, pp. 169–194. Springer, Heidelberg (2012). https://doi.org/10.1007/978-3-642-28108-2_19
3. Aalst, W.M.P., Reijers, H., Song, M.: Discovering social networks from event logs. Comput. Support. Coop. Work **14**(6), 549–593 (2005). https://doi.org/10.1007/s10606-005-9005-9
4. Alharbi, B.: Development of an ERP system design course to improve students' learning outcomes. Int. J. Emerg. Technol. Learn. **16**(12), 276–288 (2021)
5. Beranič, T., Heričko, M.: Introducing ERP concepts to IT students using an experiential learning approach with an emphasis on reflection. Sustainability **11**(18), 4992 (2019)
6. Berti, A., Park, G., Rafiei, M., Aalst, W.M.P.: A generic approach to extract object-centric event data from relational databases supporting SAP ERP. J. Intell. Inf. Syst. **61**, 835–857 (2023)
7. Er, M., Arsad, N., Astuti, H., Kusumawardani, L., Utami, R.: Analysis of production planning in a global manufacturing company with process mining. J. Enterp. Inf. Manag. **31**(2), 317–337 (2018)
8. Fleig, C., Augenstein, D., Maedche, A.: Designing a process mining-enabled decision support system for business process standardization in ERP implementation projects. In: Weske, M. (ed.) BPM Forum 2018, LNBIP, vol. 329, pp. 228–244. Springer, Heidelberg (2018). https://doi.org/10.1007/978-3-319-98651-7_14

9. Fluxicon. https://fluxicon.com/disco/. Accessed 25 Feb 2024
10. Grigorova, K., Mironov, K., Malysheva, E.: Applying process mining techniques and neural networks to creating and assessment of business process models. In: Zaitsev, V.D. (eds.) International Conference on Information Technology and Nanotechnology, pp. 278–286 (2018)
11. Lu, X., Nagelkerke, M., Wiel, D., Fahland, D.: Discovering interacting artifacts from ERP systems. IEEE Trans. Serv. Comput. **8**(6), 861–873 (2015)
12. Nisula, K., Pekkola, S.: ERP based business learning environment as a boundary infrastructure in business learning. Educ. Inf. Technol. **24**(4), 2547–2566 (2019). https://doi.org/10.1007/s10639-019-09889-0
13. Pourmasoumi, A., Bagheri, E.: Business process mining. Encyclopedia Semantic Comput. Robotic Intell. **1**(1), 1630004 (2017)
14. Simovic, A., Babarogić, S., Pantelić, O.: Towards a domain-specific modeling language for extracting event logs from ERP systems. Appl. Sci. **11**(12), 5476 (2021)
15. Varela-Vaca, Á., Galindo, J., Ramos-Gutiérrez, B., Gómez-López, M., Benavides, D.: Process mining to unleash variability management. In: Proceedings of the 23rd International Systems and Software Product Line Conference, pp. 265–276. Association for Computing Machinery, New York (2019)
16. Yurtay, Y.: Process mining in manufacturing: a literature review. Sakarya University J. Comput. Inf. Sci. **5**(3), 341–355 (2022)

Digital Discussion Game on Values: Development, Use and Possibilities for Measuring Its Functionality

Mari-Liisa Parder[1], Anu Tammeleht[1](✉), Marten Juurik[1], Triin Paaver[1], Katrin Velbaum[1], and Halliki Harro-Loit[2]

[1] Centre for Ethics, University of Tartu, Tartu, Estonia
anu.tammeleht@ut.ee
[2] Institute of Social Studies, University of Tartu, Tartu, Estonia

Abstract. To develop dialogic communication for ethical decision-making and value clarification, a digital discussion game on values was designed as there was a lack in methodological tools targeting different age-groups and involving people in communities. The current article gives an overview of the methodology and development of a digital discussion game on values and proposes possibilities for measuring its effectiveness. The innovative game has a strong methodological grounding and initial feedback on the game's functionality indicates positive outcomes. Possibilities for measuring effectiveness of the game as well as future development ideas are suggested.

Keywords: digital game · value clarification · communication ethics · dilemma method

1 Introduction

During the 21st century, questions related to communication ethics and deliberative democracy are becoming increasingly important as value-conflicts and disagreements happen daily and challenge peoples' everyday lives. For influencing the societal decisions that have implications on people's lives, public engagement and participation is needed. This participation can happen through dialogic communication [1] which has been seen as an ethical approach to decision-making [2].

More specifically, dialogic communication is a skill consisting of four competences: 1) skills of listening and responding; 2) openness; 3) empathy; 4) mutual orientation [3–5]. These four competences are needed to facilitate dialogic communication and to understand other people better. To develop dialogic communication, a discussion game on values was designed as there was a lack in methodological tools for facilitating value clarification [6, 7].

The aim of the discussion game on values is to support people's ability to recognize moral choices of a given situation as well as to explain the moral choice that reflect their moral values. It is thus an educational ethics game which is based on understanding

Y.-P. Cheng et al. (Eds.): ICITL 2024, LNCS 14785, pp. 193–202, 2024.
https://doi.org/10.1007/978-3-031-65881-5_21

that most ethically problematic situations are "complex and inherently ambiguous" [8]. Ethical decision-making is a competence that may need special tools for training because of the complexities involved in many situations.

There are numerous examples [9–14] on how games have been used to facilitate ethical decision-making (from training business ethical decision-making to learning research integrity) and teaching ethics to different target groups (from organisations to student groups).

While there are various games available for development of values and ethics competencies, to our knowledge, none of them target different age-groups in the society and that would be aimed at developing ethical decision-making in communities. The current article will give an overview of the methodology and development of a digital discussion game on values and proposes possibilities for measuring its effectiveness.

2 Development of the Discussion Game on Values

The discussion game on values is fourth in the sequence developed by the University of Tartu Centre for Ethics. In the past decade discussion games on values have been developed for teachers [15] and medical workers [16] to practice professional values. There is also a game for pupils [17] to train skills relevant for having discussion on values.

The target group for the discussion game on values is considerably larger than the previous groups of teachers and medical workers, therefore choosing the values that the game concentrates on, was challenging. In addition, one of the aims of the game was simply to encourage meaningful discussion and deliberation between different age groups. Therefore, the focus was put on the types of moral decision-making as a starting point instead of specific values.

The narratives presented in the discussion game on values are based on ideas, themes and cases collected in the initial phase of the game in 2016 from discussion rounds with different stakeholders in the Estonian society as well as from media narratives. In addition, the work on methodological approach started in the initial phase of developing the game. When the methodological blueprint of the game was modelled, the development continued with working on the case narratives, blueprint, and testing simultaneously. In 2019 the narratives included in the game were finalised and the production of the paper form of the game kit was finished.

2.1 Methodology for the Discussion Game on Values

The value game consists of two basic ingredients: a narrative that includes a moral dilemma and 4 pre-given possible choices. The game uses the narrative approach, is based on people's written and told stories that are partly "products of their life experience which reflect their diverse cultural background" [18], and facilitates case-based learning [19].

The central element for the methodology narratives that include ethical considerations [20] and pre-given choices. Therefore, the methodology draws from narrative inquiry [21] where lived experiences can be expressed as narratives [22]. The central narrative has most of the elements of fully-fledged narrative [23], however, the resolution and coda are left for the participants to narrate based on their lived experiences. The constructed narrative (based on real life examples) is used to facilitate the personal narratives of the participants to facilitate dialogic communication.

The game does not encourage participants to select the "right" course of action. Instead, it emphasizes the process where participants consider various moral choices, carry out moral reasoning, listen to other players' justifications and finally negotiate and try to come to a solution everyone would agree on. As pointed out by Bucciarelli and Daniele [24]: "During our daily life we are often faced with choices that presuppose moral judgements, many of which elicit a moral conflict. Understanding the processes involved in moral judgements in general and the experience and resolution of conflict, have wide implications for all contexts involving intra- and inter-individual conflicts".

For gamification element, narrative approach also included well-known fairy tales and Estonian folk stories that are constructed into new narratives as well as fictional and humorous stories developed by the authors of the game.

All the narratives included in the game were carefully reconstructed by the development team according to the following aspects:

1. The viewpoint of the protagonist. Choosing the right protagonist is crucial, as the players need to make a choice from the protagonist's perspective. For this to work, the protagonist must be easy to identify with and cannot be too negative or exclusive. We also tried to provide a diversity of perspectives by having different protagonists, for example a balance of young, middle-aged, and elderly characters.
2. The actors and their relations. Our narratives are relatively short and provide only the minimal amount of information about the actors and their relations to understand the situation and the protagonist's dilemma. All superfluous descriptions and characteristics were left out, to make the narratives easily relatable to players with different life experience.
3. Deconstructing the dilemma to values and loyalties. In the original narratives the underlying values and loyalties in the protagonist's dilemma were intertwined, therefore we had to choose which values or loyalties to focus on. The narrative itself does not explicitly identify any values or loyalties, but the values and loyalties were used to construct the pre-given choices for players. The main aim of identifying the values and loyalties was to set a clearer focus for the dilemma and help us exclude additional value or loyalty conflicts that could shift the focus to new issues. Quite often we had to rewrite the whole narrative, add, or remove characters to achieve this.
4. The information about the motives of the actors were minimized. We provided minimal information about the motives of the actors to give more room for interpretation based on the lived experience and life narratives of players. The aim was to imitate similar situations in real life, where the actual motives of other people are often not explicit, verbalised or otherwise known. This also directs the players to think why the actors act in a certain way, which presumes at least some level of empathy.
5. Limiting the temporal dimension. The temporal scope of the narrative should be focused on the narrative. Sometimes the narrative provided some background information from previous events, but the pre-given choices for the player were always related to the dilemma at hand and decisions were related to one temporal moment

in the narrative. Sometimes we provided the choice not to do anything. The aim was again to have a clear focus. If the narrative covered more than one episode, there would be more conditions that should be taken into consideration.

6. Balancing the dilemma. As in real life there is no easy and obvious right answer for each situation in the value game. We tried to write the narrative in a neutral way and to make sure that all the pre-given choices were morally acceptable from a certain perspective or moral theory. We specifically tried to avoid choices or options that were too good or too bad, otherwise the players would choose the obviously best option and the game would not work.

One of the key features of the game is that players can choose between four pre-given courses of action. These choices are constructed on the basis of main moral theories and are named for gamification moment as characters: deontological (character: hero); teleological/utilitarian (character: ruler); care ethics (character: healer) and the fourth approach that could be labelled as "keeping good relations" (character: merchant).

There were several reasons to have pre-given choices. Firstly, the pre-given ethical choices enable save the time concerning the recognition of a moral situation, secondly, it helps to focus on reasoning about the selected choice and negotiating with other players, and thirdly, it facilitates the discussion over the choices (instead of just agreeing with the first suitable solution that might come to people's minds). An example case from the game can be found in Fig. 1.

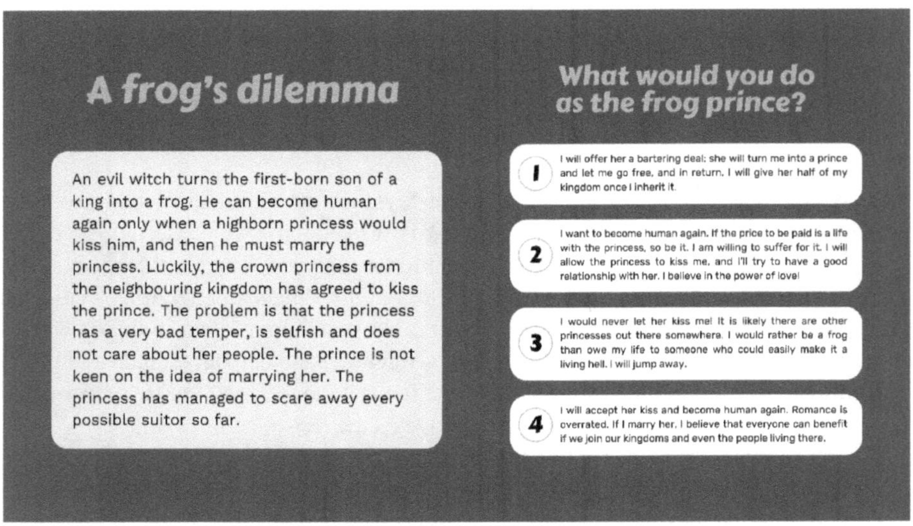

Fig. 1. Visual representation of the example case.

2.2 Digitalisation of the Game

As the paper game weighed 2,6 kg and used a considerable amount of non-sustainable material (6 books, 104 cards), it was decided to digitalise the game to make it available for a larger number of users, and to use fewer resources. The challenge of digitalisation was to preserve the essence of the game – discussion. In addition, the digital game had to be as intuitive as the paper game. The first version of the digital game was developed on the platform Mockitt Wondershare [25] showing some previews and having minimal functionality.

The digitalisation process began with prototyping at the University's Sandbox as part of the course "Digital Product Management Industry Project". Students from the Institute of Computer Science worked out how to digitalise the game by finding a suitable format. Our preference was to be browser-based and with mobile first views, to be as accessible as possible and usable with all devices (computers, laptops, smart devices). From the work of the students, a game prototype in the *Figma* [26] design platform was developed with documentation of the process, including user personas, playing scenarios, and testing.

Parallel to the Sandbox development, a philosophy PhD student started to develop the game on *Unity Technologies* [27] to try to build the application version. Unfortunately, it was a dead end due to extensive workload and the cost of app-building in general. In addition, browser-based online game is more accessible and provides similar gaming experience to different age groups.

Based on the students' initial prototype, a professional developer was searched to build the game. The company *Redwall* [28] took on the task and all the previous work was also shared with them. The process began with the company familiarizing itself with the game and drawing main development points from the interview with us as the client. Main functionalities of the game were focused on making the digital game as similar to the paper version as possible. The development of the digital game took 6 months with additional 2 months for user/client testing, which includes technical and user-based testing with different target groups (those who were already familiar with the paper game as well as those who had no experience with the game) and deciding on the final narratives to be added to the digital game. The game was released on 30th of October 2023 and includes 30 narratives. Currently, the game is available only in Estonian. Link here: https://100valikut.ut.ee/.

3 Preliminary Evaluation of the Functionality and Perceived Influence of the Game

We are constantly collecting feedback on the game: firstly, the digital game collects statistics about gameplay; in addition, the game (both the paper version and the digital version) has been used in various settings from ethics courses to community building activities where user experience and general feedback has been collected (as part of Tartu World University events). Data has not been collected for research purposes.

Our research team has also piloted data collection from participants using the digital game with focusing on monitoring the group dynamics and development of values during the discussion. During the piloting our goal was to investigate the *CoTrack* application possibilities for the game played solely online. We did not intend to draw significant conclusions on the data, instead we could affirm the suitability of the application for monitoring group dynamics

For the pilot we invited four volunteers to play the digital value game and utilised the *CoTrack* [29] application (see more about the development and functionality of the application at [30]) to monitor the group dynamics (no recordings were made), took notes on the discussed values and conducted a short focus group at the end of the discussion. All the group members were familiar with the boardgame format of the game. The piloting group chose two narratives in the digital game to discuss (the Big Bad Wolf and seven Goat Kids – juvenile delinquency; Snow-white and seven Dwarves in the emergency room). The first case was discussed for about 10 min until the group consensus was reached, the second took about 11 min (the game has a function to take time during the discussion). The group dynamics is displayed in Fig. 2.

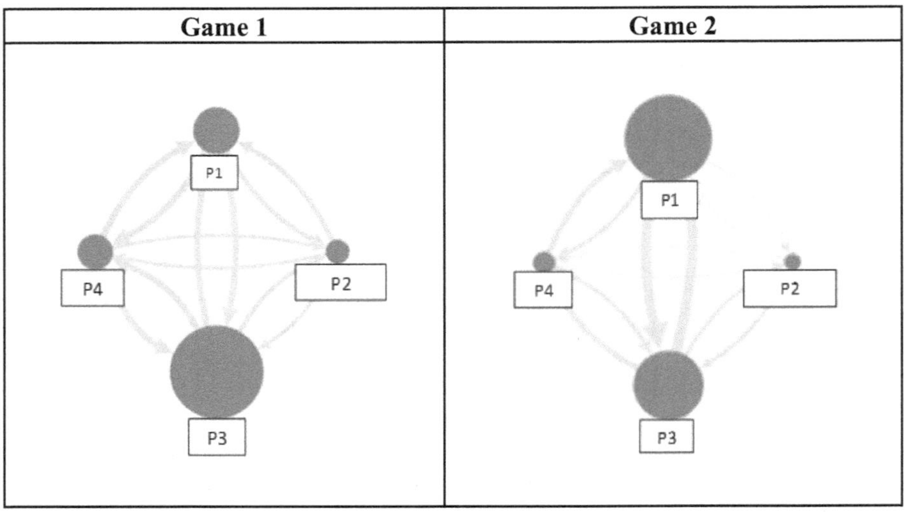

Fig. 2. Group dynamics of playing the digital discussion game on values for the pilot study group (P1–4 – participants 1–4).

The *CoTrack* graphs (in Fig. 2) display the dominance the participants had during the game. During the first case P3 (Participant 3) spoke more as this was the only participant who had played the digital game before, so others needed scaffolding to manage the game. In addition, equal lines between participants indicate that they all addressed each other and took turns to speak. The second case took a bit more time to speak and here the group dynamics indicate that some participants communicated more than others – P1 and P3 have bigger dots and the lines between them are thicker – they talked to each other more than others. P2 spoke less to P1 and P4 – the lines are thin, P3 seems to be linked to all participants.

Monitoring the content of the discussion indicated that while all participants came to the game with their own values and opinions, they were inclined to finding a group response. During the first game three participants picked the same option, even though they all had different reasons for doing it (one wanted to address the group as a leader, one considered that option the 'softest' and it would bring about the least harm, one thought that this course of action could be threatening but perhaps the result would be the best). One participant (P2) picked a different option (treating everyone in the group equally), at the end of the discussion P2 agreed to join the option others had chosen. During the second game all participants chose a different option (the reasons being: the principle of justice, speculation, compassion, seriousness of the situation). Choices of participants can be seen in Fig. 3.

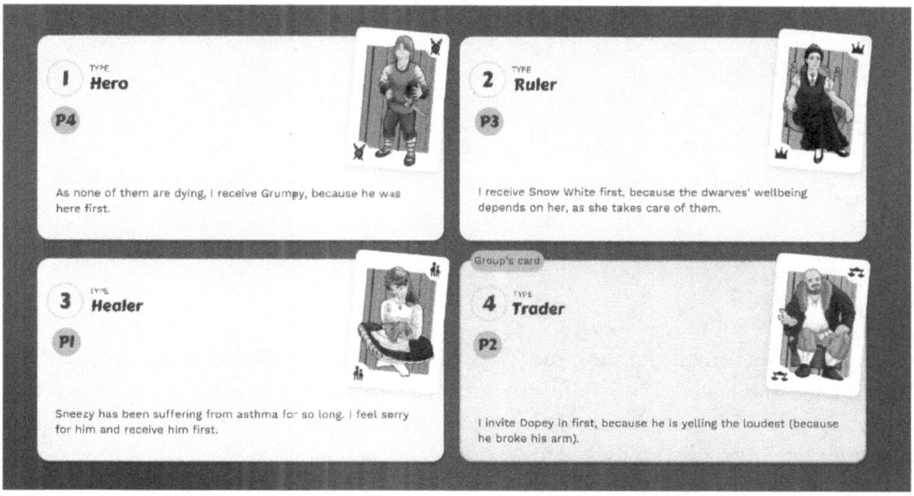

Fig. 3. Choices made by participants during the second game.

The second time the discussion took a bit longer, but eventually all participants agreed to vote for the option chosen by P2 – the arguments were convincing but not oppressive. Based on the group dynamics graph (see Fig. 2) it can be concluded that even if the person is not the most dominant in the group, others will listen and accept their arguments and they can have an impact on the group decision.

At the end of the game the group can also receive feedback about their moral compass by the digital platform – in both cases the group decision followed the 'merchant's' profile (Fig. 4 on the right), even though the original decisions may have been different (Fig. 4 on the left).

During the focus group conducted after the game the participants displayed satisfaction with the digital game. They said that the digital game looked appealing, it was clear and engaging. It was easy to play as everything was intuitively grasped (the game was perceived as user-friendly), functionality was considered good. The group thought it would be easier to play on the computer than on the smartphone or tablet. The group found that the elderly may need help to engage with the activity, but playing the value game could be organised in the daycentres for the elderly. Other age-groups would probably find it easy to play the game online. Also, engaging with more than one narrative increases the smoothness of the discussion and understanding each other's values and opinions.

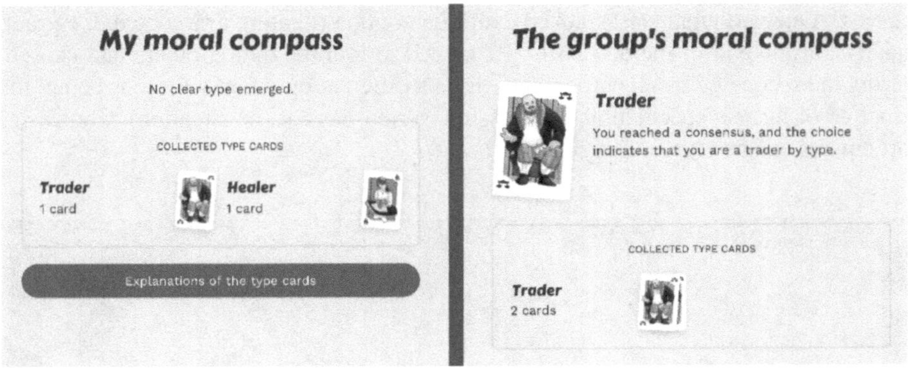

Fig. 4. Feedback to the players after playing the game: individual (on the left) and group (on the right).

4 Conclusion

In this article we provided a short overview of the methodology and development of the digital game and tested a possibility for measuring functionality of the game as a tool for raising people's awareness of their own and other people's moral thinking and moral reasoning.

The general feedback gathered from communities and the initial findings of the pilot study indicate that the game may be effective in enhancing ethical decision-making as well as moral reasoning. In everyday life, discussions about value choices usually need a catalyst, and this catalyst may be a situation where a value conflict is already heating up the conversation. The discussion game on values allows people to come together and listen to each other in playful situations. For example, some of the narratives are constructed as parodies of fairy tales or as humorous stories. However, most of the narratives are similar to people's everyday lives and encourage players to think about moral choices from different perspectives of the protagonists.

We are aware of the limitations of the pilot study - the sample size was small and personal characteristics could have played their role. Still the main goal of the pilot was to test the suitability of the *CoTrack* application as well as other means to collect data on group and individual competence development. For the future studies we are interested in evaluating the effectiveness of the game on value development and ethical sensitivity of the players. The pilot study has indicated possibilities to monitor group dynamics, there are also tools available for measuring ethical sensitivity that could be used.

We intend to continue development of the digital game as there has been international interest towards sharing it. The next step is to include the language options starting with English even though translations may be challenging as many of the stories are well-known only in Estonia and would carry values and loyalties of Estonians.

Based on the methodology, there are possibilities for developing the game in different directions. One of the directions currently in progress is communication ethics where players can take different perspectives in the same situation.

Acknowledgments. We would like to thank authors of the first paper version who are not authors of this article: Õnne Allaje, Tiia Kõnnussaar, Laura Lilles-Heinsar, Heidy Meriste, Kertu Rajando, Professor Margit Sutrop and the individuals and groups who helped to test different versions of the game and gave valuable feedback. For developing the digital game our special thanks go to Õnne Allaje-Kukk who made the first mock-up and pushed us to develop it with the help of computer science master students. We thank Redwall OÜ for developing the product and ongoing cooperation. Developing the paper version of the game was supported by the Ministry of Education and Research program "Values Development in Estonian Society 2009-2013" follow-up program for years 2014-2020. The digitalisation process was supported by the University of Tartu Developing Fund grant to a project "Developing values games to be accessible in virtual environment". The game has been used in the activities of Tartu World University, which is an official part of the main program of the European Capital of Culture Tartu 2024. Writing of this article was supported by DIACOMET ("Fostering capacity building for civic resilience and participation: Dialogic communication ethics and accountability") project funded from the European Union's Horizon Europe research and innovation grant agreement No 101094816.).

Disclosure of Interests. The authors have no competing interests to declare that are relevant to the content of this article.

References

1. Kent, M.L., Taylor, M.: Building dialogic relationships through the World Wide Web. Public Relat. Rev. **24**(3), 325 (1998)
2. Browning, N.: The ethics of two-way symmetry and the dilemmas of dialogic Kantianism. J. Media Ethics **30**(1), 3 (2015)
3. Kent, M.L., Taylor, M.: Toward a dialogic theory of public relations. Public Relat. Rev. **28**(1), 21–37 (2002)
4. Taylor, M., Kent, M.L.: Dialogic engagement: clarifying foundational concepts. J. Public Relat. Res. **26**(5), 384–398 (2014)
5. Yang, S.-U., Kang, M., Cha, H.: A study on dialogic communication, trust, and distrust: testing a scale for measuring organization–public dialogic communication (OPDC). J. Public Relat. Res. **27**(2), 175–192 (2015)
6. Simon, S.B., Olds, S.W.: Helping Your Child Learn Right From Wrong: A Guide to Values Clarification. Simon and Schuster, New York (1976)
7. Kirschenbaum, H.: Values clarification in counselling and psychotherapy. Practical strategies for individuals and group settings. Oxford University Press, New York (2013)
8. Nardo, A., Gaydos, M.: 'Wicked problems' as catalysts for learning in educational ethics games. Ethics Educ. **16**(4), 492–509 (2021)
9. Cohen, H.: The citicorp interactive work ethic game: sociological practice use in the classroom. Clin. Sociol. Rev. **11**(1), 14 (1993)
10. Nelson, J.: The market ethic: moral dilemmas and microeconomics. J. Bus. Ethics **11**, 317–332 (1992). https://doi.org/10.1007/BF00872174
11. Baldor, R.A., Field, T.S., Gurwitz, J.H.: Using the 'question of scruples' game to teach managed care ethics to students. Acad. Med. **76**(5), 510–511 (2001)
12. Bekir, N., Cable, V., Hashimoto, I., Katz, S.: Teaching engineering ethics: a new approach. In: ASEE/IEEE Frontiers in Education Conference (2001)
13. Dilemma: A board game for teaching sustainable development. http://www.jonerikdahlin.com/dilemma/. Accessed 14 Mar 2024

14. Dilemma Game: Professionalism and Integrity in Research. https://www.eur.nl/en/about-eur/policy-and-regulations/integrity/research-integrity/dilemma-game. Accessed 14 Mar 2024
15. Sutrop, M.: Can values be taught? The myth of value-free education. Trames **19**(2), 189–202 (2015)
16. Values Game for Medics: Centre for Ethics, University of Tartu. https://eetika.ee/en/content/values-game-medics. Accessed 14 Mar 2024
17. Discovering Values – a values game for students. Centre for Ethics, University of Tartu. https://eetika.ee/en/content/discovering-values-values-game-students. Accessed 14 Mar 2024
18. Hyry-Beihammer, E.K., Lassila, E.T., Estola, E., Uitto, M.: Moral imagination in student teachers' written stories on an ethical dilemma. Eur. J. Teach. Educ. **45**(3), 435–449 (2022)
19. Bagdasarov, Z., et al.: An investigation of case-based instructional strategies on learning, retention, and ethical decision-making. J. Empir. Res. Hum. Res. Ethics **7**(4), 79–86 (2012)
20. Pawlukewicz, J., Ondrus, S.: Ethical dilemmas: the use of applied scenarios in the helping professions. J. Soc. Work Values Ethics **10**(1), 2–12 (2013)
21. Bamberg, M.: Why narrative? Narrat. Inq. **22**(1), 202–210 (2012)
22. Riessman, C.: Narrative Methods for the Human Sciences. Sage Publications, Thousand Oaks (2008)
23. Labov, W.: Language in the Inner City. Univ. of Pennsylvania Press, Philadelphia (1972)
24. Bucciarelli, M., Daniele, M.: Reasoning in moral conflicts. Think. Reason. **21**(3), 265–294 (2015)
25. Mockitt Wondershare. https://mockitt.wondershare.com/home.html. Accessed 14 Mar 2024
26. Figma design. https://www.figma.com/. Accessed 14 Mar 2024
27. Unity Technologies. https://unity.com/. Accessed 14 Mar 2024
28. Redwall: Mõtleme. Loome. Lahendame. https://www.redwall.ee/. Accessed 14 Mar 2024
29. CoTrack website. https://www.cotrack.website/et/. Accessed 25 Apr 2024
30. Chejara, P., Prieto, L.P., Ruiz-Calleja, A., Rodríguez-Triana, M.J., Shankar, S.K., Kasepalu, R.: EFAR-MMLA: an evaluation framework to assess and report generalizability of machine learning models in MMLA. Sensors **21**(8), 2863 (2021)

Strategies in Digital Child Protection

Synnøve Thomassen Andersen(✉)

UiT, The Arctic University of Norway, Follumsvei 31, 9510 Alta, Norway
Synnove.T.Andersen@uit.no

Abstract. Digital child protection faces numerous challenges in ensuring the safety and well-being of children in the digital age. This chapter highlights key strategies for handling these challenges and discusses Norway's digital strategy, which focuses on leveraging digitalization for societal development and public services, including child protection. The strategy encompasses initiatives related to digital transformation, infrastructure, skills and education, data security and privacy, and digital inclusion. Digital transformation is a crucial aspect of child protection, involving the integration of technology for early detection, streamlined reporting, and collaboration between relevant stakeholders. A competence model for digital guides on the essential skills and competencies needed within government agencies to navigate digital transformation effectively. The new administrative digital system for child welfare is presented. In conclusion, addressing challenges in digital child protection requires comprehensive strategies encompassing legislation, collaboration, education, technology, and international cooperation. These strategies aim to create a safer digital environment for children and ensure their protection from online risks and harm.

Keywords: Digital Child Protection · Public Services · Digital System

1 Introduction

This paper presents strategies for handling some challenges related to integrated child and youth protection systems, more specifically the digital in child protection. The digital in child protection is a large and comprehensive topic, including different levels and user groups in society. Norway is used as an example to refine this topic. The article first briefly presents the work with digital transformation for the Norwegian government, second, the model for knowledge/learning of technology by the Directorate for Digitalization (Digdir), and at last the new administrative digital system for Norwegian Child welfare. The digital strategy for Norway (2019–2025) follows up Meld. St. 27 [15]. The strategy is cross-sectoral and defines the common goals and focus areas for digitalization activities towards 2025 and will support digital transformation throughout the entire public sector[1].The Directorate of Digitization is the Norwegian government's foremost tool for faster and more coordinated digitization of society[2]. Part of the presentation of

[1] Kommunal- og moderniserigsdepartementet, 2019.
[2] Digdir.no.

Y.-P. Cheng et al. (Eds.): ICITL 2024, LNCS 14785, pp. 203–212, 2024.
https://doi.org/10.1007/978-3-031-65881-5_22

the digital strategy for Norway, Digdir, and the new administrative system is translated by the author from the website regjeringen.no, Digdir, and Bufdir.

1.1 Digital Transformation

There is no unique definition of the term Digital Transformation. There are also inconsistencies in the existing literature [3], and several researchers claim that there is a lack of a universal and comprehensive understanding of the digital transformation concept [6, 8, 9, 13]. This situation can lead to researchers and practitioners having challenges in promoting the theory and practice of the subject [19]. Research and review of the term Digital Transformation shows that it has implications at several levels of analysis [24]. However, the term Digital Transformation is also used inconsistently by managers in various businesses to describe various strategies and organizational activities [25], which can trigger different disciplines within research and influencing practice [10]. Consistent definition of digital transformation provides clearer means for researchers to communicate with practitioners and to provide them with better prescriptions to understand and develop digital transformation [14]. A unified definition of digital transformation has been developed to bring some clarity about this concept and its associated core primitives and defining attributes [7]. The unified definition of digital transformation is as follows:

> *"A fundamental change process, enabled by the innovative use of digital technologies accompanied by the strategic leverage of key resources and capabilities, aiming to radically improve an entity* and redefine its value proposition for its stakeholders."* (*An entity could be: an organization, a business network, an industry, or society.) [7, p.12, 2021].

1.2 The Norwegian Strategy

The Norwegian Digitalization Agency is the Norwegian government's foremost tool for faster and more coordinated digitalization of the Norwegian public sector. The Norwegian Digitalization Agency are subordinate to the Ministry of Local Government and Regional Development[3]. The Norwegian government's digital strategy [20] describes digital transformation as:

- *a process where the business changes how it performs its tasks, offers better services, works more efficiently, or creates entirely new services*
  - where user focus and the user experience are the core of the change
  - which is based on the use of digital technology
- *a fundamental and comprehensive change, and not a minor adjustment*
- *redesign of the business at all levels – people, processes, technology, and management*

The Norwegian strategy (Digdir.no, 2019–2025[4]) points out 6 topic as particularly important for public administration related to digital transformation, 1) User Orientation

[3] Digdir.no.
[4] Hva er digital transformasjon? | Digdir.

and Experience, 2) Digital Technology, 3) Business and management, 4) Innovation, 5) (Exploit) data and 6) The Ecosystem. The citizens' expectations of more connected services and new enabling technologies place great demands on the public sector. To meet some of these challenges, you need digital transformation.

2 Competence-Model for Digital Transformation

The Norwegian government by Digdir has developed a competence model[5] for digital transformation. The model has three levels that build on each other and should provide a comprehensive picture of the need for expertise in your business and the public sector. The three levels are:

1. **Policy and overall guidelines -** Provide an overall introduction to the political guidelines in the area and understand the social significance of working with digital transformation, and how your business can change the fundamental ways in which it solves its tasks with the help of technology.
2. **Management of digital transformation** - Introduce what digital transformation entails for the business and what it requires of managers inspire how to work with the development of digital transformation in the business.
3. **Professional knowledge and skills -** Contribute to managers being able to work systematically both with their expertise and to provide support for building expertise in the business giving academia and suppliers an incentive to package current and future offers in a way that supports the government's goals.

Digdir has developed an overview that shows specialist knowledge and skills for digital transformation.

3 The Norwegian Child Welfare Services

3.1 Child Welfare

The primary aim of child welfare services is to ensure that children and young people living under conditions that may harm their health and development will receive the necessary assistance when they need it, and to contribute to giving children and youth safe conditions for growing up[6]. See a short introductory film from Bufdir[7].

3.2 Division of Responsibility in the Child Welfare Services

Both the local and central authorities have duties and responsibilities in the child welfare field, and the municipality is responsible for performing those functions under the Child Welfare Services Act which are not assigned to a central government body. All municipalities must have child welfare services that are responsible for the day-to-day work

[5] Kompetansemodell for digital transformasjon | Digdir.

[6] Child Welfare - regjeringen.no.

[7] How can Child Welfare Services help? YouTube.

under the Act[8]. The child welfare services are responsible for providing advice and guidance, undertaking investigations, and making administrative decisions under the Child Welfare Services Act. The purpose of the Act is to ensure that children and young people who live in conditions that may be detrimental to their health and development receive the necessary assistance, care, and protection at the right time. Anyone can find themselves in a situation where they need help and support to provide proper care for their children. The Child Welfare Services must provide help to families in such cases. The Act is intended to help ensure that children and young people are met with security, love, and understanding [12]. The ministry ensures that experiences gained from the application of the Act are evaluated and then undertakes the necessary amendments.

3.3 BUFDIR and BUFETAT

The Norwegian Directorate for Children, Youth and Family Affairs (Bufdir) and five regional offices under the central authority; Office for Children, Youth and Family Affairs (Bufetat) are responsible for matters relating to state-funded child welfare services, family counseling, and adoption (Directorate for Children, Youth and Family Affairs). The main task is to provide children, young people, and families in need of help and support with appropriate, high-quality assistance nationwide.

4 The Project: Digibarnevern

The social mission of the Child Protection Agency is to help children and young people. The municipal child welfare service manages values and power and manages legal security for children and families. To achieve this, child welfare services need good tools and solutions. But neither the families who were in contact with child welfare, the employees, the managers nor the child welfare partners have received sufficient support and information from the digital solutions that were used before 2023. However, not all county in Norway have implemented the new digital solution which is presented in this chapter. The Bufdir presented some feedback from the different actors before the project Digibarnevern were established (DigiBarnevern I Bufdir). The main points were:

- Employees receive too little help in existing subject systems to work efficiently and responsibly.
- Managers get too little and too much poor information to lead and report.
- Child welfare services cooperate too little with other services and lack good one's solutions for digital communication and transfer of information.
- Children, youth, and guardians lack an overview of their own cases, and assessments, and connections in the child protection case are not documented, and the possibility of the desired degree of digital participation.

Based on this, a national project called DigiBarnevern (Digital Child Welfare) was established in 2016 to increase child welfare services' ability to provide good and effective help to children and youth who need it. DigiBarnevern consists of two projects, a 8th

[8] Division - regjeringen.no.

municipal, and a state project. The project´s aim was to increase the quality of municipal childcare, among other things by providing better technological solutions.

Children and families who need help must receive help that works at the right time. They must meet a cooperative child protection system that provides real participation and must provide strengthened legal certainty. DigiBarnevern will also contribute to ensuring that child welfare services are experienced as safe for the children, provide equal services, and that trust in child welfare services is strengthened.

Digdir points out four major challenges associated with Child protection [18]:

- The task solution in child protection
- The distribution of responsibility between the state and the municipality
- The need for competence in child protection
- Use of private actors in child protection

4.1 National Portal for Reporting Concerns

The first part of DigiBarnevern, the National portal for reporting concerns, was presented in 2020. The reports of concern are sent securely and quickly to the child welfare services digitally and contribute to messages being more specific about what the concern is about. This contributes to a more secure assessment of the content of the reports of concern. The solution also allows you to send messages of concern directly from specialist systems in other sectors (no time delays) for example schools, kindergartens, and health and both the child welfare service and the dispatcher service achieve savings by avoiding double registration and improved work processes. The municipalities that have adopted the service report that the content of the messages is more specific and aimed at the conditions surrounding the children that are considered worrying. By the end of 2021, the portal had been used by over 187 municipalities and made available to more than 4 million residents.

4.2 Child Welfare Professional Quality System (CPS)

The next part of the project was presented in 2022. The Child welfare professional quality system (CPS) is a framework that provides child welfare professional and legal quality support, especially for the discretionary parts of case management. The system helps to strengthen the quality and legal certainty of the proceedings. Bufdir points out that the knowledge on which the Child Protection quality system is anchored contributes to a common and solid child protection professional platform for the employees in the service. "The child's needs in the Centre" forms a central part of the content of CPS, in addition to other forms of support. Attention directed to the child's needs and the child's best interests provides both a structure and a knowledge base for the child protection service's work in all phases of a child protection case. When the case manager receives quality-assured support in the case management itself, this has an impact on the manager's overview, control, and time spent. Bufdir maintains and updates the content according to changes of both a legal and child welfare nature. Bufdir, in collaboration with Statistics Norway, is also working on establishing a new reporting solution for the state.

4.3 National Child Protection Register

National Child Protection Register simplifies and streamlines reporting through automatic reporting via new professional systems safer and faster-updated knowledge base for the central government. The reporting solution will also ensure automatic extraction of data from the municipalities' professional system, and ensure a better data basis for management, service development, and research. Concept catalog improves communication through unambiguous, official definitions of terms used in child protection. National Child Protection Register solution will free up time for both the manager and employees of the municipal child welfare since they will spend significantly less time on reporting. There is no need to check that the data is correct and that you report within the deadline, and thus have time to extract insights from the figures, among other things.

4.4 Dialogue Between Partners

These three systems interact with each other and make better dialogue between partners. The child welfare professional quality system provides, support for cooperation and dialogue, implementation and documentation of analysis and assessments and a clearer decision-making basis. Most important is better information for children and parents and a clear connection between the phases and processes in the child protection case. The child welfare professional quality system emphasizes participation and involvement from children, young people, and parents throughout the entire course of the child welfare case. This includes, among other things, good information for those about whom the case is concerned, and about planning so that children, young people, and parents can recognize the information in the case. The case manager receives support to document analyzes and assessments in the case, so that the basis for ongoing and final decisions is presented in the case's documentation.

5 Challenges in Digital Child Protection

Digital child protection faces several challenges that need to be addressed to ensure the safety and well-being of children in the digital age.

Existing Legislation: One of the primary challenges in digital child protection is the need for adequate legislation that can effectively address the evolving risks and harms children face online. Existing laws may not be comprehensive enough or may not have kept pace with the rapid advancements in technology. However, the UN Convention on the Rights of the Child (CRC) recognizes children as rights holders and provides them with individual rights. It is crucial to have clear and updated laws that can appropriately deal with issues such as online grooming, cyberbullying, child pornography, and exploitation. Child welfare workers are bound by the requirements of the law and follow the guidelines for child welfare with children and youth in general. Researchers claim that "*we must also address the question of access to technologies which has important social justice implications beyond the question of solely whether ICT can be utilized*" [21, p.1495]. New laws and guidelines need to be developed that take into account the particularities of the Internet and where it intersects with the child welfare services' exercise of public authority. There are certainly challenges in digital child protection and existing legislation. Artificial intelligence has been used in products targeting children for several years, but legislation protecting them from the potential impacts of the technology is still in its infancy. UNICEF has developed a draft Policy Guidance on AI for Children to promote children's rights and raise awareness of how AI systems can uphold or undermine these rights.

Education: Lack of awareness and education among children, parents, and educators about online risks and safety measures is a significant challenge. Child welfare and social workers need to move thoughtfully and assisted by research, develop applications that enhance service user participation [21]. Children need to be educated about responsible digital citizenship, privacy protection, recognizing and responding to online threats, and seeking help when needed. Parents and educators also need to be equipped with the knowledge and skills to guide and support children in their online activities. How child welfare workers understand, navigate, and use social media and different digital systems is of central importance to the future of child welfare work.

Ethics: Balancing the ethical considerations of child protection with the need for privacy and freedom of expression is a complex challenge. While it is crucial to protect children from harm, it is equally important to respect their rights and autonomy. Ensuring ethical practices in digital child protection requires careful navigation of these competing interests. Researchers claim that "*an ethical dilemma in the tension between children's need for protection, provisions, and participation. The Internet offers both pleasures and worries, risks and possibilities. It is complex, a different arena for children to navigate and for social workers to follow in the digital landscape. One aspect of this is that even very young children have access*" [4, p.241].

Digital Competence: Digital competence is becoming a critical factor for the digital transformation capability of government agencies and their ability to realize benefits from digitalization. Due to intensive digitalization in the public sector, employees and managers in welfare sectors need to have the necessary competence to see and utilize the opportunities provided by new technologies. For social workers in Norway, like many in other technology-driven societies, digital competence is now a professional capability measure. The Norwegian Regulation on National Guideline for Social Work Education requires explicitly that higher education institutions should help their students to 'master digital tools, including knowledge of digital security, and be able to assist in the development and use of suitable technology, and know their opportunities and limitations in practice' [16]. UNESCO has identified a strong demand for initiatives to strengthen the capacities of government officials to leverage digital technologies. With the right digital competencies, policymakers and regulators are empowered to digitally transform their institutions with policies that take advantage of the opportunities offered by new technologies, while navigating the many risks and challenges they can bring. By digitizing processes and making organizational changes, governments can enhance services, save money, and improve citizens' quality of life.

As technology continues to advance, digital competence becomes increasingly important for government agencies and relevant stakeholders involved in child protection [1, 2]. They must understand and effectively use digital tools and platforms to prevent and respond to online risks. This includes the ability to leverage technologies for early detection, reporting, and intervention in cases of online child abuse. Researchers [26] point out that *"We need more in-depth discussions with social work educators and students across institutions to determine how digital competence can be better integrated and evaluated into the formal curriculum level and the actual teaching and learning process"* [26, p.13]. Digital competence in social work practice and education: experiences from Norway. A recent study discusses which knowledge areas of digital competence are vital for Norwegian social work education today, based on the EU Digital Competence framework (DigComp) and expectations from frontline practice [26]. The results reveal that the integration of digital competence knowledge areas across Norwegian social work education is still highly limited. There is a significant gap between the EU's digital competence requirement and the Norwegian social work curricula, although the DigComp framework demonstrates its limitation in conceptualizing digital competence that is relevant to the social work domain. There is also a gap between the practice in NAV and Norwegian social work curricula regarding digital competence [26].

Information Security: There is a legal dilemma in striking a balance between information and secrecy. Protecting children's personal information and data privacy is a critical aspect of digital child protection. The increasing amount of personal data being collected, stored, and shared online poses a risk if not adequately protected. Ensuring robust information security measures, including encryption, secure storage, and data handling practices, is essential to safeguard children's privacy and prevent unauthorized access or misuse of their information.

Another fact is that risk factors, such as bullying and parental neglect, as well as protecting factors, such as communicating with friends, take new forms that demand not only new skills but also a new understanding of how to fulfill the societal mandate of protecting children [4, p.241].

Addressing these challenges requires a multi-faceted approach involving collaboration between governments, law enforcement agencies, educational institutions, technology companies, and civil society organizations. It necessitates the development of comprehensive legislation, promoting digital literacy and education, fostering ethical practices, enhancing digital competence, and prioritizing information security in the context of child protection.

6 Concluding Remarks

The digital revolution has greatly changed our society over the past three decades. There is a constant need for knowledge about how digitization affects children and youth so that we can give good professional advice and develop our service offering adapted to the times in which we live. It is therefore necessary to develop a separate strategy for digital competence in the public sector. Future competence needs are essentially based on how the opportunities that lie in technology can be exploited in the agencies. Digitalization and digital transformation are ongoing and grow apace, transforming the relationship between businesses, individuals, and governments internationally. International cooperation strengthens initiatives to combat cross-border online crimes against children and promotes the harmonization of legal frameworks. Collaboration and partnerships between government agencies, law enforcement, educational institutions, technology companies, and civil society organizations play a critical role in developing coordinated strategies and sharing knowledge and resources related to the digital child protection.

References

1. Andersen, S.T.: Diffusion of innovative digital work practices. In: Huang, Y.M., Cheng, S.C., Barroso, J., Sandnes, F.E. (eds.) ICITL 2022. Lecture Notes in Computer Science, vol. 13449, pp. 278–284. Springer, Cham (2022). https://doi.org/10.1007/978-3-031-15273-3_31
2. Andersen, S., Riise, R.: Hvilken IKT Kompetanse Bør En Helsearbeider Ha? Which ICT competence a health worker should have. In: Helse [Health], edited by Blix, Anderssen & Størdal, Digital, pp. 66–93. Cappelen Damm AS, Oslo (2012)
3. Besson, P., Rowe, F.: Strategizing information systems-enabled organizational transformation: a transdisciplinary review and new directions. J, Strat. Inf. Syst. **21**(2), 103–124 (2012)
4. Björktomta, S.-B., Hansen, H.A.: Social work, children and the digital knowledge landscape: new possibilities and challenges. In: Svalastog, A.L., Gajović, S., Webster, A. (eds.) Navigating Digital Health Landscapes. HTS, pp. 223–244. Springer, Singapore (2021). https://doi.org/10.1007/978-981-15-8206-6_11
5. Directorate for Children, Youth and Family Affairs, Barne-, ungdoms- og familiedirektoratet, How can Child Welfare Services help? YouTube (2021)
6. Goerzig, D., Bauernhansl, T.: Enterprise architectures for the digital transformation in small and medium-sized enterprises. Paper Presented at the 11th CIRP International Conference on Intelligent Computation in Manufacturing Engineering, CIRP ICME (2018)
7. Gong, C., Ribiere, V.: Developing a unified definition of digital transformation. Int. J. Technol. Innov. Entrep. Technol. Manag. Technovation **102**, 102217 (2021)
8. Gray, J., Rumpe, B.: Models for the Digital Transformation. Springer, Heidelberg (2017). https://doi.org/10.1007/978-3-658-36158-7
9. Haffke, I., Kalgovas, B.J., Benlian, A.: The role of the CIO and the CDO in an organization's digital transformation. Paper Presented at the Thirty Seventh, International Conference on Information Systems, Dublin (2016)
10. Hausberg, J.P., Liere-Netheler, K., Packmohr, S., Pakura, S., Vogelsang, K.: Research streams on digital transformation from a holistic business perspective: a systematic literature review and citation network analysis. J. Bus. Econ. **89**(8–9), 931–963 (2019). https://doi.org/10.1007/s11573-019-00956-z
11. Kommunal- og moderniserigsdepartementet: Én digital offentlig sektor, Digitaliseringsstrategi for offentlig sektor 2019–2025, Departementenes sikkerhets- og serviceorganisasjon, Publikasjonskode: H-2448 B, 06/2019 Én digital offentlig sektor - regjeringen.no (2019)
12. Lovdata: Lov om barnevern (barnevernsloven),kapittel 1 (2023). https://lovdata.no/dokument/NL/lov/2021-06-18-97/KAPITTEL_1#KAPITTEL_1
13. Matt, C., Hess, T., Benlian, A.: Digital transformation strategies. Bus. Inf. Syst. Eng. **57**(5), 339–343 (2015). https://doi.org/10.1007/s12599-015-0401-5
14. McKnight, D.H., Chervany, N.L.: Trust and distrust definitions: one bite at a time. In: Falcone, R., Singh, M., Tan, Y.H. (eds.) Trust in Cyber-Societies. Lecture Notes in Computer Science, vol. 2246, pp. 27–54. Springer, Heidelberg (2001). https://doi.org/10.1007/3-540-45547-7_3
15. Meld. St. 27: Digital agenda for Norge. IKT for en enklere hverdag og økt produktivitet, Kommunal- og distriktsdepartementet, Meld. St. 27 (2015–2016) - regjeringen.no (2015–2016)

16. Nasjonale retningslinjer for helse- og sosialfagutdanningene, RETHOS. Nasjonale retningslinjer for helse- og sosialfagutdanningene (RETHOS) - regjeringen.no (2023)
17. Om Digitaliseringsdirektoratet | Digdir Hentet 14. juni fra (2023). https://www.digdir.no/digdir/om-digitaliseringdirektoratet/1547
18. Proposisjon 73 L.: Endringer i barnevernloven (barnevernsreform), Barne- og likestillingsdepartementet (2017)
19. Stock, J.R., Boyer, S.L.: Developing a consensus definition of supply chain management: a qualitative study. Int. J. Phys. Distrib. Logist. Manag. **39**(8), 690–711 (2009)
20. The digital strategy for Norway (2019–2025) Digitalisering i offentlig sektor - regjeringen.no (2019)
21. Tregeagle, S., Darcy, M.: Child welfare and information and communication technology: today's challenge. Br. J. Soc. Work. **38**, 1481–1498 (2008). https://doi.org/10.1093/bjsw/bcm048
22. UNESCO: Digital Capacity Building for Governments, unesco.org (2023)
23. UNISEF: Child protection: Digital opportunities, challenges and innovations across the Region, unicef.org (2023)
24. Vial, G.: Understanding digital transformation: a review and a research agenda. J. Strateg. Inf. Syst. **28**(2), 118 (2019)
25. Warner, K.S.R., Wäger, M.: Building dynamic capabilities for digital transformation: an ongoing process of strategic renewal. Long. Range Plan. **52**(3), 326–349 (2019). https://doi.org/10.1016/j.lrp.2018.12.001
26. Zhu, H., Andersen, S.T.: Digital competence in social work practice and education: experiences from Norway. (fulltekst) Nordic Soc. Work Res. ISSN 2156-857X.s 1-16 (2021). https://doi.org/10.1080/2156857X.2021.1899967

Exploring Teaching Experiences in Technology and Engineering MOOCs with High Enrollments in Medium-Sized Public Universities

Chi-Cheng Chang, Yao-Hua Wang, and Wan-Hsuan Yen(✉)

National Taiwan Normal University, Taipei 106, ROC
gordonwyen@gmail.com

Abstract. The study aimed to explore the teaching experiences in popular MOOCs. The two teachers, whose courses were most popular with the largest number of students in a platform of MOOCs—ShareCourse, were selected for exploring their teaching experiences. The interview data based on teaching experiences was coded into three themes and nine sub-themes, including: (a) teachers' teaching experiences of problems and challenges in MOOCs, with the sub-themes on challenges caused by student behaviors, course quality, and video production; (b) teachers' teaching experiences of attracting students, with the sub-themes on delivery of effective information, leading students with different backgrounds, and preparing and teaching MOOCs; (c) teachers' descriptions of personal reflections on teaching motivation and innovations, with sub-themes on recognition of course features, holding an altruistic attitude, and reflections on innovative instruction. According to these themes, the teaching experiences in MOOCs were explored. Finally, reflections, implications and suggestions were provided.

Keywords: MOOC · Phenomenology · Reflection · Teaching experience

1 Introduction

In these years, Massive Open Online Courses (MOOCs) have attracted much attention of educators and researchers in higher education. MOOCs are online courses that are open to the public and massively recruit students from everywhere [1]. MOOCs allow students to select the subject knowledge that they prefer to learn and control their learning progressions. Students can participate in MOOCs with either an informal way of learning with a certification or a formal way with an academic degree [2]. The development of web technology makes peer knowledge exchanges and cooperative mechanisms become convenient. Therefore, MOOCs are helpful for autodidact, empowerment, interpersonal association, social networking teaching and learning, and innovative teaching [3, 4].

The instruction in MOOCs has a different way compared with the face-to-face teaching in classroom, but it does not tend to replace the face-to-face teaching and learning in universities [2]. Teachers should pay special attention to their students during the process

Y.-P. Cheng et al. (Eds.): ICITL 2024, LNCS 14785, pp. 213–221, 2024.
https://doi.org/10.1007/978-3-031-65881-5_23

of the MOOC implementation [5], as the teacher and the students would encounter problems and challenges in the process of MOOCs' implementation. Teachers of MOOCs are facing many challenges [1, 6–9], barriers [10], and limitations [11], and have negative experiences [12]. MOOC students participated in the course voluntarily, and they are not under the control of the current educational systems or school norms. Under this circumstance, how MOOC programs and teachers attract students to register and continue to learn without a certification or other incentives becomes a research issue that researchers are curious about and desire to explore [13].

Research on MOOCs has been more focused on student issues, but there are few studies examining the teachers' experiences on MOOCs [14, 15]. MOOC teaching experiences are positively beneficial to teachers' professional development [16] and teacher teaching quality affect student continuance intention of MOOCs [13]. Schools usually reward emerging curricula depending on teachers' experiences of innovative instruction. Therefore, the study was interested in the teachers' teaching experiences in MOOCs through a phenomenological study. A qualitative study using phenomenography conducted by Blackmon [14] was to examine professors' experiences with developing and teaching a MOOC. Bhaskar et al. [10] used an interpretative phenomenological analysis approach to identify barriers and motivating factors of adopting MOOCs. However, they focused on neither the experiences nor the reflection on the experiences that are important for a phenomenological study.

Based on the research context above, the study aimed to explore the teaching experiences in popular MOOCs. The research questions were as follows: (a) What were the teachers' teaching experiences of problems and challenges in MOOCs? (b) How did teachers develop MOOC content and instruction to attract students of MOOCs? (c) How did teachers reflect on teaching motivation and innovations in MOOCs?

2 Theoretical Basis - Dewey's Theory of Experience

Experience refers to the nature of the events someone or something has undergone. Dewey' [17] theory of experience stated that experiences formed are based on two principles, continuity and interaction. Continuity is that each experience a person has will influence his/her future, for better or for worse. In other words, an experience is cumulative, with each experience influenced by prior experience and in turn shaping future experiences [18]. Interaction denotes that the situational influence on one's experience. In other word, individuals create meaning from an experience as they interact with its physical and social settings [18]. The two principles provide the educative significance and value of an experience that leads the growth of the individuals [17, p.44–45]. The value of the experience can be identified by the effect that experience has on the individual's present and future, and the extent to which the individual can contribute to society.

Dewey's theory of experience early focused on educational or learning experiences, but may extend to teacher teaching experiences. Schmidt [18] used Dewey's theory of experience to evaluate preservice teachers' teaching experience. Dewey [17] stated that an experience should present the knowledge of facts; otherwise, the experience would become unmeaningful (p.82). Through the experiences of reflective thinking, individuals may effectively transform unreflective and primary experiences to deeper, reflective and secondary experiences. In Dewey's theory, experience is always the starting point of an educational process, while it is never the result. The critical challenge of the education through experience is to select the types of present experiences that exist plentifully in subsequent experiences.

3 Method

3.1 Subject

The two popular teachers, who taught in a platform of MOOCs—ShareCourse (http://www.sharecourse.net), had the largest amounts of students taking their courses based on the records of the platform over the past few years. Therefore, they were selected for exploring their teaching experiences. The platform provides science, engineering, and social science courses on college level. Teacher X teaches a course named "Ocean Windows-Oceanographic Museum and Sea World (technology)", which is about applications of marine technology with the feature of live-action shootings. Teacher Y teaches a course named "Introduction of Internet of Things (engineering)", which is about basic concepts and various technologies in Internet of Things. The two teachers have taught the two MOOCs for several years.

3.2 Data Gathering

The interview focuses and questions were determined according to three stages of the deep interview with phenomenology including: (a) helping interviewees to construct their experienced contexts—asking interviewees to describe their experience contexts about why and how they teach MOOCs; (b) assisting interviewees to reconstruct the meanings of their experiences—asking interviewees to explain how they choose and decide their plans and designs toward MOOCs, and what they have done for the practice of choices and innovations that differ from the normality; and (c) encouraging interviewees to reflect on their experiences—asking interviewees to describe their teaching experiences of MOOCs by inquiring their thoughts toward future plans for MOOCs, which allows interviewees to reflect on how they changed and what they gained after teaching MOOCs. The interviewed data were finally transcribed to text data by the researcher and then were delivered to the interviewees for further correction and confirmation.

3.3 Data Analysis

According to the phenomenology, steps for the analyses in the study were [19]: (a) collecting text data; (b) reading text data; (c) categorizing text data into individual themes; (d) reorganizing and elaborating common themes, which are the core meanings of the experiences; and (e) integrating and describing the meanings of the experiences. Based on the steps above, the coding scheme was derived from the deep discussion between two coders, one was the interviewer and the other was a colleague who was knowledgeable about MOOCs and was responsible for filming the MOOCs. We also referred to Thomas and Harden's [20] three stages of thematic analysis to reinforce the coding process. The three stages are: the coding of text line-by-line; the development of descriptive themes; and the generation of analytical themes.

The coders/researchers began data analysis by reading the transcripts and deriving preliminary/tentative themes (sometimes called open codes) for categories based on the techniques above and the important terms/keywords related with the concepts of instruction. The coders then refined the categories of the preliminary themes through adding, collapsing, combining, dividing, expending, or revising actions until sub-themes (sometimes called focused codes) and main themes (sometimes called selective codes) describing the teaching experiences emerged. Ultimately, three themes and nine sub-themes were derived to formulate the coding scheme shown as Table 1.

Table 1. Code chart for themes on teaching experiences

First letter (Teacher code)	Second letter (Three themes)	Third letter (Three sub-themes)	Last two numbers (Order of descriptive sentence in the sub-theme)
Teacher X Teacher Y	M(MOOCs) - teaching experiences of problems and challenges in MOOCs	S(challenges caused by student behaviors) C(challenges of course quality) V(challenges of video production)	01, 02, 03, ….., 09, 10, 11, ……, 20, 21, ….
	W(way) - teaching experiences of attracting students	I(information) - how to deliver effective information L(lead) - how to lead students with different backgrounds T(teaching) - how to prepare and teaching MOOCs	01, 02, 03, ….., 09, 10, 11, ……, 20, 21, ….
	P(personal) - personal reflections on teaching motivation and innovations	F(feature) - recognition about course features A(attitude) - holding an altruistic attitude R(reflections) - reflections on innovative instruction	01, 02, 03, ….., 09, 10, 11, ……, 20, 21, ….

3.4 Reliability and Validity

The triangulation method was conducted for the reliability and validity of the data. The researcher (also the interviewer and coder) first transcribed the tape and wrote down interviewees' experiences. Afterwards, the other coder confirmed the consistency between the descriptions of experiences and the tape. Finally, the descriptions of experiences were re-checked by interviewees for feedback and revisions. All transcripts were imported into the qualitative analysis software - Nvivo by two coders who worked independently on the same transcript.

4 Results and Discussion

The content of the interview is presented in part as follows.

4.1 Teaching Experiences of Problems and Challenges in MOOCs (M)

Challenges Caused by Student Behaviors (S). In interviewees' experiences, it was obvious that students in MOOCs were of all backgrounds, different from the students in the traditional classroom. Moreover, students, who are attracted by MOOCs, are neither from a specific group, nor from the same level of knowledge. "We not only teach elites in MOOCs, but also people of all backgrounds. (XMS01)" "In MOOCs, we teach students with diverse backgrounds. (YMS01)".

Challenges of Course Quality (C). One of the frustrations of MOOC teachers was less interaction in MOOCs [6, 11, 16], that would influence the course completion of learners. Therefore, how to attract students to take courses was a big problem. "How to attract students to enroll? How to keep students to continue taking the course? (XMC01)" The similar challenge emerges that teachers of MOOCs face the challenge in customizing the course for students [8].

Challenges of Video Production (V). The challenge in teaching MOOCs is that a lot of time and money will be spent in the process. Time for developing teaching materials and completing a course would cost more than traditional instruction [6]. One of the frustrations of MOOC teachers was insufficient time for developing MOOCs [16]. As for teaching materials, Teacher X: *"Photos and profiles can be used in teaching materials, and theories can be shown by animations.* (XMV01)*"*.

4.2 Teaching Experiences of Attracting Students (W)

How to Deliver Effective Information (I). Teacher Y watched many teaching videos, which helped him understand how to demonstrate teaching materials effectively. "*The time for lectures is always not enough. I would ponder how to make people understand what I want to say in a few minutes.* (YWI01)" The opinions from the two teachers are quite consistent with the argument of Dooa et al. [16] and Alemayehu and Chen [6] that previous online teaching experiences are beneficial to MOOC teaching.

How to Lead Students with Different Backgrounds (L). Teacher X: "I will not only talk about my stuff but also other things, which can help them develop their own things. (XWL01)" Teacher Y had many cooperative experiences with industries, which can help students realize how the concepts he taught could work in reality. "In MOOCs, I teach a kind of concept, trying to make them understand the development of industries from the past 20 years to the present. (YWL01)".

How to Prepare and Teach MOOCs (T). Owing to Teacher X's experience, which might be helpful when preparing and teaching MOOCs through filming videos, he was able to clearly express his ideas and communicate with directors, photographers, editors, post producers, and other teachers in the same online course. *"We should know how to express our ideas completely and how this program will be presented in the future."* (XWT01)" *"Ideas of products can be inspired by new knowledge. What I want to teach is what kind of products will be made in the future.* (YWT01)".

4.3 Teachers' Descriptions of Personal Reflections (P)

Recognition of Course Features (F). How teachers feel about courses is part of teaching experiences. The position of a course will affect what a teacher prepares for the teaching content. *"First of all, we must define what this course is, and then we can find its content.* (XPF01)" In MOOC courses, teachers cannot lecture in detail because what they teach will be diffused. *"If I am unsure about the complete course content, I will avoid teaching in detail.* (YPF01)" *"There are aims of each phase to achieve in my course. (XPF02)" "There are a variety of sea stories, not only my stories!* (YPF02)".

Holding an Altruistic Attitude (A). The mental processes of teachers who are willing to teach MOOCs are quite positive. *"I am interested in teaching MOOCs because everyone in the society is allowed to take the courses.* (XPA01)" *"In response to the school's requirements, I participate in MOOCs.* (YPA01)" This is consistent with the argument of Dooa et al. [16] that teachers were motivated in MOOC teaching by service to the public and community as well as institutional goals.

Reflections on Innovative Instruction (R). The teaching method should be appropriate and innovative to MOOCs. *"If I feels satisfied with the current traditional instruction, I will not be innovative.* (XPR02)" The reality would not be difficult to reach, since MOOC creates the opportunity for innovative instruction [21]. How do MOOC teachers take the responsibility for disseminating knowledge? The correctness and completeness of instruction will influence the dissemination of knowledge in MOOCs. *"The more important things are your voice, thoughts, and teaching methods.* (YPR01)".

5 Conclusion

5.1 Contributions for Theories and Practices

Theoretically, the study provides the understanding of teaching experiences in MOOCs through both the Dewey's theory of experience and phenomenological approach. It provides the alternative concept that the Dewey's theory of experience initially focused on student learning experiences may be extended to teacher teaching experiences, which present the knowledge of facts. Through the meaningful experiences of reflective thinking, the MOOC teachers may effectively transform unreflective and primary experiences to deeper, reflective and secondary experiences based on the Dewey's two principles – continuity and interaction.

Practically, the MOOC teachers' descriptions about teaching experiences and the integrations of two MOOC teachers' teaching experiences can provide MOOC teachers a practical experience to follow. The study results can help instructors understand and reflect on the modern emerging instructional styles and technologies, which are beneficial for instructors and educators to be willing to try MOOC instruction, and contribute to the MOOC instructors in course designs and instructional plans.

5.2 Implications for Theories and Practices

There are three inspirations obtained from the reflections on the MOOC teachers' teaching experiences: (a) MOOCs are different from the traditional classroom teaching, and thus teachers should know and try new teaching methods, for example, how to utilize media to facilitate students' interests, how to use multimedia's visual effects to attract students' concentration, as well as how to broaden resources to enrich courses; (b) Before class, teachers have to understand the basic teaching features of MOOCs, and then think about what kind of student is appropriate for the course. The course property, which includes general education and functional course (e.g., certification or employee training) and images for course demonstrations should be under teachers' control before class; (c) teachers need to hold a learning attitude by exploring teaching methods from practices in response to such an emerging trend of online courses.

The Dewey's theory of experience and the approach of phenomenology may provide the basis for reflection on the similarities and differences in the MOOC teaching experiences that both teachers described. Other teachers who are interested in MOOCs may think about the teachers' teaching experiences of problems and challenges in MOOCs in the study and consider how to attract students of MOOCs. Other teachers may think about the teachers' reflections on teaching motivation and innovations on MOOCs and further understand the meanings of the teachers' teaching experiences in MOOCs.

5.3 Limitations and Recommendations

The key for the study is to explore the teachers' teaching experiences and provide researchers and teachers a chance to reflect, not for finding a solution or an effective teaching skill. The future study may be explained through reference to the local or institutional context and provide a focal point for what is otherwise a very broad exploratory study.

The study is not for empirical analyses, and hence the results cannot be generalized empirically, such as a comparison of pedagogy. Therefore, experimental research is recommended to examine the differences in MOOC teaching effects between different MOOC teaching methods or teachers with various MOOC experiences.

References

1. Turan, Z., Yilmaz, R.M.: Are MOOCs a new way of learning in engineering education in light of the literature? A systematic review and bibliometric analysis. J. Eng. Educ. (2024). https://doi.org/10.1002/jee.20580
2. Almatrafi, O., Johri, A., Rangwala, H.: Needle in a haystack: Identifying learner posts that require urgent response in MOOC discussion forums. Comput. Educ. **118**, 1–9 (2018). https://doi.org/10.1016/j.compedu.2017.11.002
3. Joksimović, S., et al.: Exploring development of social capital in a cMOOC through language and discourse. Internet and Higher Education **36**, 54–64 (2018). https://www.learntechlib.org/p/199287/
4. Kovanović, V., et al.: Exploring communities of inquiry in Massive Open Online Courses. Comput. Educ. **119**, 44–58 (2018). https://doi.org/10.1016/j.compedu.2017.11.010
5. Gregori, E.B., Zhang, J., Galván-Fernández, C., Fernández-Navarro, F.D.A.: Learner support in MOOCs: Identifying variables linked to completion. Comput. Educ. **122**, 153–168 (2018). https://doi.org/10.1016/j.compedu.2018.03.014
6. Alemayehu, L., Chen, H.-L.: Learner and instructor-related challenges for learners' engagement in MOOCs: A review of 2014–2020 publications in selected SSCI indexed journals. Interact. Learn. Environ. **31**(5), 3172–3194 (2023). https://doi.org/10.1080/10494820.2021.1920430
7. Eacute, J., Esteve, M.: The transformation of the teachers' role at the end of the twentieth century: New challenges for the future. Educ. Rev. **52**(2), 197–207 (2000). https://doi.org/10.1080/713664040
8. Ponnaiah, M., et al.: Design and implementation challenges of massive open online course on research methods for Indian medical postgraduates and teachers – descriptive analysis of inaugural cycle. BMC Med. Educ. **22**(1), 369 (2022). https://doi.org/10.1186/s12909-022-03423-6
9. Wadams, M.L., Schick-Makaroff, K.: Teaching assistant development and contributions in online, MOOC and blended synchronous settings: an integrative review. J. Furth. High. Educ. **46**(8), 1023–1039 (2022). https://doi.org/10.1080/0309877X.2022.2038100
10. Bhaskar, P., Joshi, A., Dayalan, P.: Investigating the barriers and motivators to MOOCs adoption: A qualitative analysis of teacher's perspective. Int. J. Knowl. Learn. **15**(2), 120–147 (2022). https://doi.org/10.1504/IJKL.2022.121989
11. Chong, S.W., Khan, M.A., Reinders, H.: A critical review of design features of LMOOCs. Comput. Assist. Lang. Learn. **35**(7), 1594–1619 (2022). https://doi.org/10.1080/09588221.2020.1825094
12. dos Santos, V.M., Cernev, A.K., Saraiva, G.M.M., Bida, A.G.: Faculty experience and digital platforms in education. Revista de Gestao **29**(3), 252–266 (2022). https://doi.org/10.1108/REGE-05-2021-0090
13. Shanshan, S., Wenfei, L.: Understanding the impact of quality elements on MOOCs continuance intention. Educ. Inf. Technol. **27**, 10949–10976 (2022). https://doi.org/10.1007/s10639-022-11063-y
14. Blackmon, S.J.: MOOC makers: Professors' experiences with developing and delivering MOOCs. Int. Rev. Res. Open and Distrib. Learn. **19**(4), 77–91 (2018). https://doi.org/10.19173/irrodl.v19i4.3718
15. Lin, J., Cantoni, L.: Decision, implementation, and confirmation: Experiences of instructors behind tourism and hospitality MOOCs. Int. Rev. Res. Open and Distance Learn. **19**(1), 1–293 (2018). https://doi.org/10.19173/irrodl.v19i1.3402
16. Dooa, M.Y., Tang, Y., Bonkc, C.J., Zhu, M.: MOOC instructor motivation and career development. Distance Educ. **41**(1), 2647 (2020). https://doi.org/10.1080/01587919.2020.1724770

17. Dewey, J.: Experience and education. Macmillan (1963)
18. Schmidt, M.: Learning from teaching experience: Dewey's theory and preservice teachers' learning. J. Res. Music Educ. **58**(2), 131–146 (2010). https://doi.org/10.1177/0022429410368723
19. Giorgi, A.: Sketch of a psychological phenomenological method. In: Giorgi, A. (ed.) Phenomenology and Psychological Research, pp. 1–12. Duquesne University Press (1985)
20. Thomas, J., Harden, A.: Methods for the thematic synthesis of qualitative research in systematic reviews. BMC Med. Res. Methodol. **8**, 45 (2008). https://doi.org/10.1186/1471-2288-8-45
21. Ratnasari, W., Chou, T.C., Huang, C.-H.: From hype to reality: the changing landscape of MOOC research. Library Hi Tech (2024). https://doi.org/10.1108/LHT-07-2023-0320

Exploring the Impact of the Pingtung Wannian River Basin Educational App on the Learning Motivation of Upper Elementary Students: An Analysis Based on the Technology Acceptance Model

C. M. Chen[1,2](✉) and P. H. Wu[2]

[1] Tajen University, Pingtung 908, Taiwan
tshaq.chen@gmail.com
[2] National University of Tainan, Tainan 700, Taiwan

Abstract. As the rapid development of information technology continues, the application of digital learning tools in the educational sector has increasingly gained attention, particularly in the field of humanities and history education. Interactive learning applications offer students richer and more diverse learning experiences, helping them understand local culture and history in a more dynamic way. This study focuses on a learning application named "Wannian River Treasure Hunt," designed specifically for upper elementary students. Through gamified learning, it aims to enhance students' interest in and knowledge of the humanities and history surrounding the Pingtung Wannian River area. Utilizing the Technology Acceptance Model (TAM), this research investigates the app's impact on the learning attitudes of fifth-grade students, aiming to identify key factors that influence students' acceptance and use of this educational application.

The findings reveal significant positive relationships between learning attitudes, perceived ease of use, perceived usefulness, and actual use, suggesting that the design of educational applications should consider not only the quality of their educational content but also their usability and the real assistance they provide to students' learning. However, the influence of entertainment on perceived usefulness did not receive significant support, indicating that merely pursuing entertainment in the design of educational applications without substantial educational content may not significantly enhance students' acceptance of the app. Additionally, the impact of perceived ease of use on actual use was not supported, implying that even if an application is easy to use, it may not lead to increased frequency of use if students do not find it useful. These insights are valuable for developers of educational applications, highlighting the need to balance entertainment with educational value to ensure the app not only engages students but also genuinely facilitates learning.

Keywords: Learning Motivation · Digital Learning · Technology Acceptance Model (TAM)

Y.-P. Cheng et al. (Eds.): ICITL 2024, LNCS 14785, pp. 222–232, 2024.
https://doi.org/10.1007/978-3-031-65881-5_24

1 Research Background, Motivation, and Purpose

1.1 Research Background

With the rapid development of information technology, the education sector is increasingly valuing the application of digital learning tools, hoping to integrate technology into teaching to stimulate students' interest and motivation in learning. Particularly for humanities and history education, interactive learning applications can provide students with a richer and more diverse learning experience, helping them understand local culture and history in a more vivid way. This study focuses on a learning application named "Wannian River Treasure Hunt," which is designed specifically for upper elementary students. It aims to enhance students' knowledge and interest in the humanities and history surrounding the Pingtung Wannian River through gamified learning.

1.2 Research Motivation

The application of technology in education has become one of the significant trends in global educational innovation. However, despite the abundance of educational applications on the market, students' learning attitudes and acceptance of these digital learning tools vary, posing a significant challenge for educators and app developers. Especially for upper elementary students, how to effectively promote their interest in learning through educational applications and improve their learning outcomes is a topic worth exploring. This study aims to investigate the impact of the " Wannian River Treasure Hunt" app on the learning attitudes of fifth-grade elementary students through the Technology Acceptance Model (TAM), to understand the key factors influencing students' acceptance and use of this learning application.

1.3 Research Purpose

1. Evaluate students' perceptions of the "Wannian River Treasure Hunt" app's ease of use and its potential to enhance learning efficiency and interest using the TAM model.
2. Analyze how students' attitudes towards learning affect their performance in humanities and history when using the "Wannian River Treasure Hunt" app, including motivation, interest, and behaviors.
3. Enhance theoretical and practical understanding of applying the Technology Acceptance Model (TAM) in elementary education, specifically in assessing elementary students' acceptance of educational technology tools for learning humanities and history through empirical research.

2 Literature Review

The primary purpose of this study is to explore the impact of applications on the learning attitudes of upper elementary students, thereby understanding the factors behind students' behavior when using this application. In this chapter, we will provide a detailed and in-depth introduction to the models influencing users' adoption of innovative technologies, including the Technology Acceptance Model, as well as other relevant theoretical frameworks.

In addition to "perceived usefulness and perceived ease of use" affecting attitudes and behavioral intentions in the Technology Acceptance Model, "external variables" also impact perceived usefulness and ease of use, indirectly influencing the final attitudes and behavioral intentions. Therefore, in this study, "entertainment and learning attitudes" are selected as variables to explore factors that may influence students' behavioral intentions.

2.1 Technology Acceptance Model (TAM)

The Technology Acceptance Model (TAM) [2], aims to clarify the key factors for the acceptance of information technology, especially in understanding technology usage behavior. This model, built upon the Theory of Reasoned Action, has been widely used to predict and explain an individual's level of acceptance of information systems. According to TAM, the user's behavioral attitude is a critical factor influenced primarily by two elements: perceived usefulness and perceived ease of use; and perceived usefulness positively affects perceived ease of use. Furthermore, both perceived usefulness and perceived ease of use are influenced by external factors.

2.2 Perceived Usefulness

In the Technology Acceptance Model (TAM) [2], it is suggested that if users find a system easy to use, they might accomplish more work with less effort, thereby increasing work efficiency. This implies that potential users would subjectively anticipate that adopting a specific information system could enhance their work performance or learning outcomes. In other words, perceived usefulness reflects the system users' expectations for improving work or learning efficiency, such as when users realize that smartphones can aid learning, reduce the time needed for work, enhance operational efficiency, or that navigation systems can prevent getting lost while driving. In these cases, the higher the perceived utility of the system, the more positive the attitude towards the system. Simply put, when potential users believe the system to be highly useful, their positive attitude towards it is likely to increase accordingly.

2.3 Perceived Ease of Use

According to Davis (1989) [2], potential users make subjective judgments about the ease of learning to operate a specific information system technology. Specifically, when system operations become more convenient, users will feel more confident in their performance, making them more willing to adopt the system; if the system is easy to operate, with clear and understandable processes and flexibility in operation, users will have high confidence in their performance. Conversely, if the technology is complex, difficult to master, or requires a significant amount of effort to learn, it may create a psychological burden for users, lead to negative emotions, and ultimately result in resistance to using the technology. In summary, when users perceive that operating a new technology, such as the functionalities of a smartphone information system, does not require excessive mental effort to master, their attitude towards using the system tends to be more positive. Moreover, perceived ease of use also has a positive effect on perceived usefulness.

2.4 Usage Attitude

Taylor and Todd (1995) [8] revealed that users' perceptions of the benefits and drawbacks of adopting a specific information system influence their attitudes towards information technology. These attitudes are doubly influenced by perceived usefulness and perceived ease of use. That is, the more useful the system is deemed by the user, the more positive their attitude towards the system becomes. Specifically, if users believe that the functionalities of innovative technologies, such as smartphones, are easy to learn and can significantly improve learning or work efficiency, their favorable opinion and positive evaluation of the technology will increase.

2.5 Entertainment

Kim and Moon (2001) [5] explored "entertainment" as an intrinsic motivation or belief formed through individual experience and interaction with the environment, considering it a key internal belief affecting an individual's use of mobile services.

Maignan and Lukas (1997) [6], in their study on user attitudes towards internet adoption, also found "entertainment" to be a positive factor to consider.

Furthermore, Kim and Moon (2001) [5] subdivided the concept of perceived entertainment into three main dimensions: (1) Concentration: In the state of entertainment, users focus entirely on the current activity, with external distractions naturally blocked, leading to users not easily perceiving the passage of time during the activity. (2) Curiosity: The interaction process arouses users' curiosity, encouraging further exploration. (3) Enjoyment: In the state of entertainment, users find the interaction itself highly enjoyable, feeling pleasure and entertainment rather than pursuing other external rewards.

2.6 Learning Attitude

In the field of educational psychology, attitude is seen as an individual's long-term emotional response and behavioral tendency towards people, events, and objects encountered in life. This concept, as described by Chang, C.H. (2011) [1], encompasses the individual's judgment and thinking about their own attitude and has a lasting impact on their behavior. The learning attitude formed under the combined influence of education, family background, peer interaction, and personal expectations directly relates to the learner's efforts, learning strategies, coping methods, and self-value recognition, which are all key factors affecting learning outcomes [3]. Previous research [4, 10] has indicated that learners' self-directed learning expectations and positive learning attitudes have a significant positive impact on learning effectiveness, with further evidence [9] showing that learners with positive learning attitudes tend to achieve better learning outcomes.

Regarding the impact of teaching methods on learning attitudes, Zhang, Y.Y. (2012) [11] found that designing a variety of teaching activities (such as group cooperation, multimedia teaching, game-based learning, etc.) could significantly enhance learners' confidence, interest, and value beliefs in learning, having a significant impact on learners' overall learning attitudes compared to traditional teaching methods. Moreover, Qian, Z.P., & Liang, L.Z. (2017) [7] further applied diversified teaching strategies such as digital picture book teaching, multimedia animation teaching, poetry and painting presentation teaching, and internet image and video-assisted teaching to learning groups of different disciplines and genders. Their research results showed that, compared to traditional lecture-based teaching, diversified teaching strategies were more capable of arousing learners' interest in learning, promoting positive learning attitudes, and thereby significantly improving learning outcomes.

3 Research Method

3.1 Research Design

This study focuses on Pingtung Minhe elementary students who used the Wannian River Treasure Hunt app. After completing the game, a survey will gather data. The research follows an empirical approach with an estimated participation of 50 to 70 students. Figure 1 illustrates the software operation, while Fig. 2 shows the app interface.

Fig. 1. Students operating the software.

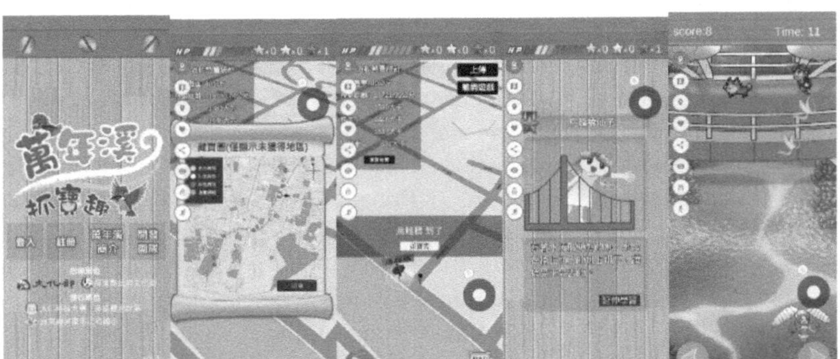

Fig. 2. Wannian River Treasure Hunt app interface.

3.2 Research Framework

Based on the literature review discussed earlier, this study primarily focuses on investigating the impact of applications on the learning motivation of upper elementary students. This research attempts to apply external variables "entertainment and learning motivation" to the Technology Acceptance Model to explore their effects on perceived usefulness and ease of use, and further examine whether perceived usefulness and ease of use influence students' usage attitudes and have an effect on their behavioral intentions. Integrating the various research variables discussed in the literature review above, this study has developed a research framework, as shown in Fig. 3.

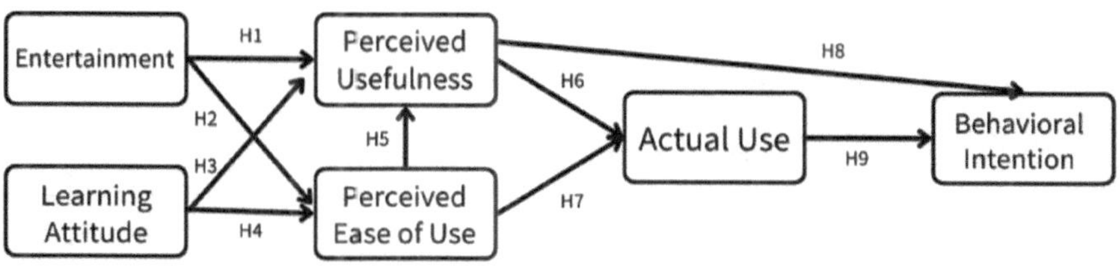

Fig. 3. This Study's Framework Diagram.

3.3 Research Hypothesis

H1: "Entertainment" has a significant positive effect on "Perceived Usefulness".
H2: "Entertainment" has a significant positive effect on "Perceived Ease of Use".
H3: "Learning Attitude" has a significant positive effect on "Perceived Usefulness".
H4: "Learning Attitude" has a significant positive effect on "Perceived Ease of Use".
H5: "Perceived Ease of Use" has a significant positive effect on "Perceived Usefulness".
H6: "Perceived Usefulness" has a significant positive effect on "Actual Use".
H7: "Perceived Ease of Use" has a significant positive effect on "Actual Use".
H8: "Perceived Usefulness" has a significant positive effect on "Behavioral Intention".
H9: "Actual Use" has a significant positive effect on "Behavioral Intention".

3.4 Reliability Analysis

In this study, a total of 70 questionnaires were distributed, and 63 were collected. After checking for incompleteness or lack of variation in responses, no invalid questionnaires were identified, resulting in a total of 63 valid questionnaires with a 100% response rate. After conducting reliability analysis for each construct, all Cronbach's α values exceeded 0.7, indicating a high level of internal consistency in this study. The results of reliability analysis for each construct are presented in Table 1.

Table 1. The results of reliability analysis.

Research Dimension	Cronbach's α
Entertainment	0.881
Learning Attitude	0.934
Perceived Usefulness	0.858
Perceived Ease of Use	0.820
Actual Use	0.877
Behavioral Intention	0.861

3.5 Validate Research Hypotheses

This study will utilize multiple regression analysis to explore and explain the strength and direction of the relationship between the independent and dependent variables, identify the best predictive model for the dependent variable, and investigate the interaction effects among the independent variables as well as their relationship with the dependent variable.

Analysis of the Impact of Entertainment, Learning Attitude, and Perceived Ease of Use on Perceived Usefulness. Regarding the perceived usefulness of the "Wannian River Treasure Hunt" app, there are three hypothesis tests as follows:

H1: *"Entertainment" has a significant positive effect on "Perceived Usefulness".*

H3: *"Learning Attitude" has a significant positive effect on "Perceived Usefulness".*

H5: *"Perceived Ease of Use" has a significant positive effect on "Perceived Usefulness".*

As shown in Table 2. Regression analysis for each dimension reveals that both "learning attitude" and "perceived ease of use" have significant positive impacts on perceived usefulness. Therefore, it can be concluded that research hypotheses H3 and H5 are supported, while H1 is not supported.

Analysis of the Impact of Entertainment and Learning Attitude on Perceived Ease of Use. Regarding the perceived ease of use of the "Wannian River Treasure Hunt" app, there are two hypothesis tests as follows:

H2: *"Entertainment" has a significant positive effect on "Perceived Ease of Use".*

H4: *"Learning Attitude" has a significant positive effect on "Perceived Ease of Use".*

As shown in Table 3. Regression analysis for each dimension reveals that "learning attitude" has a significant positive impact on perceived ease of use. Therefore, it can be concluded that research hypothesis H4 is supported, while H2 is not supported.

Analysis of the Impact of Perceived Usefulness and Perceived Ease of Use on Actual Use. Regarding the perceived usefulness of the "Wannian River Treasure Hunt" app, there are two hypothesis tests as follows:

Table 2. Multiple regression analysis of the impact of entertainment, learning attitude, and perceived ease of use on perceived usefulness.

Independent Variable	Unstandardized Coefficients		Standardized Coefficients β	T-value	P-value	VIF
	B	Standard Deviation				
Constant	0.487	0.428		1.138	0.26	
Entertainment	0.15	0.146	0.12	0.99	0.921	2.505
Learning Attitude	0.276*	0.140	0.269	1.969	0.049	3.252
Perceived Ease of Use	0.603***	0.111	0.592	5.435	<0.001	2.070
Adjusted $R^2 = 0.645$ $F = 38.605$ $P < .001$						

* $p < 0.05$ ** $p < 0.01$ *** $p < 0.001$

Table 3. Multiple regression analysis of the impact of entertainment, learning attitude on perceived ease of use.

Independent Variable	Unstandardized Coefficients		Standardized Coefficients β	T-value	P-value	VIF
	B	Standard Deviation				
Constant	1.027	0.481		2.136	0.37	
Entertainment	0.155	0.169	0.12	0.917	0.363	2.470
Learning Attitude	0.620***	0.140	0.142	4.358	<0.001	3.470
Adjusted $R^2 = 0.501$ $F = 32.113$ $P < .001$						

* $p < 0.05$ ** $p < 0.01$ *** $p < 0.001$

H6: "Perceived Usefulness" has a significant positive effect on "Actual Use".

H7: *"Perceived Ease of Use" has a significant positive effect on "Actual Use".*

As shown in Table 4. Regression analysis for each dimension reveals that "perceived usefulness" has a significant positive impact on actual usage. Therefore, it can be concluded that research hypothesis H6 is supported, while H7 is not supported.

Analysis of the Impact of Perceived Usefulness and Actual Use on Behavioral Intention. Regarding the perceived usefulness of the "Wannian River Treasure Hunt" app, there are two hypothesis tests as follows:

H8: *"Perceived Usefulness" has a significant positive effect on "Behavioral Intention".*

H9: *"Actual Use" has a significant positive effect on "Behavioral Intention".*

Table 4. Multiple regression analysis of the impact of perceived usefulness and perceived ease of use on actual use.

Independent Variable	Unstandardized Coefficients		Standardized Coefficients β	T-value	P-value	VIF
	B	Standard Deviation				
Constant	0.186	0.365		0.510	0.612	
Perceived Usefulnes	0.728	0.128	0.671	5.682	<0.001	2.666
Perceived Ease of Use	0.209	0.131	0.189	1.599	0.115	2.666
Adjusted $R^2 = 0.676$ $F = 65.587$ $P < .001$						

* $p < 0.05$ ** $p < 0.01$ *** $p < 0.001$

As shown in Table 5. Regression analysis for each dimension reveals that "actual usage" has a significant positive impact on behavioral intention. Therefore, it can be concluded that research hypothesis H9 is supported, while H8 is not supported.

Table 5. Multiple regression analysis of the impact of perceived usefulness and actual use on behavioral intention.

Independent Variable	Unstandardized Coefficients		Standardized Coefficients β	T-value	P-value	VIF
	B	Standard Deviation				
Constant	0.26	0.326		0.079	0.938	
Perceived Usefulnes	0.218	0.129	0.193	1.690	0.096	3.056
Actual Use	0.726***	0.119	0.697	6.110	<0.001	3.056
Adjusted $R^2 = 0.736$ $F = 87.290$ $P < .001$						

* $p < 0.05$ ** $p < 0.01$ *** $p < 0.001$

4 Conclusion and Recommendations

4.1 Research Conclusion

This study investigates the impact of the "Wannian River Treasure Hunt "APP on the learning attitudes of fifth-grade elementary school students through the Technology Acceptance Model (TAM). The results indicate significant positive relationships between learning attitude, perceived ease of use, perceived usefulness, and actual use. This demonstrates that the design of educational applications should consider not only the quality of their educational content but also their ease of use and actual assistance to students' learning.

The influence of entertainment on perceived usefulness was not significantly supported, suggesting that merely pursuing entertainment in educational app design, while neglecting the substantial help of its educational content, may not significantly enhance students' acceptance of the app. Additionally, the lack of significant support for the impact of perceived ease of use on actual use might imply that even if an app is easy to use, it might not increase its actual usage frequency if students do not perceive it as useful.

4.2 Recommendations

1. For Educators and Developers: Developers should prioritize the educational content and utility of applications over merely their entertainment value. Applications should be designed to not only engage students but also to significantly improve learning outcomes. Furthermore, enhancing the usability of applications to make them powerful tools for daily learning is crucial.
2. For Future Research: Future studies could explore how other factors, such as individual differences and social influences, affect learning attitudes and app usage, and how these factors interact with entertainment, perceived ease of use, and perceived usefulness. This would help to understand more comprehensively students' acceptance and usage behavior towards educational apps.

References

1. Chang, C.H.: Zhang's Psychology Dictionary (Concise Edition), 1st ed. Donghua, Taipei City (2011)
2. Davis, F., Bagozzi, R., Warshaw, P.: User acceptance of computer technology: a comparison of two theoretical models. Manage. Sci. **35**(8), 982–1003 (1989)
3. Hammouri, H.A.M.: Attitudinal and motivational variables related to mathematics achievement in Jordan: Findings from the Third International Mathematics and Science Study (TIMSS). Educational Research **46**(3), 214–257 (2004)
4. Lin, P.Q., Qi, B.X.: A study on the learning attitudes, achievement motivation, and their correlation with academic achievement of students with hearing impairments in vocational high school. J. Spec. Edu. Res. **8**, 17–32. (TSSCI) (1992)
5. Moon, J.W., Kim, Y.G.: Extending the TAM for a World-Wide-Web Context. Information and Management **38**, 217–230 (2001)
6. Maignan, I., Lukas, B.A.: The natural and social use of the internet: a qualitative investigation. The Journal of Consumer Affairs **31**(2), 346–371 (1997)
7. Qian, Z.P., Liang, L.Z.: The effects of cognitive styles and multiple intelligences on learning motivation and outcomes - A case study of digital teaching in freshman Chinese courses at a technology university. J. Humanit. Soc. Sci. Nation. Taiwan Univ. Sci. Technol. **13**(4), 325–358 (2017)

8. Taylor, S., Todd, P.: Decomposition and crossover effects in the theory of planned behavior: a study of consumer adoption intentions. Int. J. Res. Mark. **12**, 137–155 (1995)
9. Wang, Z.T.: The relationship between learning attitudes towards English and mathematics, parenting styles, and academic achievement among junior high school students: Data from the TEPS database. J. Second. Edu. 55–76 (2007)
10. Wu, W.D.: Adjustment types and psychological counseling of gifted students. Measurement and Counseling **166**, 3481–3484 (2001)
11. Zhang, Y.Y.: An exploration of the effects of diversified teaching and assessment on elementary school students' attitudes towards music learning and achievement. J. Edu. Nation. Hsinchu Univ. Edu. **29**(2), 1–33 (2012)

Exploring the Integration of Phenomenon-Based Learning Approach in Programming and Critical Thinking Intent

Meng-Chun Tsai[1](✉) and Hao-Chiang Koong Lin[2]

[1] General Competency Center, National Penghu University of Science and Technology, Penghu, Taiwan
cherrybearpipi@gmail.com

[2] Department of Information and Learning Technology, National University of Tainan, Tainan, Taiwan

Abstract. Students who are not information technology (non-IT) majors ($N = 63$) mostly appear to be frightened and bored when it comes to programming. In this study, the phenomenon-based learning (PhBL) approach would be applied to programming to focus the pedagogical process on students so that they could be inspired through thinking about daily issues. Then, cross-disciplinary integration would take place to apply the acquired programming techniques to visual inventions to generate the creative word cloud. It was indicated in this study that the whole process contributed to significantly enhanced systematic analytical capabilities, open-mindedness, intellectual curiosity, overall and reflective thinking, critical thinking intent and growth needs, with all applicable coefficients greater than 0.7, demonstrating significant high levels of correlation. Both critical thinking intent and interest in the course among students with high growth needs were greater than students with low growth needs and were highly significant with $p < .001$. The correlation with interest in the course and growth needs was nearly highly relevant ($.69^{**}$), proving that the growth needs among students could be reinforced if they have abundant pleasant learning experience.

Keywords: Critical thinking · Phenomenon-based learning · PhBL · Growth needs

1 Introduction

Critical thinking has become one of important educational goals, particularly for university students, because of its diverse nature, that is, multi-dimensional perspectives and the attempt to solve problems and the fact that it is also part of fundamental core competencies. Research has revealed that the programming learning process helps boost the development of critical thinking and advanced train of thought [1]. As such, such capability has been included in the center of the educational framework in many countries and made a paramount task to be fulfilled in education [2]. Programming education is believed to be an important route to the development of advanced thinking in students

Y.-P. Cheng et al. (Eds.): ICITL 2024, LNCS 14785, pp. 233–243, 2024.
https://doi.org/10.1007/978-3-031-65881-5_25

[3]. In fact, it helps students analyze, organize, express, and evaluate their thoughts while solving problems [4]. Meanwhile, programming is a form of exploratory learning where students constantly get boosted in their computing and creative thinking capabilities while they try to fulfill the exploratory programming task and create a bond between old and new knowledge [5, 6]. Moreover, programming is a learning process where students need to try and error repeatedly in order to realize self-reflection and to accordingly boost critical thinking [7, 8]. For most teachers or researchers, however, it remains quite challenging to develop advanced thinking capability in students through programming education [9]. Research has revealed that, with abundant and pleasant learning experience in activities, it helps reinforce students' learning behavior in terms of participation and persistence, such as concentration and perseverance. Once the creative train of thought is inspired in students, they can solve problems more effectively and clearly applying the programming technique. However, non-IT majors mostly appear to be frightened and bored while dealing with programming. In light of this, the PhBL approach will be applied to programming through this study to focus the pedagogical process on students. Students will be inspired through thinking about daily issues. Then, the programming technique acquired in class is applied to visual inventions to generate the creative word cloud. Hopefully, students will be fond of programming and enjoy it.

2 Literature Review

2.1 Critical Thinking (CT)

Boosting critical thinking is an important goal in many fields in society, especially in education, and particularly in higher education. In as early as 1987, JH MacMillan [10] pointed out that critical thinking should be a main goal of education, particularly during the university stage, as it aims to inspire students' capabilities, such as critical thinking, making inferences, and making judgment that help them make better decisions. Many ideas about critical thinking have been introduced [11]. It means, for example, the internal motivation of a person in the face of problems to be solved, ideas to be evaluated, or decisions to be made [12]. In other words, critical thinking is a "required" occupational skill in terms of problem-solving, evidence collection, and information assessment, which is even more important for a vocational university. Research has revealed that critical thinking is paramount to the promotion of deep learning among students [6, 7] as it helps them reflect and generate corresponding ideas and approaches making the best use of evidence and evaluating the materials provided. As a result, enhancing students' critical thinking is set as a paramount educational goal by many schools; they want to nurture independent critical thinkers [13, 14]. Education of the 21st century aims to prepare students with the capability to solve problems and critical thinking. By supporting this process with scientific and technical attainments, students are able to think and thinking becomes a skill that contributes the nurturing of individuals that possess originality and are more educated and open-minded [15].

2.2 Phenomenon-Based Learning, PhBL

PhBL was first developed in the late 1990s. During the 1990s, Maijaliisa Rauste-von Wright [16], in charge of educational psychology in normal education, developed PhBL accordingly. Learning was believed to be "a context-based and situated interaction process" and also "a self-correcting model of curriculum" [16] and aim at minimizing the distance between theory and practice by emphasizing the capability of students to apply what they learned in class to daily life. In other words, learning is a dynamic process and is yet also cognitive, sensitive, responsive, individual, and collective [17]. It contributes to the generation of ethical awareness in learners so that they reflect upon their prior assumptions about themselves, each other, and the world they live in and share the goal to link the learning topic to their living environment and experience. This will accordingly free them from restrictions in the field of learning [18] and reach out wherever possible with the existing pedagogical approach while at the same time retaining the depth integral of the specific discipline [19]. This is why PhBL can be referred to as a cross-disciplinary learning approach.

2.3 Growth Needs

Hackman and Lawler [20] indicated that growth needs are desires of individuals to learn and take challenges in the pursuit of self-fulfillment and growth needs vary from one person to another in extent. In other words, growth needs are individualized. Research has revealed that people's mindset is crucial to accomplishments in many aspects of life. Those who believe that capability can be developed (with a growth mindset) are more determined and passionate in realizing long-term goals [21, 22]. If students know that they can fortify their belief in growth (new and even stronger neural links take shape while they strive to learn difficult things), they are even more motivated to learn and can render higher scores and reap better learning efficacy [21]. Fundamental psychological needs and relevant characteristics of personal and academic growths have gained quite some prominence [23–25]. The satisfaction of psychological needs in students are positively related to respective development outcomes [26–29]. Besides, the satisfaction of psychological needs also contributes to spontaneous involvement [30] and the search for more assistance [23]. Based on literature review, the following questions are raised for the study: What are the effects of integrating the PhBL approach into programming courses for non-IT majors on their systematic analytical capabilities, open-mindedness, intellectual curiosity, reflective and critical thinking, and overall growth needs, including any differences observed between students with low and high growth needs?

3 Methods

3.1 Participants

The study subjects were non-IT majors, 63 in total, from a national university in Taiwan. They chose "Emerging Technology and Logical Thinking" as their elective course. Each student spent a semester in finishing the "Emerging Technology and Logical Thinking" course.

3.2 Experimental Design

The 18-week "single group pre-test and post-test design" was adopted for the curriculum. There was one class session a week that lasted for 2 h. Students completed the "Critical Thinking Intent Questionnaire" in the beginning and at the end of the semester. A total of 63 valid copies of the questionnaire were recovered. The steps taken to apply the PhBL approach to the programming course are as follows Fig. 1, students' class work creative word cloud works as follows Fig. 2.

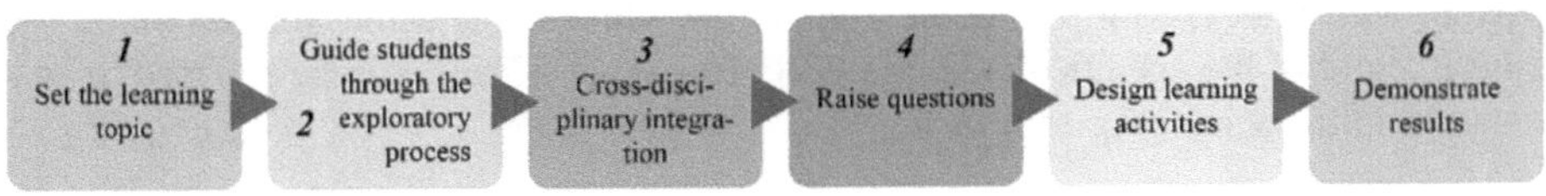

Fig. 1. PhBL course flow chart

The foregoing steps enable students to learn programming knowledge and skills and also to understand in depth daily life issues and phenomena and to develop important skills such as problem-solving and creative thinking.

Fig. 2. Creative word cloud works (Source: From students' class work)

3.3 Research Tool

Critical Thinking Intent Scale. The critical thinking intent scale of Yeh [31] is divided to four sub-constructs in total, namely, systematic analytical capabilities, open-mindedness, intellectual curiosity, and overall and reflective thinking. The overall critical thinking scale consists of 20 questions that are rated by the Likert 5-point scale of 1 (highly disagree) to 5 (highly agree). A higher score means a higher level of consent to what is described for the specific question. Reliability analysis was performed as part of the pre-test and post-test of each scale for this study. Analysis results showed that the pre-test and post-test Cronbach's α of internal consistency coefficient are .938 and .883 respectively for the 9 questions under systematic analytical capabilities, .868 and .750 respectively for the 4 questions under open-mindedness, .829 and 794 respectively for the 3 questions under intellectual curiosity, .860 and .840 respectively for the 4 questions under overall and reflective thinking, and .969 and .934 respectively for the 20 questions of the critical thinking intent scale. The reliability appeared to be optimal, as is shown in Table 1.

Growth Demand Scale. In the Job Diagnostic Survey (JDS) introduced by Hackman and Oldham [32], personal growth needs were meant mainly to weigh the individual needs in the pursuit of a higher level and consisted a total of 5 questions that were measured by the Likert 5-point scale of 1 (highly disagree) to 5 (highly agree). A higher score means a higher level of consent to what is described for the specific question. In this study, the pre-test Cronbach's α of internal consistency was .943 and the post-test one was .935; the reliability was quite desirable. See Table 1.

Table 1. Reliability of respective constructs of the critical thinking intent, growth needs and the interesting nature of course scale

-	Cronbach's α		Number of items
	pre-test	post-test	
Systematic analytical capabilities	.938	.883	9
Open-mindedness	.868	.750	4
Intellectual curiosity	.829	.794	3
Overall and reflective thinking	.860	.840	4
Critical thinking intent	.969	.934	20
Growth Needs	.943	.935	5
Interesting nature of course	.945	.958	6

4 Results

This study mainly explores the correlation between the integration of the PhBL approach in the programming course of non-IT majors and systematic analytical capabilities, open-mindedness, intellectual curiosity, overall and reflective thinking, critical thinking intent and growth needs? Are their capabilities enhanced? Are there differences between students with low growth needs and those with high ones in their critical thinking intent and the interesting nature of course? For this sake, SPSS is applied in this study for Pearson's correlation analysis, paired sample T-test, and independent sample T-test. Detailed results are provided below.

4.1 Analysis of Correlation of Respective Constructs

The Pearson's correlation analysis results revealed that the correlation coefficients among systematic analytical capabilities [$r(61) = .97, p < .01$], open-mindedness [$r(61) = .77, p < .01$], intellectual curiosity [$r(61) = .80, p < .01$], overall and reflective thinking [$r(61)$

$= .91, p < .01$], and critical thinking intent were consistently greater than 0.7, indicating significantly high positive correlation; those among systematic analytical capabilities [$r(61) = .50, p < .01$], intellectual curiosity [$r(61) = .46, p < .01$], overall and reflective thinking [$r(61) = .43, p < .01$], critical thinking intent [$r(61) = .50, p < .01$], and growth needs were between 0.4 and 0.7, indicating significantly moderate positive correlation; that with open-mindedness [$r(61) = .30, p < .05$] was smaller than 0.4, indicating significantly low positive correlation; those among systematic analytical capabilities [$r(61) = .44, p < .01$], intellectual curiosity [$r(61) = .41, p < .01$], overall and reflective thinking [$r(61) = .41, p < .01$], critical thinking intent [$r(61) = .46, p < .01$], growth needs [$r(61) = .69, p < .01$], and interesting nature of course were between 0.4 and 0.7, indicating significantly moderate positive correlation while that with open-mindedness [$r(61) = .35, p < .05$] was smaller than 0.4, indicating significantly low positive correlation. See Table 2.

Table 2. Correlation matrix of respective constructs upon Pearson's correlation analysis (N = 63) after the course

	1	2	3	4	5	6
1. Systematic analytical capabilities	-					
2. Open-mindedness	$.69^{**}$	-				
3. Intellectual curiosity	$.71^{**}$	$.50^{**}$	-			
4. Overall and reflective thinking	$.84^{**}$	$.60^{**}$	$.67^{**}$	-		
5. Critical thinking intent	$.97^{**}$	$.77^{**}$	$.80^{**}$	$.91^{**}$	-	
6. Growth needs	$.50^{**}$	$.30^{*}$	$.46^{**}$	$.43^{**}$	$.50^{**}$	-
7. Interesting nature of course	$.44^{**}$	$.35^{**}$	$.41^{**}$	$.41^{**}$	$.46^{**}$	$.69^{**}$

$^{*}p < .05$ ** p <. 01 *** p < .001

4.2 Analysis of Related Competencies After Participation in Course

In order to know if students' applicable competencies were enhanced after the course, the paired sample T-test was adopted for analysis and it revealed significant differences between pre-test and post-test means in systematic analytical capabilities ($t(62) = 2.13$, $p = .04$, $d = 0.27$). The post-test systematic analytical capabilities (M = 4.15, SD = 0.60) were significantly greater than the pre-test ones (M = 3.88, SD = 0.75). Open-mindedness differed significantly between pre-test and post-test means ($t(62) = 2.57, p = .01$, $d = .32$). The post-test open-mindedness (M = 4.28, SD = 0.50) was significantly greater than the pre-test one (M = 3.97, SD = 0.73). Intellectual curiosity differed significantly between pre-test and post-test means ($t(62) = 3.77$, $p = .00$, $d = .48$). The post-test intellectual curiosity (M = 4.25, SD = 0.66) was significantly greater than the pre-test one (M = 3.74, SD = 0.79). Overall and reflective thinking differed significantly between pre-test and post-test means ($t(62) = 2.16$, $p = .03$, $d = .27$). The post-test overall and reflective thinking (M = 4.09, SD = 0.72) was significantly greater than the pre-test one (M = 3.79, SD = 0.78). Critical thinking intent differed significantly between pre-test and post-test means ($t(62) = 2.65, p = .01, d = .33$). The post-test critical thinking intent (M = 4.18, SD = 0.55) was significantly greater than the pre-test one (M = 3.85, SD = 0.72). Growth needs differed significantly between pre-test and post-test means ($t(62) = 2.41, p = .02, d = .30$). The post-test growth needs (M = 3.99, SD = 0.88) were significantly greater than the pre-test ones (M = 3.62, SD = 0.84). They indicate that students' systematic analytical capabilities, open-mindedness, intellectual curiosity, overall and reflective thinking, critical thinking intent, and growth needs were all significant. See Table 3. In other words, the integration of the PhBL approach in the programming course of non-IT majors did significantly enhance the systematic analytical capabilities, open-mindedness, intellectual curiosity, overall and reflective thinking, critical thinking intent and growth needs.

Table 3. T-test of pre-test and post-test differences (N = 63)

Dimension	*M(SD)*		*df*	*t-value*	*p*	*d*
	pre-test	post-test				
Systematic analytical capabilities	3.87 (0.75)	4.15 (0.60)	62	2.13	$.04^{*}$	0.27
Open-mindedness	3.97 (0.73)	4.28 (0.50)	62	2.57	$.01^{*}$	0.32
Intellectual curiosity	3.74 (0.79)	4.25 (0.66)	62	3.77	$.00^{***}$	0.48
Overall and reflective thinking	3.79 (0.78)	4.09 (0.72)	62	2.16	$.03^{*}$	0.27
Critical thinking intent	3.85 (0.72)	4.18 (0.55)	62	2.65	$.01^{**}$	0.33
Growth needs	3.62 (0.84)	3.99 (0.88)	62	2.41	$.02^{*}$	0.30

$^{*}p < .05$ $^{**}p <. 01$ $^{***}p < .001$

4.3 Analysis of Low and High Growth Needs

In order to know the differences, if any, between low growth needs and high ones in terms of critical thinking intent and interesting nature of course, the independent sample t test was adopted for analysis in this study. Results are shown in Table 4. The results showed significant differences between low growth needs and high ones in critical thinking intent ($t(31) = -4.26, p = .000, d = 0.75$). Low growth needs ($M = 3.89, SD = 0.55$) were smaller than high ones ($M = 4.61, SD = 0.40$), with significant correlation. Significant differences were found in interesting nature of course ($t(31) = -6.33, p = .000, d = 1.12$). Low growth needs ($M = 2.72, SD = 0.57$) were smaller than high ones ($M = 4.35, SD = 0.89$), with significant correlation.

Table 4. Independent sample t-test of low and high growth needs

Dimension	*M (SD)*		*df*	*t-value*	*p*	*d*
	Low growth needs ($N = 17$)	High growth needs ($N = 16$)				
Critical thinking intent	3.89 (0.55)	4.61 (0.40)	31	−4.26	$.000^{***}$	0.75
Interesting nature of course	2.72 (0.57)	4.35 (0.89)	31	−6.33	$.000^{***}$	1.12

$^{*}p < .05$ $^{**}p < .01$ $^{***}p < .001$

5 Conclusion

What are the effects of integrating the PhBL approach into programming courses for non-IT majors on their systematic analytical capabilities, open-mindedness, intellectual curiosity, reflective and critical thinking, and overall growth needs, including any differences observed between students with low and high growth needs? We will answer questions about this study in more details below.

Through Table 2, we know that correlation coefficients of respective constructs with the overall scale were consistently greater than 0.7, indicating significantly high positive correlation. This answers to the research findings of Yeh [31]. In terms of growth needs and interesting nature of course, except for the correlation coefficient of open-mindedness, which was smaller than 0.4 and demonstrated significantly low positive correlation, the remainder was between 0.4 and 0.7, indicating significantly moderate positive correlation. This answers to the research findings of Marcos-Vílchez et al. [13]. Throughout critical thinking, competency and character are complementary to each other because they help students take advantage of evidence and evaluate the provided materials and reflect upon ideas. As far as interesting nature of course is concerned, its correlation with growth needs is close to highly relevant ($.69^{**}$), which proves that it helps reinforce students' motivation for growth needs if they have enriched and pleasant learning experience and it will convert to participation and persistence of learning behavior [9].

Through Table 3, we know that, in terms of pre-test and post-test means, post-test ones were consistently greater than pre-test ones, indicating that the integration of the PhBL approach in the programming course of non-IT majors did significantly enhance the systematic analytical capabilities, open-mindedness, intellectual curiosity, overall and reflective thinking, critical thinking intent and growth needs. The sub-construct of intellectual curiosity reached significance ($p < .001$), indicating that the integration of PhBL approach allowed the students to begin with daily life issues and link their living environment and experience [18] and the combination of programming and visual design and it contributed to enhanced intellectual curiosity of the students. Such an exploratory learning process enhanced the critical thinking intent [18].

Through Table 4, we know that the critical thinking intent and interesting nature of course among students with high growth needs were both greater than those among students with low ones and highly significant ($p < .001$). This is because high growth needs are associated with the pursuit of self-fulfillment and the desire to take challenges [20] and growth needs vary from one person to another in extent. In other words, growth needs are individualized. Learners with high growth needs will reinforce the positive correlation between the characteristics of the task and their key psychological states. In addition, they will strengthen the correlation between their psychological states and satisfaction as well as efficacy. This falls in line with the findings of related studies. As such, learners with high growth needs reinforce the scenario of curricular design and curricular innovation and create positive correlation with their mindset. Such a mindset can exercise an important effect on their accomplishments in many aspects of life. Those who believe that capability can be developed (with a growth mindset) are more determined and passionate in realizing long-term goals [21, 22]. Once students fortify their belief in growth (new and even stronger neural links take shape while they strive to learn difficult things), they are even more motivated to learn and will have even greater learning accomplishments.

Disclosure of Interests. It is now necessary to declare any competing interests or to specifically state that the authors have no competing interests.

References

1. Almerich, G., Suárez-Rodríguez, J., Díaz-García, I., Cebrián-Cifuentes, S.: 21st-century competences: The relation of ICT competences with higher-order thinking capacities and teamwork competences in university students. J. Comput. Assist. Learn. **36**(4), 468–479 (2020)
2. Assaly, I., Jabarin, A.: Arab Israeli EFL teachers' perceptions and practices vis-à-vis teaching higher-order thinking skills: a complicated relationship. Language Teaching Research, 13621688211032426 (2021)
3. Liu, D., Zhang, H.: Improving students' higher order thinking skills and achievement using WeChat based flipped classroom in higher education. Educ. Inf. Technol. **27**(5), 7281–7302 (2022)
4. Buitrago Flórez, F., Casallas, R., Hernández, M., Reyes, A., Restrepo, S., Danies, G.: Changing a generation's way of thinking: teaching computational thinking through programming. Rev. Educ. Res. **87**(4), 834–860 (2017)
5. Garcia, M.B.: Cooperative learning in computer programming: a quasi-experimental evaluation of Jigsaw teaching strategy with novice programmers. Educ. Inf. Technol. **26**(4), 4839–4856 (2021)
6. Wu, T.T., Chen, J.M.: Combining Webduino programming with situated learning to promote computational thinking, motivation, and satisfaction among high school students. J. Edu. Comp. Res. **60**(3), 631–660 (2022)
7. Liu, C.Y., Li, W., Huang, J.Y. Lei, L.Y., Zhang, P.R.: Collaborative programming based on social shared regulation: An approach to improving students' programming achievements and group metacognition. J. Comput. Assist. Learn. **39**(5), 1714–1731 (2023)
8. Psycharis, S., Kallia, M.: The effects of computer programming on high school students' reasoning skills and mathematical self-efficacy and problem solving. Instr. Sci. **45**(5), 583–602 (2017)

9. Popat, S., Starkey, L.: Learning to code or coding to learn? A systematic review. Computers & Education **128**, 365–376 (2019)
10. McMillan, J.H.: Enhancing college students' critical thinking: a review of studies. Res. High. Educ. **26**, 3–29 (1987)
11. Rui, W., et al.: The research design of the 5Cs framework for twenty-first century key competences. Journal of East China Normal University (Educational Sciences) **38**(2), 20 (2020)
12. Facione, P.A., Facione, N.C., Giancarlo, C.A.: Professional judgment and the disposition toward critical thinking (1997). Retrieved 21 Nov2020
13. Marcos-Vílchez, J.M., Sánchez-Martín, M., Muñiz-Velázquez, J.A.: Effectiveness of training actions aimed at improving critical thinking in the face of disinformation: a systematic review protocol. Thinking Skills and Creativity, 101474 (2024)
14. Halpern, D.F.: Thought and knowledge: an introduction to critical thinking. Psychology press (2013)
15. Altun, E., Yildirim, N.: What does critical thinking mean? Examination of pre-service teachers' cognitive structures and definitions for critical thinking. Thinking Skills and Creativity **49**, 101367 (2023)
16. Rauste-von Wright, M.: The function of curriculum and the concept of learning. Curriculum approaches. Readings and activities for educational studies, 21–34 (2001)
17. Küpers, W.: Phenomenology of learning. In: Seel, N.B., (ed.) Encyclopedia of the Sciences of Learning, pp. 2611–2615 Springer, Cham, Switzerland (2012)
18. Tian, M., Risku, M.: A distributed leadership perspective on the Finnish curriculum reform 2014. J. Curric. Stud. **51**(2), 229–244 (2019)
19. Wolff, L.A.: Phenomenon-based learning. In: Encyclopedia of Sustainable Management, pp. 1–9. Springer International Publishing, Cham (2022)
20. Hackman, J.R., Lawler, E.E.: Employee reactions to job characteristics. J. Appl. Psychol. **55**(3), 259 (1971)
21. Toding, M., Mädamürk, K., Venesaar, U., Malleus, E.: Teachers' mindset and attitudes towards learners and learning environment to support students' entrepreneurial attitudes in universities. The Int. J. Manage. Edu. **21**(1), 100769 (2023)
22. Hochanadel, A., Finamore, D.: Fixed and growth mindset in education and how grit helps students persist in the face of adversity. J. Int. Edu. Res. (JIER) **11**(1), 47–50 (2015)
23. Earl, S.R., Taylor, I.M., Meijen, C., Passfield, L.: Trajectories in cognitive engagement, fatigue, and school achievement: The role of young adolescents' psychological need satisfaction. Learn. Individ. Differ. **101**, 102248 (2023)
24. Guay, F.: Applying self-determination theory to education: regulations types, psychological needs, and autonomy supporting behaviors. Can. J. Sch. Psychol. **37**(1), 75–92 (2022)
25. Howard, J.L., Bureau, J.S., Guay, F., Chong, J.X., Ryan, R.M.: Student motivation and associated outcomes: A meta-analysis from self-determination theory. Perspect. Psychol. Sci. **16**(6), 1300–1323 (2021)
26. Tian, L., Chen, H., Huebner, E.S.: The longitudinal relationships between basic psychological needs satisfaction at school and school-related subjective well-being in adolescents. Soc. Indic. Res. **119**, 353–372 (2014)
27. Huhtiniemi, M., Sääkslahti, A., Watt, A., Jaakkola, T.: Associations among basic psychological needs, motivation and enjoyment within finnish physical education students. J. Sports Sci. Med. **18**(2), 239 (2019)
28. Carmona-Halty, M., Schaufeli, W.B., Llorens, S., Salanova, M.: Satisfaction of basic psychological needs leads to better academic performance via increased psychological capital: A three-wave longitudinal study among high school students. Front. Psychol. **10**, 474273 (2019)
29. Alivernini, F., et al.: Positive youth development among youth living in poverty: the role of psychological needs satisfaction. Youth & Society **55**(5), 947–969 (2023)

30. Bureau, J.S., Howard, J.L., Chong, J.X., Guay, F.: Pathways to student motivation: a meta-analysis of antecedents of autonomous and controlled motivations. Rev. Educ. Res. **92**(1), 46–72 (2022)
31. Yeh, Y.C.: A study of substitute teachers' professional knowledge, personal teaching efficacy, and teaching behavior in critical-thinking instruction. Journal of Chengchi University **78**, 55–84 (1999)
32. Hackman, J.R., Oldham, G.R.: Development of the job diagnostic survey. J. Appl. Psychol. **60**(2), 159 (1975)

The Effect of Integrating Task Scaffolding into MakeCode Arcade with WiFiBoy on Students' Learning Motivation, Cooperative Tendency, and Altruistic Behaviors in Programming Learning

Wei-Ting Wu[1], Po-Han Wu[1](✉), Ming-Chia Wu[1], Tosti H. C. Chiang[2], and Jan-Pan Hwang[3]

[1] Department of Information and Learning Technology, National University of Tainan, Tainan City, Taiwan
d11055001@stumail.nutn.edu.tw, phwu@mail.nutn.edu.tw

[2] Department of Graduate Institute of Mass, Communication National Taiwan Normal University, Taipei City, Taiwan

[3] Department of Information, Management National Chin-Yi University of Technology, Tauchung City, Taiwan

Abstract. This study investigates how Task Scaffolding in MakeCode Arcade with WiFiBoy affects elementary school students' motivation and altruism in programming. The study adopted a quasi-experimental research design with 39 sixth-grade students from two classes in an elementary school. The classes were divided into task scaffolding in MakeCode Arcade with WiFiBoy and web-based simulator groups. Both groups implemented the same MakeCode Arcade platform programming curriculum. They conducted a three-lesson teaching experiment, which was preceded and followed by pre-test and post-tests of the programming learning motivation questionnaire, and the whole teaching experiment was video recorded to observe students' altruistic behavior.

The study results showed that the Make Code Arcade with task scaffolding could help students improve their learning effectiveness and the number of altruistic behaviors. In terms of the altruistic behavior conversion mode, it is suggested that when designing the teaching activities, in addition to combining the hardware objects and task scaffolding in the programming courses, teachers should also give students more opportunities for discussion, peer feedback, and encourage them to assist their peers in completing programming tasks in the learning environment, so that the students can show more altruistic behaviors, to enhance the learning effectiveness of the learners in the programming learning and the altruistic behaviors.

Keywords: Learning motivation · Cooperative learning · Altruistic behavior · Programming

Y.-P. Cheng et al. (Eds.): ICITL 2024, LNCS 14785, pp. 244–252, 2024.
https://doi.org/10.1007/978-3-031-65881-5_26

1 Introduction

Rapid technological advancements have complicated the problems individuals face, necessitating more efficient solutions. Computational thinking, a concept introduced by Wing in 2006 [1], offers a framework for creatively solving problems using computer science principles [2]. This skill, essential not just for computer scientists but for everyone, applies to problem-solving, system design, and understanding human behavior [3]. It's also integrated into Taiwan's 12-year National Basic Education Curriculum, emphasizing programming within Information Technology.

Cognitive tasks in programming education are crucial for fostering computational thinking [1]. Scratch, a visual programming language (VPL) developed by MIT in 2007, is widely used in elementary schools to promote creative, collaborative, and systematic thinking through visual programming [4]. VPLs like Scratch employ visual elements in programming, providing an intuitive interface that enhances student motivation more than traditional textual languages [5–7].

Using Scratch, students develop computational thinking and problem-solving skills [8]. However, its single-player focus may limit cooperative learning and restrict collaborative skills development [9]. Over time, students might lose interest, feeling the learning process ends once they can operate the computer, potentially decreasing motivation. Recently, a Taiwanese company introduced WiFiBoy, a handheld gaming console that lowers the entry barrier for programming [10]. The researcher plans to integrate WiFiBoy into the elementary curriculum to boost motivation and extend learning goals beyond solo game creation, including cooperative play. This integration aims to enhance peer interactions, empathy, and experience sharing, enriching the learning environment.

Slavin (1985) [11] defines cooperative learning as a structured strategy where teachers organize students into diverse groups based on ability, gender, and ethnicity, applicable across various subjects and grade levels. Parker (1985) [12] describes it as an environment for students to assist and share with peers in heterogeneous groups [13]. Johnson & Johnson (1994) [14] state that effective cooperative learning involves positive interdependence, personal responsibility, direct interaction, social skills, and group processing [15], enhancing learning performance [16]. In constructivism, Vygotsky & Cole (1978) [17] introduced the Zone of Proximal Development (ZPD), where a child learns with the aid of a more capable individual, enhancing their potential [18]. However, as students differ in their programming abilities and learning rates, their willingness to help peers can vary, influenced by personal gain or loss considerations, reflecting altruistic behaviors such as helping, sharing, and empathizing [19–22].

Altruism is crucial in elementary school group dynamics, enhancing interpersonal relationships and social connections. Studies show altruistic behaviors improve academic performance and personal happiness [23, 24]. Cooperative learning is an effective method to foster altruism, supported by Vygotsky's social constructionist framework. Digital games are practical tools within this framework, offering immediate motivation and scaffolding for educational purposes. Both digital and traditional games that promote altruistic and cooperative behaviors have proven to significantly influence children's altruistic tendencies, encouraging them to cooperate and share objectives through interactive gameplay.

This study integrates task scaffolding with WiFiBoy and MakeCode Arcade in programming courses for senior elementary students. WiFiBoy, depicted in Fig. 1, is the primary interactive tool, enhancing motivation by visualizing programming languages and incorporating cooperative learning techniques. Students collaborate on game design and share their creations, gaining practical experience and developing cooperative problem-solving skills through interactive learning.

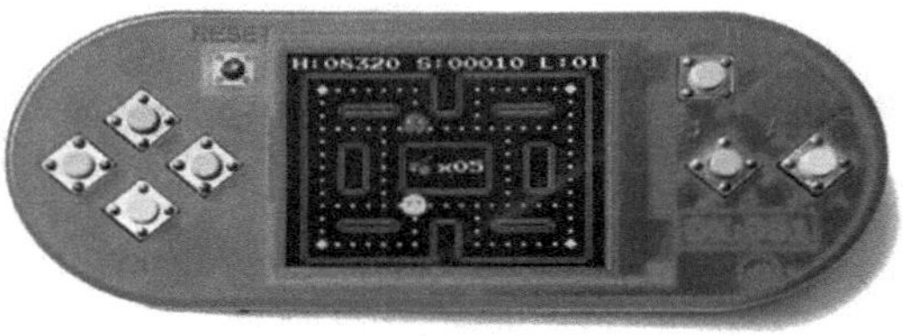

Fig. 1. OK-D51 Model WiFiBoy Gaming Console

2 Material and Research Method

2.1 Research Question

RQ1. To investigate whether using WiFiBoy Arcade with task scaffolding significantly affects elementary school students' programming motivation and cooperation tendency. RQ2. What are elementary school students' different learning patterns of altruistic behaviors when using Task Scaffolding in MakeCode Arcade with WiFiBoy in programming teaching?

2.2 Task Scaffolding Environment

The MakeCode Arcade platform interface includes the simulator, block-based command area, and coding area. Researchers enhanced this setup with the Block Mask Extension Kit on Google Chrome, positioned on the upper right side of the coding area. This extension divides the curriculum into ten progressive units for game creation, each featuring a 'Unit Description Area,' 'Hints Area,' and 'Submit Assignment Area,' as detailed in Fig. 2. The 'View Hint' and 'Show Answer' buttons provide staged guidance: the former overlays the first hint, while the latter shows the complete solution, effectively scaffolding learning. This selective visibility reduces cognitive load by limiting interaction to relevant blocks, thus improving engagement and motivation. Teachers can track student progress through these assignments.

2.3 Research Design and Sample

This study involved 39 sixth-grade students from an elementary school in Kaohsiung City, Taiwan, who had basic programming knowledge. Employing a quasi-experimental

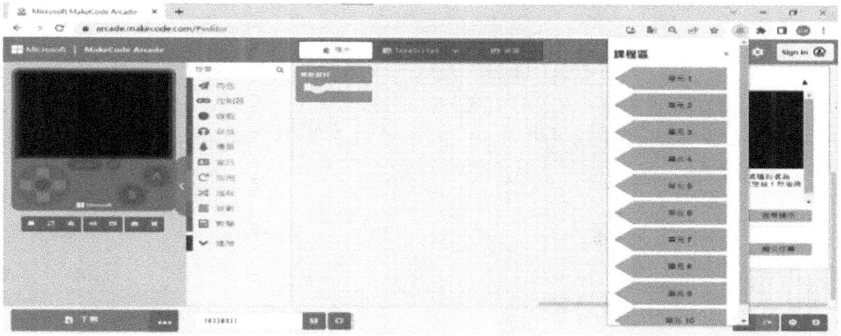

Fig. 2. The Function and Interface of Block Mast Extension Kit on Google Chrome

design, students were divided into experimental and control groups. Before the experiment, pre-test questionnaires on programming motivation and cooperation tendencies were administered. During the experiment, the experimental group used Task Scaffolding in MakeCode Arcade with WiFiBoy and a block mask expansion kit, while the control group used web-based simulators. Both groups were recorded with two cameras for the entire teaching process. Post-test cooperation questionnaires were given right after the experiments, and video recordings were analyzed for altruistic behavior coding.

2.4 Research Tool

Programming Learning Motivation Questionnaire. This questionnaire, adapted from Wang and Chen (2010) and based on a scale by Pintrich et al. (1991), aimed to measure students' motivation levels in programming. It demonstrated reliability with a Cronbach's α of 0.79, indicating a credible level of consistency.

Cooperation Tendency Questionnaire. This study used the Collaborative Inclination Scale by Lai and Hwang (2014) to assess students' inclination toward collaborative programming. The scale's reliability ranged from 0.69 to 0.84, with an overall Cronbach's α of 0.85, reflecting good stability and consistency.

Altruistic Behavior Coding Table. Researchers developed a coding table for altruistic behaviors, divided into four groups: Sharing Resources, Praise and Encouragement, Helping Others, and Collaborative Contribution. This table, encompassing nine specific behaviors (e.g., Sharing, Inviting, Feedback, Assistance), was used to record observed behaviors during the experiment. Experts reviewed and refined it to ensure content validity.

3 Result

3.1 Learning Motivation in Programming

The programming learning motivation questionnaire utilized a Likert five-point rating scale, where higher scores denote a more positive and proactive learning motivation within that dimension for learners. Table 1 presents the average and standard deviation of both pre-and post-test scores from the programming learning motivation questionnaire across different programming learning tools.

Table 1. Mean and standard deviation of pre-and post-tests for the programming learning motivation questionnaire with different learning tools.

Motivation	Learning Tools	N	Pre-test		Post-test	
			Mean	SD	Mean	SD
Learning Motivation	Task Scaffolding WiFiBoy Group	20	4.01	.58	4.24	.55
	Web Simulator Group	19	4.05	.76	4.25	.80
	Total	39	4.03	.67	4.25	.67
Internal Motivation	Task Scaffolding WiFiBoy Group	20	4.00	.63	4.35	.60
	Web Simulator Group	19	3.97	.90	4.21	1.01
	Total	39	3.98	.76	4.25	.81
External Motivation	Task Scaffolding WiFiBoy Group	20	4.00	.72	4.12	.67
	Web Simulator Group	19	4.18	.72	4.35	.71
	Total	39	4.09	.72	4.23	.69

In the pre-test, the web simulator group scored higher overall and external learning motivation than the Task Scaffolding into MakeCode Arcade with WiFiBoy Group, which scored slightly higher in internal motivation. The web simulator group showed more significant variance in overall and internal motivation scores, suggesting more variability within this group. In contrast, the variance in external motivation was similar between the groups.

In the post-test, the web simulator group scored higher in external motivation, whereas the Task Scaffolding group had higher internal motivation scores. The mean scores for overall learning motivation were relatively similar between the two groups. Again, the web simulator group displayed more significant score variability in overall and internal motivation. Covariance analysis was used to assess the impact of the different learning tools on programming motivation, with results indicating a consistent distribution pattern across both groups.

Table 2 illustrates that after adjusting for pre-test scores as covariates, the covariance analysis showed an F-value of .01 and a significance level of .94 ($p > .05$). This indicates that there was no statistically significant difference in post-test learning motivation between the groups using different programming tools. Essentially, the type of learning tool did not significantly impact the student's learning motivation.

3.2 Descriptive Statistics of Programming Cooperation Tendency

The programming cooperation tendency questionnaire uses a five-point Likert scale, with higher scores indicating stronger cooperation tendencies. Table 3 shows both groups' mean and standard deviation of pre-test and post-test scores. In the pre-test, the Task

Table 2. Post-test Covariate Analysis of Programming Motivation Questionnaires with Different Learning Tools.

Post-test of Learning Motivation	Group	Number	Mean	Standard Deviation	Adjusted Mean	F	Significance
Total Score	Task Scaffolding WiFiBoy Group	20	4.24	.55	4.24[a]	.01	.94
	Web Simulator Group	19	4.25	.80	4.25[a]		

a. The covariate present in the model is estimated at the following value: Learning Motivation Pre-test = 4.11

Scaffolding into MakeCode Arcade with WiFiBoy Group had an average score of 4.22 (SD = .49) compared to the web simulator group's 4.17 (SD = .61). In the post-test, the Task Scaffolding group scored higher again with an average of 4.45 (SD = .65). In contrast, the web simulator group scored 4.34 (SD = .70).

Table 3. The Mean and standard deviation of the pre-test and post-test scores of the programming cooperation tendency questionnaire for different learning tools.

Motivation	Learning tools	N	Pre-test		Post-test	
			Mean	Standard Deviation	Mean	Standard Deviation
Cooperative Tendency	Task Scaffolding WiFiBoy Group	20	4.22	.49	4.45	.65
	Web simulator group	19	4.17	.61	4.34	.70
	Total	39	4.20	.55	4.40	.66

The table shows that the average cooperation tendency of the Task Scaffolding into MakeCode Arcade with WiFiBoy Group was higher than that of the web simulator group in both the pre-test and post-test. Additionally, the standard deviation data for both groups were similar, indicating a comparable distribution pattern.

Table 4 indicates that after excluding the influence of pre-test scores on post-test scores, the result shows an F-value of 0.50, with a significance of 0.49 ($p > .05$). This suggests no significant difference between the groups. The performance of the two groups of students on the cooperative tendency questionnaire did not vary due to the different learning tools.

Table 4. Summary of Covariance Analysis for Post-test of Cooperative Tendency in Programming Among Different Learning Tools.

Post-test of cooperation tendency	Group	N	Mean	Standard Deviation	Adjusted Mean	F	Significance
Final Score	Task Scaffolding WiFiBoy Group	20	4.45	.65	4.45[a]	.50	.49
	web simulator group	19	4.34	.70	4.34[a]		

3.3 Altruistic Behavior Sequence Analysis

The altruistic behavior code used in this study was compiled based on relevant literature. According to the recording of the experimental process, two groups were selected from Task Scaffolding into MakeCode Arcade with WiFiBoy Group and a web simulator group to analyze the frequency and sequence of altruistic behaviors among students within each subset. To improve the reliability of the behavioral sequences, two experts were invited to verify the validity of the sequences by the Kappa test, and the Kappa consistency coefficient was .76 ($p < .001$), which is a significant consistency. The number of times the two groups of students produced the altruistic behavior items is shown in Table 5.

Table 5. Altruistic behavior code generation ratio of Task Scaffolding into MakeCode Arcade with WiFiBoy Group and web simulator groups.

Group	Count	SH	SI	PB	PF	HA	HI	CD	CC	CE	Total
Task Scaffolding Group	Number	18	16	2	18	32	24	86	6	3	205
	Ratio	9%	8%	1%	9%	16%	12%	42%	3%	0%	100%
Web simulator group	Number	4	11	3	3	25	13	63	4	0	126
	Ratio	3%	9%	2%	2%	20%	10%	50%	3%	1%	100%

Table 5 shows that the number of altruistic behaviors generated by the Task Scaffolding into MakeCode Arcade with WiFiBoy Group is higher than that of the web simulator group. In terms of the distribution of altruistic behaviors, the four altruistic behaviors that generated more altruistic behaviors were SH (sharing), PF (feedback), HI (instructing), and CE (contributing). Both groups' most frequent altruistic behavior was CD (discuss), followed by HA (assist).

The main differences in altruistic behavior sequences between the two groups are considered statistically significant if the z-score exceeds 1.96 ($p < .05$). The Task Scaffolding into MakeCode Arcade with WiFiBoy Group exhibited three behavior sequences that were statistically significant and absent in the web simulator group. Conversely, the Web Simulator group displayed eight behavior sequences that reached statistical significance, which were not present in the Task Scaffolding into MakeCode Arcade with WiFiBoy Group (Fig. 3).

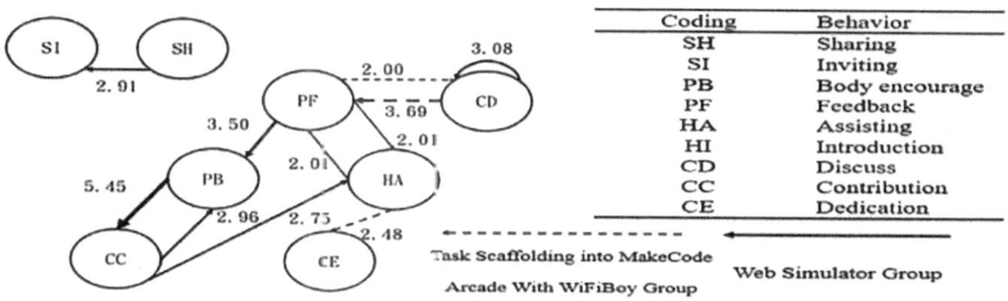

Fig. 3. The Difference Between the Two Groups of Altruistic Behavior Transitions

Figure 3 highlights significant behavioral sequences in the Task Scaffolding Group: CD → PF, PF → CD, HA → CE. During interactions, students look at the screen or discuss (CD) to assist each other, provide positive feedback (PF), and then return to discussing (CD) to complete tasks. They also help peers by physically approaching the screen (HA) and then getting invited to assist further (CE). For the Web Simulator group, significant sequences include SH → SI, CD → CD, PF → PB, PB → CC, CC → PB, CC → HA, PF → HA, HA → PF. Students share (SH) and invite peers to engage (SI). Discussions are repeated (CD → CD), with affirming gestures (PB) leading to more active requests for assistance (CC) and continued support (PB → CC). Help offered (HA) results in further positive feedback (PF), enhancing collaborative interactions.

4 Conclusion

The study found no significant differences in learning motivation or cooperative tendency between students using Task Scaffolding with MakeCode Arcade and those using web simulators, suggesting that the type of learning tool did not affect these outcomes. Despite this, intrinsic motivation in both groups improved after the experiment. Notably, the Task Scaffolding group displayed more altruistic behaviors and fewer transitions between these behaviors than the web simulator group. In particular, students in the Task Scaffolding group were more proactive in giving positive feedback and sharing resources, such as inviting peers to use the WiFiBoy console. These actions boosted cognitive engagement and confidence, facilitating cooperative learning and mutual benefits. While the learning tools did not influence motivational levels or cooperation, the specific interactions and feedback mechanisms enabled by Task Scaffolding significantly enhanced altruistic behaviors and peer interaction dynamics.

References

1. Grover, S., Pea, R.: Computational thinking in K–12: A review of the state of the field. Educ. Res. **42**(1), 38–43 (2013)
2. Shute, V.J., Sun, C., Asbell-Clarke, J.: Demystifying computational thinking. Educ. Res. Rev. **22**, 142–158 (2017)
3. Wing, J.M.: Computational thinking. Commun. ACM **49**(3), 33–35 (2006)
4. Denning, P.J., Tedre, M.: Computational thinking. MIT Press, Cambridge (2019)
5. Burnett, M.M., McIntyre, D.W.: Visual programming. Computer-Los Alamitos **28**, 14 (1995)
6. Prensky, M.: Digital natives, digital immigrants part 1. On the Horizon **9**(5), 1–6 (2001)
7. Funkhouser, C.: The influence of problem-solving software on student attitudes about mathematics. J. Res. Comput. Educ. **25**(3), 339–346 (1993)
8. Resnick, M., et al.: Scratch: programming for all. Communications of the ACM 52(11), 60–67 (2009)
9. Seyed, T., et al.: MakerArcade: using gaming and physical computing for playful making, learning, and creativity. Extended Abstracts of the 2019 CHI Conference on Human Factors in Computing Systems, pp. 1–6. ACM, New Tork (2019)
10. Stevenson, A.: Oxford dictionary of English. Oxford University Press, USA (2010)
11. Slavin, R.E.: Cooperative learning Applying contact theory in desegregated schools. J. Soc. Issues **41**, 45–62 (1985)
12. Parker, R.E.: Small-group cooperative learning—Improving academic, social gains in the classroom. NASSP Bull. **69**(479), 48–57 (1985)
13. Kagan, S., Kagan, S.: Cooperative learning. Kagan, San Clemente (1994)
14. Johnson, D.W., Johnson, R.T.: Leading the cooperative school. Interaction Book Company Edina, MN (1994)
15. Deutsch, M.: A theory of co-operation and competition. Human Relations **2**(2), 129–152 (1949)
16. Van Ryzin, M.J., Roseth, C.J., Biglan, A.: Mediators of effects of cooperative learning on altruistic behavior in middle school. Int. J. Appl. Posit. Psychol. **5**(1–2), 37–52 (2020)
17. Vygotsky, L.S., Cole, M.: Mind in society: Development of higher psychological processes. Harvard University Press, Cambridge (1978)
18. Doolittle, P.E.: Understanding Cooperative Learning through Vygotsky's Zone of Proximal Development (1995)
19. Gilligan, C.: In a different voice: Psychological theory and women's development. Harvard University Press, Cambridge (1993)
20. Johnson, D.W., Johnson, R.T.: Cooperative, competitive, and individualistic learning environments. Int. Guide Stude. Achiev. 372–374 (2013)
21. Grusec, J.E., Sherman, A.: Altruistic Behavior. Social development Relationships in infancy, childhood, and adolescence, 263–286 (2011)
22. Honig, A.S.: Prosocial development in children. Young Children 51–62 (1982)
23. Fehr, E., Fischbacher, U.: The nature of human altruism. Nature **425**(6960), 785–791 (2003)
24. Istiqomah, I., Supriatna, M., Budiman, N.: Fostering Altruism in Elementary School. In: International Conference on Educational Psychology and Pedagogy-" Diversity in Education" (ICEPP 2019), pp. 110–113. Atlantis Press, Paris (2020)

The Impact of Prior Knowledge on the Motivation and Effectiveness of Using the English Sentence Rearrangement Practice System

Jui-Chi Peng[1](✉) and Gwo-Haur Hwang[2]

[1] Holistic Education Center, Cardinal Tien Junior College of Healthcare and Management, Taipei City, Taiwan
kikipeng@ctcn.edu.tw

[2] Graduate School of Intelligent Data Science, National Yunlin University of Science and Technology, Taipei City, Taiwan

Abstract. The study explores the impact of prior knowledge on the motivation and effectiveness of using the English Sentence Rearrangement Practice System. Through an empirical investigation involving 87 first-year students from a nursing department in northern Taiwan, the research investigates the relationship between prior knowledge, learning motivation, and learning effectiveness. The study consisted of an 8-week experimental teaching program, with 100 min of instruction each week. In the first week, participants received an introduction to the system and completed a pre-test. Through the second to the seventh weeks, learners engaged in individual practice using the system either during or after class. In the eighth week, participants underwent a post-test examination and completed the ARCS (Attention, Relevance, Confidence, and Satisfaction) learning motivation questionnaire. Findings suggest that while there is no significant difference in learning motivation between learners with high and low prior knowledge levels, the use of the English Sentence Rearrangement Practice System effectively sustains learners' motivation levels, as evidenced by consistently high average values of the ARCS. Moreover, the system significantly enhances learning effectiveness, particularly for learners with low prior knowledge, indicating its potential to bridge performance gaps. These results underscore the importance of instructional approaches and the integration of digital technologies in language learning contexts. The study contributes certain observations into enhancing language teaching strategies to support learners in their language acquisition journey.

Keywords: Sentence Structure · Prior knowledge · Learning Motivation · Learning Effectiveness · English Sentence Rearrangement Practice System

1 Introduction

Research on sentence structure and English learning has underscored the pivotal role of sentence structure in expressing thoughts and ideas [1]. English learners frequently face challenges in mastering sentence structure due to various factors, including the influence

Y.-P. Cheng et al. (Eds.): ICITL 2024, LNCS 14785, pp. 253–263, 2024.
https://doi.org/10.1007/978-3-031-65881-5_27

of their native language and the inherent complexity of English sentence structure [1]. This difficulty often leads to errors in sentence variety, with learners showing a tendency to favor certain structures over others [2]. Effective language teaching methods and strategies are crucial to address these challenges [1]. Proficiency in understanding English sentence structure is not only vital for effective writing, reading, and critical thinking [3], but also for facilitating accurate sentence production, which can be influenced by the statistical properties of learners' native language input [4].

In language learning, prior knowledge plays a significant role and can influence learning strategies [6]. Several studies have highlighted the substantial impact of prior knowledge, learning motivation, and instructional behaviors on learning effectiveness. Usman [7] observed that learning motivation, cognitive strategy, and prior knowledge all positively affect learning satisfaction. Prior knowledge serves as a robust predictor of second language (L2) proficiency, especially in receptive vocabulary knowledge and speaking skills [8]. Moreover, leveraging prior knowledge schemas in foreign language teaching and learning is crucial, with organizational and personal dimensions identified as key factors [9]. These dimensions encompass not only the organization of existing knowledge but also the personal interpretation and application of that knowledge in learning contexts, thus shaping learners' approaches to language acquisition.

The integration of digital technology into English language teaching and learning has become increasingly vital, particularly in response to the COVID-19 pandemic [10, 11]. Both students and teachers demonstrate high digital literacy and utilize digital technology for various language learning activities, with a preference for mobile devices [12]. Despite the challenges posed by digital learning, students generally perceive its effectiveness for English language acquisition beyond the traditional classroom setting [13]. These findings underscore the importance for policymakers and educators to incorporate digital technologies into English language classrooms and to support learners in utilizing digital devices for language learning outside of class.

Hence, this study proposes the development of a digital learning system – the English Sentence Rearrangement Practice System – to address the aforementioned issues. This system aims to enhance English language learning by providing learners with opportunities to practice rearranging sentences, thereby improving their understanding of sentence structure and syntax. The study seeks to investigate the impact of prior knowledge levels on the utilization of this system and its effects on the learning motivation and effectiveness of English learners. Through exploring these factors, this research aims to contribute to the development of effective language teaching methods and strategies to support English language learners in their educational journey.

2 System Introduction

This study has developed an English Sentence Rearrangement Practice System, which is deployed on computers and mobile devices as well. The system consists of learner interface and teacher interface. The learner interface includes "Personal Practice", "Learning Progress", "Pre-test", "Post-test", and "System Instructions", as shown in Fig. 1. The teacher interface allows monitoring of learner progress and pre/post-test scores.

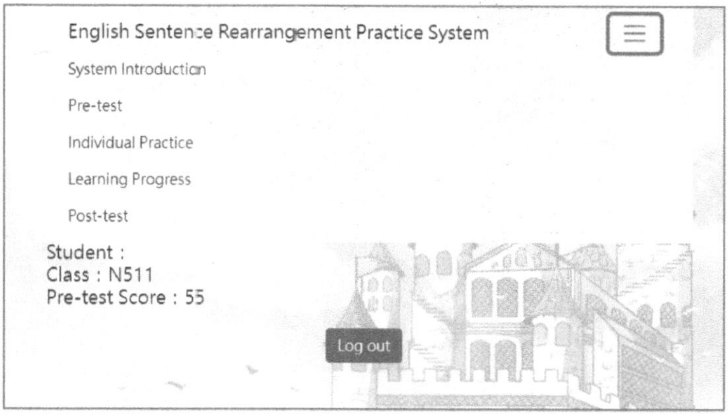

Fig. 1. Learner Interface

In the "Personal Practice", "Pre-test", and "Post-test" sections, learners are required to arrange the English vocabulary provided by professional English teachers into sentences by filling in the numbers, as illustrated in Fig. 2. In the "Personal Practice" feature, upon completing the exercises, the system will indicate the correct and incorrect positions and offer a function to revise the answers. Learners can make corrections based on the questions answered incorrectly, as shown in Fig. 3. The "Pre-test" and "Post-test" are only available for testing in the first and last weeks of the instructional experiment.

Fig. 2. Sentence Rearrangement Interface

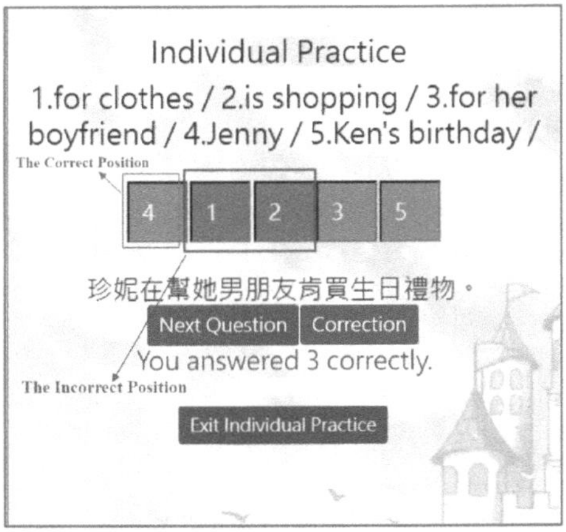

Fig. 3. Personal Practice Prompt Interface

In the "Learning Progress" feature of this system, learners can view the chapters practiced during personal exercises, the number of correct and incorrect answers, practice duration, and more. Learners can use this function to reinforce practice in chapters where they have made more mistakes, as illustrated in Fig. 4.

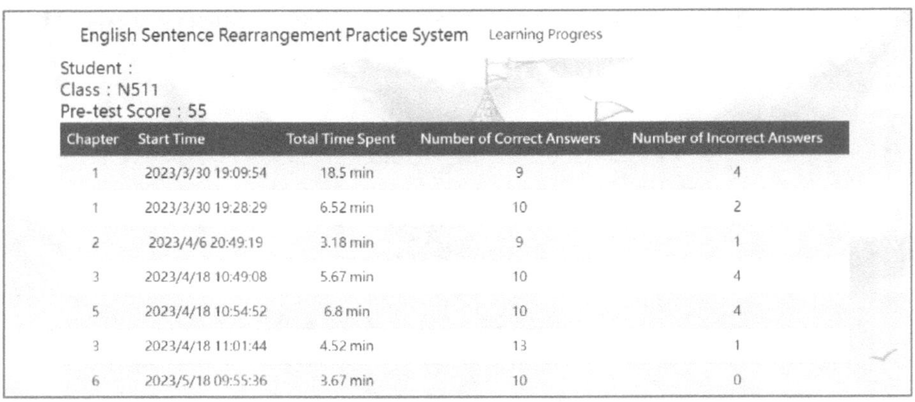
English Sentence Rearrangement Practice System Learning Progress

Student :
Class : N511
Pre-test Score : 55

Chapter	Start Time	Total Time Spent	Number of Correct Answers	Number of Incorrect Answers
1	2023/3/30 19:09:54	18.5 min	9	4
1	2023/3/30 19:28:29	6.52 min	10	2
2	2023/4/6 20:49:19	3.18 min	9	1
3	2023/4/18 10:49:08	5.67 min	10	4
5	2023/4/18 10:54:52	6.8 min	10	4
3	2023/4/18 11:01:44	4.52 min	13	1
6	2023/5/18 09:55:36	3.67 min	10	0

Fig. 4. Learning Progress Interface

3 Research Methodology

3.1 Research Hypotheses

This study has developed an "English Sentence Rearrangement Practice System" to enhance learners' motivation and learning effectiveness. However, different levels of prior knowledge may influence learners' motivation and learning effectiveness after using the system. Therefore, this study proposes the following two hypotheses. The research architecture diagram is shown in Fig. 5.

H1: There is a significant difference in the influence of prior knowledge on learning motivation.
H2: There is a significant difference in the influence of prior knowledge on learning effectiveness.

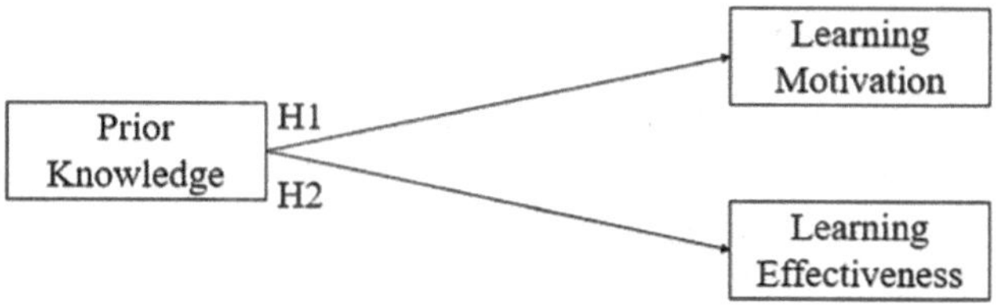

Fig. 5. Research Architecture

3.2 Research Participants

The participants in this study were 87 first-year students from three classes of a nursing department at a vocational college in northern Taiwan. The sample consisted of 43 students with high prior knowledge and 44 students with low prior knowledge, as shown in Table 1. Prior knowledge in this study was determined based on the average scores of the pre-test, categorizing learners into those with high and low prior knowledge.

Table 1. Sample Size of Prior Knowledge Study

Group	Number	Percentage	Total
High Prior Knowledge	43	49.43%	87
Low Prior Knowledge	44	50.57%	

3.3 Research Tools

This study investigates the impact of prior knowledge on learning motivation and learning effectiveness when using the English sentence structure practice system. The research tools include:

1. English Pre-test and Post-test Papers: The pre-test and post-test papers for the English Sentence Structure Practice System in this study were developed with the assistance of professional English teachers. Both the pre-test and post-test papers consist of 20 sentence rearrangement questions drawn from the system, covering the same scope of content.

2. ARCS Learning Motivation Scale: The learning motivation scale adopts the ARCS Learning Motivation Questionnaire designed by Keller [14]. The ARCS Learning Motivation Questionnaire comprises four dimensions: A (Attention), R (Relevance), C (Confidence), and S (Satisfaction), with each dimension consisting of five questions plus one reverse-scored question, totaling 24 questions.

3.4 Experimental Procedure

The experimental procedure of this study consisted of an 8-week teaching experiment with two sessions per week. The pre-test examination was conducted in the first week of the instructional experiment to assess the participants' level of understanding in the subject. Both the pre-test and post-test of this study were administered by the same English teacher, based on the scope of instruction. The questions in the pre-test and post-test were different. According to the average scores obtained from the pre-test, participants were categorized into high prior knowledge and low prior knowledge groups. There were a total of 20 English sentence rearrangement questions in each test, with each question carrying 5 points, resulting in a total score of 100 points.

From the 2nd to the 7th week, regular classes were conducted, allowing learners to use the English Sentence Structure Practice System. In the final week, the post-test and ARCS learning motivation questionnaire were administered. The experimental procedure diagram is shown in Fig. 6.

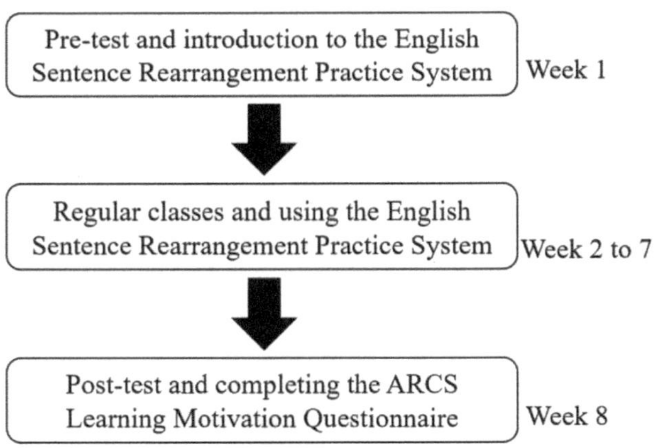

Fig. 6. Experimental Procedure Diagram

4 Results and Discussion

The study employed SPSS for the following analyses: utilizing independent samples t-test to examine the impact of prior knowledge on learning motivation and employing paired samples t-test to analyze the effect of prior knowledge on learning outcomes. The discussions are divided into two sections accordingly.

4.1 Impact of Prior Knowledge on Learning Motivation

This study first analyzed the impact of prior knowledge on the motivation to use the English Sentence Rearrangement Practice System. The reliability analysis of the ARCS questionnaire in this study yielded Cronbach's α coefficients ranging from 0.908 to 0.956 across the four dimensions. These values were all greater than 0.7, indicating high reliability of the ARCS questionnaire [15], as shown in Table 2.

Table 2. The reliability analysis of the ARCS questionnaire

	Cronbach's α
A (Attention)	0.949
R (Relevance)	0.955
C (Confidence)	0.908
S (Satisfaction)	0.956

The results indicated that there was no significant difference in learning motivation between learners with high prior knowledge and those with low prior knowledge after using the English Sentence Rearrangement Practice System, as shown in Table 3. However, the average values of the ARCS dimensions were all greater than 3, indicating that using the English Sentence Rearrangement Practice System could help learners maintain higher levels of learning motivation.

Table 3. Independent Sample t-test for the Impact of Prior Knowledge on Learning Motivation

Item	Prior Knowledge	Count	Mean	Standard Deviation	*t*
A (Attention)	High	43	3.865	0.940	1.570
	Low	44	3.559	0.877	
R (Relevance)	High	43	3.921	0.917	1.155
	Low	44	3.705	0.829	
C (Confidence)	High	43	3.819	0.858	1.654
	Low	44	3.541	0.702	
S (Satisfaction)	High	43	3.735	0.900	0.719
	Low	44	3.605	0.788	

4.2 Impact of Prior Knowledge on Learning Effectiveness

This study further analyzed the effect of prior knowledge on the improvement in learning effectiveness through the use of the English Sentence Rearrangement Practice System.

The results indicate a significant difference in the improvement in learning outcomes based on prior knowledge levels *($t = -4.960$, $p = 0.001$)*, as shown in Table 4. This suggests that the English Sentence Rearrangement Practice System effectively enhances the learning effectiveness of learners with low prior knowledge.

Table 4. Independent Sample *t*-test for the Effect of Prior Knowledge on Learning Effectiveness

Prior Knowledge	Count	Mean	Standard Deviation	*t*
High	43	6.40	14.365	-4.960^{***}
Low	44	26.14	22.043	

*** $p < .001$

Additionally, this study employed paired sample t-tests to analyze the self-improvement of learning effectiveness concerning prior knowledge. The results revealed significant differences in self-improvement between high prior knowledge learners and low prior knowledge learners *($t = 2.919$, $p = 0.01$), ($t = 7.865$, $p = 0.001$)*, as shown in Tables 5 and 6. Once again, it demonstrates that the English Sentence Rearrangement Practice System effectively enhances learners' learning effectiveness.

Table 5. Paired Sample t-test for Self-Improvement of Learning effectiveness among High Prior Knowledge Learners

Test	Count	Mean	Standard Deviation	*t*
Pre-	43	62.56	6.111	2.919^{**}
Post-	43	68.95	17.305	

** $p < .01$

Table 6. Paired Sample t-test for Self-Improvement of Learning effectiveness among Low Prior Knowledge Learners

Test	Count	Mean	Standard Deviation	*t*
Pre-	44	38.07	11.625	7.865^{***}
Post-	44	64.20	15.399	

*** $p < .001$

4.3 Discussion

Despite the absence of a significant difference in learning motivation between learners with high and low prior knowledge after engaging with the English Sentence Rearrangement Practice System, the consistently high average values of the ARCS dimensions suggest the system's efficacy in sustaining learners' motivation levels. This aligns with existing research indicating the effectiveness of the ARCS model in maintaining motivation across diverse learner populations, especially in language learning contexts [16]. The use of a mobile-assisted tool with multimedia-based instructions enhances learners' motivational attitudes and consequently leading to improved learning outcomes. [17].

The study demonstrates a significant improvement in learning effectiveness for low prior knowledge learners through the uses of the English Sentence Rearrangement Practice System, a finding of particular significance. Further analysis reveals that self-improvement among low prior knowledge learners significantly exceeds that of high prior knowledge learners, indicating a notable impact of prior knowledge levels on learning effectiveness. According to Alsadoon [18] and Komarudin [19], prior knowledge significantly impacts learning effectiveness, particularly for low prior knowledge learners. This is further influenced by the use of an adaptive e-course, which can minimize the performance gap between beginner and advanced learners [17]. Additionally, L2 proficiency can influence the effectiveness of learning direction in vocabulary learning, with lower proficiency learners benefiting more from L2-to-L1 learning [20].

Overall, the English Sentence Rearrangement Practice System effectively enhances learning motivation and outcomes for learners across different levels of prior knowledge. It not only helps maintain high levels of motivation but also significantly improves learning effectiveness, with a more substantial impact observed among learners with low prior knowledge.

5 Conclusion and Future Outlook

Based on the analysis conducted, several key conclusions can be drawn regarding the impact of prior knowledge on learning motivation and effectiveness in language learning contexts.

Firstly, while there may not be a significant difference in learning motivation between learners with high and low prior knowledge levels, the consistently high average values of the ARCS dimensions suggest that instructional strategies, such as the English Sentence Rearrangement Practice System, effectively sustain learners' motivation levels. This finding aligns with previous research demonstrating the efficacy of the ARCS model in maintaining motivation across diverse learner populations, particularly in language learning contexts.

Secondly, the use of mobile-assisted tools with multimedia-based instructions has been shown to enhance learners' motivational attitudes, thereby leading to improved learning outcomes. This highlights the importance of integrating digital technologies into language learning environments to support learners in their educational journey.

Furthermore, the significant impact of prior knowledge on learning effectiveness, particularly for low prior knowledge learners, underscores the importance of tailored instructional approaches. Adaptive e-courses and strategies that address the specific needs of learners at different proficiency levels can help minimize performance gaps and optimize learning outcomes.

In conclusion, the study reveals the relationships between prior knowledge, learning motivation, and instructional strategies in language learning.

By understanding and leveraging these dynamics, educators may have the capacity to explore more efficient methods in aiding learners throughout their language acquisition journey. Looking forward, the consideration of developing a system focused on sentence rearrangement appears to be a promising avenue for facilitating the acquisition of contextualized sentence-level representations. Through the incorporation of sentence-level exercises and learning contextualized sentence-level representations, learners could potentially gain a more comprehensive understanding of the language, thereby enhancing their language comprehension abilities. These changes and advancements are positioned to potentially offer English learners a more flexible, engaging, and efficient learning experience, potentially enabling them to master the English language more effectively.

References

1. Tạ Thành, H.: Sentence structures in learning English. Tạp chí Nghiên cứu Dân tộc **12**(3), 51–56 (2023)
2. Charpentier-Jiménez, W.: Quantifying sentence variety of english learners. Revista Electronica Educare **24**(3), 537–551 (2020)
3. Freidin, R.: Adventures in English Syntax. Cambridge University Press, Cambridge UK (2020)
4. Thothathiri, M., Braiuca, M.C.: Distributional learning in English: the effect of verb-specific biases and verb-general semantic mappings on sentence production. J. Exp. Psychol. Learn. Mem. Cogn. **47**(1), 113 (2021)
5. Zanetti, A., Volodina, E., Graën, J.: Automatic generation of exercises for second language learning from parallel corpus data. Int. J. TESOL Stud. **3**(2), 55–70 (2021)
6. Nguyen, M.H.: Beyond the washback of the English National Exam on learning: subsequent impact on language learning strategies of first-year English majors. Lang. Educ. Assess. **3**(2), 38–57 (2020)
7. Usman, O., Miranda, V.: The Influence of Learning Motivation, Cognitive Strategy, Prior Knowledge on Learning Satisfaction. https://ssrn.com/abstract=3641269 30 June 2020
8. De Wilde, V., Brysbaert, M., Eyckmans, J.: Young learners' L2 English after the onset of instruction: Longitudinal development of L2 proficiency and the role of individual differences. Bilingualism: Lang. Cognition **24**(3), 439–453 (2021)
9. Valunaite Oleskeviciene, G., Lobato Miranda, G., Mockienė, L., Gulbinskiene, D.: Discourse-Annotated Corpus for Foreign Language Teaching/Learning: Prior Knowledge Meaning. Pedagogika. Kaunas: Vytauto Didžiojo universiteto Švietimo akademija **147**(3) (2022)
10. Yasseen Shukr, H., Adnan Jameel, T.: Digital technology in English language teaching and learning. NTU J. Adm. Hum. Sci. (JAHS) **2**(2), 164–177 (2022)
11. Alakrash, H.M., Abdul Razak, N.: Technology-based language learning: Investigation of digital technology and digital literacy. Sustainability **13**(21), 12304 (2021)
12. Muharom, F., Nugroho, A., Ramadhan Putra, P.H.: Self-directed use of digital devices for out-of-class English learning. Int. J. Educ. Math. Sci. Technol. **10**(1), 257–271 (2021)
13. Nugroho, A., Atmojo, A.E.: Digital learning of English beyond classroom: EFL learners' perception and teaching activities. JEELS (J. English Educ. Linguist. Stud.) **7**(2), 219–243 (2020)
14. Keller, J.M.: Development and use of the ARCS model of instructional design. J. Instr. Dev. **10**(3), 2–10 (1987)
15. Nunnally, J.C., Bernstein, I.H.: Psychometric Theory. McGraw-Hill, New York (1994)

16. Kim, B.J.: A study of the effects of Keller's ARCS Motivational Model on learning motivation and academic achievement in business major English class. J. Dig. Convergence **18**(2), 213–221 (2020)
17. Refat, N., Kassim, H., Rahman, M.A., Razali, R.B.: Measuring student motivation on the use of a mobile assisted grammar learning tool. PLoS ONE **15**(8), e0236862 (2020)
18. Alsadoon, E.: The impact of an adaptive e-course on students' achievements based on the students' prior knowledge. Educ. Inf. Technol. **25**(5), 3541–3551 (2020)
19. Komarudin, M., Sutadji, E., Widiyanti: Increase the problem solving ability through improved prior knowledge. J. Phys.: Conf. Ser. 1700(1) (2020)
20. Terai, M., Yamashita, J., Pasich, K.E.: Effects of learning direction in retrieval practice on EFL vocabulary learning. Stud. Second. Lang. Acquis. **43**(5), 1116–1137 (2021)

Collaborative Problem-Solving on Learning Performance in Simulation-Based Learning: A Quasi-Experimental Study

Astrid Tiara Murti[1], Budi Dharmawan[2], Chia-Chen Chen[1], and Ting-Ting Wu[3](✉)

[1] National Chung Hsing University, Taichung, Taiwan, R.O.C.
[2] Jenderal Soedirman University, Purwokerto, Indonesia
[3] National Yunlin University of Science and Technology, Douliu, Taiwan, R.O.C.
ttwu@yuntech.edu.tw

Abstract. Simulation-based learning utilizes information technology to replicate real-world environments, aiding in the comprehension of complex phenomena. However, optimizing learners' efforts remains a challenge. Collaborative problem-solving integrates collaboration and problem-solving, enhancing learning performance, and is commonly employed in technology-enhanced classrooms. This study investigates the integration of collaborative problem-solving in simulation-based learning to enhance learner performance. A quasi-experimental design compared a control class to an experimental class where collaborative problem-solving was integrated. The results confirm that collaborative problem-solving in simulation-based learning had significantly higher learning performance compared to the learner in the traditional instructions. These findings suggest that collaborative problem-solving enhances learner understanding and practical skills, offering pedagogical insights for effective simulation-based learning.

Keywords: simulation · collaborative problem-solving · performance · quasi-experiment

1 Introduction

Simulation-based learning involves the use of information technology to simulate real-world environments [1]. Computer-based simulation learning can tailor real-world phenomena that are difficult to observe, which is appropriate to the learner's knowledge level, and facilitates a deeper understanding of these phenomena [2]. For teachers, simulation has become a valuable instructional aid for teaching. Studies have demonstrated that effective simulation-based learning can improve learning outcomes [1, 3, 4]. However, some drawbacks need to be considered, primarily on how to coordinate learners' efforts effectively for optimal outcomes.

Collaborative problem-solving integrated collaboration and problem-solving, encouraging learners to solve problems in a collaborative learning environment. Collaborative learning has been shown to develop learners' ability to identify and work

Y.-P. Cheng et al. (Eds.): ICITL 2024, LNCS 14785, pp. 264–270, 2024.
https://doi.org/10.1007/978-3-031-65881-5_28

toward goals, communicate ideas, identify problems and solutions, and make complex decisions [5]. Moreover, collaboration can effectively improve the learning performance of the learners. Problem-solving strategies are often adopted for teaching and learning [6], and have been explored in classes utilizing technologies [3, 5, 7]. Problem-solving is a process that requires brainstorming, analysis of problems, and developing solutions according to what is known and unknown [4, 8].

In consideration of coordinated instruction in collaborative problem-solving, learners construct the knowledge of shared ideas and understanding to process different aspects of a problem. This study employs a quasi-experimental approach to investigate whether integrating collaborative problem-solving into simulation-based learning could enhance learners' performance. Therefore, this study seeks to address whether any differences detected in learners' performance when collaborative problem-solving is integrated into simulation-based learning.

2 Literature Review

2.1 Simulation-Based Learning

Computer-based instruction, such as simulation in education has become an increasingly widespread trend. Learners frequently encounter constraints, such as time, cost, and risk that prevent them from directly addressing real-world problems [2, 3]. Simulation serves to replicate those situations, overcoming the limitations for educational purposes. It is an effective teaching tool that supports a holistic approach to problem-solving [5, 7]. Teachers employ simulation-based learning in their teaching to provide opportunities for practicing real-world problem-solving. Through repeated activities facilitated by simulation, learners acquire a deeper understanding of the phenomena and how the real world operates. Moreover, dynamic and interactive computer simulations can improve learner performance [1, 4].

Simulations are focused on specific functional areas. The simulation in this study was called Valuation Technology (V-Tech) Simulation of the patent-oriented process, and was developed by Universitas Jenderal Soedirman [9]. V-Tech simulation evaluates the value of technology assets by simulating market conditions and assessing them against specific criteria. This process involves analyzing various factors such as market demand, competitive landscape, intellectual property rights, and technological advancement to determine the potential value and marketability of a technology asset. By simulating different scenarios and market dynamics, stakeholders can make informed decisions regarding patent valuation, licensing agreements, investment strategies, and technology commercialization efforts.

2.2 Collaborative Problem-Solving and Learning Performance

Nelson [10] proposed collaborative problem-solving to foster learners' active learning within the collaborative setting that reflects real-world contexts, tasks, and challenges. The pedagogy of collaborative problem-solving guides the development of learners' cooperation and communication abilities [1, 11]. During collaborative problem-solving, the learners need to work together and communicate with each other by sharing ideas, knowledge, and abilities. Griffin et al. [12] mentioned that the collaborative problem-solving process usually consists of: 1) defining the problems, 2) understanding the process, 3) identifying the root causes, 4) developing solutions, and 5) sustaining the improvement.

Some research has indicated that group work significantly affects learner performance [1, 4, 8, 13]. As a form of scaffolding, collaborative problem-solving requires social interactions to tackle complex tasks. This approach allows learners to exchange ideas, perspectives, and strategies, leading to deeper understanding and more comprehensive solutions. Through collaboration, learners can leverage the collective knowledge and skills of the group, leading to improved problem-solving outcomes and enhanced performance [14]. The experimental group of this study, aside from using the simulation, the collaborative problem-solving strategy was also integrated as the instructional approach to investigate whether this pedagogy could enhance learners' performance.

3 Methodology

3.1 Research Method

This study employed a quasi-experimental approach, in which one intact class of learners was randomly designated as the control class, and another class was designated as the experimental class. Both classes utilized V-Tech Simulation as the instructional tool for the management information systems course. In the experimental class, the learning activities were integrated with collaborative problem-solving steps. The independent variable in this study was the participation in the learning activities, and the dependent variable was the learner's performance assessed by the teacher.

The study included 60 learners from two intact classes enrolled in the university course in Indonesia. The control class comprised 30 learners, consisting of 8 males and 22 females, whereas the experimental class had 20 females and 10 males.

3.2 Research Procedures

The simulation environment of V-Tech replicates the licensing value of the technology according to specific criteria, parameters, market conditions, and risk assessments. The simulation was performed in the latter half of the semester for six sessions, and lasted for 100 min each. Before using the simulation, all participants signed the consent form. In the first session, all participants in both classes received instruction on operating V-Tech simulation, which they will use from sessions 2 through 5. The two classes have different learning instructions implemented in their class activities. The control class is instructed using the traditional instruction method. The traditional instruction emphasizes more on delivering lectures to cover the principles of the course. Whereas, the experimental class is instructed using collaborative problem-solving instruction, placing greater emphasizes on discussions during classroom activities. The steps of collaborative problem-solving and the implementation in this study for the experimental class are presented in Table 1. From sessions 2 through 5, participants are tasked to resolve all problems within the simulation. In the last session, session 6th, the participants presented their outcomes to the teacher and class (Fig. 1).

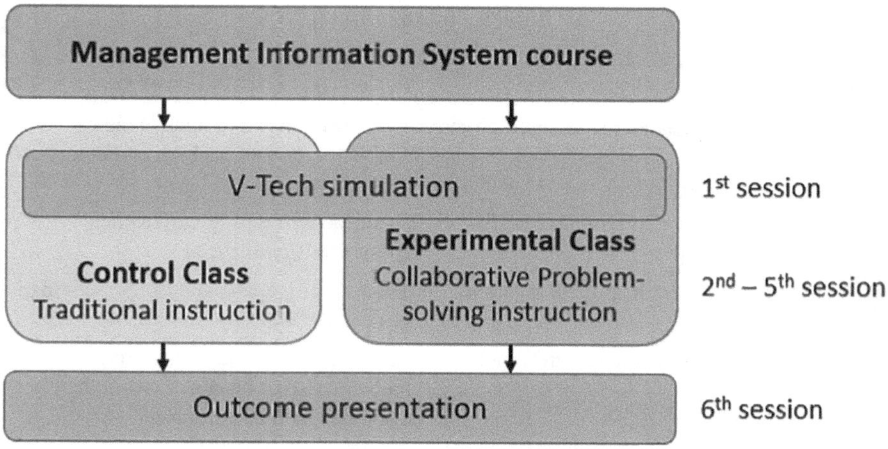

Fig. 1. The experimental procedure.

Table 1. The nine steps of collaborative problem-solving [10] and implementation.

Steps	Collaborative problem-solving	Implementation in the classroom
1	The teacher establishes the foundational understanding of the learners	The teacher establishes learners' foundational knowledge of patent valuation, licensing agreements, investment strategies, and technology commercialization efforts
2	The learners form small heterogeneous groups	The teacher organized the learners into heterogeneous groups, with each group comprising 4 learners, resulting a total of 10 groups
3	The preliminary process of defining the tasks and problems	The teacher provided explanations and guidance on defining the problems and directions for problem-solving to the learners
4	Each group member defines what roles are necessary for the tasks	Learners were tasked with determining the strategies and dividing tasks based on their roles within the group
5	Groups engage in V-Tech simulation	Learners participated in group discussions, sharing ideas, perspectives, and knowledge related to the task. The group collaboratively worked towards completing simulation tasks, accumulating upon the collective expertise and insights of its members

(*continued*)

Table 1. (*continued*)

Steps	Collaborative problem-solving	Implementation in the classroom
6	Learners finalize their simulation project	The groups began to finalize their simulation project package and completed the tasks
7	Learners reflect and synthesize their experiences	As the activities progress, learners' comprehension increases
8	Learner prepared the project outcome presentation	The learner prepares their presentation of project outcomes
9	The teacher and learners reflect on the activities	Led by the team leader, the group shared their simulation results in which the teacher evaluated their performance

3.3 Instruments

The learners' performance was evaluated by the teacher using the assessment rubric of V-Tech designed by [9]. The rubric consists of five criteria as shown in Fig. 2, in which each criterion evaluates learners' ability to explores, explain, organize, and discuss the main issues of technology value predictions and forecast-based planning. Each criterion was scored between 1 (insufficient) to 4 (exemplary), with a maximum score of 20 points.

Assessment Rubric for V-Tech

Criteria	Description	Assessment
1	The student is able to explore the main issues in assessing the technology value prediction and forecast-based planning, while also considering contextual factors.	4 = Exemplary 3 = Proficient 2 = Development 1 = Insufficient
2	The student successfully explains why/how the technology value prediction and forecast-based planning works, identifying embedded or implicit issues and addressing their relationship to each other.	
3	Critical elements of the technology value prediction and forecast-based planning are appropriately developed and described.	
4	Organizes evidence to reveal important patterns, differences, or similarities related to technology value prediction and forecast-based planning.	
5	State conclusions or assertions focused solely on the findings. Discuss relevant limitations and/or supported implications of technology value predictions and forecast-based planning.	

Fig. 2. The experimental procedure.

4 Result

In this study, the learner performance was assessed by the teacher using a rubric and analyzed using analysis of variance (ANOVA) to determine the significant differences between the control and experimental classes. The resulting analysis of learner performance is presented in Table 2. The results indicated that learners in the experimental class had higher performance (M = 16.8, SD = 1.21) compared to the control class (M = 14.3, SD = 1.15). Further analysis of variance shows that these differences are significant ($F = 67.0, p < 0.05, {\eta_p}^2 = 0.536$). The value of ${\eta_p}^2 = 0.536$ indicates that approximately 53.6% of the variance of learner performance can be explained by the differences in learning activities. Therefore, the learner who uses collaborative problem-solving has a higher understanding of how the technology is valued in forecast-based planning.

Table 2. The ANOVA results of learners' performance.

	Mean	SD	Mean Squares	F	p	${\eta_p}^2$
Control class	14.3	1.15	93.75	67.0	0.000*	0.536
Experimental class	16.8	1.21				

$^* p < 0.05$

5 Discussion and Conclusion

The characteristic of simulation-based learning is its ability to facilitate exploring real-world problems. Accordingly, this study adopts a quasi-experimental design to examine the influence of collaborative problem-solving in simulation-based learning on learner performance. Furthermore, two intact classes were divided into the experimental class and control classes to assess whether collaborative problem-solving strategies can develop higher learning performance.

The results confirm that collaborative problem-solving in simulation-based learning had significantly higher learning performance compared to the learner in the traditional instructions. It indicates that the pedagogical approach of collaborative problem-solving improved learning outcomes. This finding is consistent with prior studies. In Lu & Lin's [1] quasi-experimental study, the learner who participated in simulation-based learning alongside collaborative problem-solving strategies positively influenced learner outcomes. Similar results were also presented by Lin et al. that illustrated that integrating collaborative problem-solving in educational activities was beneficial to learners.

The results of this study provide teachers with suggestions for pedagogical approaches that can enhance learner performance. The simulation-based learning requires high cognitive demands, highlighting the need for thoughtful instructions that promote effective learning experiences. The designed collaborative problem-solving enhances practical skills. Furthermore, this approach facilitates peer interaction and discussion in the classroom, fostering knowledge construction and teamwork abilities among learners.

Acknowledgment. This research was funded by the National Science and Technology Council, Taiwan, R.O.C. under Grant no. MOST 110-2511-H-224-003-MY3 and MOST 111-2628-H-224-001-MY3.

References

1. Lu, H.-K., Lin, P.-C.: A study of the impact of collaborative problem-solving strategies on students' performance of simulation-based learning — a case of network basic concepts course. Int. J. Inform. Educ. Technol. **7**(5), 361–366 (2017). https://doi.org/10.18178/ijiet.2017.7.5.895
2. Ambrosio Mawhirter, D., Ford Garofalo, P.: Expect the unexpected: simulation games as a teaching strategy. Clin. Simul. In Nurs. **12**(4), 132–136 (2016). https://doi.org/10.1016/j.ecns.2015.12.009
3. Huang, Y.-M., Silitonga, L.M., Wu, T.-T.: Applying a business simulation game in a flipped classroom to enhance engagement, learning achievement, and higher-order thinking skills. Comput. Educ. **183**, 104494 (2022). https://doi.org/10.1016/j.compedu.2022.104494
4. Lin, P.-C., Hou, H.-T., Chang, K.-E.: The development of a collaborative problem solving environment that integrates a scaffolding mind tool and simulation-based learning: an analysis of learners' performance and their cognitive process in discussion. Interact. Learn. Env. **30**(7), 1273–1290 (2022). https://doi.org/10.1080/10494820.2020.1719163
5. Peterková, J., Repaská, Z., Prachařová, L.: Best practice of using digital business simulation games in business education. Sustainability **14**(15), 8987 (2022). https://doi.org/10.3390/su14158987
6. Gagné, R.M.: Learnable aspects of problem solving. Educ. Psychol. **15**(2), 84–92 (1980). https://doi.org/10.1080/00461528009529218
7. Aqlan, F., Zhao, R.: Assessment of collaborative problem solving in engineering students through hands-on simulations. IEEE Trans. Educ. **65**(1), 9–17 (2022). https://doi.org/10.1109/TE.2021.3079523
8. Rojas, M., et al.: Assessing collaborative problem-solving skills among elementary school students. Comput. Educ. **175**, 104313 (2021). https://doi.org/10.1016/j.compedu.2021.104313
9. Dharmawan, B., Sukardi, Setyowati, K.: Model of technology valuation system of patent-oriented process (case study on composition of cajuput candy as throat relief). Jurnal Teknologi Industri Pertanian. **20** (2010)
10. Nelson, L.M.: Collaborative problem solving. In: Reigeluth, C.M. (ed.) Instructional-Design Theories and Models: A New Paradigm of Instructional Theory. pp. 241–267. Erlbaum Associates (1999)
11. Vygotsky, L.S.: Mind and Society: The Development of Higher Psychological Processes (1978)
12. Griffin, P., Care, E.: Assessment and Teaching of 21st Century Skills Methods and Approach (2015)
13. Chen, L., et al.: Exploring factors that influence collaborative problem solving awareness in science education. Technol. Knowl. Learn. **25**, 337–366 (2020). https://doi.org/10.1007/s10758-020-09436-8
14. Chen, L., et al.: Direction of collaborative problem solving-based STEM learning by learning analytics approach. Res. Pract. Technol. Enhanc. Learn. **14**, 24 (2019). https://doi.org/10.1186/s41039-019-0119-y

Extracting the Semantic Representation of Chinese-Japanese Homophones with Word2Vec for Teaching Chinese as a Second/Foreign Language

Min-Chi Lo[1], Li-Yun Chang[1], and Hou-Chiang Tseng[2](✉)

[1] Department of Chinese As a Second Language, National Taiwan Normal University, Taipei, Taiwan

[2] Graduate Institute of Digital Learning and Education, National Taiwan University of Science and Technology, Taipei, Taiwan

tsenghc@mail.ntust.edu.tw

Abstract. The purpose of this study was to quantify the semantic distance between Chinese-Japanese homophones, and to further examine whether the traditional classification of Chinese-Japanese homophones reflects varying semantic distances. Ultimately, this study aimed to offer corresponding teaching suggestions for teachers' reference. We introduced a novel approach to classifying Chinese-Japanese homophones by combining the Revised Hierarchical Model with the Word2Vec technology to extract semantic representations and calculate the semantic distance of meanings in Chinese-Japanese homophones across "Same", "Overlap", and "Different" types. Through cluster analysis of semantic distances, we found that semantic distance indeed reflects the traditional classification of Chinese-Japanese homophones. The "Same" type had the average semantic distance of 0, showing the high degree of similarity between the meanings in Chinese and Japanese within this category. The "Different" type had the greatest average semantic distance, indicating the lowest similarity. The "Overlap" type had the average semantic distance between the "Same" and "Different" types, representing the complex nature of this category. Based on these findings, this study proposed teaching suggestions to help Chinese teachers determine the teaching sequence among Chinese-Japanese homophones.

Keywords: Chinese-Japanese homophones · semantic representation · teaching Chinese as a second/foreign language · Word2Vec

1 Introduction

Among the writing systems worldwide, Chinese greatly influenced Japanese. Although belonging to different language families, both utilize Chinese characters (Kanji). Many believe that Japanese learners of Chinese benefit from their knowledge of Kanji when learning Chinese. Despite the significant overlap in form, pronunciation, and meaning between Japanese Kanji and Chinese characters, which allows Japanese learners

Y.-P. Cheng et al. (Eds.): ICITL 2024, LNCS 14785, pp. 271–280, 2024.
https://doi.org/10.1007/978-3-031-65881-5_29

to utilize their Japanese knowledge to infer the meaning of Chinese characters, not all homophones share the same meaning in both languages. Past research has also indicated that homophones can lead to both positive and negative transfer in learning [1]. Thus, adapting teaching methods to different types of homophones can improve learning.

The classification of Chinese-Japanese homophones currently lacks an objective, quantifiable approach, relying instead on relatively subjective methods. Researchers subjectively determine whether the meanings of a homophone in Chinese and Japanese are the same. In monolingual research, the calculate of cosine similarity allows for the objective measurement of the semantic similarity between words and sentences.

Therefore, this study aims to start from lexical processing models from psycholinguistic theory to simulate the process of learners processing first language (L1) and second language (L2). Further, utilizing Word2Vec as a tool and through the construction of semantic space, we aim to quantitatively represent the objective distance between the Chinese and Japanese meanings of homophones. These semantic representations may assist teachers in developing corresponding teaching strategies for vocabularies at different distances. Specifically, the objectives of this study are as follows:

1. To quantify the semantic distance between Chinese-Japanese homophones using Word2Vec.
2. To further examine whether the traditional classification of Chinese-Japanese homophones reflects different semantic distances.
3. To propose teaching suggestions for homophones of different classifications and semantic distances.

2 Literature Review

2.1 Classification of Chinese-Japanese Homophones

Modern Japanese primarily consists of phonetic characters (Hiragana, Katakana, and Romaji) and ideographic characters (Kanji). At the character level, the Japanese Ministry of Education issued the Jōyō (Common) Kanji List in 2010, which includes a total of 2,136 Kanji characters. According to Chang [2], approximately 90% of these Kanji have forms that are identical or similar to the standard characters used in Taiwan. Furthermore, at the vocabulary level, "Chinese-Japanese Homophones" refer to words in both language that correspond in form and pronunciation, constituting nearly 50% of the Japanese lexicon [3]. In addition, Chang [4] analyzed A1 vocabulary from a corpus of Test of Chinese as a Foreign Language (TOCFL) 8,000 Chinese Vocabulary Item and common Japanese vocabulary. The findings revealed that Chinese-Japanese homophones constitute up to 60.76% of the A1 level Chinese vocabulary, highlighting their importance in teaching Chinese to Japanese learners.

Classification of homophones, based on previous research, is traditionally divided into two categories based on their form: "identical in form" and "not identical in form" [5]. The present study adopts a broader definition of homophones, including words "not identical in form" (e.g. 國/国in Chinese and Japanese). Besides form, the Japanese Agency for Culture Affairs [6] also categorizes homophones based on meaning into four types: Same (S), Overlap (O), Different (D), and Nothing (N, Japanese-specific Kanji words). Many studies have also classified homophones based on it and further suggested subcategories based on the nuances within each main category [4, 7].

In terms of teaching research, previous studies have shown that both Chinese and Japanese native speakers are influenced by their native language when learning Chinese-Japanese homophones [1]. Learners are more likely to make errors with the "O" and "D" type than with the "S" type. This has led to suggestions for teachers to be mindful of the differences between the two languages to prevent negative transfer [1].

2.2 L2 Lexical Processing Model

In psycholinguistic research, various models are proposed to explain how bilinguals understand and produce language, as well as how they switch between different languages. The Revised Hierarchical Model (RHM) suggests semantic concepts are shared across multiple languages, with a stronger connection between the L1 and concepts, but a weaker connection between the L2 and concepts [8]. Therefore, bilinguals must access L2 semantics through their L1. In other words, when learners with Japanese as their native language process Chinese-Japanese homophones, they first access the semantics of their native language, Japanese, before reaching the semantics of the second language, Chinese. Prior research on Chinese-Japanese homophones has also indicated that RHM can explain the lexical processing of Chinese native speakers learning Japanese Kanji vocabulary [9, 10]. Similarly, we may infer that this model is also applicable to Japanese native speakers learning Chinese.

2.3 Extracting of Chinese Semantic Representation by Using Word2Vec

Semantic representations derived from corpora, known as embeddings (i.e., LSA, Word2Vec), utilize the patterns within text to embed words in a vector space. Within this space, words with similar meanings are positioned closely together. These approaches reflect the semantic relationships between mental representations of vocabulary within a reader's mind [11, 12]. Through semantic representation, we can enable the objective, precise, and automated analysis of semantic connections between words, sentences, and even entire texts. Many researchers have utilized Word2Vec [13] for reading-related research, such as text readability studies [14, 15], or text classification research [16]. Furthermore, in recent years, studies have been using large corpora to compare and delineate the semantic relationships between vocabularies. For example, Sung et al. [17] employed a massive corpus to construct a "Chinese Corpora-based Conceptual Space" (CCCS) which consists of approximately 7.82 million cross-disciplinary and cross-age Chinese texts, containing about 1.3 billion Chinese words as training data. Through Word2Vec, they established a conceptual space based on a Chinese corpus, representing a semantic memory space that closely approximates the general domain knowledge of the Taiwanese population.

Although there is a wealth of research on Chinese-Japanese homophones in learning and teaching Chinese as a second/foreign language, studies that provide teaching suggestions from the perspective of semantic representation are limited. Therefore, by combining the theories of psycholinguistics, this study aims to use Word2Vec to simulate the L2 semantic processing proposed by the RHM. Given the following two reasons, this study chose to utilize CCCS for extracting semantic representations of Chinese-Japanese homophones with Word2Vec in our study. Firstly, CCCS contains a large amount of data across multiple fields, suitable for the varied situations in teaching. Secondly, the Chinese corpus is appropriate for understanding the semantic discrepancies between the actual meanings and meanings extracted by Japanese learners of Chinese when reading Chinese texts that include Chinese-Japanese homophones from the perspective of Chinese learning and teaching. To the best of our knowledge, this study is the first to offer teaching suggestions for Chinese-Japanese homophones by quantifying semantic discrepancies through this approach. The following section details our research methodology.

3 Methodology

3.1 Materials

All the Chinese-Japanese homophones used in this research were sourced from the self-learning materials, "Chinese-Japanese Homophone Learning Strategy I-III" [18–20] which were designed specifically for Japanese learners of Chinese. These materials categorize the Chinese-Japanese homophones into three categories: Same (S), Overlap (O), and Different (D). We selected a total of 296 entries composed purely of Kanji characters as the research materials.

3.2 Data Collection Procedures

To quantify the semantic distance between Chinese-Japanese homophones using Word2Vec, and to further examine whether the traditional subjective classification of homophones into three categories "S", "O" and "D" accurately reflects varying semantic distances, we organized and selected data as follows.

Compilation of Vocabulary List. For the selected homophones, we listed their categories as defined in the "Chinese-Japanese Homophone Learning Strategy I-III" and consulted the Japanese-Chinese Dictionary published by Shogakukan [21] to list the Chinese meanings associated with each term. Considering the context of this study was in Taiwan, the vocabulary list incorporates each Chinese meaning's corresponding level and word frequency as per the Taiwan Benchmarks for the Chinese Language (TBCL) wordlists of three grades/seven levels proposed by the National Academy for Educational Research (NAER) in Taiwan [22]. Additionally, since the Chinese terms used in the Japanese-Chinese Dictionary tend to follow China's usage, and the CCCS we used is based on Taiwanese corpora, any terms unique to China found in the dictionary were adjusted to reflect the usage common in Taiwan.

Calculation of Semantic Distance. The semantic cosine similarity between the Chinese meanings of the target Chinese-Japanese homophones and each of their Japanese meanings, as translated in the Japanese-Chinese Dictionary [21], was calculated within the CCCS using Word2Vec. Compound words not included in the CCCS were excluded from the analysis. The Word2Vec model used in CCCS was trained using the Continuous Bag of Words (CBOW) method with Hierarchical Softmax. The parameters used for training were a window size of 8; a minimum word count of 2; and a sampling rate of 1e-4. This resulted in word vectors of 100 dimensions for each vocabulary term. The cosine similarity was calculated by taking the cosine of the angle between the corresponding word vectors. This transformation ensures that the cosine values range between 1 and −1. The semantic distance between the Chinese and Japanese meanings was then calculated by subtracting each cosine similarity from 1, which followed procedures used by previous research [23]. The semantic distance is a value between 0 and 2, where a value closer to 0 indicates greater semantic similarity between the two terms.

Comparison between Traditional Subjective Classification and Objective Semantic Distance. Given that each Chinese term among the homophones may correspond to multiple meanings in Japanese, to select representative Japanese meanings for further cluster analysis and to compare traditional classification with semantic distance, the approach taken by Yang et al. [24] was referenced for data processing. For homophones categorized as "S" type, the Japanese meaning with the smallest semantic distance to the Chinese term was selected for each homophone. For terms categorized as "O" and "D" types, the levels of each Japanese meaning were reviewed in the TBCL wordlists. The term that had the highest frequency within the lowest level and had a non-zero semantic distance was selected as the representative term.

3.3 Data Analysis

Utilizing the calculated semantic distance, further analyses were conducted to assess the discrepancies between traditional subjective classifications and objective categorizations of homophones. Semantic distances of each selected homophone ($N = 296$) were analyzed using cluster analysis with $k = 3$ to identify distinct clusters or groups of homophones. Subsequently, ANOVA tests were conducted to examine the differences among clusters in the homophones.

4 Results and Discussion

4.1 Results of Cluster Analysis

The cluster analysis was conducted based on the variable of "semantic distance". According to the number of homophone categories, three clusters were analyzed. Table 1 shows the results. An ANOVA on the semantic distances calculated through Word2Vec revealed a significant difference among the three clusters ($F = 2784.53$, $p < .001$). This indicated that cluster analysis can effectively differentiate between groups of homophones. As presented in Table 1, the results indicated that the homophones in cluster 1 had a semantic distance of 0. The homophones in cluster 2 had a short semantic distance. The homophones in cluster 3 had the longest semantic distance among them.

To further examine whether cluster analysis reflects the traditional classification of homophones, we analyzed the number of different categories of homophones within each cluster (see Table 2).

Table 1. The clusters of the semantic distance of Chinese-Japanese homophones.

Cluster	Cluster 1 (*N* = 143)	Cluster 2 (*N* = 137)	Cluster 3 (*N* = 16)	*F*
Semantic distance (*M, SD*)	.00 (.02)	.47 (.11)	.82 (.11)	2784.53***

***p < .001

Table 2. Distribution of Chinese-Japanese homophones across categories after cluster analysis.

Type of homophones	Cluster 1	Cluster 2	Cluster 3
Same (*N* = 143)	**143**	0	0
Overlap (*N* = 137)	3	**71**	**63**
Different (*N* = 16)	0	5	11

*The bolded text with a gray background indicates the majority homophones of the three different types within each cluster.

4.2 Discussion

Cluster analysis results shows that quantified semantic distance values can reflect the traditional classification of homophones. Tables 1 and 2 show that homophones categorized as "S" were all placed in cluster 1, with an average semantic distance of 0, which shows a high degree of similarity between the meanings in Chinese and Japanese. For the "D" type, the majority were in cluster 3, with the greatest average semantic distance, which indicates the lowest similarity between the Chinese and Japanese meanings among the three categories. Lastly, "O" type homophones were mostly found in clusters 2 and 3, with the majority in cluster 2. Their semantic distance fell between those of "S" and "D" types, reflecting the complex nature of these homophones where some meanings align with Chinese and others do not.

Previous studies [1] on homophones have often pointed out that homophones can lead to both positive and negative transfer, especially with a higher likelihood of errors occurring in the "O" and "D" types. Therefore, teachers should consciously conduct comparisons of homophones to help students distinguish between the differences in the two languages. Although there has been considerable research on teaching homophones, studies on the teaching sequence for vocabulary within the same type are rare. The following are the teaching suggestions based on our findings.

The Suggestion of Teaching Sequence of Different Types of Homophones. Table 3 provides examples of each type of homophones and the semantic distance between Chinese and Japanese meanings across different levels from the TBCL wordlists of three grades/seven levels of NAER. Based on our research findings, we offer the following suggestions of teaching sequence for teachers as a reference.

For "S" type homophones, which have zero semantic distance across all levels, indicating a high degree of similarity in form and meaning between Chinese and Japanese,

Table 3. Examples of semantic distance of different types of homophones across different levels from the TBCL wordlist.

	TBCL level	Level 1	Level 2	Level 3	Level 4	Level 5	Level 6	Level 7	X*
Same (S type) N=143	Chinese	去年 (last year)	文化 (culture)	父母 (parents)	外國 (foreign country)	簡單 (simple)	美術 (fine arts)	電源 (power supply)	職員 (member of staff)
	Japanese	去年 (last year)	文化 (culture)	父母 (parents)	外国 (foreign country)	簡単 (simple)	美術 (fine arts)	電源 (power supply)	職員 (member of staff)
	Semantic Distance	0.00	0.00	0.00	0.00	0.00	0.00	0.00	0.00
	Subtotal	22	23	23	49	14	1	3	8
Overlap (O type) N=137	Chinese	便利 (convenient)	期待 (await)	婚姻 (marriage)	風景 (scenery)	意見 (feeling)	完成 (complete)	上映 (unspool)	球場 (court)
	Japanese	便利 (convenience)	期待 (hope)	婚姻 (get married)	風景 (scene)	意見 (lately)	完成 (be finished)	上映 (put on a film)	球場 (baseball stadium)
	Semantic Distance	0.15	0.27	0.40	0.34	0.34	0.35	0.30	0.36
	Chinese	活動 (activity)	大家 (everybody)	種 (type)	結果 (in the end)	多少 (how much)	告訴 (tell)	單身 (single)	花 (flower)
	Japanese	活動 (work)	大家 (landlord)	種 (reason)	結果 (consequence)	多少 (a little)	告訴 (file a lawsuit)	単身 (alone)	花 (flower arrangement)
	Semantic Distance	0.86	0.88	0.85	0.88	0.95	0.96	0.90	0.96
	Subtotal	21	17	7	36	22	15	9	10
Different (D type) N=16	Chinese	先生 (Mr.)	結局 (outcome)	作法 (method)	嚴重 (serious)	結束 (end)	迷路 (lose your way)	N/A	N/A
	Japanese	先生 (teacher)	結局 (after all)	作法 (manners)	厳重 (strict)	結束 (unite)	迷路 (maze)	N/A	N/A
	Semantic Distance	0.93	0.77	0.78	0.68	1.03	0.78	N/A	N/A
	Subtotal	4	1	6	2	2	1	0	0

*The TBCL levels were identified based on the Chinese translation of the meaning of the Japanese homophones, instead of the meaning of Chinese homophones.

*The English translations of the Chinese-Japanese homophones were primarily sourced from the Collins Dictionary [25]. If no information was available in the Collins Dictionary, the Cambridge Dictionary [26] and goo Dictionary [27] were consulted in that order.

*X: vocabularies that are not included in the 7 levels

teachers can prioritize teaching "S" type without being restricted to specific TBCL levels. However, attention must be paid to differences in word classes and collocations. For instance, when teaching a Level 4 term like "foreign country," teachers should remind students that the Chinese character is "國" not "国".

On the other hand, for "O" type homophones, whose meanings partially overlap between Chinese and Japanese, there is a higher complexity of meanings. Teachers could start teaching words with shorter semantic distances at specific levels because this type of word has a relatively higher similarity in meaning between Chinese and Japanese. Then, words with longer semantic distances can be introduced. Since a longer semantic distance indicates a lower correlation between the Chinese and Japanese meanings, teachers should highlight the differences between the two languages. For example, when teaching Level 2 term, teachers might begin with words like "期待", which have a shorter semantic distance, before moving on to "大家", which has a longer semantic distance. By adopting a teaching method that progresses from low to high semantic distance, students can gradually learn words ranging from simple to complex.

Lastly, for the "D" type, given that these homophones have the longest semantic distance and the greatest difference in meaning between Chinese and Japanese, this type can be taught starting from the vocabulary with shorter semantic distance within the same level after completing the teaching of "S" and "O" types. This is because, compared to the "D" type, the meanings of "S" and "O" types in Chinese and Japanese are more similar, making it easier for students to grasp them in their learning.

Collectively, the suggested teaching sequence outlined above can be used not only for course design and teaching strategies but also as a reference for developing educational materials such as textbooks. Currently, there are not many available resources specifically focused on Chinese-Japanese homophones, and most are in dictionary forms. The few self-learning materials available often arrange vocabulary thematically. Therefore, we suggest that teachers may refer to our proposed teaching sequence when developing materials regarding Chinese-Japanese homophones.

5 Conclusion and Future Work

This study applied an innovative method to classify Chinese-Japanese homophones by calculating the semantic distance through Word2Vec. The findings of this study may contribute to theory, methodology, and practical application. Firstly, from a theoretical perspective, we integrated the Revised Hierarchical Model (RHM) from psycholinguistics into natural language processing (NLP) to simulate how learners use their L1 to access concepts in an L2 when processing homophones. Although RHM primarily focuses on the human learning processes, its insights into lexical access can inform cross-linguistic knowledge transfer methods in NLP. Secondly, in terms of methodology, this study offered an alternative method to traditional classification. We used Word2Vec to calculate the semantic distance between Chinese and Japanese meanings. Through cluster analysis, we demonstrated that semantic distance could reflect the traditional classification of homophones. This method enables researchers to more precisely quantify the similarity between Chinese and Japanese meanings of homophones. Lastly, in terms of practical application, we provided detailed teaching suggestions for teachers' reference. By quantifying semantic distance, teachers can further determine the teaching sequence of homophones within the same category. For instance, in the "O" type, words with closer semantic distances within the same level can be taught first.

Although we have provided the suggested teaching sequence, corresponding teaching materials are currently unavailable. Thus, developing such materials serves as a subsequent work for our project in supporting teaching Chinese as a second/foreign language. Regarding future work, given the relatively limited dataset for the "D" type in this study, our next step involves expanding the dataset, especially the "D" type to further broaden the scope of research materials. Further, we plan to investigate the cognitive processes and psychological reality when Japanese learners of Chinese read homophones with different semantic distances through experiments. Based on the expected experimental findings, our ultimate goal is to conduct an empirical teaching study based on our suggested teaching sequence to provide converging evidence to support the teaching suggestions.

Acknowledgements. This work was financially supported by the "Chinese Language and Technology Center" of National Taiwan Normal University (NTNU) by the Ministry of Education (MOE) in Taiwan.

References

1. Cai, Q.Y.: The analysis of chinese character writing and words usage errors made by Chinese-Japanese learners and suggestions. Chung Yuan J. Teach. Chin. as a Secon. Lang. **13**, 53–77 (2014)
2. Chang, C.L.: Comparison of Commonly Used Characters Between Taiwan and Japan, and Suggestions for Teaching Materials Writing. TMUE J. Lang. Lit. **21**, 127–146 (2019)
3. National Institute for Japanese Language and Linguistics.: Research and Education on Vocabulary (Part 1). Ministry of Finance Printing Bureau, Tokyo (1984)
4. Chang, C.L.: A comparative analysis of chinese and japanese kanji vocabulary from the perspective of chinese language teaching: a case study of the AI vocabulary of TOCFL 8000 chinese vocabulary item. The World of Chinese Lang. **122**, 54–69 (2018)
5. Pan, J.: The Establishment and Historical Evolution of Kanji. Commercial Press, Beijing (2013)
6. Agency for Cultural Affairs, Japan: Chinese Corresponding to Kanji: Research Materials for Japanese Language Education. Ministry of Finance Printing Bureau, Tokyo (1978)
7. Miura, A.: The meaning and usage of chinese characters introduced from Japanese into China. J. Japan. Lang. Educ. **53**, 102–112 (1984)
8. Kroll, J.F., Stewart, E.: Category interference in translation and picture naming: evidence for asymmetric connections between bilingual memory representations. J. Mem. Lang. **33**, 149–174 (1994)
9. Fei, X., Zhao, S., Liu, J.: Auditory recognition of Chinese-Japanese cognates and homographs by Chinese JFL learners. Psychologia **64**, 1–22 (2022)
10. Song, Q., Fei, X., Matsumi, N.: The lexical processing of Japanese collocations by Chinese Japanese-as-a-foreign-language learners: an experimental study by manipulating the presentation modality, semantic transparency, and translational congruency. Front. Psychol. (2023). https://doi.org/10.3389/fpsyg.2023.1142411
11. Chen, M.L., Wang, H.C., Ko, H.W.: The construction and validation of chinese semantic space by using latent semantic analysis. Chin. J. Psychol. **51**(4), 415–435 (2009). https://doi.org/10.6129/CJP.2009.5104.02
12. Altszyler, E., Ribeiro, S., Sigman, M., Slezak, D.F.: The interpretation of dream meaning: resolving ambiguity using latent semantic analysis in a small corpus of text. Consciousness Cognition: An Int. J. **56**, 178–187 (2017)
13. Mikolov, T., Yih, W.T., Zweig, G.: Linguistic regularities in continuous space word representations. In: Proceedings of the 2013 conference of the North American chapter of the association for computational linguistics: Human language technologies, pp. 746–751 (2013)
14. Liu, Y.N., Chen, K.Y., Tseng, H.C., Chen, B.: A study of readability prediction on elementary and secondary Chinese textbooks and excellent extracurricular reading materials. In Proceedings of the 27th Conference on Computational Linguistics and Speech Processing (ROCLING 2015), pp. 71–86 (2015)
15. Tseng, H.C., Hung, H.T., Sung, Y.T., Chen, B.: Classification of text readability based on deep neural network and representation learning techniques. In Proceedings of 28th Conference on Computational Linguistics and Speech Processing (ROCLING 2016), pp. 255–270 (2016)
16. Wang, P., Xu, B., Xu, J., Tian, G., Liu, C.-L., Hao, H.: Semantic expansion using word embedding clustering and convolutional neural network for improving short text classification. Neurocomputing **174**, 806–814 (2016). https://doi.org/10.1016/j.neucom.2015.09.096
17. Sung, Y.T., Cheng, H.H., Tseng, H.C., Chang, K.E., Lin, S.Y.: Construction and validation of a computerized creativity assessment tool with automated scoring based on deep-learning techniques. Psychology of Aesthetics, Creativity, and the Arts (2022)

18. Chang, L.Y., Wei, Y.L.: Chinese-Japanese Homograph Learning Strategy I. Cheng Chung Book Co. Ltd, Taipei (2021)
19. Chang, L.Y., Wei, Y.L.: Chinese-Japanese Homograph Learning Strategy II. Cheng Chung Book Co. Ltd, Taipei (2022)
20. Chang, L.Y., Wei, Y.L.: Chinese-Japanese Homograph Learning Strategy III. Cheng Chung Book Co., Ltd., Taipei (in press)
21. Chinese-Japanese Dictionary, 3rd edn. Shogakukan Inc., Tokyo (2015)
22. TBCL wordlists of three grades/seven levels proposed by NAER. https://coct.naer.edu.tw/download/tech_report/. Last accessed 30 Jan 2024
23. Dumas, D., Dunbar, K.N.: Understanding fluency and originality: a latent variable perspective. Thinking Skills Creativity **14**, 56–67 (2014)
24. Yang, C.Z., Li, J.J., Lin, S.C.: Lexical complexity prediction using word embeddings. In Proceedings of the 35th Conference on Computational Linguistics and Speech Processing (ROCLING 2023), pp. 279–287. The Association for Computational Linguistics and Chinese Language Processing (ACLCLP), Taipei City (2023)
25. Collins Dictionary Homepage: https://www.collinsdictionary.com/. Last accessed 23 Mar 2024
26. Cambridge Dictionary Homepage: https://dictionary.cambridge.org/. Last accessed 23 Mar 2024
27. goo Dictionary Homepage. https://dictionary.goo.ne.jp/. Last accessed 23 Mar 2024

Does the PBL Teaching Strategy Suit Higher Education Students with Disabilities? Exploring Financial Literacy Education: Based on PjBL and PmBL

Heng-Yau Pan[1], Gou-Yang Lin[2], and Kou-Hao Lin[3](✉)

[1] Far East University, Sinshih District, Tainan City 744001, Taiwan
[2] National Cheng Kung University, East District, Tainan City 701401, Taiwan
[3] National Taitung Junior College, Taitung City 95045, Taiwan
johnlin@gm.ntc.edu.tw

Abstract. This study examines the effectiveness of Project-Based Learning (PjBL) and Problem-Based Learning (PmBL) approaches in enhancing financial literacy among students with disabilities in higher education. Seven first and second-year students from a university in eastern Taiwan participated in the study, exhibiting a diverse range of disabilities including autism, visual impairment, cerebral palsy, and learning disabilities. The study found that while both PjBL and PmBL groups showed improvements in financial literacy scores, the PjBL group demonstrated a statistically significant improvement in self-efficacy compared to the PmBL group. Motivational factors, as assessed by the Motivated Strategies for Learning Questionnaire (MSLQ), showed no significant differences in intrinsic motivation, extrinsic motivation, work values, or control beliefs between the pre-test and post-test scores for either group. However, the PjBL group exhibited a notable reduction in learning anxiety, and there is also a more positive performance in intrinsic motivation. These findings underscore the importance of tailored instructional strategies for students with disabilities, with PjBL showing promise in enhancing self-efficacy and potentially improving learning outcomes. This study provides valuable insights for universities aiming to support the educational development and financial well-being of students with disabilities.

Keywords: Financial Literacy · PjBL (Project-Based Learning) · PmBL (Problem-Based Learning) · Higher Education for students with Disabilities

1 Introduction

In pursuit of students' problem-solving abilities and employability skills, European higher education has, for decades, focused on advanced educational methodologies [1]. Financial literacy, also known as financial capability, denotes an individual's overall capacity encompassing knowledge, understanding, skills, attitudes, behaviors, and values essential for navigating potential financial crises [2–4]. Research utilizing unstructured interviews has revealed that undergraduate students in finance departments at universities may exhibit similarities to ordinary investors. Specifically, students may lack

Y.-P. Cheng et al. (Eds.): ICITL 2024, LNCS 14785, pp. 281–291, 2024.
https://doi.org/10.1007/978-3-031-65881-5_30

essential abilities such as risk-reward assessment, buy-and-hold strategy proficiency, understanding of financial regulations, and competence in financial statement analysis [5]. Consequently, there is a growing global concern regarding the improvement of financial literacy among university students, with the aim of equipping individuals with the skills necessary to navigate future financial challenges [6–8].

Therefore, 'financial literacy education' not only aims to equip typical students with essential skills but also aims to accommodate students with physiological or psychological disorders. Its objective is to empower students to develop and enhance the aforementioned abilities, ensuring their capability to make effective financial decisions in their daily lives. Moreover, it extends these capabilities to promote financial security for individuals and families in society during adulthood [4, 9], thereby contributing to the enhancement of economic and social well-being.

2 Literature Review

2.1 Problem-Based Learning (PmBL) and Project-Based Learning (PjBL)

Problem-based learning (PmBL), implemented to foster learners' active engagement in the learning process and enhance their problem-solving, diagnostic, or clinical reasoning abilities [10], is centered on individual case problems, aiding learners in improving their problem-solving skills and acquiring relevant knowledge [11]. Furthermore, PmBL encompasses several teaching characteristics, including:

(1) Facilitating the connection and retrieval of previously acquired knowledge;
(2) Encouraging the acquisition of new knowledge through small group discussions;
(3) Integrating information relevant to the presented problems;
(4) Fostering learning within real-world contexts;
(5) Stimulating learners' motivation through participation in open-ended discussions due to the interconnected nature of problems [12].

Hence, the primary objective of the PmBL instructional approach is to boost students' motivation to learn and bolster their capacity for integrating knowledge, ultimately fostering the development of their problem-solving abilities [13]."

Project-Based Learning (PjBL) is an educational approach focused on hands-on construction, offering learners intricate and genuine projects. This method empowers students to select topics, formulate problems, devise action plans, gather data, engage in problem-solving, make decisions, conduct inquiries, and present findings—a methodology rooted in inquiry-based learning [14]. According to literature, only 20% of research on Project-Based Learning (PjBL) strategies is focused on higher education [15]. Furthermore, there is evidence suggesting that the research trajectory of PjBL in higher education has notably trailed behind its development in K-12 education [16].

Although this instructional approach is beneficial in various fields such as engineering, medicine, psychology, and education, it is less commonly used in the fields of finance and economics [1].

Scholars propose a three-stage approach for implementing the Project-Based Learning (PjBL) teaching strategy in financial education[1]:

(1) Begin by introducing the PjBL method to students and organizing them into teams.
(2) Proceed with teachers providing instruction on fundamental financial concepts and financial planning.
(3) Conclude by assigning practical topics for exploration by each group, covering areas such as loans, leasing, crowdfunding, venture capital, and other financing issues.

2.2 The Special Education Act of Taiwan and the Definition and Assessment of Disabilities (Disorders)

The Special Education Act of Taiwan aims to ensure that citizens with disabilities and giftedness/talents receive adaptive and inclusive education, allowing them to fully develop their potential, foster their personality, and contribute to society. Disabilities (or disorders), as defined by the Act, include various physiological or psychological disorders that professionals identify as necessitating special education and related services [17].

Article 3 of the Special Education Act outlines the definition of disabilities (or disorders) [17]. Which professionals evaluate and identify to determine the necessity for special education and related services. These disabilities include intellectual disability, visual impairment, hearing impairment, speech or language disorders, orthopedic impairment, cerebral palsy, health impairments, emotional and behavioral disorders, learning disabilities, autism, multiple disabilities, developmental delays, and other conditions.

Under Article 12 of the Enforcement Rules of the Special Education Act [18], universities and colleges are required to establish teams to develop individualized support plans for disabled students. These plans are tailored to address the specific nature of each student's disability and their unique needs, integrating available resources within the institution. Each personalized support plan must include:

(1) Assessment of the student's current competencies, family situation, and needs.
(2) Identification of the special education, support services, and strategies required by the student.
(3) Transition counseling and services to facilitate the student's transition to post-secondary education or employment.

Overall, the Special Education Act and its enforcement rules aim to provide comprehensive support to students with disabilities, ensuring that their educational needs are met through personalized and effective interventions.

3 Methodology

3.1 PjBL and PmBL

Seven students with disabilities from the information science department participated in this study. They were divided into two groups based on their willingness to participate in teaching strategies: the PjBL group (experimental group) and the PmBL group (control group). The course content, assessment methods, and teaching instructors were the same for both groups, with the only difference being the teaching strategy. The experimental group students adopted the PjBL strategy, while the control group adopted the PmBL teaching strategy. Data collection was conducted through Google Forms surveys.

3.2 Experimental Procedure

As shown in Fig. 1, the research experiment follows a quasi-experimental research design. Both the experimental and control groups undergo an 8-week course, which includes activities such as practicing bank deposit and withdrawal receipts in the first week to stimulate learning motivation, as well as course introductions and pre-tests. The curriculum activities from weeks 2 to 7 cover topics such as savings and time deposits, life insurance, time value of money, financial lending, stock markets, ex-rights and ex-dividend. The content and instructors are consistent for both groups. However, the PjBL group (experimental group) is required to complete an e-book, while the PmBL group (control group) completes a self-directed learning report. In the eighth week, a post-test on financial literacy is conducted, along with the Motivated Strategies for Learning Questionnaire (MSLQ) to assess intrinsic motivation, extrinsic motivation, job value, control belief, self-efficacy, and learning anxiety, in order to understand the impact of different PBL learning strategies.

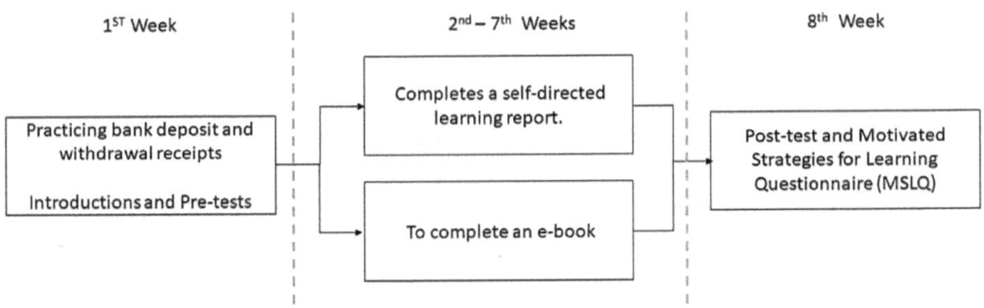

Fig. 1. Research Experiment Flowchart: Quasi-Experimental Design and Assessment Overview.

3.3 Measurement

The financial literacy test used in this study consists of 20 items, which were reviewed by experts to measure changes in students' learning activities. Additionally, the Motivated Strategies for Learning Questionnaire (MSLQ) was employed to investigate intrinsic motivation, extrinsic motivation, job value, control belief, self-efficacy, and learning anxiety [19]. The questionnaire was rated on a 5-point Likert scale, ranging from 1 (strongly disagree) to 5 (strongly agree), with a total of 31 questions. Internal consistency tests conducted in various studies indicated Cronbach's α coefficients ranging from 0.612 to 0.90 for different language versions, demonstrating good reliability and validity.

3.4 Data Analysis

Using IBM SPSS 26, non-parametric statistical analyses were conducted on the experimental and control groups, including descriptive statistics, Mann-Whitney Test, Wilcoxon Signed-Rank Test, to understand the differences between different PBL teaching strategies.

4 Results and Discussion

Among the first and second-year students enrolled in a financial literacy course at a university in eastern Taiwan, a total of 7 participants were surveyed. As shown in Table 1, in Panel A, the gender distribution revealed that 57.1% (4 participants) were male, while 42.9% (3 participants) were female. Panel B reports on student disability, indicating that 42.9% of the participants (3 students) reported having autism, 14.3% (1 student) had visual impairment, another 14.3% (1 student) had cerebral palsy, and 28.6% (2 students) had learning disabilities. Regarding student background as shown in Panel C, 42.9% (3 students) belonged to the business management group, whereas the majority, accounting for 57.1% (4 students), were enrolled in the electrical and electronics group.

Table 1. Descriptive Statistics of Participants in Financial Literacy Course

Panel A: Group by Gender (N = 7)		
Gender	N	N%
Female	3	42.9%
Male	4	57.1%
Panel B: Group by Disability (N = 7)		
Disability	N	N%
Autism	3	42.9%
Visual Impairment	1	14.3%
Cerebral Palsy	1	14.3%
Learning Disability	2	28.6%
Panel C: Group by Background (N = 7)		
Background	N	N%
Commerce and Management	3	42.9%
Electrical and Electronic	4	57.1%

Table 2 presents the Comparative Analysis of Participant Characteristics in Project-based Learning (PjBL) and Problem-based Learning (PmBL) Courses. Seven students independently selected different teaching strategy courses, with five students participating in the Project-based Learning (PjBL) experimental group course, and the remaining two students joining the Problem-based Learning (PmBL) control group course.

Table 2. Comparative Analysis of Participant Characteristics in Project-based Learning (PjBL) and Problem-based Learning (PmBL) Courses

Panel A: Group by Gender				
	PjBL		PmBL	
	N	N%	N	N%
Female	3	60%	0	0%
Male	2	40%	2	100%
Total	5	100%	2	100%

Panel B: Group by Disability				
	PjBL		PmBL	
	N	N%	N	N%
Autism	2	40%	1	50%
Visual Impairment	0	0%	1	50%
Cerebral Palsy	1	20%	0	0%
Learning Disability	2	40%	0	0%
Total	5	100%	2	100%

Panel C: Group by Background				
Background	PjBL		PmBL	
	N	N%	N	N%
Commerce and Management	3	60%	0	0%
Electrical and Electronic	2	40%	2	100%
Total	5	100%	2	100%

In Panel A, for Project-based Learning (PjBL), gender distribution indicates a relatively balanced representation, with 60% of participants identifying as female (3 students) and 40% as male (2 students). Panel B reports a varied profile regarding disability for Project-based Learning (PjBL), with 40% reporting autism (2 students), 20% with cerebral palsy (1 student), and 40% having learning disabilities (2 students). Additionally, Panel C shows that 60% of PjBL participants hail from a Commerce and Management background (3 students), whereas 40% come from an Electrical and Electronic background (2 students).

In contrast, Problem-based Learning (PmBL) showcases a different demographic landscape. Gender-wise, in Panel A, PmBL participation is dominated by male students, constituting 100% of the cohort (2 students). In Panel B, Disabilities among PmBL participants include 50% with autism (1 student) and another 50% with visual impairment (1 student). Furthermore, Panel C shows that all PmBL participants (100%) are from an Electrical and Electronic background.

Table 3 conducted a Mann-Whitney test on the pre-financial literacy assessment scores of two types of PBL teaching groups. In the PjBL group, which consisted of 5 participants, the mean rank of the scores was 3.40, resulting in a sum of ranks of 17.00. In contrast, the PmBL group comprised 2 participants, with a mean rank of 5.50 and a sum of ranks of 11.00. The comparison between these two groups did not yield significant differences ($Z = -1.230$, $p > 0.05$), this indicates that there is no difference in prior knowledge and starting points between the two groups.

Table 3. Comparison of Pre-Financial Literacy Assessment Scores between PjBL and PmBL Teaching Groups using Mann-Whitney Test

	Strategy	N	Mean Rank	sum rank	Z	p
pre-test	PjBL	5	3.40	17.00	−1.230	.219
	PmBL	2	5.50	28.00		

After undergoing group instruction in both PjBL and PmBL, students from both groups took a post-test for financial literacy. Table 4 displays the Wilcoxon Signed-Rank Test results for the difference between post-test and pre-test scores in the PjBL and PmBL groups. In the PjBL group, the mean of the post-test (pre-test) scores was 55 (45), with a standard deviation of 7.071 (7.071). There were 4 positive ranks indicating an increase in scores from pre-test to post-test. Additionally, one tied rank was observed in this group. A Wilcoxon signed-rank test revealed a difference ($z = -1.890$, $p < 0.1$).

In contrast, in the PmBL group, the mean of the post-test (pre-test) scores was 50 (55), with a standard deviation of 14.142 (7.071). One negative rank was recorded, implying a decrease in scores from pre-test to post-test. No positive ranks were observed in this group. Similar to the PjBL group, one tied rank was also observed. A Wilcoxon signed-rank test revealed no difference ($z = -1.000$, $p > 0.1$). This suggests that compared to the PmBL instructional strategy, the PjBL instructional strategy provides more cognitive assistance in implementing financial literacy courses in university special education programs.

Table 4. Wilcoxon Signed-Rank Test for Pre and Post-Test Scores in PjBL and PmBL

	Post-test – Pre-test	N	Mean Rank	Sum of Ranks	Z	p
	Negative Ranks	0	0	0	−1.890*	.059
PjBL	Positive Ranks	4	2.50	10.00		
	Tied	1				
	Negative Ranks	1	1	1	−1.000	.317
PmBL	Positive Ranks	0	0	0		
	Tied	1				

* represent 10% significance levels.

Table 5. Wilcoxon Signed-Rank Test for MSLQ

Panel A: Intrinsic Motivation						
	Post-test – Pre-test	N	Mean Rank	Sum of Ranks	Z	p
PjBL	Negative Ranks	3	2.00	6.00	−0368	.713
	Positive Ranks	1	4.00	4.00		
	Tied	1				
PmBL	Negative Ranks	1	1.00	1.00	−1.000	.317
	Positive Ranks	0	0	0		
	Tied	1				
Panel B: Extrinsic Motivation						
PjBL	Negative Ranks	0	0	0	−1.604	.109
	Positive Ranks	3	2.00	6.00		
	Tied	2				
PmBL	Negative Ranks	2	1.50	3.00	−1.342	.180
	Positive Ranks	0	0	0		
	Tied	0				
Panel C: Work Values						
PjBL	Negative Ranks	1	5	5.00	−0.677	.498
	Positive Ranks	4	2.50	10.00		
	Tied	0				
PmBL	Negative Ranks	1	2.00	2.00	−0.447	.655
	Positive Ranks	1	1.00	1.00		
	Tied	0				
Panel D: Control Beliefs						
PjBL	Negative Ranks	4	2.50	10.00	−0.677	.498
	Positive Ranks	1	5.00	5.00		
	Tied	0				
PmBL	Negative Ranks	2	1.50	3.00	−1.414	.157
	Positive Ranks	0	0	0		
	Tied	0				
Panel E: Self-Efficacy						
PjBL	Negative Ranks	0	0	0	−2.032**	.042
	Positive Ranks	5	3.00	15.00		
	Tied	0				

(*continued*)

Table 5. (*continued*)

Panel A: Intrinsic Motivation						
	Post-test – Pre-test	N	Mean Rank	Sum of Ranks	Z	p
	Negative Ranks	1	1.50	1.50	0.000	1.000
PmBL	Positive Ranks	1	1.50	1.50		
	Tied	0				
Panel F: Learning Anxiety						
	Negative Ranks	3	2.67	8.00	−0.137	.891
PjBL	Positive Ranks	2	3.50	7.00		
	Tied	0				
	Negative Ranks	0	0	0	−1.342	.180
PmBL	Positive Ranks	2	1.50	3.00		
	Tied	0				

** represent 5% significance levels.

Table 5 presents the outcomes of the Wilcoxon Signed-Rank Test for MSLQ (Motivated Strategies for Learning Questionnaire), aimed at evaluating the efficacy of diverse instructional approaches on various facets of learning motivation and behavior. Here, we investigate whether the impact of different learning strategies on intrinsic motivation, extrinsic motivation, work values, control beliefs, self-efficacy, and learning anxiety is statistically significant, as elaborated in Panels A through F.

In Panel A, for the PjBL group, the analysis revealed that there were no significant differences between pre-test and post-test scores for intrinsic motivation ($p = 0.713 > .1$). Specifically, the negative ranks indicated instances where post-test scores were lower than pre-test scores, with a mean rank of 2.00 and a sum of ranks of 6.00. The lone positive rank demonstrated that in one case, the post-test score surpassed the pre-test score, with a mean rank of 4.00 and a sum of ranks of 4.00. Similarly, for the PmBL group, no significant differences were found between pre-test and post-test scores for intrinsic motivation ($p = 0.317 > .1$). Only one negative rank was observed, reflecting a scenario where the post-test score was lower than the pre-test score, with a mean rank of 1.00 and a sum of ranks of 1.00. However, the performance of the experimental group (PjBL group) was more positive compared to the control group (PmBL).

In Panel B, These findings suggest that neither teaching approach significantly influenced extrinsic motivation scores, as evidenced by the non-significant p-values of 0.109 for the PjBL group and 0.180 for the PmBL group.

In Panel C, the analysis showed no significant differences be-tween pre-test and post-test scores for work values. These findings suggest that neither teaching approach significantly influenced work values scores, as evidenced by the non-significant p-values of 0.498 for the PjBL group and 0.655 for the PmBL group.

In Panel D, the analysis revealed no significant alterations be-tween pre-test and post-test scores for control beliefs. These results suggest that neither teaching approach significantly impacted control beliefs scores, as supported by the non-significant p-values of 0.498 for the PjBL group and 0.157 for the PmBL group.

In Panel E, the Wilcoxon Signed-Rank Test was employed to assess the influence of teaching methodologies on self-efficacy in university financial literacy courses targeted at students with special needs. For the PjBL group, a statistically significant improvement in self-efficacy was observed from pre-test to post-test, as indicated by the large negative rank sum of −15.00 and a mean rank of 3.00 for positive ranks. Notably, no negative ranks were recorded for this group, suggesting that all post-test scores were higher than pre-test scores. This improvement is further supported by a significant p-value of 0.042, denoting a 5% level of significance. Conversely, for the PmBL group, no statistically significant changes in self-efficacy were detected, this suggests that the PmBL teaching approach did not lead to significant improvements in self-efficacy scores among students.

Finally, as shown in Panel F, for the PjBL group, a modest reduction in learning anxiety was observed from pre-test to post-test, indicated by the sum of ranks for negative ranks (8.00) exceeding that of positive ranks (7.00), resulting in a slightly negative rank sum (−1.00). However, this difference did not reach statistical significance ($p = 0.891 > .1$). Although neither PjBL nor PmBL instructional strategies demonstrated a significant effect on reducing learning anxiety among students with special needs in financial literacy courses, a reduction in anxiety was observed in the PjBL group.

5 Conclusion

Based on the findings of the study involving first and second-year students enrolled in a financial literacy course at a university in eastern Taiwan, this research encompassed seven participants with diverse backgrounds. Participants independently selected their preferred teaching strategy, leading to two groups: five students in the PjBL experimental group and two in the PmBL control group. Disabilities varied among participants, including autism, visual impairment, and cerebral palsy, with both Project-Based Learning (PjBL) and Problem-Based Learning (PmBL) approaches being utilized.

While both groups exhibited improvements in financial literacy scores from pre-test to post-test, the PjBL group notably showed a statistically significant improvement compared to the PmBL group. Moreover, it is noteworthy that the PjBL group displayed a significant enhancement in self-efficacy compared to the PmBL group. This indicates that PjBL might offer greater cognitive support in implementing financial literacy courses for students with special needs, leading to an improvement in self-efficacy.

Analysis of the Motivated Strategies for Learning Questionnaire (MSLQ) revealed that, while not statistically significant, the PjBL group showed a slight reduction in learning anxiety and a more positive trend in intrinsic motivation.

In summary, this study underscores the effectiveness of Project-Based Learning in enhancing self-efficacy and potentially reducing learning anxiety among students with disabilities in financial literacy courses. By employing innovative teaching methods like PjBL, universities can better support the educational development and financial well-being of students with diverse learning needs.

Acknowledgments. This research was supported by the National Science and Technology Council, Taiwan, R.O.C [grant numbers NSTC 111-2410-H-602-002].

References

1. Parrado-Martínez, P., Sánchez-Andújar, S.: Development of competences in postgraduate studies of finance: a project-based learning (PBL) case study. Int. Rev. Econ. Educ. **35**, 100–192 (2020). https://doi.org/10.1016/j.iree.2020.100192
2. Altman, M.: The implications of behavior economics for financial literacy and public policy. J. Soc.-Econ. **41**(5), 677–690 (2012). https://doi.org/10.1016/j.socec.2012.06.002
3. Organization for Economic Co-operation and Development: PISA 2012 results: Students and money: Financial literacy skills for the 21st Century (Volume VI). PISA, OECD Publishing, Paris (2014)
4. Opletalová, A.: Financial education and financial literacy in the Czech education system. Procedia Soc. Behav. Sci. **171**, 1176–1184 (2015)
5. Chin, L.C., Lin, G.Y., Lin, K.H.: Exploratory research on the improvement of financial literacy flipped learning effectiveness-based on guiding scaffold via Project-Based Learning approach. J. Insur. Financ. Manag. **7**(3), 22–34 (2022)
6. Office of Financial Education: Integrating financial education into school curricula: Giving America's youth the educational foundation for making effective financial decisions throughout their lives by teaching financial concepts as part of math and reading curricula in elementary, middle, and high schools. Department of Treasury, Washington, DC (2002)
7. Greenspan, A.: The importance of financial education today. Soc. Educ. **69**(2), 64–65 (2005)
8. Organization for Economic Co-operation and Development: Guidelines on financial education at school and guidance on learning framework (2011). Retrieved from http://www.oecd.org/dataoecd/15/57/48493142.pdf
9. Lusardi, A.: Financial literacy and the need for financial education: evidence and implications. Swiss J. Econ. Stat. **155**(1), 1–8 (2019)
10. Barrows, H.S., Tamblyn, R.M.: Problem-based Learning: An Approach to Medical Education. Spring Publishing Company, New York (1980)
11. Albanese, M.A., Mitchell, S.: Problem-based learning: a review of literature on its outcomes and implementation issues. Acad. Med. **68**(1), 52–81 (1993)
12. Schmidt, H.G.: Foundations of problem-based learning: some explanatory notes. Med. Educ. **27**(5), 422–432 (1993)
13. Albion, P.R., Gibson, I.W.: Problem-based learning as a multimedia design framework in teacher education. J. Technol. Teach. Educ. **8**, 315–326 (2000)
14. Blumenfeld, P.C., Soloway, E., Marx, R.W., Krajcik, J.S., Guzdial, M., Palincsar, A.: Motivating project-based learning: sustaining the doing, supporting the learning. Educ. Psychol. **26**(3 & 4), 369–398 (1991)
15. Guo, P., Saab, N., Post, L.S., Admiraal, W.: A review of project-based learning in higher education: student outcomes and measures. Int. J. Educ. Res. **102**, 101586 (2020). https://doi.org/10.1016/j.ijer.2020.101586
16. Lee, J.S., Blackwell, S., Drake, J., Moran, K.A.: Taking a leap of faith: Redefining teaching and learning in higher education through project-based learning. Interdisc. J. Problem-Based Learn. **8**(2), 19–34 (2014)
17. Ministry of Education, Taiwan (R.O.C.): The Special Education Act. (2023)
18. Ministry of Education, Taiwan (R.O.C.): The Enforcement Rules of the Special Education Act. (2023)
19. Pintrich, P.R.: A manual for the use of the Motivated Strategies for Learning Questionnaire (MSLQ) (1991)

Effects of ASQ-Based E-books on Nursing Students' Learning Performance

Chia-Lin Chen and Han-Yu Sung(✉)

Department of Allied Health Education and Digital Learning, National Taipei University of Nursing and Health Science, Taipei, Taiwan
hanyu.sung@gmail.com

Abstract. Congenital heart diseases are commonly seen in the pediatrics department. Knowledge content related to such diseases involve cardiac anatomy, cardiac hemodynamics, systemic circulation, and fetal circulation. Traditional teaching processes mostly use images and textual descriptions to demonstrate the content. However, most of the traditional teaching process is only presented through graphic descriptions, and it is difficult for students to connect the knowledge of dynamic heart structure and its blood flows. Accordingly, the present study used interactive e-books based on annotation, summarizing, and questioning (ASQ) strategies as the teaching intervention approach to explore the effects of the approach on students' learning effectiveness in a course unit of congenital heart diseases in pediatric nursing. The experimental results revealed that the participants exhibited significant improvement in learning achievement and learning motivation. The results implied that the use of "interactive e-books incorporated with ASQ strategies" on nursing students effectively helped their thinking and knowledge construction, thereby benefiting their understanding of knowledge regarding congenital heart diseases.

Keywords: Congenital heart disease · ASQ strategies · Interactive e-book

1 Introduction

Cardiovascular disease is one of the important units that nursing students must study in pediatric nursing. According to the Ministry of National Examination and Election (MNEA) Nursing Question Outline from 1998-110, this unit has been included in the question scope every year, and its knowledge includes the physiological characteristics of the heart and blood vessels of children, the common health problems of heart disease in children, the common heart diseases in children, and the nursing care of heart disease in children [1].

The care of children with congenital heart disease is relatively complex and requires the learner to have a good understanding of the anatomy of congenital heart defects. It is very difficult for the learner to understand the anatomy of the defects, especially when the teacher teaches multiple complex defects at the same time, the learner is more likely to be confused, and when there is no expertise in the structure of the defects,

Y.-P. Cheng et al. (Eds.): ICITL 2024, LNCS 14785, pp. 292–297, 2024.
https://doi.org/10.1007/978-3-031-65881-5_31

not only is it not possible to understand the physiological conditions caused by the defects, but also it is not possible to provide the appropriate care for the child and his/her family. The lack of expertise in the structure of defects, in addition to the inability to understand the physiological conditions caused by each defect, and the inability to provide appropriate nursing interventions for the child and his/her family [2], should be examined and attempted to be overcome in order to improve the teaching and learning situation.

With the advancement of technology, the mode of learning has shifted from viewing printed books to the use of multimedia and highly interactive digital teaching materials. However, this contrasts sharply with the traditional lecture method, and the use of multimedia teaching materials for learning allows learners to learn without the constraints of time and place, and also allows for "learner-centered" learning. However, some researchers have pointed out that although the use of interactive teaching materials in the teaching process can stimulate students' interest in learning, their learning outcomes may not be achieved without appropriate learning strategies or tools [3, 4]. Kirch (2012) proposed the WSQ (Watch-Summary-Question) strategy, which means "watch, summarize, and ask questions", where learners summarize the key points and ask questions after watching the video [5]. However, Lin et al. (2019) pointed out that learners' failure to correctly identify key concepts during the viewing stage would affect their thinking and the compilation of knowledge content [6]. Therefore, this study attempted to change Watch to Annotation to identify key concepts of knowledge content through learners' use of graphic annotations, and to use interactive e-books incorporating the ASQ strategy as a An interactive e-book incorporating ASQ strategies was used as a pedagogical intervention to explore the learning effectiveness of nursing students in a pediatric nursing course on congenital heart disease.

2 Literature Review

Kirch (2012) proposed the WSQ (Watch-Summary-Question) strategy, which guides learners to ask questions after watching and summarizing the content of the instructional video [5]. This learning strategy encourages learners to take notes while watching the teaching materials, and the process consists of three phases of watching, summarizing, and questioning, which is called the WSQ (Watch, Summary, and Question) strategy. This is called the WSQ (Watch, Summary, and Question) strategy. The WSQ strategy helps learners identify key questions, summarize what they know, and then ask questions. However, if learners cannot identify the key concepts correctly in the Watch stage, it will affect their performance in the Summary and Question [6]. Therefore, this study changed the Watch stage to Annotation, in which learners are guided to define and annotate the important concepts in the content. In this stage, learners are guided to define and annotate the important concepts in the content to facilitate students' progress in the higher levels of Summary and Question.

1. Annotation:

Annotation is one of the important learning strategies, which aims to identify the key points in a large amount of learning content and conduct the learning process of highlighting or writing notes [7]. Wolfe (2002) pointed out that the use of annotations can help learners to learn and also improve their learning efficiency through annotations [8]. Ball et al. (2009) also pointed out that if the annotation strategy can be used to annotate the meaning of learning materials, it can not only enhance the learners' understanding of the contents of the materials, but also improve their learning effectiveness [9].

2. Summary:

The purpose of the summary is to select the key points of the chapter or essay and describe them concisely, so that the content can be understood when reading [10]. The purpose of a summary is to assist learners in understanding and clarifying the key points of learning, so that learners can reason and connect the content with prior knowledge.

3. Questioning:

By observing and summarizing the written notes, students move from low to high level thinking and ask questions related to the content knowledge. Questioning is not only about memorization and comprehension, but also about actively constructing knowledge and thinking about relevant issues during the learning process [11, 12].

According to the analysis of related literature, the use of ASQ strategies in teaching interventions can effectively enhance students' learning effectiveness and improve their learning outcomes and self-efficacy. However, a review of previous studies shows that ASQ strategies have not been used with interactive e-books in teaching and learning, and have not been applied to the curriculum of congenital heart disease. Therefore, this study developed an interactive e-book based on the Annotation, Summary, and Question (ASQ) strategy to investigate the effects of this learning model on the learning achievement and motivation of nursing students in a course on congenital heart disease in pediatric nursing. The impact of this learning model on the learning achievement and motivation of nursing students in a pediatric congenital heart disease course was investigated.

3 Method

This study was a one-group pretest-posttest design in which the researcher explained the purpose of the study and the flow of the experimental activities, and the experimental activities were conducted after obtaining the written consent of the study participants. The pretest and posttest were conducted before and after the teaching activities. The pretest and pretest questionnaire were congenital heart disease knowledge test and learning motivation questionnaire, respectively, and the congenital heart disease knowledge test posttest and learning motivation posttest questionnaire were administered after the intervention of the teaching activity.

The curriculum design for Pediatric Congenital Heart Disease is based on the Oliva Model of curriculum development, which collects data from environmental background factors and learner needs, and develops the objectives of the course so that the goals and objectives of the course and the objectives of the course and the goals and objectives of the classroom correspond to each other. The development of the objectives will follow Bloom's statement that educational objectives should include knowledge, affect and skills. The content of the pediatric congenital heart disease curriculum was developed according to the research objectives and was divided into three units: understanding normal heart structure, understanding non-growth heart disease, and understanding growth heart disease.

3.1 Participants

This study was conducted in a private medical university in northern Taiwan with a convenience sample of 35 postgraduate nursing students who had passed the medical and surgical nursing program and were willing to participate in this study and had completed a consent form. The study will be conducted through a human subjects committee with the consent and support of the Academic Affairs Office and the instructors.

3.2 Measuring Tools

The knowledge test on congenital heart disease covers the pathology, clinical symptoms and medical management of congenital heart disease. The questions were taken from the national nursing examination of the past 5–10 years, and the questions were of multiple-choice type, while the content of the questions was assessed by three experts in the field for expert validity. The expert content validity was assessed for relevance, representativeness, and clarity of the learning effectiveness test, and the pre-test consisted of 20 multiple-choice questions, with expert content validity of 1.0 and 1.0 for the S-CVI. The post-test consisted of 15 multiple-choice questions and 5 quizzes, with an expert content validity of 1.0 and an S-CVI of 1.0, indicating good content validity.

The learning motivation questionnaire in this study was based on the learning motivation scale proposed by Wang and Chen (2010) [13], which was modified from Pintrich et al. (1991), with a Cronbach's alpha of 0.79, and the scale was scored on a five-point Likert scale, with five levels of agreement, 1 being strongly disagree and 5 being strongly agree [14]. This questionnaire was used to investigate the performance of learners' motivation and consisted of 6 questions, the first 3 questions were to understand the learners' internal motivation and the last 3 questions were to investigate the learners' external motivation. Both the pre- and post-questionnaires used positive narratives, e.g., Question 1: "In this program, I prefer challenging materials because I can learn new things"; Question 2: "Getting a good grade in this program is the most satisfying thing for me". The pre-motivation questionnaire and post-motivation questionnaire were administered once before and once after the teaching-learning activities, in order to find out whether the students' feelings about using the ASQ-based E-books in the learning process throughout the learning activities would have an impact on their motivation to learn about the congenital heart disease program.

4 Experimental Results

This study was conducted to find out whether the use of ASQ-based E-books in the unit of Pediatric Nursing "Congenital Heart Disease" has a significant effect on students' learning achievement. This study was analyzed using a paired-sample t-test. The results of the statistical analysis are shown in Table 1, which shows that the mean score of students' learning achievement on the pre-test was 76.31 with a standard deviation of 9.20, and the mean score of students' learning achievement on the post-test was 80.14 with a standard deviation of 9.78, which is a significant difference between pre- and post-test scores ($t = 3.25$, $p < 0.01$). It can be inferred that the use of ASQ-based E-books can significantly and effectively improve students' learning achievement in the congenital heart disease course.

Table 1. t-test result of the students' learning achievement

Group	Mean	SD	t	*p*
post-test	80.14	9.78	3.25^{**}	.003
pre-test	76.31	9.20		

$^{**}p < .01$

In order to find out whether the use of ASQ-based E-books in the "Congenital Heart Disease" module of pediatric nursing had a significant effect on students' motivation, this study was conducted by asking students to complete a motivation questionnaire after the teaching activities and analyzing it using a paired-sample t-test. The results of the statistical analysis are shown in Table 2, which shows that the mean score of students' learning motivation on the pre-questionnaire was 4.07 with a standard deviation of 0.33, while the mean score of the post-questionnaire was 4.31 with a standard deviation of 0.51, and the difference in the scores of students' learning motivation before and after the learning activities reached a significant difference ($t = 3.10$, $p < 0.01$). It can be inferred that the use of ASQ-based E-books can significantly and effectively enhance students' learning motivation.

Table 2. t-test result of the students' learning motivation

Group	Mean	SD	t	*p*
post-questionnaire	4.31	0.51	3.10^{**}	.002
pre-questionnaire	4.07	0.33		

$^{**}p < .01$

References

1. Ministry of National Examination and Election (MNEA) Global Information Network: Nursing Question Outline from 1998–110, MNEA Global Information Network (2022)
2. Aldridge, M.D.: Using models to teach congenital heart defects: a hands-on approach. Dimens. Crit. Care Nurs. **28**(3), 116–122 (2009). https://doi.org/10.1097/DCC.0b013e31819aef15

3. Cheng, M.H.M., Wan, Z.H.: Unpacking the paradox of Chinese science learners: Insights from research into Asian Chinese school students' attitudes towards learning science, science learning strategies, and scientific epistemological views. Stud. Sci. Educ. **52**(1), 29–62 (2016)
4. Peng, H.Y., Chuang, P.Y., Hwang, G.J., Chu, H.C., Wu, T.T., Huang, S.X.: Ubiquitous performance-support system as mindtool: a case study of instructional decision making and learning assistant. Educ. Technol. Soc. **12**(1), 107–120 (2009)
5. Kirch, C.: My favorite WSQ. Retrieved from http://flippingwithkirch.blogspot.com/2012/01/my-favorite-wsq.html (2012)
6. Lin, H.C., Hwang, G.J., Hsu, Y.D.: Effects of ASQ-based flipped learning on nurse practitioner learners' nursing skills, learning achievement and learning perceptions. Comput. Educ. **139**, 207–221 (2019)
7. Kiryakov, A.: Semantic annotation, indexing, and ndexing, and retrieval. Elseviers J. Web Sem. **2**, 26–41 (2005)
8. Wolfe, J.: Annotation technologies: a software and research review. Comput. Compos. **19**, 471–491 (2002)
9. Ball, E., Franks, H., Jenkins, J., McGrath, M., Leigh, J.: Annotation is a valuable tool to enhance learning and assessment in student essays. Nurse Educ. Today **29**(3), 284–291 (2009)
10. Ministry of Education: Revised Mandarin Dictionary (2015)
11. Silver, E.A., Cai, J.: Assessing students' mathematical problem posing. Teach. Child. Math. **12**, 129–135 (2005)
12. Wang, X.M., Hwang, G.J.: A problem posing-based practicing strategy for facilitating students' computer programming skills in the team-based learning mode. Educ. Tech. Res. Dev. **65**(6), 1655–1671 (2017)
13. Wang, L.C., Chen, M.P.: The effects of game strategy and preference-matching on flow experience and programming performance in game-based learning. Innov. Educ. Teach. Int. **47**(1), 39–52 (2010)
14. Pintrich, P.R., Smith, D.A.F., Garcia, T., McKeachie, W.J.: A manual for the use of the motivated strategies for learning questionnaire (MSLQ). National Center for Research to Improve Postsecondary Teaching and Learning, MI (1991)

CD-ROM in Chinese Character Education: Streamlining Material Complication with Multi-level Features

Li-Yun Chang[1], Jung-En Haung[2], Min-Chi Lo[1], and Hou-Chiang Tseng[2](✉)

[1] National Taiwan Normal University, Taipei, Taiwan (ROC)
[2] Graduate Institute of Digital Learning and Education, National Taiwan University of Science and Technology, Taipei, Taiwan (ROC)
tsenghc@mail.ntust.edu.tw

Abstract. This study introduced the "Character Difficulty–Research on Multi-features (CD-ROM)", a pioneering tool developed to streamline the compilation of materials for Chinese literacy enhancement. By leveraging a comprehensive database of multi-level features of characters and empirical data on learner performance, CD-ROM provided a significant leap forward in material preparation. Specifically, the "Instructional Content Suggestion" functionality was designed to exemplify technology-enhanced language education by offering customized instructional content across the "radical-character-word" continuum, tailored to the input text. Moreover, employing a mixed-methods research design, the capacities of CD-ROM was assessed through an evaluation involving 68 educational practitioners in Chinese pedagogy, evidencing its superiority over conventional material compilation methods within the framework of the Technology Acceptance Model. Results highlighted CD-ROM's effective and efficient role in providing explicit instruction, enabling dynamic pedagogical customization, and facilitating the creation of test items in reading materials. The findings not only underscored the utility of CD-ROM in educational technology integration but also set the stage for future advancements in Chinese character education.

Keywords: Chinese-as-foreign/second language (CFL/CSL) learning and instruction · Character difficulty · orthographic features of Chinese characters · technology · enhanced language learning

1 Introduction

Chinese characters possess unique and multi-level characteristics in terms of their form, pronunciation, and meaning, especially considering their vast number and the visual complexity of their compositions [1]. To achieve basic reading proficiency in Chinese, learners typically need to master around three thousand characters and understand how these characters are formed from different character orthographic features (e.g., strokes, components/radicals) arranged in tens of configurations (e.g., positions within structures) within a two-dimensional space [2], further mapping to their pronunciations and

Y.-P. Cheng et al. (Eds.): ICITL 2024, LNCS 14785, pp. 298–308, 2024.
https://doi.org/10.1007/978-3-031-65881-5_32

meanings with interrelated lexical constituent connections [3]. These characteristics of multi-level features make character learning a significant challenges to Chinese-as-Foreign/Second-Language (CFL/CSL) learners [4]. To support learners overcome the challenge, educational practitioners in Chinese character pedagogy have made efforts to design instructional materials which leverage the distinctive features of characters to enhance literacy competencies and such efforts have gained considerable success (e.g., [5–7]). However, the procedure to compile such character-based instructional materials involves repeatedly manual search in textbooks and dictionaries; the process is notably laborious and time-intensive [8]. Specifically, in the compilation of character-based instructional materials, breaking down words into characters, and subsequently into smaller orthographic features (e.g., radicals, strokes, and positions within structures) demands significant time. Moreover, even with character databases (e.g., [2]), searching entry by entry, coupled with linking to character grades (e.g., [9]), are labor-intensive. Thus, there is an urgent demand for facilitative technological tools to equip Chinese educational practitioners with enhanced functional capabilities in preparing lessons which focus on enhancing literacy competences.

To fulfill the above-mentioned needs, this research aims to streamline and scientize the compilation of Chinese pedagogical materials, focusing on character-based instruction, for educational practitioners (e.g., Chinese language teachers). Building upon the "Chinese Orthography Database Explore (CODE)" by Chen et al. [2] and its documented achievements (e.g., [4–7]), and by integrating character features and learner performances [10], this research aims to devise a technological tool and substantiate this tool's efficacy. The specific aims of this study included:

1. Developing "Suggested Learning Content" based on a needs analysis of Chinese language teachers for the tool "Character Difficulty – Research on Multi-features (CD-ROM).
2. Employing a mixed-design framework to substantiate CD-ROM's efficacy by comparing it with an existing material-compiling platform, and to refine functions of CD-ROM based on both qualitative and quantitative feedback.

2 Related Work

2.1 The Importance of Character Features in Learning to Read Chinese

The importance of mastering multi-level features of characters in learning to read Chinese, a foundational skill underpinned by word decoding, cannot be overstated [11]. Mastering the 2,328 commonly-used characters essential for basic daily life tasks [12], a process that often takes several years, presents a significant time cost compared to the alphabetic writing systems that can be mastered in mere weeks [13]. Chinese educational community frequently underscores the challenges associated with learning characters, attributed to their rich and multilevel orthographic features. Moreover, psycholinguistics research illuminates the challenges posed by complex compositions, inconsistent form-sound correspondences, and elevated visual complexity of Chinese orthographic units relative to single English letters.

Decomposing characters into smaller orthographic units, based on the CODE [2], positions within structure have been categorized into 22 distinct types, with the number of radicals reaching up to 419. The extensive arrangement of radicals, locating in various positions, results in tens of thousands of characters. For Chinese-as-first-language (L1) readers, mastering at least 4,500 characters is required for casting off illiteracy and further for meeting the literacy standards mandated by higher education [14]. Similarly, for CSL/CFL leaner, they are expected to be proficient in approximately 3,000 characters [9]. The gradual incorporation of characters into instructional materials, integrating the pedagogical rationale of using i+1 principle [15] to consider difficulty of input for second/foreign language instruction, emerges as a critical area of research.

2.2 The Influence of Explicit Instruction on Character Features for Enhancing Chinese Literacy and Vocabulary Size

Echoing Krashen's i+1 principle [15], in Chinese character education, the concept of "character-based" pedagogical approach aims to scaffold learners' learning by presenting characters slightly above their current proficiency level, enabling a structured yet dynamic experience that promotes effective character learning. For example, when CSL/CFL students encounter the radical "馬" (horse), Chinese language teachers may guide the students' attention to deriving characters where the radical "馬" is located on the left position of a left-right structure. Characters derived in such a manner, including "騎" (ride), "馭" (control), and "駛" (drive), typically signify actions associated with the use of a horse. Conversely, when the radical "馬" appears of the right position within the left-right structure, the pronunciation of the derived characters (e.g., "瑪/mǎ/", "碼/mǎ/," "媽/mā /," and "嗎/mā /") resembles that of "馬/mǎ/." This explicit instruction not only elucidates the position-structure relations underlying spatial configuration but also the enhances learners' awareness to semantic/phonetic cues of stroke patterns, thereby enriching the students' orthographic knowledge. This pedagogical approach, transition from "radical" to "characters" and then to "words," proves beneficial for both L1 learners [16] and CFL learners [4].

Nevertheless, if Chinese teachers intend to employ such "radical-character-word" instruction to facilitate character learning, it necessitates the decomposition of words to characters and further dissection of characters into radicals; this process is labor-intensive [8]. Even with the use of character database or dictionaries, searching through data entry by entry can be exceptionally draining and time-consuming. Thus, in the preparation of instructional materials or the drafting of test items, language teachers frequently resort to Chinese character websites as tools, aiming to streamline the material compilation process for enhanced efficiency.

2.3 Comparison of Websites for Inquiring Chinese Character Features

Most existing technological tools for Chinese characters are primarily websites, offering data retrieval functions. Yet, few websites deliver a "one-stop" solution capable of addressing the preparatory requirements of Chinese language teachers—for instance, furnishing essential insights such as non-character forming radicals, frequencies of radicals/structures/characters, and difficulty level grading (e.g., character classifications from authoritative lists such as the TBCL or learning difficulty based on empirical data from Chinese learners). Huang et al. [10] conducted evaluations of notable websites for extracting character feature information, underscoring that the majority are deficient in textual analysis capabilities (as observed in resources like the Chinese University of Hong Kong's Humanities Computing Research Center's "Multi-function Chinese Character Database" [17] and Academia Sinica's "International Encoded Han Character and Variants Database" [18]). Even websites capable of providing character gradings based on input text, like Mandarin Training Center's "Advanced Chinese Character Electronic Search System (ACCESS)" [19] or National Academy for Educational Research (NAER)'s "System for Application of Chinese Language Teaching Standards–Character Grading Standard Search System", [20] still leave room for improvement.

Specifically, these tools do not provide comprehensive feedback based on the input text, including the delineation of character difficulty levels, identification of simpler characters, and delineation of more challenging characters. Thus, Huang et al. [10] integrated the CODE [2] and character difficulty data derived from learners' performances, culminating in the development of a system endowed with three functions: (1) analyzing a text and providing its difficulty regarding Chinese characters; (2) decomposing characters into radicals and calculating the frequency of radicals/structures based on the analyzed text; and (3) affording radical-deriving characters based on the analyzed text and downloadable images as instructional materials. Although this system has provided tailor-made instructional information, its efficacy has not been substantiated, leaving its validity to be further explored. Additionally, this system's function independently presents information on the radical and structure level. Integrating these features to offer Chinese language teachers a more comprehensive selection of instructional materials could significantly enhance lesson preparation.

To address these gaps, the present study built upon the system developed by Huang et al. [10], developing an integrated, novel function for "Instructional content suggestion", with the aim to collect user feedback, verify the system's efficacy, thereby contributing to the refinement of technological tools designed for the intricate process of material complication for character-based explicit instruction.

3 Research Methodology

To fulfill the aims, the present study encompassed two stages: (1) system construction with the added "Instructional content suggestion", and (2) system evaluation.

3.1 Stage 1: System Construction

Rationale: leveraging technology to bridge words, characters, and radicals. The system was architected with a focus on user-centric design, leveraging needs analyses with Chinese language educators [21] which called for a comprehensive digital tool for supporting material complications. This study expanded upon "the System for Chinese Character Difficulty and Features" [10] by developing "Instructional content suggestion" functionality, consequently rebranding it as "Character Difficulty – Research on Multi-features (CD-ROM)": http://chenchang.tcsl.ntnu.edu.tw/CD_ROM/ana.aspx.

This enhancement introduced the "words-characters-radicals" connections and subsequent functions, providing a comprehensive tool for Chinese character instruction.

Environment: utilizing Visual Studio.NET for multi-level data presentation. The CD-ROM system was developed using Microsoft's Visual Studio.NET, a web development framework renowned for its compatibility and programming stability, thereby aligning with the generic specifications anticipated by a broad user base. In the pursuit of optimizing the system's aesthetics and enhancing user experience, frontend programming methodologies, including CSS and jQuery, were applied to amplify user engagement and augment the visual allure of the interface.

Moreover, the system utilized Visual Studio.NET's suite of programming instruments for development purposes, employing the GridView function to present datasets of Chinese characters in a structured table format. This facilitated users' comprehension of analytical outcomes and streamlined the access to intricate information of character features. Furthermore, harnessing the "C# Dictionary" for data organization, this system facilitated text analyses of up to two thousand Chinese characters, excluding non-relevant symbols. Leveraging CODE [2], the extensive database of 6,097 Chinese characters categorized by multi-level features, this system could dynamically present critical feature information (e.g., difficulty levels of words/characters, frequencies of characters/radicals) based on users' input. Additionally, tailored algorithms enabled multi-level analysis, such as decomposing characters into radicals and positions and calculating frequencies of linguistic features. Compatibility with major web browsers ensured wide accessibility for educational research and practice purposes.

Function: streamlining radial, character and word with user-centric suggestions. The function "Instructional content suggestion" encompassed two options for users: "radicals derive characters", and "characters derive words". Below were examples with Fig. 1 showing the corresponding screenshots:

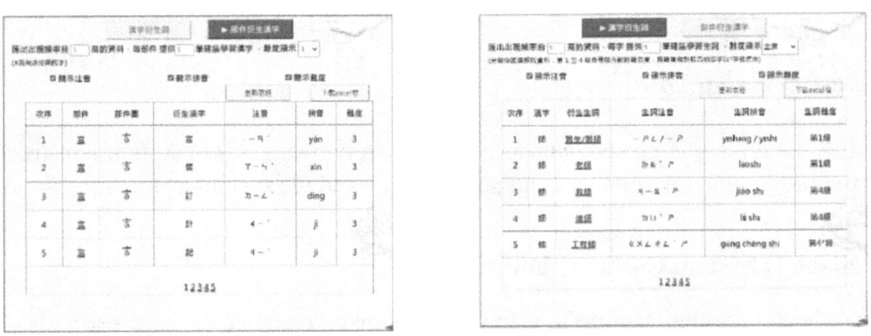

Fig. 1. Two options (left panel: "radicals derive characters"; right panel: "characters derive words".) of CD-ROM's "Instructional content suggestion" function.

Instructions to users:

Step 1. Enter text in the left box and click "Analyze".

Step 2. In the right box, select either "Radicals derive character" or "character derive words" based on your needs and set the conditions; this offers references across "radical-character-word" levels.

Step 3. Click "Update" to view the results that meet the criteria; clicking "Download" provides an Excel file.

Results based on user input: The "Instructional content suggestion" function facilitated a user-oriented customization, enabling precise retrieval of targeted information, such as the frequencies of radicals and that of characters, difficulty level of words/characters within the input text, and suggestions for either simpler or more difficult words/characters tailored to user preferences. Following the suggestions, the system provided users with additional resources, including downloadable flashcards for character study, modifiable example sentences incorporating selected characters, and an Excel spreadsheet designed for data categorization according to user needs. Notably, while character difficulty levels retrieved from empirical learner performance, word difficulty information aligned with the TBCL [9]. This way enhanced the educational content's reliability and validity, further facilitating unified modulation of "radical-character-word" difficulty within an integrated system, the CD-ROM.

3.2 Stage 2: System Evaluation

To evaluation the efficacy of the CD-ROM system, this stage implemented focus group methodologies to garner user insights. The objectives were twofold: firstly, to delineate user comparisons—specifically, Chinese language teachers—between this innovation CD-ROM and the extant system by NAER (https://coct.naer.edu.tw/sentedit/); secondly, to amass both quantitative and qualitative data to inform system enhancements.

Research design and procedure: Employing a mixed-methods design, quantitative data were collected via the Technology Acceptance Model (TAM) [22] given that TAM has consistently proven to be a reliable and widely recognized framework for evaluating the efficacy of digital learning tools [23], supplemented by qualitative insights drawn from open-ended survey inquiries and subsequent interviews reflecting users' opinions.

To compare users' feedback on the CD-ROM system with the NAER system, two focus groups were conducted in professional development workshops in Taiwan (for demographics, refer to the "Participations"). Each workshop comprised seven segments: introductions to, hands-on engagements with, and evaluations of each system (i.e., CD-ROM and NAER system), interspersed by a brief 10-min intermission, following by an in-depth interview for using two systems. The sequence of introducing two systems was counterbalanced to mitigate potential biases. Workshops spanned 90 min, with ethical clearance from a premier Taipei research university's review board (i.e., institutional review board); informed consent was procured pre-event.

Participants: Using convenience sampling at a comprehensive university in the north Taiwan, 68 educational practitioners specializing in Chinese character pedagogy were enlisted (3 males, 65 females; $M_{\text{age}} = 41$, $SD_{\text{age}} = 13.41$), boasting a minimum of one-year teaching experience. One group ($n = 42$) experienced CD-ROM first and then the NAER system while the other group ($n = 26$) experienced the NAER system first and then the CD-ROM. All ancillary elements (e.g., facilitators and assistants) remained constant.

Instruments: Comprising the CD-ROM and NAER system, we devised user-feedback surveys grounded in scholarly discourse and research objectives. The primary quantitative instrument was the TAM [18], widely adopted in the digital learning domain. The scale employed a Likert seven-point scale with 10 items across three constructs: perceived usefulness (4 items), perceived ease of use (4 items), and behavioral intention (3 items). The Chinese version of TAM has shown robust validity and reliability [23]. Semi-structured questionnaires following the TAM also collected user feedback on each system's functionality as well as users' positive and negative experiences. Qualitative discussions in focus groups were framed by Rosell-Aguilar's [24] framework, spanning pedagogical efficacy, technological integration, and user experience.

4 Results and Discussion

4.1 Results of Stage 1: System Construction

The construction of CD-ROM, anchored in user-centric design, has provided a pedagogical framework with the support of technology, assisting in the assembly of instructional materials. Figure 2 depicted the system's interface, not only presenting lucid instruction for each function but also supplemented by YouTube tutorials to enhance user comprehension and engagement.

Specifically, the highlights of CD-ROM were its robust exploitation of diverse, multi-level character features (e.g., position-structure relations, radicals, and fonts of archaic Chinese scripts, etc.), providing dynamic pedagogical customization within the "radical-character-word" continuum. It further afforded Chinese language teachers with meticulously curated resources: a repository of 419 downloadable radical images, inclusive of non-character radicals, personalized flashcards for lexical constituents, editable sample words, phrases, and sentences, as well as reliable difficulty levels of characters and words, thereby enhancing the functional prowess of this digital apparatus in supporting material compilation for Chinese language teaching practitioners.

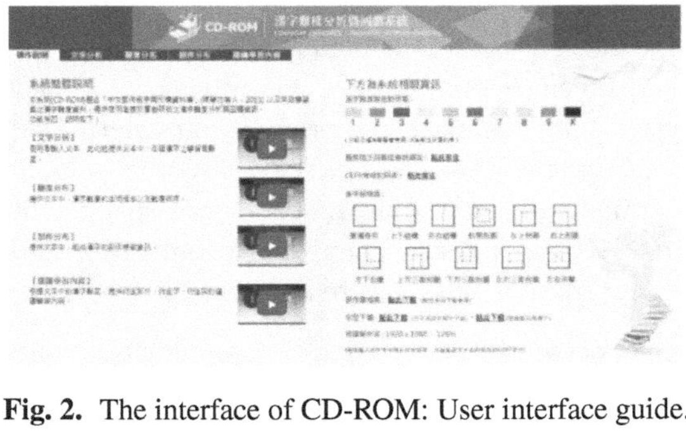

Fig. 2. The interface of CD-ROM: User interface guide.

4.2 Results of Stage 2: System Evaluation

A comparative analysis via the TAM: CD-ROM vs. NERA system. To elucidate the comparative evaluation of the CD-ROM versus the NAER system by 68 Chinese language teachers, influential statistical analyses were conducted with the TAM framework, encompassing perceived usefulness, ease of use, and behavioral intention. For perceived usefulness, the CD-ROM system achieved a mean score of 5.73, overshadowing the NAER system's 5.24. A paired samples t-test underscored a significant disparity (t=3.44, p=.002) with a moderate Cohen's d effect size of 0.42. Regarding ease of use, the CD-ROM system attained a mean score of 6.00 against the NAER system's 5.50, evidencing a notable difference (t=2.83, p=.009) and a moderate Cohen's d of 0.46. For behavioral intention, the CD-ROM system scored a mean of 6.10, exceeding the NAER's 5.63, with significant statistical divergence (t=2.21, p=.037) and a moderate Cohen's d of 0.39. Collectively, these quantitative findings corroborated the CD-ROM's supremacy over the NAER system in all assessed TAM constructs, affirming the CD-ROM's enhanced acceptability.

Quantitative feedback for the novel function "Instructional content suggestion". In addition to the comparative analysis on overall acceptance with the TAM model, a focused quantitative evaluation of the "Instructional content suggestion" function was undertaken with descriptive statistics (refer to Table 1). Across a seven-point scale, all ten items garnered mean scores exceeding 5.78, indicative of Chinese language educators' favorable views towards this functionality. This positive feedback was substantiated by the left-skewed distribution of responses, which showed that the mass of the distribution is concentrated on the right of the graphical representation, namely stronger agreement on the item description.

Qualitative feedback for the novel function "Instructional content suggestion". In the qualitative evaluation, most of the Chinese language teachers commended the "Instructional content suggestion" function. Endorsements included: "*Usually, when I'm preparing for lessons, I have to use many websites to look up information for a single Chinese character and its deriving words. CD-ROM integrates features like radicals, structures, characters, the Six Writings, and more. It also proffers text-based analysis, which saves me a lot of time and is super convenient*". "*After analyzing the difficulty based on the input text, the CD-ROM also provided me with the frequency of occurrence for radicals, characters and derived words and phrases. This is invaluable for deciding which content helps students learn characters and words*". In response to requests for enhancements, several Chinese teachers referenced the utility of stroke order animations in character pedagogy. Despite initially excluding such animations due to copyright constraints, we acknowledged recommendations for a more detailed breakdown of characters and the linkage of the "word-character-component-stroke" continuum. Thus, this study has incorporated this suggestion into CD-ROM's future work.

Table 1. Summary of users' quantitative feedback with the Technology Acceptance Model.

Question items	M	S.D.	Skewness
1. The "character derive words" functional design provides learners with additional words, complemented by systematic scaffolding	6.04	1.11	−1.69
2. The "radical derive characters" functional design provides learners with additional characters, complemented by systematic scaffolding	6.06	0.96	−0.95
3. Using this function has streamlined my lesson planning in Chinese character education, marking a significant improvement over previously used website	5.78	1.10	−1.05
4. Using this function has accelerated my lesson preparation process, facilitating quicker readiness	5.85	1.06	−1.11
5. Using this function allows me to acquire more comprehensive information for lesson preparation in Chinese reading education	5.85	1.14	−1.14
6. This function has contributed to the efficiency of preparing for Chinese language teaching	5.93	1.14	−1.17
7. I can easily use this function to complete the preparatory work for teaching Chinese characters and words	5.87	1.12	−0.98
8. I perceive the function is easily adoptable, indicating its ease of integration into teaching practices	6.13	0.95	−0.92
9. I find the interface of this function is intuitively designed, offering clarity and ease of understanding	6.16	1.05	−1.62
10. Engaging with this function does not require extensive cognitive effort, indicating its user-friendly nature	6.16	1.02	−1.38

Note. "This function" refers to the "Instructional content suggestion" of CD-ROM

5 Conclusions and Future Work

In sum, this study presented CD-ROM, a facilitative technological aid designed to equip Chinese educational practitioners with enhanced functional capabilities in preparing explicit character instruction. By integrating technological advancements with the "radical-character-word" continuum, this study affords the innovation "Instructional content suggestion", offering bespoke functionalities such as "radical derive characters" and "character derive words" to meet specific pedagogical needs. This innovation endeavored to present a comprehensive solution capable of addressing the material complications issues of Chinese language teachers, thereby enhancing the preparatory process by leveraging technology to bridge words, characters, radicals, and their orthographic features. Particularity, CD-ROM dynamically presented information and feedback based on users' input text. Empirical assessments employing the TAM and focus group analysis substantiated its superiority in usability and pedagogical efficacy relative to extant educational resources (e.g., the NEAR system).

Based on both the quantitative and qualitative feedback, future endeavors would focus on enhancing specific aspects of this technological aid, CD-ROM, including the integration of stroke order animations to facilitate deeper understanding of character formation, broadening its linguistic accessibility through the development of an English interface, and executing targeted improvements informed by feedback from more diverse Chinese educational practitioners. These strategic enhancements aim to bridge existing gaps in Chinese language pedagogy, reaffirming our commitment to refining educational technology tools in response to practitioner insights.

Acknowledgements. This work was financially supported by the "Chinese Language and Technology Center" of National Taiwan Normal University (NTNU) within the framework of the Higher Education Sprout Project by the Ministry of Education (MOE) in Taiwan as well as a grant from the Ministry of Science and Technology award (MOST 112–2410-H-003 -073 -MY3).

References

1. Chang, L.Y., Chen, Y.C., Perfetti, C.A.: GraphCom: A multi-dimensional measure of graphic complexity applied to 131 written languages. Behav. Res. Methods **50**(1), 427–449 (2018). https://doi.org/10.3758/s13428-017-0881-y
2. Chen, H.C., Chang, L.Y., Chiou, Y.S., Sung, Y.T., Chang, K.E.: Construction of Chinese orthographic database for Chinese character instruction. Bulletin of Educational Psychology. **43**(Special Issue on Reading), 269–290 (2011)
3. Perfetti, C.A., Liu, Y., Tan, L.H.: The lexical constituency model: some implications of research on Chinese for general theories of reading. Psychol. Rev. **112**(1), 43–59 (2005). https://doi.org/10.1037/0033-295X.112.1.43
4. Xu, Y., Chang, L.Y., Perfetti, C.A.: The effect of radical-based grouping in character learning in Chinese as a foreign language. Mod. Lang. J. **98**(3), 773–793 (2014)
5. Lin, Z.X., Chen, H.C.: Chinese Characters: Building Blocks Character-based Learning Method I. Cheng Chung Book Co., Ltd, Taipei (2015)
6. Lin, Z.X., Chen, H.C.: Chinese Characters: Building Blocks Character-based Learning Method II. Cheng Chung Book Co., Ltd, Taipei (2015)
7. Chang, L.Y., Tang, Y.Y., Lee, C.Y., Chen, H.C.: The effect of visual mnemonics and the presentation of character pairs on learning visually similar characters for CSL learners. Front. Psychol. **13**, 783898 (2022). https://doi.org/10.3389/fpsyg.2022.783898
8. Chang, L.Y., Tseng, C.C., Perfetti, C.A., Chen, H.C.: Development and validation of a Chinese pseudo-character/ non-character producing system. Behav. Res. Methods **54**, 632–648 (2022). https://doi.org/10.3758/s13428-021-01611-8

9. TBCL wordlists of three grades/seven levels proposed by NAER, https://coct.naer.edu.tw/download/tech_report/, last accessed 2024/1/30
10. Haung, J.E., Tseng, H.C., Chang, L.Y., Chen, H. C., Sung, Y.T.: The design and development of a system for Chinese character difficulty and features. In Proceedings of the 34th Conference on Computational Linguistics and Speech Processing, pp. 256–262. The Association for Computational Linguistics and Chinese Language Processing, Taipei (2022)
11. Gough, P.B., Tunmer, W.E.: Decoding, reading, and reading disability. Remedial and Special Education **7**(1), 6 (1986). https://doi.org/10.1177/074193258600700104
12. Shu, H., Chen, X., Anderson, R.C., Wu, N.: Properties of school Chinese: Implications for learning to read. Child Dev. **74**(1), 27–47 (2003)
13. Seymour, P.H.K., Aro, M., Erskine, J.M.: Foundation literacy acquisition in European orthographies [Electronic version]. Br. J. Psychol. **94**, 143–174 (2003). https://doi.org/10.1348/000712603321661859
14. Wang, C.C., Huang, L.Y., Chang, Y.W., Chen, H.F.: Number of characters school students know from grade 1 to G9. Bulletin of Education Psychology **39**(4), 555–568 (2008)
15. Krashen, S.D.: Second Language Acquisition and Second Language Learning. Pergamon Press Inc., Oxford (1981)
16. Ho, C.S., Yau, P.W., Au, A.: Development of orthographic knowledge and its relationship with reading and spelling among Chinese kindergarten and primary school children. Chinese children's reading development 51–71 (2003)
17. Multi-function Chinese Character Database Homepage, https://humanum.arts.cuhk.edu.hk/Lexis/lexi-mf/
18. International Encoded Han Character and Variants Database Homepage, http://chardb.iis.sinica.edu.tw/
19. Advanced Chinese Character Electronic Search System (ACCESS) Homepage, http://huayutools.mtc.ntnu.edu.tw/mtchanzi
20. System for Application of Chinese Language Teaching Standards–Character Grading Standard Search System Homepage, https://coct.naer.edu.tw/standsys/
21. Chang, L.Y., Tseng, H.C., Chen, H.C., Sung, Y.T.: Developing and implementing a system integrating character features and learners' performance. The 13th International Conference on Han Characters Education and Research. USA. (2024)
22. Davis, F.D.: Perceived usefulness, perceived ease of use, and user acceptance of information technology. MIS Q. **13**(3), 319–340 (1989). https://doi.org/10.2307/249008
23. Lai, Y.H., Huang, F.F., Yang, X.H.: Construction and related study of the inventory of Technology Acceptance Model. Journal of Oriental Institute of Technology **35**, 201–221 (2015)
24. Rosell-Aguilar, F.: State of the app: A taxonomy and framework for evaluating language learning mobile applications. The CALICO Journal **34**(2), 243–258 (2017)

Embodied Learning – Are We Losing It?

Merja Bauters[1,2(✉)]

[1] School of Digital Technologies, Tallinn University, Narva Mnt 29, Tallinn, Estonia
merja.bauters@tlu.ee, merja.bauters@helsinki.fi
[2] University of Helsinki, PL 4 (Yliopistonkatu 3), Helsinki, Finland

Abstract. New knowledge from various fields of cognitive neuroscience is incorporated into the learning sciences. This research highlights interactions between embodied learning and philosophical approaches from phenomenology and pragmatism to cognitive neurosciences. These research threads direct attention to embodied learning and the need for further research on the hindrances and benefits of using digital tools to scaffold and enhance learning. The methods derived from Peirce's advice to reason in a critical and self-controlled manner describe the method used in the study, which could be called to follow the hermeneutic tradition of being interpretative. I will end with three intriguing examples of experimental studies (two tools from one project and one neuroscientific experiment) that provide insights into embodied learning. The aim is to persuade more research on how our emerging digital learning tools and practices enhance or hinder the embodied aspect of learning.

Keywords: Embodied learning · tangible learning · phenomenology · cognitive neuroscience

1 Introduction

Embodied, sometimes called tangible learning, has been discussed for some time by various disciplines. Phenomenological and pragmatism approaches have taken the environmental, embodied and thinking as intertwined and essential for learning. These approaches have underscored learning as the central aspect of human abilities to reason and collaborate. Ingold describes it well, and he has formed his view on Gibson's [1], Vygostky's, [2] and Merleau-Ponty's [3] writings. Pragmatism (for instance, Dewey) [4], has emphasised the experience in learning, which often is comprised of "learning by doing". In a brief summary, Ingold [5] states that learning is not the passing on ready-formed knowledge but the productive collaboration of concurrent and overlapping generations. Learning is social with observation and attention. Observing, attention, imitation, and social aspects are currently the focus of those mentioned above in cognitive neuroscientific studies, especially imitation, which was connected with mirror neurons in the recent past (2000–2019) [6]. The crucial aspect that Ingold stresses is the processual nature of learning, namely, through participation in the developmental process, that system elements become meaningful. It means that practitioners draw from the collective experience of carrying out a range of tasks in an environment where their cultural

Y.-P. Cheng et al. (Eds.): ICITL 2024, LNCS 14785, pp. 309–316, 2024.
https://doi.org/10.1007/978-3-031-65881-5_33

knowledge resides—regrown in each through their practical overlap as generations carry on their lives together. What every generation brings to the next are the conditions of development for this regrowth to occur [7].

Philosophical and cognitive neuroscience research point to the same aspect: human corporality, the transforming body-brain that forms meaning within interaction with the environment. The paper draws attention to the tangible physicality of our thinking and reflection abilities because it is often neglected when designing learning tools or pedagogical practices. It is a crucial aspect of learning, into which there are scarce guidelines or best practices [see 16].

The structure is as follows: I will first explain the methods used; secondly, I shall briefly describe the neuro-scientifical findings from brain plasticity affecting thinking, bodily practices transforming thinking abilities, and cross-cognitive transfer. Then, I will describe crucial aspects of the philosophical ponderings that describe similar aspects that recent and current cognitive neuroscience has discovered. Lastly, I provide descriptive examples of digital tools designed to promote awareness of our bodily influence on our reflection and thinking.

2 Methods

Peirce's advice for reasoning in a critical and self-controlled manner describes the method used in the study. "[The reasoning] operation is not worthy to be called reasoning unless it be deliberate, critical, self-controlled. In such genuine reasoning, we are always conscious of proceeding according to a general rule, which we approves" [8].

Others should follow the reasoning so that anyone can point out its flaws. Valsiner [9] describes scientific knowledge as a construction process: "The psychological processes involved in scientific knowledge construction are similar to everyday knowledge construction in its main feature – semiotic mediation" [9].

The methodology adopted could be called to follow the hermeneutic tradition of being interpretative.

3 Cognitive Neuroscientific Findings

The cognitive neuroscientific research field has discovered various aspects of how the body and practices affect thinking and reasoning. Some examples include, for instance, evidence of the effects of brain plasticity growing and allowing better abilities for thinking and reasoning. Some are based on our physical activities, which positively influence the brain; for instance, practicing musical instruments [10, 11] or playing music at home. [12, 13]. The authors discovered that individual differences between children's capabilities to perform complex mental tasks, such as set-shifting, which require the use of attention and executive functions, were closely related to both their musical activities and brain responses. These examples point to the impact of the training that is not only seen in advanced skills in music but also translates into more potential capacity for any auditory or fine motor tasks. Similar aspects have been discovered in practising crafts and visual arts. These have been shown to enhance the integration of multiple motor, perceptual, and cognitive functions; it has a strong potential for cross-cognitive transfer. Tyler and Likova [14] described how increased inter-brain synchrony is related to improved collaborative task performance. Since inter-brain synchrony can occur without physical presence, its role in online interaction and remote work becomes an interesting question. Apart from professional performance, inter-brain synchronisation could also be expected to positively affect social relationships online, as previous studies have often demonstrated links between interpersonal and inter-brain synchronisation and affiliation, cooperation and prosocial tendency in face-to-face interaction [15].

These selective examples aim to show that research connects physical actions to thinking abilities, but also that the digital environment, especially the distance environment, is a novel area in which we are only trying to understand how it enhances or hinders our abilities to act, collaborate, and think.

However, the strictly specified methods that need to be applied in experimental brain research settings are still the most significant restricting factor in the whole research area, and there are several phenomena that cannot be studied [16]. The main challenges lie in the inability to capture phenomena occurring during creative activity, as most brain imaging devices require the phenomenon or event to be replicated several times and the participant to be still.

The current cognitive neuroscientific phenomenological studies have commonalities, which are scarcely discussed. I aim to bring up some of these commonalities. However, in this paper, I will not discuss whether these studies are compatible with their worldviews. I hope to increase interest in what we should know of embodiment with our increasing development of digital learning environments.

Next, I will discuss the phenomenological and pragmatism views on embedded learning in more depth. After that, I will provide two examples of studies designing and using digital tools for embodied learning. Lastly, I will try to raise interest in more experiments on embodied learning designed from the phenomenological perspective.

4 Embodied Learning as Lifelong Learning

I am approaching learning as a lifelong process through intriguing research projects, namely, Chemero's [17] radical embodied cognitive science project. The roots of the project come from William James [18]. James's interest in Darwinian thinking is in psychology, which takes meaning-making as a tool for adapting animals to their environments. However, Chemero does not include Charles Peirce's [8] ideas but rather discusses John Dewey's pragmatism. Dewey [4] is also discussed by Ingold, who builds on the critiquing part of the Darwinian view but uses parts of Gibson's perception action and cognition – ecological psychology. Perception is an unmediated relationship between an animal and the environment. The unmediated perceiving qualities in pragmatism are the essential connection to the environment. Gibson argues that an unmediated relationship with the environment is sufficient for guiding action because the environment contains affordances, opportunities for behaviour and information sufficient to specify them. However, in this unmediated connection with affordances for action, there is a difference between Gibson's and Chemero's or Ingold's descriptions. Chemero and Ingold understand that information and meaning are created within an action; information does not just lie in the environment but is created within actions. It can be seen in braid or continuous cyclical reciprocal collaborative "work/action." The reciprocal interaction between humans/animals and the environment is the core of pragmatism, Vygosky and later on, Cultural Historical Activity Theory [19]. The added aspect is the social nature of learning. These fundamental elements of learning are the same in all mentioned parties.

Chemero is exempt from the above writers as he also has executed experiments to prove his point. Chemero and Ingold also ground their thinking on phenomenological philosophers such as Meurleau-Ponty. His statement from 1956 sums up the aim of learning as embodied interaction with the environment well: "[Meaning] is inseparable from the subjectivity and from the intersubjectivity which forms their unity by taking up my past experiences in my present experiences and experience of others in my own" [20].

In summary, embodied knowledge focuses on – what could also be called – habit. The habits are not automated practices but enacted in an attentive and kinaesthetic correspondence with tools, materials and environment. In this view, habits can hold symbolic and abstract aspects, such as working with words [21]. In Ingold's writing, meaning, thinking, and reflection require awareness of feeling others feeling you—or, in a word, haptically and that "[…] thinking is that of a mind that is not confined within the body, but that extends outwards to include tools, materials and surrounding conditions" [7].

Although Ingold does not mention Chemero's radial ecological phenomenology or recent cognitive neuroscientific findings, such as the synchronising studies of brain waves and mirror neurons, he has beautifully nailed the crucial focus of learning.

Most of the recent cognitive neuroscientific findings have been gathered from crafts and the arts, such as the article "Why our brains love arts and crafts implications of creative practices on psychophysical well-being" by [6], which emphasises the need for children to learn by doing creative works, gestures, and crafting. Such learning does not diminish at adult age [6]. It can be more difficult to determine in adults, but a language deficit can make embodied learning visible.

Next, I will present more in-depth examples from art-related projects. These examples were chosen because they present the co-design of the digital tools and feedback from the artist using the tools. The examples are also clear and easy to grasp, even for those who do not participate in art or enjoy artistic events.

5 Research Examples and Results

Different disciplines provide worthwhile but varied views of the importance of interaction with the environment and on learning, for instance, the neurosciences, embodied cognition [22, 23], the extended phenomenological–cognitive system [24] and the profound role of feelings and emotions in decision-making and meaning-making in conscious activities [25]. Silberstein and Chemero [24] described this "system" as a heterogeneous composition of brain, body, and niche, which are non-linearly coupled to one another. It is a relational and dynamic system, and interactions occur among the heterogeneous parts on multiple spatial and temporal scales. The spatial and temporal scales underline the situation of the process and the continuous interaction with all non-linearly linked parts.

I will provide some examples that describe how digital tools can be used with embodiment. I wish to request more such research, which will provide insights into the hindrances and benefits digital tools can provide for embodied learning.

The first example is from Nuno Correia et al. [26], who researched how machine learning-based tools could support dancers and choreographers. The study was informed by soma design [27] with a co-design perspective and aimed to make apparent non-visible bodily aspects of dancers. The proposal was to design interactive visuals from body maps using Machine Learning and Composite Animation. A multi-stage study involving 12 dancers was conducted. The tools designed were Machine Learning Interactive Visuals (MLIV) and Composite Animation Interactive Visuals (CAIV).

Machine Learning Interactive Visuals tool used body maps, sensors, and detected gestures to create an interactive animation mapped to the choreography. The other tool, Composite Animation Interactive Visuals (CAIV), was designed to create interactive visuals from free-form body maps. The animator created ten motion graphics sequences, one per dancer chosen from the respective body map for animation while covering five section themes. The tool was thought to be used as an onstage virtual "partner" for the dancers. Next, I will describe the dancers' comments related to learning and how the tools increase or decrease body knowledge and reasoning.

The dancers described the tool Machine Learning Interactive Visuals (MLIV) as externalising the subjective live body experience and the feeling of the movement. They felt that the tools enhanced imagination and awareness of oneself, promoting reflection but also being monotonous. In addition, one dancer felt that it created a loop from biological to digital and back, allowing new movement possibilities. Dancers felt like they had been involved in the design process of the tool but wished for more interactions so they could try things out and learn from them.

Composite Animation Interactive Visuals (CAIV) promoted feelings and ideas, such as revealing the dancers' unconscious decisions, which could be used for teaching and learning in interactive installations and could create connections between the image and body.

An essential aspect of this research is the co-design of the tools. It allowed to have feedback throughout the process and not only validation. Therefore, it is not a cognitive neuroscientific experiment. Thus, it is impossible to understand what occurs in dancers' brains while using the tools. It reflects the earlier studies that mentioned the problem is live experimental cognitive neuroscientific research [6, 16]. However, it is possible to see new insights coming to the dancers while using the tools about themselves and "their embodied reflections". Thus, further research could be even more interdisciplinary, namely, having the cognitive neuroscientists invited, just like [16] requested more research, where the laboratory settings are not constraining the research.

The following study from Martikainen et al. [28] on emotions and synchronisation between persons in collaborative tasks in physical and digitally mediated environments. They research how pairs' empathy skills and dispositional empathy meet their counterparts' evaluations of social closeness and subjective workload in a collaborative problem-solving task completed face-to-face and in virtual reality. The pairs solved the task of building a structure from three-dimensional blocks. The pair were given two different two-dimensional viewpoints, shown on cards. They were not allowed to show the cards to their counterparts. Still, they could communicate with each other to reach a structure that reflects both of their perspectives when viewed from different angles. This study found that similarity in personality was rated higher among participants face-to-face compared to the VR experiment. The pair's dispositional empathy was associated with likeability ratings in the face-to-face experiment. In contrast, in VR, dispositional empathy was associated with the task, rated as less effortful by the counterpart. The authors provide two possible reasons. The first explanation for the results is that more nonverbal cues are available in face-to-face situations. Dispositional empathy is experienced and interpreted differently depending on the information available. Secondly, it could be possible that in the face-to-face situation, participants paid more attention to each other and the relationship quality in the presence of more social cues. In VR, in the absence of these cues, the focus is more on the quality of collaborative problem-solving [28].

The last study is a perfect example of research I am asking to increase. Such research can provide us with knowledge of how and what kind of technologies can support and enhance learning while still considering the embodied and tangible nature of human learning.

6 Limitations

There are limitations. Firstly, I have not executed case studies myself. I am using research from projects I have been involved in or know more about. This is a conscious decision because articles do not tell everything, and knowing the research's background is essential to understanding it in more depth. Therefore, I feel confident reflecting on the research, setting, and outcomes.

7 Discussion and Conclusion

The presented studies and brief theoretical background will bring food for thought about whether we are thinking about embodiment and tangibility. The need for digitally mediated collaborative problem-solving is increasing [29]. There is a need to understand better the differences between virtual and other digitally mediated environments and physical ones [30].

The theoretical aspects highlight the great potential of corporeality and physical education as actors in learning. However, simultaneously, it places the need to experiment and disseminate new learning approaches and perspectives in the foreground. The theoretical frameworks and approaches focusing on bodily states and the consequent sensorimotor interactions with the environment provide knowledge and an understanding of the relationship between the environment and the different cognitive states and learning [31]. According to Barsalou, the meaning is created by the bodily interaction of its surrounding elements using sensorimotor networks [32].

I hope that executing more of the cognitive neuroscientific experiments set by the phenomenological perspective will have broad significance for the theoretical development in education and renewed nuanced knowledge of the embodied learning process.

Acknowledgments. I wish to thank the reviewers and all my colleagues with whom I have worked. Without you, I would not have enough common ground to think forward and beyond the mainstream.

Disclosure of Interests. No research grants were received for the research.

References

1. Gibson, J.J.: The ecological approach to visual perception. Houghton Mifflin, Boston (1979)
2. Vygotsky, L.: Mind in society. In: Cole, M., John-Steiner, V., Scribner, S. (eds.) Cambridge, MA: Harvard University Press (1978)
3. Merleau-Ponty, M.: Phenomenology of Perception. Translated by Smith, C. London: Routledge & Kegan P (1962)
4. Dewey, J.: Experience and education. New York, NY: Simon and Schuster. (1938/1997)
5. Ingold, T.: Evolution without inheritance: steps to an ecology of learning. Curr. Anthropol. **63**(S25), S32–S55 (2022)
6. Huotilainen, M., Rankanen, M., Groth, C., Seitamaa-Hakkarainen, P. Mäkelä, M.: Why our brains love arts and crafts implications of creative practices on psychophysical well-being, FormAkademisk.org 1, **11**(2), 1–18 (2018) https://doi.org/10.7577/formakademisk.1908
7. Ingold, T.: Of work and words: Craft as a way of telling. European Journal of creative practices in cities and landscapes **2**(2), 5–17, 11 (2019)
8. Peirce, C.P.: Collected papers of Charles Sanders Peirce, In: CP and paragraph are used when direct quotations are used, CP 4.476, Burks, A. (ed.). Cambridge, Mass, Harvard University Press, pp. 7–8. (1958)
9. Valsiner, J.: The Guided Mind: A Sociogenetic Approach to Personality. Cambridge, Massachusetts, and London: Harvard University Press, pp. 286–287 (1998)
10. Putkinen, V., Tervaniemi, M., Saarikivi, K., de Vent, N., Huotilainen, M.: Investigating the effects of musical training on functional brain development with a novel melodic MMN paradigm. Neurobiol. Learn. Mem. **110**, 8–15 (2014)
11. Putkinen, V., Tervaniemi, M., Saarikivi, K., Huotilainen, M.: Promises of formal and informal musical activities in advancing neurocognitive development throughout childhood. Ann. N. Y. Acad. Sci. **1337**(1), 153–162 (2015)
12. Putkinen, V., Tervaniemi, M., Huotilainen, M.: Informal musical activities are linked to auditory discrimination and attention in 2–3-year-old children: An event-related potential study. Eur. J. Neurosci. **37**(4), 654–661 (2013)
13. Saarikivi, K., Chan, T.M.V., Huotilainen, M., Tervaniemi, M., Putkinen, V.: Enhanced neural mechanisms of set shifting in musically trained adolescents and young adults: converging fMRI, EEG, and behavioral evidence. Cereb. Cortex **33**(11), 7237–7249 (2023). https://doi.org/10.1093/cercor/bhad034
14. Tyler, C., Likova, L.: The role of the visual arts for enhancing the learning process. Front. Hum. Neurosci. **6**, 8 (2012). https://doi.org/10.3389/fnhum.2012.00008
15. Wikström, V., et al.: Inter-brain synchronization occurs without physical co-presence during cooperative online gaming. Neuropsychologia **174**, 108316 (2022)
16. Seitamaa-Hakkarainen, P., Huotilainen, M., Mäkelä, M. Groth, C., Hakkarainen, K.: How can neuroscience help to understand design and craft activity? The promise of cognitive neuroscience in design studies. FORMakademisk, **9**(1), 3, 1–16 (2016)
17. Chemero, A.: Radical embodied cognitive science. Rev. Gen. Psychol. **17**(2), 145–150 (2013)

18. William, J.: Essays in Radical Empiricism. Longman Green and Co., New York (1912)
19. Sannino, A., Engeström, Y.: Cultural-historical activity theory: Founding insights and new challenges.Cultural-historical psychology. **14**(3) (2018)
20. Merleau-Ponty, M., Bannan J.F.: What is Pehnomenology? CrossCurrents 6 (1) 59–70, 69. Wiley Stable (1956) https://www.jstor.org/stable/24456652
21. Gulliksen, M.S.: Making matters? Unpacking the role of practical aesthetic making activities in the general education through the theoretical lens of embodied learning. Cogent Education 4:1415108 (2017)
22. Shapiro, L.: The Routledge handbook of embodied cognition. Routledge, Taylor & Francis Books, New York (2014)
23. Clark, A.: Natural-born cyborgs: Minds, technologies, and the future of human intelligence. Oxford University Press, New York (2003)
24. Silberstein, M., Chemero, A.: Complexity and extended phenomenological cognitive systems. Top. Cogn. Sci. **4**(1), 35–50 (2012). https://doi.org/10.1111/j.1756-8765.2011.01168.x
25. Damasio, A.R.: Emotion and the human brain. Ann. N. Y. Acad. Sci. **935**(1), 101–106 (2001). https://doi.org/10.1111/j.1749-6632.2001.tb03475.x
26. Correia, N.N., Masu, R., Primett, W., Jürgens, S., Feitsch, J., Plácido da Silva, H.:. Designing Interactive Visuals for Dance from Body Maps: Machine Learning and Composite Animation Approaches. In Designing Interactive Systems Conference (DIS '22), June 13–17, 2022, Virtual Event, Australia. ACM, New York, NY, USA (2022) https://doi.org/10.1145/3532106.3533467
27. Höök, K.: Designing with the Body: Somaesthetic Interaction Design. The MIT Press, Cambridge, Massachusetts (2018)
28. Martikainen, S., Wikström, V., Falcon, M., Saarikivi, K.: Collaboration face-to-face and in virtual reality-empathy, social closeness, and task load. In: Companion Publication of the 2019 Conference on Computer Supported Cooperative Work and Social Computing, pp. 299–303 (2019)
29. Fiore, S.M., Graesser, A., Greiff, S.: Collaborative problem-solving education for the twenty-first-century workforce Nat. Human Behaviour, **2**, 367– 369 (2018) https://doi.org/10.1038/s41562-018-0363-y
30. Brynjolfsson, E., Horton, J.J. Ozimek, A., Rock, D., Sharma, G., TuYe, H.Y.: COVID-19 and Remote Work: an Early Look at US Data National Bureau of Economic Research. (2020) https://doi.org/10.3386/w27344
31. Farina, M.: Embodied cognition: dimensions, domains, and applications. Adapt. Behav. **29**(1), 73–88 (2021)
32. Barsalou, L.W.: Grounded cognition. Annu. Rev. Psychol. **59**, 617–645 (2008)

Cultivating Critical Thinking: A Competitive, Web-Enhanced Gaming Experience

Juri Mets(✉)

Tallinn University, Narva Mnt 25, 10120 Tallinn, Estonia
juri.mets@tlu.ee

Abstract. Critical thinking (CT) skills are essential in navigating the complexities of modern information landscapes This article presents a novel methodology and design guidelines for creating educational games aimed at enhancing fundamental CT skills. Utilizing a robust technological platform, the game integrates multiple game-based learning elements such as peer learning, competition, and immediate feedback, which are proven to engage and motivate learners. The game, "Brain Fitness", has been adapted for various learner groups and settings, demonstrating versatility in both online and offline formats. A case study involving employees from a food production company illustrates the game's effectiveness in improving players' abilities to identify logical fallacies and cognitive biases. Despite limitations in empirical validation, preliminary feedback highlights the game's potential in CT skills development. This work contributes to educational strategies by providing a scalable and adaptable solution that addresses the urgent need for critical thinking enhancement in educational and professional contexts.

Keywords: Critical Thinking · Educational Games · Critical Thinking Learning

1 Introduction

Reports from various authoritative entities highlight the significance of CT. These entities include international organizations such as the World Economic Forum [1], intergovernmental bodies like OECD [2], and supranational unions including the European Commission [3] and the Council of the European Union [4]. CT is essential for anyone exposed to logical fallacies and persuasion tactics. Such patterns appear in various contexts, including work, study, social media, advertisements, and political statements. Human decision-making can be significantly influenced by the intentional or unintentional use of these misleading patterns, including logical fallacies [5–7].

Acknowledging the lack of a universally accepted definition of CT in scholarly literature [8, 9], this article adopts Steven Pinker's definition. Pinker [10] defines CT as identifying and rejecting both formal and informal fallacies to ensure logical reasoning.

One major challenge in learning CT skills is their perception as cognitively demanding activities that require significant concentration and effort [11]. Additionally, humans often believe they are proficient thinkers even without CT skills, which makes them less

Y.-P. Cheng et al. (Eds.): ICITL 2024, LNCS 14785, pp. 317–324, 2024.
https://doi.org/10.1007/978-3-031-65881-5_34

likely to engage in training [12]. Therefore, a primary issue is motivating individuals to develop CT skills they find difficult and may not recognize the need for.

A recent literature review on game-based learning [13] demonstrates that games keep players actively engaged and motivated to participate in the learning process. Additionally, games can incorporate various types of intrinsic and extrinsic motivations [14–16], such as challenges, curiosity, cooperation with other players, competition, rewards (e.g., earning points), and concrete feedback. Furthermore, game-based learning has shown promising results in developing CT skills [13, 17].

Peer learning enables individuals to accomplish tasks they could not achieve alone by collaborating with more skilled partners [18]. In a group, different members may be better equipped to recognize various types of logical fallacies or deceptive patterns, thereby enhancing the learning experience. For example, in solving the classical reasoning problem—the Wason selection task [19]—fewer than 15% of participants working alone could provide the correct answer. However, about 70% succeed after discussing it in groups of three to five [20]. Cooperative learning is one of the methods widely used for teaching of thinking [21]. Additionally, research has demonstrated the cognitive and affective benefits of cooperative learning [22, 23].

Technology-based response systems, also known as clickers, and their value in learning are well documented in scholarly literature [24–26]. These systems are effective in developing CT skills [27]. Moreover, the immediate feedback provided by response systems is a key game design element that enhances the success of game-based learning [17].

This article proposes a solution to engage learners in the demanding mental activities required for CT by utilizing collaborative and competitive educational games. By combining game-based, peer, and cooperative learning with proven game design elements, it is possible to create an engaging, interactive, and socially dynamic learning environment. The primary purpose of this work is to provide methodological guidelines for designing effective games that enhance CT skills and for implementing these games in various educational settings. Section 2 reviews related research. Section 3 describes the game and its technical infrastructure. Section 4 presents an example of a game used to teach CT skills to employed adults. Section 5 discusses directions for further research. Finally, Sect. 6 presents the conclusions.

2 Related Work

Scholarly literature reviews [13, 17] highlight various games designed for learning CT skills. However, there is a notable lack of games that both cultivate fundamental CT skills and are adaptable for different educational settings and group sizes. Most existing games [e.g. 28–30] are tailored for specific population groups and lack flexibility in design and content modification. This article addresses these gaps by proposing a technological solution and design guidelines for creating versatile games that enhance CT skills.

3 Game

3.1 The Game Engine Description

The game's technical infrastructure integrates multiple components within a single web-based platform, including:

- MCQ Quiz Making Module that allows for the creation of written tasks, consisting of a problem description followed by multiple correct and incorrect answer options.
- Game Facilitation System that features a facilitator's control panel. This system enables facilitators to start and stop the game at will, display results privately or publicly, and manage team compositions and other administrative functions.
- Virtual Game Currency Betting Module that permits the game creator or facilitator to designate the total amount of game currency available per game or round, set minimum and maximum bet amounts, and apply different bet multipliers to various answers.
- Mobile Technology-Supported Response System that delivers MCQs directly to players' smartphones or computers, facilitating seamless interaction and engagement.

The design elements of this platform align with the findings from a research review on facilitating 21st-century skills, including CT, through a game-based learning approach [17]. These elements include collaboration, complexity, competition, challenge (including time limits), clear goals, communication, immediate feedback, control, interactivity, and rewards.

Once a game is created on this platform, it is ready for use with minimal preparation. Players simply need to understand the rules, discuss, and select answers using their smartphones or computers. The only other equipment required is a projector and screen, or a TV panel, to display instructions and results.

3.2 Gameplay Mechanics, Dynamics and Aesthetics

The primary goal of the game is to enhance the players' ability to identify logical fallacies and recognize cognitive biases and language patterns used in persuasion tactics. MDA (Mechanics, Dynamics, and Aesthetics) framework [31] is utilized to describe the game.

3.2.1 Gameplay Mechanics

The gameplay mechanics (Fig. 1) are structured to foster CT skills through various interactive components:

- Group Discussions: Players engage in parallel discussions within their teams, aiming to collectively identify the correct solutions to presented problems.
- Individual Betting with Selected Surety Levels: Following discussions, players place individual bets on their believed correct answers using virtual coins. They can assign different surety levels to their choices by distributing the available game currency among the various options.

- Result Summation and Feedback: The individual results of group members are summed to calculate the team's result. A feedback session then provides detailed explanations of the answers and the factors influencing the players' decision-making processes.

The formal objective of the game is to accumulate the maximum number of game coins.

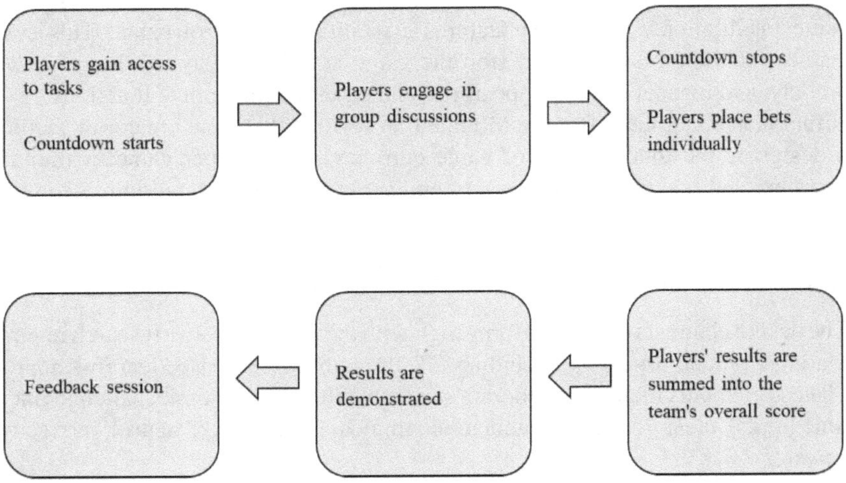

Fig. 1. Gameplay Mechanics Flowchart.

3.2.2 Gameplay Dynamics

The gameplay dynamics are designed to actively engage players and enhance their CT skills through various interactive challenges:

- Team-Based Discussions and Perspective Exchange: Uncertainty about the correct answers encourages players to engage in team-based discussions, where they share and debate different perspectives. This not only keeps players motivated but also challenges them to critically evaluate their own and others' arguments in a competitive setting.
- Learning from Peers: The exchange of perspectives allows players to learn from peers who possess greater skill in recognizing various decision-affecting patterns.
- Stimulating Disagreements: Disagreements within discussions further stimulate the application of CT skills [32].
- Time Pressure: The urgency created by time constraints enhances motivation [15] and compels players to concentrate on identifying the correct solutions.
- Individual Betting and Team Impact: Players individually bet on answers, necessitating persuasive discussions within teams to agree on the most likely correct answer, as these choices affect the team's overall results.

- Risk Management: The ability to allocate game currency to different answers, representing different levels of certainty, introduces an element of risk management and certainty assessment.
- Feedback for Deeper Learning: A feedback session at the end of each round provides detailed explanations of the answers, enhancing understanding and fostering deeper learning from each task.

3.2.3 Gameplay Aesthetics

The aesthetic experience is crafted to foster deep emotional engagement, specifically targeting:

- Challenge: Players are tested on their critical thinking skills through intricate scenarios that require identifying logical fallacies and cognitive biases.
- Fellowship: The game encourages collaboration and knowledge sharing, enhancing the social bonds among players.
- Expression: Players articulate their reasoning and strategies, allowing for personal expression within the game's framework.
- Discovery: New information and unexpected outcomes keep gameplay intriguing and educational.
- Submission: Players immerse themselves in a structured environment, submitting to game rules and challenges.
- Competition: Teams strive to outperform each other, with success deeply rooted in their collective emotional investment in winning.

4 Brain Fitness—an Example of a CT Game

"Brain Fitness" is a game developed using the proposed methodology and has been adapted for various learner groups, from school and university students to employed adults. It was implemented as part of a CT skills training program for 12 employees from a food production company with diverse backgrounds [33]. In the game, players were randomly assigned to teams of three and took on roles as members of the Management Board of a fictional company. Teams competed against each other. According to the game's storyline, the Management Board received a proposal to enhance employee efficiency by training their mental functions using a special computer program, BF-2. Players were then given a list of questions about BF-2 and tasked with selecting those that, with a high degree of probability, would help assess the feasibility of implementing the proposal.

The design of 'Brain Fitness' incorporated three key elements: the preparation of an MCQ task, the tuning of the betting system, and the setting of a time limit for discussions. The MCQ task included a list of questions, each of which could be a correct choice or a carefully designed distractor (incorrect choice). These distractors, incorporating several informal fallacies, were specifically crafted to challenge the players' CT skills. For example, the question "Has the stock value of companies whose employees use BF-2 regularly increased?" uses the informal fallacy of "irrelevant conclusion". Another question, "How many people use BF-2?" employs the "bandwagon fallacy".

Additionally, the question "Is it true that many of the world's leading politicians have been using the BF-2 for a long time?" is based on the "argument from authority". For each correct answer, two distractors were implemented, a ratio found to be sufficient in most cases according to recent research [34]. Additionally, the tasks were presented in the players' native language to avoid the potential degradation of CT skills performance that can occur when instructions are given in a foreign language [35].

The game's betting system was designed to encourage thoughtful consideration of options by limiting the number of virtual coins available. This limitation prevents players from placing bets on every option merely to mitigate risk. Additionally, setting minimum and maximum bet amounts discourages players from betting all their coins on one option they are certain about, and makes it relatively costly to place "just in case" bets on options they are less sure of.

The players evaluated 'Brain Fitness' as effective in developing CT skills and found it motivating to play [33]. More than 90% of the participants reported that the game's interface was intuitive and easy to interact with. They also noted improvements in problem-solving and identifying logical fallacies. Despite the study's limitations—such as relying solely on qualitative analysis and lacking experimental data on changes in players' CT skills independent of other educational games and pedagogical interventions—the findings highlight the game's potential as an effective tool for engaging players in CT skills development.

5 Future Work

Several promising directions for future research have been identified. First, the development of valid and reliable tests for identifying and rejecting both formal and informal fallacies could pave the way to enhance fundamental CT skills using the proposed technological solution. Second, this solution could be applied to investigate differences in fallacy detection across various demographic groups, such as different ages and educational backgrounds. Third, by collecting and analyzing data during gameplay, researchers can gain insights into the zones of proximal development [18] for individual players, potentially tailoring learning experiences more effectively. Fourth, future studies should also explore the long-term effects of game-based learning on the development of CT skills.

6 Conclusion

This article has introduced a methodology and guidelines for designing games that foster fundamental CT skills. Thanks to robust technological solutions, the game is adaptable for diverse groups and can accommodate various educational and training settings. It is designed to be versatile, supporting both offline and online gameplay for groups of varying sizes, with minimal preparation required from the players. This flexibility ensures that the game can effectively contribute to improving CT skills across different demographics and contexts.

Acknowledgements. The author wishes to thank Merja Lina M. Bauters for her invaluable support and supervision, and Peadar Charles Callaghan for his knowledge and helpful suggestions.

References

1. World Economic Forum: The Future of Jobs Report 2020. (2020)
2. OECD: OECD Skills Outlook 2019: Thriving in a Digital World. OECD (2019). https://doi.org/10.1787/df80bc12-en
3. European Commission: Communication from the Commission to the European Parliament, the Council, the European Economic and Social Committee and the Committee of the Regions: European Skills Agenda for sustainable competitiveness, social fairness and resilience (COM/2020/274 final). https://eur-lex.europa.eu/legal-content/EN/ALL/?uri=CELEX:52020DC0274 (2020)
4. The Council of the European Union: COUNCIL RECOMMENDATION of 22 May 2018 on key competences for lifelong learning, https://eur-lex.europa.eu/legal-content/EN/TXT/PDF/?uri=CELEX:32018H0604(01)&rid=7 (2018)
5. Cialdini, R.B., Goldstein, N.J.: Social Influence: Compliance and Conformity. Annu. Rev. Psychol. **55**, 591–621 (2004). https://doi.org/10.1146/annurev.psych.55.090902.142015
6. Tversky, A., Kahneman, D.: Judgment under Uncertainty: Heuristics and Biases: Biases in judgments reveal some heuristics of thinking under uncertainty. Science **185**, 1124–1131 (1974). https://doi.org/10.1126/science.185.4157.1124
7. Halpern, D.F.: Thought and knowledge: an introduction to critical thinking. Psychology Press, New York (2014)
8. Bailin, S., Case, R., Coombs, J.R., Daniels, L.B.: Conceptualizing critical thinking. J. Curric. Stud. **31**, 285–302 (1999). https://doi.org/10.1080/002202799183133
9. Hitchcock, D.: Critical Thinking, https://plato.stanford.edu/archives/win2022/entries/critical-thinking/ (2022)
10. Pinker, S.: Rationality: What it is, why it seems scarce, why it matters. Penguin (2022)
11. Valenzuela, J., Saiz, C.: Percepción sobre el coste de pensar críticamente en universitarios chilenos y españoles. Electron. J. Res. Educ. Psychol. **8**, 689–706 (2010)
12. Baron, J.: Thinking and deciding. Cambridge University Press, New York (2023)
13. Katual, D., Drevin, L., Goede, R.: GAME-BASED LEARNING TO IMPROVE CRITICAL THINKING AND KNOWLEDGE SHARING: LITERATURE REVIEW. Journal of the International Society for the Systems Sciences. **67** (2023)
14. Deci, E.L.: Intrinsic motivation and self-determination. In: Spielberger, C.D. (ed.) Encyclopedia of applied psychology. pp. 437–448. Elsevier, New York (2004). https://doi.org/10.1016/B0-12-657410-3/00689-9
15. Malone, T.W., Lepper, M.R.: Making learning fun: A taxonomy of intrinsic motivations for learning. In: Aptitude, learning, and instruction. pp. 223–254. Routledge (2021)
16. Csikszentmihalyi, M.: Intrinsic rewards and emergent motivation. In: The hidden costs of reward. pp. 205–216. Psychology Press (2015)
17. Qian, M., Clark, K.R.: Game-based Learning and 21st century skills: A review of recent research. Comput. Hum. Behav. **63**, 50–58 (2016). https://doi.org/10.1016/j.chb.2016.05.023
18. Vygotsky, L.S., Cole, M.: Mind in society: Development of higher psychological processes. Harvard university press (1978)
19. Wason, P.C.: New horizons in psychology. (1966)
20. Mercier, H., Trouche, E., Yama, H., Heintz, C., Girotto, V.: Experts and laymen grossly underestimate the benefits of argumentation for reasoning. Think. Reason. **21**, 341–355 (2015). https://doi.org/10.1080/13546783.2014.981582
21. Mercer, N., Dawes, L.: The study of talk between teachers and students, from the 1970s until the 2010s. Oxf. Rev. Educ. **40**, 430–445 (2014). https://doi.org/10.1080/03054985.2014.934087

22. Johnson, D.W., Johnson, R.T., Stanne, M.B.: Cooperative learning methods: A meta-analysis. (2000)
23. Johnson, D.W., Maruyama, G., Johnson, R., Nelson, D., Skon, L.: Effects of cooperative, competitive, and individualistic goal structures on achievement: A meta-analysis. Psychol. Bull. **89**, 47 (1981)
24. Blasco-Arcas, L., Buil, I., Hernández-Ortega, B., Sese, F.J.: Using clickers in class. The role of interactivity, active collaborative learning and engagement in learning performance. Computers & Education. **62**, 102–110 (2013)
25. Hoekstra, A.: Vibrant student voices: Exploring effects of the use of clickers in large college courses. Learn. Media Technol. **33**, 329–341 (2008)
26. Lantz, M.E.: The use of 'clickers' in the classroom: Teaching innovation or merely an amusing novelty? Comput. Hum. Behav. **26**, 556–561 (2010)
27. Mollborn, S., Hoekstra, A.: "A meeting of minds" using clickers for critical thinking and discussion in large sociology classes. Teach. Sociol. **38**, 18–27 (2010)
28. Chang, C.-Y., Kao, C.-H., Hwang, G.-J., Lin, F.-H.: From experiencing to critical thinking: a contextual game-based learning approach to improving nursing students' performance in electrocardiogram training. Education Tech. Research Dev. **68**, 1225–1245 (2020)
29. Halpern, D.F., Millis, K., Graesser, A.C., Butler, H., Forsyth, C., Cai, Z.: Operation ARA: A computerized learning game that teaches critical thinking and scientific reasoning. Thinking Skills and Creativity. **7**, 93–100 (2012). https://doi.org/10.1016/j.tsc.2012.03.006
30. Lee, H., et al.: Cooperation begins: Encouraging critical thinking skills through cooperative reciprocity using a mobile learning game. Comput. Educ. **97**, 97–115 (2016)
31. Hunicke, R., LeBlanc, M., Zubek, R.: MDA: A formal approach to game design and game research. Presented at the Proceedings of the AAAI Workshop on Challenges in Game AI (2004)
32. Levitin, D.J.: A field guide to lies: critical thinking in the information age. Dutton, New York, New York (2016)
33. Mets, J., Bauters, M.: Engaging Company Employees in Critical Thinking Through Game-Based Learning: A Qualitative Study. In: Huang, Y.-M. and Rocha, T. (eds.) Innovative Technologies and Learning. pp. 403–408. Springer Nature Switzerland, Cham (2023). https://doi.org/10.1007/978-3-031-40113-8_39
34. Haladyna, T.M., Downing, S.M., Rodriguez, M.C.: A review of multiple-choice item-writing guidelines for classroom assessment. Appl. Measur. Educ. **15**, 309–333 (2002)
35. Manalo, E., Sheppard, C.: How might language affect critical thinking performance? Thinking Skills and Creativity. **21**, 41–49 (2016). https://doi.org/10.1016/j.tsc.2016.05.005

Author Index

Y.-P. Cheng et al. (Eds.): ICITL 2024, LNCS 14785, pp. 325–327, 2024.
https://doi.org/10.1007/978-3-031-65881-5